PRIVILEGE

AUTHOR PASSMORE, Colin

TITLE PRIVILEGE

Date	
13.4.00	oc
4.7.00	Rachel Hall
28/8/01	ec wright (made ete)
18.4.02	Natalie Coleman
11.2.04	Nina Benson

AUTHOR *PASSMORE, Colin*

TITLE *PRIVILEGE*

Date	
13.99 oc	
£7.00	Rachel Hall
28/5/01	ee wright (pocket)
18.7.02	Natalie Coleman
H.2.04	Nina Benson

PRIVILEGE

Colin Passmore
Solicitor

CLT PROFESSIONAL PUBLISHING
A Division of Central Law Training Ltd

Dedicated to my wife and to Anna Kennedy

© Colin Passmore 1998

Published by
CLT Professional Publishing
A division of Central Law Training Ltd
Wrens Court
52/54 Victoria Road
Sutton Coldfield
Birmingham B72 1SX

ISBN 1 85811 078 5

Printed in Great Britain by The Ipswich Book Company Ltd

Contents

FOREWORD

In *R v Derby Magistrates Courts, ex p. B* [1996] 1 AC 487, Lord Lloyd said that 'the courts have for very many years regarded legal professional privilege as *the* predominant public interest'. In the same case the House unanimously rejected the blandishments of Counsel to carry out a balancing exercise where the privilege was invoked, and to contemplate its overriding in the interests of truth and openness. No greater testimony can be found to the importance of the subject of Colin Passmore's new book.

But the circumstances in which the privilege is engaged, and the reach that it enjoys are not always easy to ascertain. The route is a maze, not a motorway, sewn with constantly sprouting cases with an overlay, in appropriate areas, of EU law. Nor is this edition likely to be the last word on the subject. The imminent incorporation of the European Convention of Human Rights into English law, in particular Article 6, guaranteeing the right to a fair trial, will inevitably create new problems for the courts. The right of an unfettered access to the courts with legal assistance has bulked large in Convention jurisprudence. The basic domestic principle of the privilege, that a client should be able to obtain legal advice in confidence, will be fortified by this infusion of outside law.

Colin Passmore, a highly experiences city solicitor, is well familiar with the practical issues generated by his subject. It is unsurprising that he has written a book of great interest to practitioners and scholars alike.

The Honourable Michael J Beloff QC
President
Trinity College
Oxford

PREFACE

This book was originally inspired by my needs as a busy litigator for a text which would enable me to get to grips, in a practical fashion, with complex privilege issues in the shortest possible time frame. The project grew well beyond that objective as my interest in the subject increased, with the result that the final product is now considerably longer than either I or my publishers ever envisaged. I hope that the book will nonetheless serve the needs of practising lawyers.

I have received enormous support and encouragement over the years that it has taken me to reach the present stage. Thanks must go to Andrew Prideaux, my commissioning editor, for his continuing patience and kind encouragement, especially as deadlines were repeatedly missed. I also owe an enormous debt to Nicola Pittam, a former colleague now at the Law Commission, for tremendous amounts of work in enabling me to put Chapter 7 together; and also to my colleague Jonathan Goodliffe who was the principle architect of Chapters 10 and 11. I must also thank Jacqui Packham and Carmen Culmer without whose secretarial skills I would undoubtedly not have reached publication, even in 1998. Warm thanks must also go to the Honourable Michael Beloff QC not only for reviewing the book in manuscript but for also giving me the additional encouragement necessary to complete this work. At the end of the day of course all errors and omissions are mine and nobody else's.

Finally, thanks to my family, and especially my children Rachael, Sophie and Anna, who have made me promise never to write another book.

Colin Passmore
April 1998

TABLE OF CASES

British and Commonwealth cases

EU Cases

TABLE OF STATUTES

TABLE OF STATUTORY INSTRUMENTS AND EC AND INTERNATIONAL LEGISLATION

Statutory Instruments

EC Legislation

International Convention and Covenant

Chapter 1

LEGAL PROFESSIONAL PRIVILEGE: BASIC PRINCIPLES

1. PRIVILEGE: IN SUMMARY

Legal professional privilege is a part of the English law of evidence. It is a rule which entitles a litigant[1] during the course of legal proceedings to withhold from his opponent and from the court (and certain other types of judicial tribunal[2]), evidence, whether in written or oral form, which is within the scope of the privilege. The right to withhold such evidence is exercisable – subject to certain limited exceptions – notwithstanding that it is admissible evidence which may be crucial to the outcome of the proceedings in which it is relevant.[3]

The evidence which legal professional privilege permits to be withheld from a court and an opponent comprises certain types of written or oral communications which can be broadly categorised under the following two heads:

- **Advice privilege:** this covers confidential communications between a lawyer and his client made for the purposes of seeking or giving legal advice.[4]
- **Litigation privilege:** this covers confidential communications made between a lawyer and his client, or the lawyer or the client and a third party, which come into existence for the dominant purpose of being used in connection with actual or pending litigation.[5]

---

1   And his successor in title: see Chap. 6.
2   And from certain types of administrative and law enforcement bodies which have been given statutory powers which allow them to compel disclosure of evidence: see Section 5 below.
3   See The Law Reform Committee's Sixteenth Report, *Privilege in Civil Proceedings*, Cmnd. 3472, para. 1: "It is the right of a person to insist on there being withheld from a judicial tribunal information which might assist it to ascertain facts relevant to an issue upon which it is adjudicating."
4   Advice privilege is described in detail in Chap. 2.
5   Litigation privilege is described in detail in Chap. 3.

Privilege, being a rule of evidence, is part of English procedural law. It has not, as has happened in certain Commonwealth jurisdictions, developed so as to confer more substantive rights.[6] It is in England a shield, as opposed to a sword. Thus, the ability of the courts to grant an injunction to prevent a violation of a party's privilege[7] derives not from any rights conferred by the privilege (since these merely entitle a party to refuse production), but from the court's equitable jurisdiction which, by protecting the confidentiality[8] which underlies all privileged communications, is invoked as an aid to protect the privilege. Even so, legal professional privilege is no ordinary rule of evidence, because it is "a fundamental condition on which the administration of justice as a whole rests".[9]

This book is primarily concerned with issues of privilege as they arise in High Court civil proceedings. The vast majority of the principles stated in this book are nonetheless, for the most part, as equally applicable in inferior civil courts and in criminal courts.[10]

2. THE JUSTIFICATION FOR LEGAL PROFESSIONAL PRIVILEGE

The underlying rationale for legal professional privilege reflects the type of evidence which it protects from production. It also illustrates the unique nature of the privilege in the English law of evidence. This rationale has been consistently stated for well over 160 years. It is that the administration of justice requires that everyone should be able to consult a lawyer, or to prepare his case for litigation, without fear that any information given to the lawyer, or which he collects himself,[11] will later be revealed in court against his wishes and interests. There are numerous examples in the case reports of how the judges have stated the underlying principles. The following

---

6 In England, "...privilege is an aspect of the law of evidence and not of constitutional rights..." per Ebsworth, J in *Kershaw* v *Whelan* [1996] 1 WLR 358 at 370. However, it may well be a right recognised by the European Court of Human Rights: see footnote 9, below.

7 As to which see generally Chap. 7.

8 As to which see Section 9 below, Chap. 2, Section 8 and Chap. 7, Section 3.

9 See Lord Taylor, CJ in *R* v *Derby Magistrates' Court, ex p. B* [1996] 1 AC 487 at 507. In his speech, at 507, Lord Taylor also noted a possibility, on which the House did not hear any argument, that legal professional privilege "is a fundamental human right protected by the European Convention for the Protection of Human Rights and Fundamental Freedoms (1953) Cmnd. 8969...". See further Section 10 below and, generally, Chap. 11.

10 In *R* v *Derby Magistrates' Court, ex p. B* [1996] 1 AC 487, Lord Taylor noted, at 503, that "...privilege is the same whether the documents are sought for the purpose of civil or criminal proceedings, and whether by the prosecution or the defence...".

11 The position where a litigant acts in person requires separate consideration: see Chap. 4, Section 5.

examples, taken from 1833 up to the present, demonstrate a theme which the judiciary has consistently observed in applying this area of the law.[12]

The usual starting point is Lord Brougham's judgment in *Greenough* v *Gaskell*.[13] This was an important decision, not only because it was the first one in which a court held that legal professional privilege extended beyond litigation privilege to include advice privilege, but also because of Lord Brougham's description of the underlying principles. In his view, these were founded on:

> "...a regard to the interests of justice which cannot be upheld and to the administration of justice which cannot go on without the aid of men skilled in jurisprudence, in the practice of the court and in those matters which form the subject of all judicial proceedings. If the privilege did not exist at all everyone would be thrown upon his own resources: deprived of all professional assistance a man would not venture to consult any skilful person or would only dare to tell his counsel half his case".[14]

The importance of the client being able to confide in his lawyer, knowing that his innermost secrets will remain confidential, was identified as the crucial element of the privilege by Sir George Jessell, MR, over forty years later, in an oft-cited passage from a judgment which is still a leading authority on the scope of litigation privilege. He described the justification for legal professional privilege in this way:

> "...that as, by reason of the complexity and difficulty of our law, litigation can only be properly conducted by professional men, it is absolutely necessary that a man, in order to prosecute his rights or to defend himself from an improper claim, should have recourse to the assistance of professional lawyers, and it being so absolutely necessary, it is equally necessary, to use a vulgar phrase, that he should be able to make a clean breast of it to the gentleman whom he consults with a view to the prosecution of his claim, or the substantiating of his defence against the claim; that he should be able to place unrestricted and unbounded confidence in the professional agent, and that the communications he so makes to him should be kept secret, unless with his consent (for it is his privilege, and not the privilege of the confidential agent), that he should be enabled properly to conduct his litigation."[15]

More recently, Bingham, LJ identified the root of the privilege as being the public interest in ensuring that hopeless and exaggerated claims and unfounded and spurious defences are discouraged. To achieve this:

---

12 Lord Taylor, CJ's speech in *R* v *Derby Magistrates' Court, ex p. B* [1996] 1 AC 487 contains a number of additional examples.
13 (1833) 1 My & K 98.
14 *Ibid.*, p.103.
15 See *Anderson* v *Bank of British Columbia* (1876) 2 ChD 644 at 649.

"...it is necessary that actual and potential litigants, be they claimants or respondents, should be free to unburden themselves without reserve to their legal advisers, and their legal advisers be free to give honest and candid advice on a sound factual basis, without fear that these communications may be relied on by an opposing party if the dispute comes before the court for decision. It is the protection of confidential communications between client and legal adviser which lies at the heart of legal professional privilege...".[16]

So, subject to certain limited exceptions,[17] the courts will not permit any enquiry into nor require disclosure to be made of any instructions which a client gives his lawyer, or of any advice which the lawyer gives the client, nor of any communications they make with third parties in relation to litigation.[18]

3. ASSERTING PRIVILEGE: THE CONSEQUENCES

Since it involves withholding relevant evidence from a court, asserting privilege necessarily can have dramatic consequences. This was recognised by Roskill, LJ in *Causton* v *Mann Egerton (Johnsons) Limited* when he said:

"...so long as we have an adversary system, a party is entitled not to produce documents which are properly protected by privilege if it is not to his advantage to produce them, and even though their production might assist his adversary if his adversary or his solicitor were aware of their contents or might lead the court to a different conclusion from that to which the court would come in ignorance of their existence".[19,20]

A striking example of the consequences of asserting privilege is the decision in *R* v *Derby Magistrates Court ex p. B*[21] in which the House of Lords took the opportunity in 1995 to reassert the importance of privilege in emphatic terms. Here, B was charged in 1978 with murder after

---

16 Per Bingham, LJ in *Ventouris* v *Mountain* [1991] 1 WLR 607 at 611.

17 As to which see Section 6 below; and Chap. 8.

18 This is notwithstanding the fact that the English system of civil procedure "...is founded on the rule that the interests of justice are best served if parties to litigation are obliged to disclose and produce for the other party's inspection all documents in their possession, custody or power relating to the issues in the action" per Bingham, LJ, in *Ventouris* v *Mountain op. cit.*, n.16, at 611.

19 [1974] 1 WLR 162 at 170.

20 These principles do not apply in, *e.g.* proceedings under the Children Act 1989, since these are not adversarial in character. See *In re L (a minor)* [1997] AC 16 (discussed in Section 6 below); and Steyn, LJ in *Oxfordshire County Council* v *M* [1994] 2 All ER 269 at 281.

21 [1996] 1 AC 487.

admitting to the police that he had strangled a girl. He changed his story before trial, alleging instead that S had killed the girl. B was acquitted, but in 1991, together with S, was found liable in a civil action brought by the victim's mother for assault and battery. When S was then charged with murder, B gave evidence at his committal proceedings. In cross examination he declined to answer questions about instructions he had given to his solicitors in 1978 before he changed his story. The defence thereupon obtained a witness summons under section 97 Magistrates' Courts Act 1980 addressed to B's former solicitors. This sought the production of privileged documentation detailing instructions B had given in defending the murder charge.

The House of Lords quashed the witness summons for failure to satisfy certain statutory requirements. Lord Taylor, LCJ, who gave the leading judgment,[22] went on to consider the second ground of appeal which was based on the fact that the witness summons sought materials protected by legal professional privilege. The issuing magistrate, following *R v Ataou*,[23] had performed a balancing exercise, weighing the public interest in the protection of confidential communications between a solicitor and his client against the public interest in ensuring that all relevant, admissible evidence is made available to the defence. B's counsel argued that, prior to the decision in *R v Barton*,[24] there had been no precedent for carrying out such a balancing exercise. After reviewing the long history of the law of privilege – a review which ought to be required reading for any student of the subject – Lord Taylor agreed. He noted:

> "The principle which runs through all these cases … is that a man must be able to consult his lawyer in confidence, since otherwise he might hold back half the truth. The client must be sure that what he tells his lawyer in confidence will never be revealed without his consent. Legal professional privilege is thus much more than an ordinary rule of evidence, limited in its application to the facts of a particular case. It is a fundamental condition on which the administration of justice as a whole rests".[25]

The importance of the privilege is such that B's right to withhold privileged materials could not be violated, even though it meant, potentially, that S and the court were deprived of crucial information highly pertinent to S's guilt or innocence. The "absolute nature" of the privilege, which had to be upheld

---

22 He also gave the court's judgment in *Balabel v Air India* [1988] Ch. 317, the leading modern authority on the "advice" head of privilege: see Chap. 2.

23 [1988] QB 798.

24 [1973] 1 WLR 115.

25 *Op. cit.*, n.21, at 507.

> "...in the wider interests of all those hereafter who might otherwise be deterred from telling the whole truth to their solicitors",

meant there was no exception to the privilege which deprived a man of his right to withhold documents which, if produced, would enable another to establish his innocence or resist an allegation made by the Crown in a criminal trial.[26] *Ataou* and *Barton* were therefore overruled.

The sanctity of the privilege is further emphasised by the fact that evidence which the magistrate in the *Derby Magistrates* decision considered relevant and admissible was withheld from the court, even though there could be no question of B being retried for murder. However, a related issue which was canvassed in this decision and which may yet arise for determination on a future occasion is the argument that a person cannot withhold documents where he no longer has any interest in maintaining his privilege. This is a controversial issue which has not previously been aired judicially in England.[27] While reserving his final view on a point which is surely likely to arise for determination sooner or later, Lord Nicholls was:

> "...instinctively unattracted by an argument involving the proposition that a client can insist on non-disclosure, to the prejudice of a third party, when (ex hypothesi) disclosure would not prejudice the client. I would not expect a law, based explicitly on considerations of the public interest, to protect the right of a client when he has no interest in asserting the right and the enforcement of the right would be seriously prejudicial to another in defending a criminal charge or in some other way...".[28]

In *Derby Magistrates*, there was a subsisting interest in that the applicant was entitled to withhold materials which might cause him to face accusations of murder, a charge of which he had already been acquitted.

---

26 Per Lord Taylor, in *Derby Magistrates, op. cit.,* n.21, at 508–9. References to the "absolute nature" of the privilege are not entirely justified: see the statutory overrides discussed in Section 6 below. Note also that the "crime-fraud" exception established in *R v Cox and Railton* (1884) 14 QBD 153 is not a true "exception" to the privilege since this line of authority prevents the privilege from arising in the first place: see Chap. 8 below.

27 Though see *R v Craig* 1 NZLR 597 and *R v Dunbar and Logan* 138 DLR (3d) 521. For a somewhat unconvincing example of "spent privilege" being applied, see the Hong Kong decision in *Longin Investment Ltd v Johnson, Stokes and Master* (Unreported) 19 February 1997.

28 *Derby Magistrates, op. cit.,* n.21, at 513.

4. THE CLIENT'S PRIVILEGE AND THE LAWYER'S DUTY

From earliest times, the courts have recognised that privilege belongs to the client which he alone can waive.[29] In the *Derby Magistrates* case discussed above, Lord Taylor noted that *Wilson v Rastall*[30] was clear authority for this proposition and the rule that:

> "...the court will not permit, let alone order, the attorney to reveal the confidential communications which have passed between him and his former client. His mouth is shut forever".[31]

Furthermore, the solicitor is under a duty to protect his client's privilege, for example, by asserting it on his behalf if he himself is asked to produce his client's privileged documents[32] or to answer interrogatories which would involve the disclosure of privileged information.[33] Presumably, given the absolute nature of the privilege the lawyer must do so at his own expense, if necessary; and even if he is exercising a lien over privileged materials in respect of unpaid fees.

In the light of this rule, the guidance in the *Law Society's Guide to the Professional Conduct of Solicitors*,[34] to the effect that a solicitor may reveal confidential information concerning a client to the extent necessary to establish a defence to a criminal charge, a civil claim brought by the client or where the solicitor's conduct is under investigation by, for example, the Law Society's complaints bodies, must be treated with extreme caution where such confidential information is also privileged. Quite apart from the difficulties which derive from the analogous prohibition on the use, without client consent, of privileged materials to resist wasted costs applications, as noted by the Court of Appeal in

---

29   But see Chap. 7, Section 2 which discusses the lawyer's ability to waive his client's privilege.

30   (1792) 4 Term Rep 753.

31   *Ibid,* at 504-505. See also, *e.g.,* Lord Brougham in *Greenough v Gaskell* (1833) 1 My & K 98 at 103, and Jessel, MR in *Anderson v Bank of British Columbia* (1876) 2 ChD 644 at 649, quoted at p. 3 above.

32   See Lord Griffiths in *R v Central Criminal Court, ex p. Francis and Francis* [1989] 1 AC 346 who referred at 381 to the rule "...that the privilege is that of the client and not the solicitor, although it is the duty of the solicitor to protect his client's privilege unless the client waives it."

33   *Proctor v Smiles* (1886) 55 LJQB 527.

34   Seventh Edn (1996), Principle 16.02, para. 10. See also *Parry-Jones v Law Society* [1969] 1 Ch 1, discussed in Section 5 below.

Ridehalgh v *Horsefield and Isherwood*,[35] the guidance sits very unhappily with the decision in *Derby Magistrates:* if the sanctity of privilege prevents an accused obtaining another's privileged materials in order to establish his innocence on a charge of murder, it is hard to see the justification for the solicitor being allowed to do so without client consent in the circumstances suggested by the *Guide.*[36]

Furthermore, just as the court will not allow a party who refuses to waive his privilege to be questioned about his refusal,[37] neither will it draw any adverse inferences against him in consequence of that refusal: *Wentworth* v *Lloyd.*[38] It should also be noted that, because it is the client's privilege, his lawyer cannot invoke the privilege, or attempt to use it for his own benefit, if the client waives it.[39]

5. PRIVILEGE:
THE RULE OF EVIDENCE

The rules relating to privilege provide an important framework within which a lawyer and client can work together, shielded from the eyes of the world. However, because privilege is only a rule of evidence, then the circumstances in which its benefits can be enjoyed are necessarily limited. Those limitations are exemplified by the Court of Appeal's decision in *Parry-Jones* v *The Law Society.*[40] Here, the Law Society served on Mr Parry-Jones, a solicitor, a written notice pursuant to Rule 11 of the Solicitors' Accounts Rules 1945, and Rule 11 of the Solicitors' Trust Accounts Rules 1945, which required him to produce for inspection his books of account and other necessary documents relating to his practice as a solicitor and to every trust of which he was a trustee. In the course of complying with these requests, Mr Parry-Jones argued that he was not bound to produce to the Law Society documents or information which he

---

35 [1994] Ch 205, discussed in Chap. 7, Section 5 below. See the position in relation to other professionals who use their client's confidential information, as in, *e.g., R* v *Institute of Chartered Accountants of England and Wales, ex p. Brindle* [1994] BCC 297.

36 Although, if the client sues his legal adviser for negligence he runs a real risk that the Court will infer a waiver of privilege in respect of the retainer: see the discussion on this point in Chap. 7, Section 5.

37 Per Lord Taylor in *Derby Magistrates, op. cit.,* n.21, at 503.

38 (1864) 10 HL Cas, 589.

39 See *Re International Power Industries* [1985] BCLC 128 discussed in Chap. 7, Section 2; and *R* v *Peterborough Justices, ex p. Hicks* [1977] 1 WLR 1371.

40 [1969] 1 Ch 1.

regarded as privileged from production. He therefore sought an injunction restraining the Law Society and its officials from having access pursuant to the notices to confidential information relating to any of his clients' affairs without their express authority.[41]

The Court of Appeal upheld the striking out of Mr Parry-Jones' action: the Law Society had power under the Solicitors Act 1957 to make rules whereby it could inspect a solicitor's books and supporting documents in order to ensure compliance with those rules. That power was exercisable even though it meant disclosing confidential details relating to the clients' affairs. According to Lord Denning, MR, the contract between solicitor and client must be taken to contain the implication that, since the solicitor must obey the law, and in particular must comply with the rules made under the authority of statute for the conduct of his profession, if those rules required him to disclose his clients' affairs, then he must do so. Thus the two notices served on him pursuant to the Solicitors' Accounts Rules and the Trust Rules overrode any privilege or confidence which existed as between Mr Parry-Jones and his clients.[42]

In agreeing with Lord Denning, Diplock, LJ put the matter very relevantly for current purposes. He said:

> "So far as Mr Parry-Jones' point as to privilege is concerned, privilege, of course, is irrelevant when one is not concerned with judicial or quasi-judicial proceedings because, strictly speaking, privilege refers to a right to withhold from a court, or a tribunal exercising judicial functions, material which would otherwise be admissible in evidence."[43]

Inspecting documents under Rule 11 of the Solicitors Account Rules 1945 was, according to Diplock, LJ, no more in the nature of judicial proceedings than an inspection by a factory inspector under the Factory Acts.

Judicial proceedings

As the decision makes clear, privilege is only relevant, and therefore maintainable, in "judicial or quasi-judicial proceedings". For the most part, identifying judicial proceedings is easy. So in proceedings in the High

---

41 As noted in Section 1 above, privilege is a shield, not a sword, so Mr Parry-Jones' writ was framed by reference to obligations of confidentiality which underlay his clients' privilege: see Section 9 below. See also *W v Edgell* [1990] 1 Ch 359 and the discussion in Chap. 7, Section 7.

42 And see also, in relation to the privilege against self-incrimination *R v Institute of Chartered Accountants of England and Wales, ex p. Nawaz* (Unrep., 25 April, 1997) discussed in Chap. 11, Section 2.

43 [1969] 1 Ch 1 at 9.

Court, County Court, Crown Court, Magistrates Court, Industrial Tribunals, arbitration proceedings and, for example, most types of tax tribunals,[44] a litigant is entitled to assert his privilege. However, there will be certain types of investigations which may fall into a "grey area". Evidently, investigations of an administrative nature, as under the Solicitors Accounts Rules and Trust Rules, are not judicial or quasi-judicial proceedings for the purpose of the rules of privilege. Nor, arguably, are review proceedings before a Mental Health Tribunal, since they are not "adversarial" in character.[45] Similarly, as will be discussed below, the House of Lords has held that litigation privilege is not available in certain types of child care and wardship proceedings.

One type of body whose functions merit consideration in this context are the self-regulating organisations ("SRO's") created under the Financial Services Act 1986. It is a moot point as to whether these bodies would be regarded as carrying out judicial functions when, for example, conducting formal investigations into breaches of rules, such that the rules of privilege apply. On the one hand, one can draw comparisons between court proceedings and a hearing before the SRO, especially in relation to disciplinary hearings. On the other, given that it is a requirement of authorisation under that Act that a member formally contracts with his SRO to co-operate with any investigations which they institute, one can see the analogies, though imperfect, which can be drawn with the situation in *Parry-Jones*. These would suggest that privilege is not claimable as against those bodies when exercising their powers of compulsory disclosure. However, one possible distinction derives from the fact that *Parry-Jones* was concerned with the solicitor's clients' privilege, and not his own, as for example if he had consulted counsel about his own position. Arguably, such documents would not be relevant anyway to the Law Society's investigation. But in the case of the SROs, it is more likely to be those types of documents which are called for.[46] In that case, there may well be arguments available to the effect that the SROs' rules need to spell out their entitlement to seek privileged materials belonging to the member.[47]

For the present, the issue is resolved in favour of the privilege because, broadly, the SROs' rules make clear that there is no right to encroach on a

44 See for example *Alfred Crompton Amusement Machines Limited* v *Customs and Excise Commissioners (No 2)* [1974] AC 405.

45 *W* v *Edgell* [1990] Ch 359 at 422 per Bingham, LJ.

46 Though not a case concerned with privilege, the decision in *Kaufmann* v *Crédit Lyonnaise Bank* (1995) *Times* 1 February, illustrates this point.

47 See the discussion in Section 6 below. It is also notable that provisions in the Financial Services Act 1986 preserve privilege in the face of the disclosure powers conferred on inspectors by ss. 105 and 177 of that Act.

member's privilege. Thus, while the Securities and Futures Authority's enforcement powers include, on the face of it, the right (pursuant to Rule 7-8(2)) to require the production of documents and records which could include privileged materials, Rule 7-8(4) ameliorates its effect by providing that:

> "Nothing in this rule shall require the production of a document or record subject to legal professional privilege".[48]

Similarly, the Personal Investment Authority's rights to compel the production of information from its members is subject to Rule 1.1.1(2) which provides that the PIA will not:

> "Require a Member to provide it with any information or document which is subject to legal professional privilege".

Interestingly, the IMRO rules[49] do not contain a similar provision to the SFA's and PIA's rules just mentioned. IMRO has extensive powers to require the production of other information. The only concession it contains so far as concerns privilege is a Note in Chapter VI, Rule 2.7(1) which states that:

> "In the carrying out of its regulatory functions, IMRO will have regard ... to the obligation of legal professional privilege."

As suggested above, not every type of enquiry conducted by IMRO would necessarily constitute judicial or quasi-judicial proceedings, such that IMRO could arguably call for privileged materials. The issue has yet to arise for determination.

Privilege: statutory preservations

As the *Parry-Jones* decision illustrates, outside of a court room or other judicial proceeding, the protection of privilege is not available. This could mean that the law enforcement and other administrative bodies which have statutory rights to compel the production of evidence required to enable them to discharge their functions could encroach upon a person's privilege. However, the legislature has evidently been alive to this possibility, since it has chosen, for the most part, to deal with it by including in the enabling legislation an express protection of material which would qualify for legal

---

48   This rule concludes with a useful reminder that a document is not blessed with privilege merely because it is prepared by "a legally qualified person": see further on this Chap. 2, Section 9.

49   Version dated February 1996.

professional privilege in judicial proceedings.[50]

These statutory savings, to which there are exceptions (discussed in Section 6 below), have been achieved on a case-by-case base, rather than as the consequence of a general principle. This means that whenever a client is made the subject of an administrative-style investigation, it is never safe for his lawyer to assume that his papers will be protected, even if held by the lawyer, against any powers of seizure which the investigators might possess on the basis that those papers would, in a judicial context, be the subject of a valid claim to privilege. It is therefore essential to review the provisions of the enabling statute which grants the investigative powers to see what, if any, protection has been afforded to privileged material.

Of the numerous examples collected in footnote 50 of the ways in which the legislature has intervened in this way, three help to illustrate this point. First, the general powers granted to the police under section 19 of the Police and Criminal Evidence Act 1984 to seize evidence and other material is subject to the proviso contained in sub-section (6) which provides:

> "No power of seizure conferred on a constable under any enactment (including an enactment contained in a Act) passed after this Act is to be taken to authorise the seizure of an item which the constable exercising the power has reasonable grounds for believing to be subject to legal privilege".[51]

Similar restrictions are placed on the extent to which the police can execute search warrants obtained under sections 8 and 9 of that Act.[52]

---

50 This is true, *e.g.*, of the right to compel evidence in relation to investigations conducted under the Tribunals of Inquiry and Evidence Act 1921 (s. 1(3)), Taxes Management Act 1970 (s. 20B(8), s. 20C (4)), Fair Trading Act 1973 (s. 29(5) and 85(3)), the Health and Safety at Work Act 1974 (s. 20), Data Protection Act 1984 (s. 31(2)), Solicitors Act 1974 (s. 46(ii)), Evidence (Proceedings in Other Jurisdictions) Act 1974 (s. 3(1)), the Merchant Shipping Act 1977 (s. 28), Competition Act 1980 (s. 3(7)), the Insurance Companies Act, 1982 (s. 47(B)), the Police and Criminal Evidence Act, 1984 (ss. 8, 9 and 19), the Companies Act, 1985 (s. 452), the Business Names Act, 1985 (s. 7), the Drug Trafficking Offences Act, 1986 (ss. 27–29), the Building Societies Act, 1986 (s. 21), the Financial Services Act, 1986 (s. 94, 105, 123 and 177), Gas Act 1986 (as amended by Competition and Service (Utilities) Act 1982, Gas (Exempt Supplies) Act 1993, and Gas Act 1995) (s. 38(1B)), the Criminal Justice Act 1987 (s. 2), the Consumer Protection Act, 1987 (s. 47), the Prevention of Terrorism (Temporary Provisions) Act, 1989 (Schedule 7), the Companies Act, 1989 (ss. 83 and 160), the Criminal Justice (International Cooperation) Act, 1990 (s. 7), the Courts and Legal Services Act, 1990 (ss. 46 and 63), the Environmental Act, 1990 (ss. 17, 69, 115), the Northern Ireland (Emergency Provisions) Act, 1991 (s. 24), the Trade Union and Labour Relations (Consolidation) Act, 1992 (s. 37(e)) and the Pensions Act 1995 (ss. 48(5) and 102(2)). See on this subject, Millett, J's judgment in *Price Waterhouse* v *BCCI* [1992] BCLC 583 at 597, discussed in Section 6 below.
51 Items subject to legal privilege are defined in s. 10 of this Act. See further, Chap. 8, Section 5.
52 As to which, see Chap. 8, Section 5.

A second example is afforded by section 46(ii) Solicitors Act 1974. This empowers the Law Society to serve writs of subpoena on third parties, requiring them to give evidence or to produce documents in relation to investigations being conducted into the affairs of a solicitor. However, it further provides that no one can be compelled under any such writ "to produce any document which he could not be compelled to produce on a trial of an action". While the sub-section does not say so expressly, this is a clear example of the preservation of any privilege which the subpoenaed party has in relation to any relevant information or documentation.[53]

.A more recent example is provided by the "whistle blowing" provisions contained in section 48 Pensions Act 1995. These allow, *inter alia,* any professional adviser to an occupational pension scheme to report to OPRA, the statutory regulator, certain suspected breaches of duty by, for example, the scheme trustees or managers. Section 48(5) relieves the advisor of any breach of duty (*e.g.* to maintain confidentiality) which would be consequent upon him making his report. However, the sub-section makes it clear that the whistle blowing provisions do not allow the disclosure of privileged information.

6. PRIVILEGE: SOME EXCEPTIONS

Statutory Overrides

The House of Lords in *Derby Magistrates* proceeded on the basis that the "absolute nature" of privilege permitted of no exceptions. Lord Taylor acknowledged the possibility that privilege could "modified, or even abrogated by statute", but indicated that in contrast to recent inroads into the right to silence and the privilege against self-incrimination, Parliament had so far left privilege "untouched".[54] This is, strictly, true so far as concerns asserting privilege during the course of legal proceedings. Parliament has, however, made it clear that outside the courtroom there are circumstances where bodies with powers to compel production of documents can seek privileged documents.

An important example of these powers is contained in section 39 Banking Act 1987. Section 39(1) entitles the Bank of England to require an institution authorised under that Act, for example a bank, to produce

---

53 This provision contrasts with the position in relation to the rules made under s. 29 Solicitors Act 1957 (now s. 32 Solicitors Act 1974) and considered in *Parry-Jones* v *Law Society* [1969] Ch 1.

54 *Ibid.,* at 507.

specified documents. Section 39(13) provides:

> "Nothing in this section shall compel the production by a barrister, advocate or solicitor of a document containing a privileged communication made by him or to him in that capacity".[55]

In *Price Waterhouse v BCCI Holdings*,[56] Millett, J held that, on its true construction, section 39 could compel a person to produce privileged documents. Noting that express words were not necessary to exclude privileged documents from the ambit of the section 39 powers,[57] he concluded that the exception to the section 39 powers as contained in sub-section (13) – that is, those in the hands of lawyers – marked the limit of the exception. From this, it followed that privileged documents could be sought from the authorised institution.[58]

A similar example of the legislature intervening in this way is contained in the Taxes Management Act 1970, which was considered in the Court of Appeal's decision in *R. v IRC, ex parte Taylor (No.2)*.[59] This concerned a solicitor, Mr Taylor, who appealed against his personal tax assessments for particular years. While those appeals were still pending, the Board of Inland Revenue served a notice on him under section 20(2) of the Taxes Management Act 1970 requiring him to deliver to the inspector documents in his possession or power specified in an attached schedule. These included documents relating to Mr Taylor's business as a solicitor. Mr Taylor issued judicial review proceedings in which he sought to quash the notice on a variety of grounds, one of which related to the fact that some of the documents sought by the notice were protected by the duty of

---

55 Similar saving provisions are found in ss. 41 (11) and 42 (6) of the Banking Act 1987 in relation to the powers of document production conferred by those sections. See also s. 20C(4) Taxes Management Act 1970 and 29(5) Fair Trading Act 1973.

56 [1992] BCLC 583.

57 He noted (at 593) that in the absence of sub-section (13), "it might be a nice question whether the obligation to comply with a s.39 notice extended to documents covered by legal professional privilege". In *Bank of England v Riley* [1992] Ch 475, the Court of Appeal had little difficulty in concluding that although s.42 of the Banking Act 1987 did not expressly override the privilege against self-incrimination, having regard to its purpose and its proper construction, persons suspected of contravening ss. 3 or 35 of that Act were not excused from complying with a s. 42 request for information on the grounds of this privilege. See also, in the context of the Insolvency Act 1986, *Bishopsgate Investment Management v Maxwell* [1992] BCC 214. However, note the distinction which Lord Taylor drew in *Derby Magistrates* between the privilege against self incrimination and legal professional privilege, discussed at p. 13 above.

58 Millett, J briefly puzzled as to why s. 39 could not compel production from the lawyers. He suggested Parliament was concerned to protect the lawyers' interests – presumably the inconvenience or even embarrassment of having such notices served at their offices or chambers.

59 [1990] 2 All ER 409.

confidentiality which Mr Taylor owed to his clients. Giving the leading judgment, Bingham, LJ[60] said:

> "It is quite plain that Parliament had the position of professional legal advisers very much in mind. So much is plain from s. 20B(3) and (8). Parliament has expressly preserved the client's legal professional privilege where disclosure is sought from a lawyer or a tax accountant in his capacity as a professional adviser[61] and not a taxpayer ... But there is no preservation of legal professional privilege and no limited protection where the notice relates to a lawyer in his capacity as taxpayer who is served with a notice under s. 20(2). The clear inference is ... that a client's ordinary right to legal professional privilege, binding in the ordinary way on a legal adviser, does not entitle such legal adviser as a taxpayer to refuse disclosure. That is not, to my mind, a surprising intention to attribute to Parliament. In different circumstances the Court of Appeal has held that the Law Society is entitled to override a client's right to legal professional privilege when investigating a solicitor's accounts: see *Parry-Jones* v *Law Society* ... It is, as I think, altogether appropriate that the Revenue, being charged with the duty of collecting the public revenue, should enjoy a similar power".[62]

As the judgment makes clear, the Act distinguishes between the privilege of the respondent to the notice, which is preserved; and that of the respondent's clients, which is not. In this respect, the Taxes Management Act 1970 mirrors the position in *Parry-Jones;* whereas in relation to a section 39 Banking Act 1987 Notice, it is the respondent's privilege which can be overridden. Far more controversial are the "break-in and bugging" powers which have been conferred on the police and other law enforcement agencies by Part III of the Police Act 1997. These entitle an "authorising officer"[63] to authorise the entry onto or interference with property or wireless telegraphy in specified circumstances. However, unless the case is one of "urgency"[64] then such authorisation cannot be given if such action:

> "... is likely to result in any person acquiring knowledge of (1) matters subject to legal privilege...".[65]

unless it has first been authorised by a Chief Commissioner[66] appointed by the Prime Minister. Matters subject to legal privilege are defined in section

---

60 Who represented the Law Society in the *Parry-Jones* case.
61 For an example of a professional adviser claiming privilege in response to a s. 20(3) notice, see R v *Board of Inland Revenue, ex p. Goldberg* [1989] QB 267, discussed in Chap. 5.
62 [1990] 2 All ER 409 at 413–414.
63 As defined in s. 93(5): basically, a Chief Constable or other top-ranking law enforcement officer, and (s. 94) their deputies.
64 S. 97(3).
65 S. 92(2)(b).
66 A senior judicial officer: s. 91(2).

98, a definition which mirrors the common law definitions of advice and litigation privileges.

These are controversial provisions[67] which contemplate the possibility that the police can record or gather privileged information, either in urgent cases or where the Commissioner approves. These provisions could, therefore, represent a major in-road into legal professional privilege. As Lord Brown-Wilkinson commented in the House of Lords' debate on the Bill on 28 January 1997:

> "... the effect of covert surveillance is not limited to the suspected villain... If that bug is [in the villain's solicitor's office] it picks up not only what the suspected criminal says but what all other people say who come into the office... It is therefore a major infringement of perfectly innocent people's personal integrity and privacy if those bugs are placed in such places."

A further example of a statutory provision which leads to (at least partial) abrogation of privilege is section 2D of the Limitation Act 1939[68] which was considered by the Court of Appeal in *Jones* v *GD Searle & Co.*[69] This decision is considered in detail in Chapter 7.

Non-adversarial proceedings

Another exception to the usual rules of privilege has been recently confirmed by the House of Lords in relation to children's and wardship proceedings. This exception has been established by reference both to an implied statutory abrogation of the privilege and the fact that such proceedings are non-adversarial. In *Re L (a Minor), (Police Investigation: Privilege)*,[70] interim care orders were made in respect of the child of two drug addicts who asserted that the child's ingesting of methadone had been accidental. The parents were allowed by order to disclose the court papers to a medical expert, on terms that her report would be available to all parties to the proceedings. The expert's report in fact cast serious doubts on the parents' version of events with the result that the police authorities became interested and sought a copy. The mother challenged Bracewell, J's order permitting disclosure to the police, asserting that she had failed to uphold the absolute nature of the (litigation) privilege attaching to the report. In the House of Lords, the mother placed heavy reliance on Lord Taylor's judgment in *Derby Magistrates*. The majority in *Re L* recognised

---

67 Albeit a considerable improvement on earlier provisions in the Bill: see the author's article, *The Police and Privilege*, NLJ, 14 March, 1997 at 391.
68 Now s. 33 Limitation Act 1980, which is to the same effect.
69 [1979] 1 WLR 101.
70 [1997] AC 16.

the force of Lord Taylor's observations on the absolute nature of privilege.[71] However, they noted these were made by reference to advice privilege.

This enabled them to focus on distinctions between advice and litigation privilege, for example, the fact that whereas a solicitor could not, without his client's consent, be compelled to express an opinion on the factual or legal merits of the case, a third party who provides a (privileged) report to a client can be subpoenaed to give evidence by the other side including answering questions as to his factual findings and opinion thereon (see *Harmony Shipping Co* v *Saudi Europe Line Limited*).[72]

Consequently, the majority in *Re L* held that, since litigation privilege is an essential component of the English adversarial procedure, privilege could only be established for the expert's report if proceedings under Part IV of the 1989 Children Act are adversarial in nature. Approving Sir Stephen Brown P.'s judgment in *Oxfordshire County Council* v *M*[73], Lord Jauncey held that they are not. In his view,

> "... care proceedings under Part IV of the Act are so far removed from normal actions that litigation privilege has no place in relation to reports obtained by a party thereto which could not have been prepared without the leave of the court to disclose documents already filed or to examine the child".[74]

Lord Jauncey went on to hold that in Children Act 1989 proceedings litigation privilege never arises because:

> "It is excluded by necessary implication from the terms and overall purpose of the Act. This does not of course affect privilege arising between solicitor and client".[75]

Whilst the result is supportable in the special context of child-related proceedings, the reasoning is not, as Lord Nicholls' powerful dissenting speech[76] (with which Lord Mustill agreed) demonstrates. He disagreed that the Children Act 1989 intended to restrict legal professional privilege in family proceedings. Echoing Lord Taylor's comments in *Derby Magistrates*, he held that clear words or a compelling context are needed before Parliament can be taken to have intended that this "deeply imbedded"

---

71 See Section 3 above.
72 [1979] 1 WLR 1380: a case discussed in Chap. 3 below.
73 [1994] Fam 151. He had held that such proceedings are not adversarial in nature because children's cases fall into a special category where the court is bound to undertake all necessary steps to arrive at an appropriate result in the paramount interests of the welfare of the child.
74 [1997] AC 16 at 27.
75 *Ibid.*, at 27.
76 *Ibid.*, at 33.

privilege should be ousted in favour of another interest.[77] The public interest in a party being able to obtain informed legal advice in confidence prevails over the public interest in all relevant material being available to courts when deciding cases. As for Lord Jauncey's distinctions between advice and litigation privilege, Lord Nicholls' view was that the two subheads are integral parts of a single privilege:

> "In the context of court proceedings, the purpose of legal advice privilege would be frustrated if the legal advisor could not approach potential witnesses in confidence before advising the client. This is as much true in family proceedings as any other".[78]

Nor, in his view, did upholding privilege in any way conflict with the paramountcy principle which prevails in children's proceedings. The views of an expert, for example, can always be made available within the existing legal framework since it is open to any party to subpoena him. Given the court's ability to secure that result, he felt that to override or displace the privilege attaching to an expert's report made in Children Act proceedings could not be justified.

It is to be hoped that, in the light of the unanimous decision in *Derby Magistrates,* the exception established in *Re L* is confined to experts' reports prepared for care and analogous proceedings (such as wardship). While this appears to be the House's decision in *Re L,* the difficulty, as Lord Nicholls observed, is that once privilege is displaced in relation to experts' reports, then there is no logical reason why the same should not apply to an ordinary witness statement. Of more concern is the distinction between advice and litigation privilege which was deployed in *Re L.* Coupled with the unconvincing way in which the Children Act 1989 was interpreted to displace privilege, this decision may well encourage submissions that other statutes have similarly abrogated the usual rules as to privilege.

One consequences of the decision in *Re L* in that experts' reports which are not privileged because of the decision in *Re L* are therefore discoverable in any litigation in which they are relevant.[79] The Court of Appeal so held in *Vernon v Bosley (No. 2),*[80] in which it was also decided that the ratio decidendi of *Re L* was not confined to wardship or care proceedings: the principle extended to reports obtained from experts in Children Act proceedings – in this case an application for residence orders

---

77 As to this, see *Commissioner of Inland Revenue v West-Walker* [1954] NZLR 191.
78 *Ibid.,* at 33.
79 However, the right to inspect would be subject to Family Proceedings Rules 1991, r. 4.23.
80 [1997] 1 All ER 614.

in respect of children – which related to the psychiatric well-being of one of the parents. Where those reports became relevant in a subsequent "nervous shock" negligence action, then they do not acquire a privilege simply because they would have done so had they been brought into existence in other circumstances.[81]

Insolvency proceedings

Another type of proceeding in which there is scope for arguing that legal professional privilege cannot be asserted is those by which witnesses are summoned for examination or to produce documents either by a liquidator or trustee in bankruptcy pursuant to their respective powers under sections 236 and 366 of the Insolvency Act 1986. In either case, it is clear that the witness can never assert or hide behind the privilege of either the company in liquidation or of the bankrupt: the privilege is vested in the relevant office holder.[82] Nor, in such circumstances, can a witness who happens to be a solicitor for a third party who is in possession of information or documents confided to him or coming into his possession in that capacity assert any privilege in them if they would be discloseable if it were the client who was the witness at the examination.[83]

However, the point has been raised[84] whether a witness can assert a privilege which is his alone, and not that of the liquidator or the trustee, as a reason for refusing to answer questions and produce documents. This question was left open by Vinelott, J in *Re Brook Martin & Co (Nominees) Ltd*,[85] and was not raised at all in two other decisions in which the point could have been taken.[86] The Court of Appeal has, in contrast, held in *Bishopsgate Investment Management* v *Maxwell*[87] that the

---

81 Per Stuart-Smith, LJ, *ibid.*, at 628.
82 See *Re International Power Industries* [1985] BCLC 128 and *Re Konigsberg (a bankrupt)* [1989] 3 All ER 289. Further, having regard to s. 291 Insolvency Act 1986, which requires the bankrupt to deliver to the Official Receiver books and records, including "any which would be privileged from disclosure in any proceedings", relating to his estate and affairs, the bankrupt cannot himself assert his own privilege in an examination under s. 290 Insolvency Act 1986.
83 See the comments of Lightman, J in *Re Murjani (a bankrupt)* [1996] 1 All ER 65 at 72. See also the cases cited at n. 39 above.
84 See, *e.g. Insolvency*, Totty and Moss, at Section H 3.14.
85 [1993] BCLC 328.
86 *Re Highgrade Traders Ltd* [1984] BCLC 151 and *Re Aveling Barford* [1989] 1 WLR 360. Buckley on the Companies Acts (14th Edn., 1981) notes (at 651), in commentary to the predecessor provision in s. 268 Companies Act 1948 that, in *In re Mesco Properties* (unrep.), Mr Registrar Berkeley overruled a solicitor's assertion of his client's privilege on a s. 268 examination. While the note of this unreported decision suggests that the decision is supportable on the alternative basis that the crime-fraud exception (discussed in Chap. 8 below) applied, the note states that the Registrar over-ruled the privilege on the ground that otherwise the inquisitorial jurisdiction of the Court would be frustrated.
87 [1993] Ch 1.

privilege against self-incrimination does not justify a refusal to produce documents or answer questions on a section 266 Insolvency Act 1986 examination.

One of the arguments which is used to support the view that the privilege can be overridden is the fact that the examination is of a non-adversarial nature and is therefore, to that extent, akin to proceedings under the Children Act 1989. To this it might be said that it is difficult to see how questioning of a potential defendant by a liquidator could be said to be "non-adversarial";[88] further, as the House of Lords recognised in *Re L* (discussed at p. 18 above), even in children's proceedings, advice privilege can still be asserted. Another argument used to support the view that privilege is not available during these examinations is based on the fact that the Insolvency Act is silent in terms of any statutory preservation of the privilege. Since this contrasts with the approach adopted in other statutes, such as those mentioned in footnote 50 above, this supports the argument that there must be an implied abrogation of the privilege. However, this point alone cannot be conclusive, for in one instance, *Price Waterhouse* v *BCCI*,[89] where it has been held that statutory powers do exist to enable privilege to be overridden – as in section 39(13) of the Banking Act 1987 – the court took some comfort from the fact that the relevant statutory provision at least touches on the extent of the abrogation, even if it does not spell out the fact of the (partial) abrogation. In the same decision, Millet, J observed that there is authority to the effect that mere silence in a statute on this point does not override the privilege.

An additional argument in favour of abrogation of legal professional privilege in examinations under the Insolvency Act 1986 is that, otherwise, the purpose of the examinations,[90] namely, in the case of liquidators, to enable them to discover the truth of the circumstances relating *inter alia* to the affairs of the company so as to enable the liquidator as efficiently as possible to complete the liquidation, including pursuing claims, could be frustrated by wholesale reliance on privilege.

The counter-argument – quite apart from the absence of an express statutory abrogation of the privilege – is that, for example, to require a witness to divulge the privileged advice he has received in relation to legal

---

88 But an examination of a "mere" witness under s.366 of the Insolvency Act 1986 is a non-adversarial proceeding: per Lightman, J in *Re Murjani (a bankrupt)* [1996] 1 All ER 65. However, as Lord Nicholls noted in his dissenting judgment in *Re L*, to attach the "bewitching label of inquisitorial" (in that case, to family proceedings) "says nothing about whether legal professional privilege should or should not be available to a person who is a party to the proceedings": [1997] AC 16 at 31.

89 [1992] BCLC 583.

90 See, for example, *Re British & Commonwealth Holdings plc* [1993] AC 426.

proceedings which might be brought against him by the liquidators who are examining him or as to whether or not he should challenge the examination order would run directly contrary to the whole purpose of the privilege. Having regard to the House of Lords' decision in *Derby Magistrates,* and the acknowledgement in *Re L* that even advice privilege can be asserted in Children Act 1989 proceedings, it is submitted that examinations under sections 236 and 366 Insolvency Act 1986 ought, at the least, not to encroach on privileged advice relating to the witness's own position in potential litigation with the liquidator or trustee.

What though of the witness's instructions to his solicitors which might assist the liquidators' purpose? Style and Hollander[91] suggest that it might be appropriate to seek such a document if there is no other adequate source of information. Some support for this view can be detected in *Re Murjani (a bankrupt)*[92] where Lightman, J noted that the availability of legal professional privilege where a solicitor is examined under section 366 Insolvency Act 1986 is circumscribed in that it cannot extend to anything which his client can himself lawfully be required to reveal. This begs the question whether, and if so to what extent, legal professional privilege can be lawfully claimed at the examination by the client. However, while the position awaits a full judicial determination, Lightman, J's passing comments on the subject suggest that the court's approach is likely to be that, while blanket claims to privilege will not be allowed, equally, the importance of privilege is such that will not be easily overridden:

> "... the extent of the privilege is a matter to be kept in mind when considering what documents ought to be disclosed and what questions should be answered on the oral examination and, if a serious difficulty arises, it can be referred to the court for resolution".[93]

Finally, it is submitted that merely because the privilege against self-incrimination is not available in an Insolvency Act examination,[94] this does not itself undermine claims to legal professional privilege. There is a real distinction to be drawn between the privilege against self-incrimination and legal professional privilege. To uphold the former could well result in the liquidator learning nothing; upholding the latter merely results in the liquidator not learning how relevant facts might have been communicated to his solicitor. As will be seen in Chapter 2, legal professional privilege does not prevent the liquidator getting at those underlying facts.

91　*Documentary Evidence* (6th Edn.), 300.
92　[1996] 1 All ER 65.
93　*Ibid.,* at 72.
94　*Bishopsgate v Maxwell* [1992] BCC 214.

7. PRIVILEGE AS A RULE OF EVIDENCE: FURTHER LIMITATIONS

Since privilege is part of English procedural law, and the privilege itself does not confer any substantive rights (at least before the English courts), then, because a communication can be withheld from disclosure before the English courts on account of its privileged nature, it does not follow that it will be accorded the same treatment in proceedings before a foreign court or tribunal. Of course, there may well be similar – if not identical – rules applicable in the foreign court, particularly in Commonwealth and other countries whose legal system is common law based.[95] However, wherever legal advice – whether in an adversarial or non-adversarial context – is given in circumstances where it might be relevant to potential proceedings before a foreign court, the client would be well advised to seek the guidance of a foreign lawyer as to his court's approach to the issue of legal professional privilege.[96] Otherwise, he runs the danger that evidence which would be shielded from the eyes of the English courts is afforded no such protection abroad. In such a case, if used in evidence in the foreign proceedings, the argument may then arise that the privilege has been lost for the purposes of the English proceedings.

In the converse situation, the English courts are generous: communications falling within the scope either of advice or litigation privilege as those concepts are applied in English law[97] will be protected, irrespective of how a foreign court would treat them. Thus, an English court will not oblige a litigant involved in foreign civil proceedings who is resident in this country to produce documentation pursuant to letters rogatory issued by a foreign court for use in proceedings before that court where such documentation is susceptible to a claim for legal professional privilege under the English rules.[98] This is so even if the foreign court does

---

95 The European Court of Justice noted a "common law" of legal professional privilege in EC countries: see *AM&S Ltd v EC Commission* [1982] ECR 1575. The decision is discussed in Chap. 4. In Hong Kong, s.39A(2) of the Legal Practitioners Amendment Ordinance (No 60/1994) provides: "Solicitor–client privilege exists between a foreign lawyer and his client to the same extent as the privilege exists between a solicitor and his client".

96 See *Bonzel v Intervention Ltd (No 2)* [1991] RPC 231 discussed in Chap. 7, section 4.

97 Including under s. 10 Police and Criminal Evidence Act 1984: see *Crown Prosecution Service (on behalf of DPP of Australia) v Holman, Fenwick & Willan,* Unreported 13 December 1993, discussed in Chap. 2, Section 4.

98 See by way of example *Re Sarah C Getty Trust v Getty and Another* [1985] QB 956 discussed in Chap. 2. In a criminal context, see the Criminal Justice (International Co-operation) Act 1990 s. 4 and Sched. 1 para. 4(1)(a), whereunder an English court will not oblige a person to give evidence in this country for use in connection with a criminal proceeding or investigation overseas if it is evidence he would not be compelled to give in criminal proceedings before an English court.

not recognise the concept of legal professional privilege or, as in the case of some foreign jurisdictions, particularly in states in the United States of America, has its own rules as to privilege which are not precise equivalents to the English rules.

International litigation frequently gives rise to these types of problems. Such litigation inevitably involves parties, witnesses and thus evidence from a number of different countries. Often the same dispute will spawn related proceedings before the courts of a number of countries. This can give rise to difficult problems as to the admissibility in evidence, on a jurisdiction-by-jurisdiction basis, of materials which may be susceptible to a claim to privilege in one country but not in another. Which law is to apply in determining the question of what material is privileged and what is not may become important, particularly where one law would allow material to be withheld, and another would force its production. This question was first examined by the English courts in *Lawrence* v *Campbell*.[99] This concerned which law governed the privilege applying to communications between a Scottish solicitor practising in London and his client based in Scotland. The report does not spell this out, but evidently the Scottish lawyer could only advise on Scots law. The Vice Chancellor, Sir R.T. Kindersley, said:

> "A question has been raised as to whether the privilege in the present case is an English or a Scotch privilege; but sitting in an English court, I can only apply the English rule as to privilege ..."

This decision was cited with approval in *Re Duncan, deceased,*[1] which also applied the rule that the *lex fori* governs the question whether a document which a party seeks to have produced in proceedings before an English court is privileged. Ormrod, J held:

> "These matters are matters to be decided according to the practice of this court. I, therefore, hold that all the documents which are communications passing between the Plaintiff and his foreign legal advisors are privileged, whether or not proceedings in this or any other court were contemplated when they came into existences".[2]

In summary, the position in England is as follows:

- Before an English court a communication which would satisfy the requirements of privilege under English law will be upheld even though the communication is between a foreign lawyer (albeit one

---

99 (1859) 4 Drew 485.

1 [1968] P 306.

2 *Ibid.* at 312. This decision was followed in *Minnesota Mining & Manufacturing Co.* v *Rennicks (UK) Ltd* [1991] FSR 97 where Hoffmann, J refused an application for discovery of documents "subject to litigant's privilege arising in U.S. proceedings".

practising from England) and a foreign client relating to foreign legal advice: see *Lawrence* v *Campbell.*

- Similarly, communications between an English client and his foreign lawyer relating to foreign proceedings will also be regarded as privileged: see *Re Duncan.*[3]

- Communications between a foreign lawyer and his English client in which foreign legal advice is sought and proffered in relation to a business transaction are privileged (even though litigation is not then in prospect): *Great Atlantic Insurance Co* v *Home Insurance Co.*[4]

- Privilege also attaches to communications between a foreign lawyer and his client where the foreign lawyer advises on English law. This was recently decided by Aldous, J in *IBM Corp* v *Phoenix International (Computers) Ltd* where the Judge said:

> "The fact that the advice given [by American attorneys] related predominantly to English law is irrelevant. It was advice of foreign lawyers, acting as lawyers, to be used by Phoenix to decide what strategy to adopt in carrying on business ... The correct approach is to look at the substance and reality of the document, the circumstances in which it came into existence and also its purpose. It was advice given by lawyers in circumstances where litigation was contemplated to enable the recipient to decide what strategy to adopt, both from a legal and business standpoint. Such a document is privileged".[5]

While this is not yet a direct authority on the point, there is little reason to doubt, given the foregoing, that the advice of an English lawyer on a foreign law will be entitled to a similar protection before the English courts.

8. PRIVILEGE:
OTHER PROFESSIONS?

Lord Brougham's judgment in *Greenough* v *Gaskell*[6] makes clear that privilege is confined to communications involving members of the legal profession (hence legal professional privilege), albeit Lord Brougham could not easily justify this limitation.

As will be seen in the next chapter, to qualify for privilege, the lawyer must be acting in a professional capacity at the time the relevant

---

3' [1968] P 306. And see also *Bunbury* v *Bunbury,* (1839) 2 Beav 173.
4' [1981] 1 WLR 529. See also *Derby & Co Ltd* v *Weldon* (No 7) [1990] 1 WLR 1156 at 1179 and *Macfarlan* v *Rolt* (1872) LR 14 Eq 580.
5' [1995] 1 All ER 413, at 429.
6' [1833] 1 My & K 98.

communication is made. This means that he must have been professionally consulted. It does not, however, appear that he needs to hold a full English practising certificate or to have been called to the Bar: the decision in the *IBM* case (referred to at p. 24) shows that a foreign lawyer who advises on English law can enter into privileged communications.[7] The solicitor's employees such as a legal executive, a trainee solicitor, a licensed conveyancer and a paralegal can all create privileged documents in the course of their employment so long as they are acting in a capacity in which they are giving, or are helping to give, legal advice pursuant to the professional relationship which subsists between their solicitor employer and his client.[8] In-house lawyers can also create privileged communications.[9] The mere holder of a legal qualification cannot, without more, engage in privileged communications unless employed in a lawyer's office where he dispenses legal advice under appropriate supervision.

From time to time, attempts have been made to establish privileges beyond those accorded to dealings with lawyers. Whether or not one agrees with the importance placed by the courts on the relationship which exists between client and lawyer, from earliest times courts have refused to recognise any privileges arising from dealings with others in confidence, or relationships with other types of professionals.

Thus in *Wilson* v *Rastall* Buller, J stated in emphatic terms in 1792 that:

> "The privilege is confined to the cases of Counsel, solicitor, and attorney... I take the distinction to be now well settled, that the privilege extends to those three enumerated cases at all times, but that it is confined to these cases only. There are cases, to which it is much to be lamented that the law of privilege is not extended; those in which medical persons are obliged to disclose the information which they acquire by attending in their professional characters".[10]

There have been some minor relaxations of these principles. Thus, patent agents and trade mark agents can now, pursuant to sections 280 and 284 respectively of the Copyright, Designs and Patents Act 1988,[11] enter into

---

7' [1995] 1 All ER 413. In *Re Duncan* [1968] P 306, Ormrod, J noted at 311 that the principles relating to privilege had not been developed so as to require all qualifying lawyers to be on the Roll of solicitors: "The basis of the privilege is just as apt to cover foreign lawyers...provided only that the relationship of lawyer and client subsists between them".

8' See also s. 33 Administration of Justice Act 1985 and s. 63 Courts and Legal Services Act 1990.

9' As to whom see Chap. 4.

10' (1792) 4 Durn. & E 753, at 759.

11' As recently as 1983, trade mark agents were refused a privilege at common law: *Dormeuil Trade Mark* [1983] RPC 131; and beyond the statutory concessions, patent agents likewise have no privilege: *Wilden Pump Engineering Co* v *Fusfield* [1985] FSR 159, CA.

privileged communications where they are advising, whether or not in relation to litigation, on for example passing off matters, and matters concerning the protection of designs, trademarks or service marks. Auditors and tax advisers enjoy a limited privilege which entitles them to withhold documents which are their property and which they have created for the purposes of their auditing function or for giving tax advice in the face of statutory notices served by the Revenue in the exercise of the latter's powers under sections 20 and 20A of the Taxes Management Act 1970 (see section 20B(9)). Like the patent and trade mark agents', this privilege is a creature of statute.[12] Otherwise, a professional who is not a lawyer but who dispenses advice on the law, such as an accountant tax adviser, and members of the construction industry, cannot communicate with his client under the cloak of privilege. The ability of certain professionals to instruct counsel directly does not appear to have changed this.

Otherwise, Buller, J's laments have had no effect. Thus, ninety years later, in *Wheeler* v *Le Marchant*,[13] the Court of Appeal confirmed that the principle protecting confidential communications is of a very limited character:

> "It does not protect all confidential communications which a man must necessarily make in order to obtain advice, even when needed for the protection of life, or of his honour, or of his fortune. There are many communications which, though absolutely necessary because without them the ordinary business of life cannot be carried on, still are not privileged".[14]

The Master of the Rolls noted that communications with a medical man and a priest in the confessional, and to a friend with respect to matters of the most delicate nature, were never protected in the same way as privileged communications with a lawyer. In some respects, the court's stance is not easy to justify. Accountants, for example, now tend to dispense the majority of tax law advice in this country. It is difficult not to accord qualifying communications between (a non-legal) tax adviser and his clients a privileged status, having regard to the rationale underpinning privilege generally: namely, full and frank disclosure as between (legal) adviser and client. Yet it is extremely unlikely that a court will ever recognise such a privilege.[15]

12'   S. 20B(9), Taxes Management Act 1970.

13'   (1881) 17 Ch D 675.

14'   Per Jessel, MR, *ibid.* at 681.

15'   It is unlikely that the creation of a multi-disciplinary practice which includes lawyers and accountants would change these restrictions without more: only the lawyers could engage in privileged communications with their clients. However, nice questions might arise as to who is a lawyer in such a practise: *e.g.*, what of the accountant who dispenses tax advice under a lawyer's supervision?

So, the Employment Appeal Tribunal in *New Victoria Hospital* v *Ryan*[16] refused to recognise any privilege in communications between the Industrial Relations Personnel Consultants Group – a firm of personnel consultants – and the hospital. Though employing no legally qualified staff, the IRPC apparently dispensed legal advice. The EAT declined to follow a suggestion in *Phipson on Evidence* (14th Edition), based on the decision in *M and W Grazebrook* v *Wallens*,[17] that such advice could be privileged. Tucker, J, delivering the EAT's judgment, held that:

> "...the privilege should be strictly confined to legal advisers such as solicitors and counsel, who are professionally qualified, who are members of professional bodies, who are subject to the rules and etiquette of their profession, and also owe a duty to the Court.[18] This is clearly defined, and is an easily identifiable qualification for the attachment of privilege. To extend the privilege to unqualified advisers such as personnel consultants is in our opinion unnecessary and inadmissible."

Attempts to extend the range of available privileges have similarly failed. Thus in *Chantrey Martin & Co* v *Martin*,[19] in which a firm of chartered accountants sued their former employee for breach of his contract of service, an issue arose at the discovery stage as to whether the plaintiffs were obliged to produce all their working papers and schedules relating to the audit of the books of a client company, a company which was otherwise unconnected with the issues raised in the litigation. The accountants contended that these documents, though their own property, should not be produced because they embodied information which was the subject of professional confidence as between them and the client company: disclosure of the contents to the defendants would, it was argued, be a breach of their duty to the client company. Rejecting this submission, Jenkins, LJ commented:

> "Outside the area of legal professional privilege, which is not in question here, we do not think this is a sufficient ground for refusing an order for production".[20]

He went on to note a general proposition, to be found in *Bray on Discovery* (1885), to the effect that:

> "it is no ground for resisting production that a person not before the court

---

16[1] [1993] ICR 201; [1993] IRLR 202.
17[1] (1973) ICR 256.
18[1] This statement does not sit happily with the cases concerning foreign lawyers discussed in Section 7 above.
19[1] [1953] 2 QB 286.
20[1] *Ibid.*, at 293–294.

has an interest in the document ... unless it is an interest in the nature of property".[21]

The issue arose again ten years later in a *Attorney-General* v *Clough*[22] when the Court of Appeal was asked to recognise the confidential relationship which apparently exists between the press and a press informant as falling into a recognised category of privilege. The background was an enquiry established under the Tribunals of Inquiry (Evidence) Act 1921 following the imprisonment of an admiralty clerk for an offence under the Officials Secrets Act 1911. A journalist who had published an article about the clerk's imprisonment gave evidence to the inquiry but refused to reveal the identity of an informant who had given him information on which he had based his article. For the journalist it was argued that, legally and constitutionally, the press is in a special position, different from ordinary members of the public, such that it is entitled to special privileges which would extend to immunity from giving the names of the source of their information. Particular reliance was placed on the importance of confidential communications. Rejecting this claim, Lord Parker, CJ had not the slightest hesitation in concluding that, in regard to the press,

> "... the law has not developed and crystallised the confidential relationship in which [the press] stand[s] to an informant into one of the classes of privilege known to the law".[23]

Despite these authorities, Lord Denning, MR attempted to sanction an alternative ground of privilege in *Alfred Crompton Amusement Machines Limited* v *Customs and Excise Commissioners (No 2)*.[24] The facts of this litigation are considered in detail in Chapter 3. He held that tax commissioners were entitled to claim privilege on the grounds of confidence, a privilege which he described in this way:

> "... a party to litigation is not obliged to produce documents, or copies of documents, which do not belong to him, but which have been entrusted to his custody by a third party in confidence".[25]

The decision in *Chantry Martin* was prayed in aid of this "new" privilege. However, although apparently supported by Karminski, LJ, when the matter proceeded to the House of Lords[26] it was quickly, and decisively, killed off.

21' *The Principles and Practice of Discovery*, 194 (hereafter to be called "Bray").
22' [1963] 1 QB 773.
23' *Ibid.*, at 792. This case considers the position at common law. Subsequently, some protection has been afforded to confidential press sources under, for example, the Contempt of Court Act 1981 and the Police and Criminal Evidence Act 1984. See also *Saunders* v *Punch Limited (t/a Liberty Publishing)* [1998] 1 All ER 234.
24' [1972] 2 QB 102.
25' *Ibid.*, at 134.
26' [1974] AC 405.

Another "head" of privilege which has recently been sought, but rejected as being unknown to the law, is a "foreign state" privilege. In *Buttes Oil Co v Hammer (No 3)*[27] a submission was made that a foreign state could intervene and claim a privilege for itself, so as to entitle the foreign state to prevent the disclosure of any documents it considered "inimical to its own public interest". Lord Denning MR refused to admit such a principle into the law because it would give a foreign state a veto which is not available even to our own government.

Finally, it is relevant to note, albeit briefly, the so-called "matrimonial reconciliation" privilege. This privilege probably has considerably less importance than in former days when contested divorce proceedings were far more frequent than under the present divorce laws. This privilege, established by the Court of Appeal in *McTaggart v McTaggart,*[28] is to the effect that where proceedings between husband and wife are imminent and either or both consults an intermediary (such as a probation officer, marriage guidance counsellor or even a priest)[29] for the purposes of attempting to effect a reconciliation between them, then any statement, whether written or oral, made to the intermediary is privileged.[30] The rationale for excluding the reconciliation conversations from the courts is more akin to the justification for rendering inadmissible the contents of without prejudice discussions.[31] As with legal professional privilege, the privilege is that of the husband or wife, and not the intermediary. Thus, so long as neither of them objects (where they have both attended the same reconciliation meeting) or the husband or wife individually (where they have attended such a meeting alone), then there is no independent privilege in the intermediary entitling him to refuse to give evidence of the reconciliation discussions.[32]

27' [1981] QB 223, a decision discussed in more detail in Chap. 6 Section 3.

28' [1949] P 94

29' See *Pais v Pais* [1970] 3 WLR 830. Accordingly, the intermediary need not be legally qualified nor acting in a legal capacity for the purposes of this privilege.

30' See also *Mole v Mole* [1951] P 21, *Pool v Pool* [1951] at 470, *Henley v Henley* [1955] at 202, *Broome v Broome* [1955] P 190 and *Theodoropoulas v Theodoropoulas* [1964] at 311. In *R v Nottingham Justices, ex p. Bostock* [1970] 1 WLR 1117, it was held that conversations between an adoption society case worker and the alleged father of an unborn child concerning its possible adoption were not made with a view to compromising subsequent affiliation proceedings brought by the mother in which they were held to be admissible.

31' See Denning, LJ in *McTaggart v McTaggart* [1949] at 94.

32' See *Pais v Pais* [1970] 3 WLR 830.

9. PRIVILEGE AND
CONFIDENTIALITY

The concept of confidentiality is closely bound up with legal professional privilege.[33] Thus, as will be discussed in Chapter 2, any communication which is to qualify for privilege must have been made in confidential circumstances. The consequence is that all privileged communications are necessarily confidential ones; but it by no means follows that all confidential communications are privileged, since it is only the confidential relationship between lawyer and client which can give rise to a claim to privilege. Furthermore, once the underlying confidentiality is lost, this will usually result in the loss of the privilege, as will be discussed in Chapter 7.

The interplay between privilege and confidentiality is neatly highlighted by the decision in *Parry-Jones* (discussed in Section 5 above), where Diplock, LJ (having decided that it was not open to the solicitor to claim privilege in the circumstances then before the court), noted:

> "What we are concerned with here is the contractual duty of confidence, generally implied though sometimes expressed, between a solicitor and client...".[34]

The decision also illustrates an important distinction between the two concepts, namely that the strength of the relationship of confidence as between a professional and client is as nothing when compared to the strength of the relationship of confidence which exists where that professional is a lawyer and where it is open to that client to make a claim to privilege in respect of qualifying communications between them. As Lord Wilberforce made clear in *Science Research Council* v *Nassé*,[35] confidentiality – in contrast to privilege – is never sufficient of itself to exempt a document from discovery to an opponent.[36]

This applies as much to the solicitor's duty of confidentiality – where privilege is not available[37] – as to any other professional's duty. Indeed, the solicitor's duty:

> "...is subject to, and overridden by, the duty of any party to that contract [between solicitor and client] to comply with the law of the land. If it is the duty of such a party to a contract, whether at common law or under statute, to disclose in defined circumstances confidential information, then he must

---

33' See generally Toulson & Phipps, *Confidentiality* (1996).
34' [1969] 1 Ch 1 at 9.
35' [1980] AC 1028 at 1065.
36' See also, Staughton, LJ in *Arbuthnot* v *Fagan* [1996] Lloyd's Rep 135 at 152.
37' See *CHC Software Care Ltd* v *Hopkins & Wood* [1993] FSR 241.

do so, and any express contract to the contrary would be illegal and void. For example, in the case of banker and customer, the duty of confidence is subject to the overriding duty of the banker at common law to disclose and answer questions as to his customer's affairs when he is asked to give evidence on them in the witness box in a court of law".[38]

The same distinction is applied outside the court room. So, for example, police powers of seizure exercised under the Police and Criminal Evidence Act 1984 will entitle them in an appropriate case to take possession of confidential communications between a banker and customer[39] and a doctor and patient. They will not, however, allow them to seize privileged communications between a client and his lawyer.[40]

This difference is not affected by the public interest in the administration of justice, which brings with it the general requirement that all relevant evidence, including confidential materials, should be before a court . Thus, while a judge will be able to exercise some discretion as to whether or not information covered by an obligation of confidentiality should be disclosed, in most cases the balance comes down in favour of disclosure if he considers the material concerned to be relevant and admissible.[41] Thus, rare are the circumstances in which a subpoena *duces tecum* will fail to compel the production to a court of a confidential communication passing between a banker and customer. In contrast, there is no balancing exercise to be performed where those confidential materials are also privileged, for here the prevailing interest is the need to protect and preserve the privilege. As Lord Taylor, CJ commented in *Derby Magistrates:*

38[1] Per Diplock, LJ, in *Parry-Jones,* [1969] 1 Ch 1.
39[1] The decision in *Tournier v National Provincial and Union Bank of England* [1924] 1 KB 461 contains four well known exceptions to the banker's duty of confidentiality.
40[1] See Section 5 above.
41[1] In relation to confidential documents, see the recent Court of Appeal decision in *Wallace Smith Trust Co Ltd (in liq) v Deloitte Haskins & Sells* [1996] 4 All ER 403. Note also the Court of Appeal's decision in *Marcel v Commissioner of Police of the Metropolis* [1992] 2 WLR 50 which concerned the status of documents seized by the police under the Police and Criminal Evidence Act 1984 which a party to parallel litigation wanted to assist his civil claim. As to these, Sir Christopher Slade said (at pp. 70–71): "... there is a public interest in ensuring a proper observance by the police of the obligation of confidentiality in respect of documents seized under relevant powers. ... I cannot, however, see why that public interest should in all cases and in all circumstances outweigh the public interest in ensuring a full and fair trial on full evidence in cases where the police have seized documents under Part II of the Act of 1984 and wish to use them for the purpose of assisting the supposed victim of an alleged crime to obtain a fair trial of a claim for damages in a civil case on full evidence. Everything must depend on the circumstances of the particular case."

"... if a balancing exercise[42] was ever required in the case of legal professional privilege, it was performed once and for all in the 16th century...".[43]

The distinction between the status of a communication for which legal professional privilege can be claimed and one which is confidential is further illustrated by the decision in *Price Waterhouse* v *BCCI Holdings*.[44] Here, Price Waterhouse was served with notices by the Serious Fraud Office and the Bank of England under, respectively, section 2 Criminal Justice Act 1987 and section 39 Banking Act 1987. In both cases, the notices required them to produce documents which those authorities intended to pass on to the Bingham Inquiry which had been set up to investigate the collapse of the BCCI Banking Group in 1991. The documents included communications between Price Waterhouse and former client companies within the BCCI Group. The accountants wished to co-operate in that enquiry but were concerned that to hand the documents over without the protection of a court order might expose them to civil or criminal sanctions in the event it was found that those documents were subject to legal professional privilege or a duty of confidentiality owed to the former BCCI Banking Group. They therefore applied to the High Court by way of originating summons for declarations aimed at determining whether they could comply with the SFO and the Bank of England notices, notwithstanding any privilege which could be claimed over the documents concerned and any obligations of confidentiality owed to the Bank.

Although Millett, J ruled[45] that the question of privilege could not arise because Price Waterhouse were not legal advisers, his answer to a third question raised, namely whether any obligation of confidentiality attaching to their client communications precluded the intended disclosure, lead him to comment that:

> "Whereas legal professional privilege is normally an answer to compulsory disclosure to a court of law or, in most cases, to a body having statutory powers to require disclosure, confidentiality alone affords protection only against voluntary disclosure without the consent of the person to whom the duty of confidentiality is owed ... It is now well settled that where one party is in possession of information in respect of which he owes a duty of confidentiality to another, he is not ordinarily at liberty to divulge that

---

42' See also the Court of Appeal's decision in the *Aegis Blaze* [1986] 2 Lloyds Rep. 203 which similarly rejected a submission that it should conduct a balancing exercise to determine whether or not disclosure of privileged materials should be ordered. The decision is discussed in Chap. 4, Section 5.

43' [1996] AC 487 at 508.

44' [1992] BCLC 583.

45' *Ibid.*, at 588.

information to a third party without the consent or against the wishes of that other: see *A-G v Guardian Newspapers Ltd (No 2)*,[46] per Bingham, L.J. It is also well established that although there is a strong public interest in maintaining confidentiality, this may be outweighed by some countervailing public interest in disclosure, and that the latter is not limited to the public interest in detecting or preventing wrong-doing."[47]

On the facts of the case, the judge ruled that the public interest outweighed the duty of confidentiality owed to the bank, with the result that the accountants were at liberty to make disclosure to the Inquiry. In the process, he reaffirmed that the task of balancing competing interests has no bearing whatsoever on the question of whether privileged documents should be adduced in evidence.

10. CAN PRIVILEGE GIVE RISE TO SUBSTANTIVE (OR HUMAN) RIGHTS?

Although privilege is a cornerstone of the English justice system, it remains, primarily, a "mere" rule of evidence (albeit one which may now be capable of conferring "human rights").[48] Elsewhere, however, the rule of evidence is being slowly transformed into a more substantive right. Two decisions of the Canadian courts illustrate how privilege is tending to lose its temporal connection with the tendering of evidence inside a court room. This has the result that, in contrast to the position in England, it gives rise to rights which can be invoked at a much earlier stage, and not necessarily with direct reference to "judicial proceedings".

In *Solosky v The Queen*,[49] a prison governor opened certain items of correspondence which had passed between Mr Solosky, an inmate, and his solicitors. The correspondence was opened in the interests of prison security and pursuant to regulations – whose validity was not challenged – made under Canada's prison discipline laws. Mr Solosky objected to this and so asked the Supreme Court of Canada to declare that the correspondence passing between him and his solicitors should be treated as privileged correspondence which should be forwarded unopened.

46' *Ibid.*, at 596.
47' [1990] 1 AC 109 at 214.
48' See footnote 9 above which quotes Lord Taylor in *Derby Magistrates* who averted to the possibility of privilege being a fundamental human right. Lord Nicholls, in his dissenting speech in *Re L*, suggested that the unavailability of litigation privilege in family proceedings might deny a parent the right to a fair hearing to which he is entitled under Art. 6(1) (read with Art. 8) of the Human Rights Convention: [1997] AC 16 at 32. See further p. 36 below.
49' [1980] 1 SCR 821.

The court recognised that Canadian case law had begun to develop the traditional approach to privilege in such a way that it was:

> "... no longer regarded merely as a rule of evidence which acts as a shield to prevent privileged materials from being tendered in evidence in a court room".[50]

So, in a number of cases involving police search warrants, the Canadian courts had ruled that privileged documents seized in the execution of those warrants could not be tendered in evidence at the trial in connection with which they had been obtained. However, even in those cases the "evidential connection" of the privilege had been retained such that they could be rationalised "as merely shifting the time at which the privilege can be asserted".[51] This was not enough to assist Mr Solosky. Rejecting the submission that privilege had come to be recognised as a "fundamental principle" more properly characterised as a "rule of property", the court ruled that privilege was still aimed at improper use or disclosure of evidence, and not at the mere opening of letters. It was therefore difficult to see how the privilege could be engaged within prison walls and far from a court or quasi-judicial context.[52]

Two years later, the Supreme Court of Canada in *Descoteaux* v *Mierzwinski*[53] held that it was quite apparent that the court in *Solosky* had applied a standard that had nothing to do with privilege as a rule of evidence, but instead had applied a substantive rule, albeit without actually formulating it.[54] The facts in *Descoteaux* were that police officers searched the premises of a legal aid office searching for a legal aid application form completed by L who was suspected of having reported a low income in order to qualify for public funding. As the warrant was being executed, a lawyer made a claim for privilege with the result that the documents concerned were placed in a sealed envelope.[55] Application was then made for a writ of certiorari requesting that the seizure be quashed

---

50' Per Dickson, J in *Solosky* at 836.

51' *Ibid.*, Dickson, J at 836 and 837.

52' There was a small crumb of comfort for Mr Solosky in that the court noted that interference with a prisoner's mail required the prison authorities to adopt a minimalist approach so as to ensure that the solicitor–client privilege is established in each case. For Dickson, J, this would allow (i) opening an envelope to inspect for contraband; (ii) reading a letter only to the extent necessary to ensure it contains a confidential communication; and (iii) maintaining the confidentiality of its contents: *ibid.*, at 841–842.

53' 141 DLR 590.

54' At 604, per Lamer, J who gave the judgment of the court.

55' For an account of the English practice of sealing documents for which a disputed claim to privilege is made in the course of attempts by the police to execute a search warrant see *R* v *Leeds Magistrates' Courts, ex p. Dumbleton* (unrep., 27 April 1993) (CA).

and the documents in the envelope returned unread to the legal aid office.

Arguments were raised as to whether or not the application form was privileged, issues which the court resolved in the favour of L.[56] As to whether the question of privilege was relevant at this stage the court held that it was no longer necessary to wait for a trial or other form of judicial enquiry at which a privileged communication is to be adduced in evidence before questions as to its admissibility can be raised:

> "The fundamental right to communicate with one's legal advisor in confidence has given rise to a rule of evidence and a substantive rule. Whether through the rule of evidence or the substantive rule, the client's right to have his communications to his lawyer kept confidential will have an effect when [a] search warrant ... is being issued and executed".[57,58]

The debate in England has taken a slightly different course, where by and large similar results are achieved to those reached in the two Canadian cases through the use of statutory protections.[59] The closest that the English courts have come so far in this country to developing a substantive rule is the Court of Appeal's decision in *R v Secretary of State for the Home Department, ex parte Leach (No 2)*.[60] Like *Solosky*, this decision concerned the right of a prisoner to correspond with his legal advisors without that correspondence being read by the prison governor. The statutory context was section 47(1) of the Prison Act 1952, pursuant to which rule 33(3) of the Prison Rules 1964 had been made whereby a governor could read every letter to or from a prisoner. An exception to this provision was contained in rule 37A which disentitled him from reading or stopping correspondence between a prisoner and his legal advisor where the prisoner was party to proceedings in which a writ had already been issued. Leach, who contemplated commencing legal proceedings, but had not yet started them, applied by way of judicial review for a declaration that rule 33(3) was *ultra vires* the regulation – making powers contained in the Prison Act 1952 on the ground that it

---

56' This case is discussed further in this context in Chap. 3 below.

57' *Ibid.,* at 618.

58' In the event, since the legal aid form had allegedly been completed with a view to committing a criminal offence, this gave rise to the so called crime/fraud exception to privilege – discussed in Chap. 8 below – thus robbing the form of the protection with which it would otherwise have been blessed. So the Justice of the Peace had jurisdiction to order seizure of the document. However, that jurisdiction was limited to his examining the form, once seized, for the purposes of determining whether it contained anything confidential/privileged and, if it did, to photocopying only that part which was relevant to the applicant's financial means. Thereafter, the original form was to be replaced into the sealed envelope for eventual return to the legal aid office.

59' See Section 5 above.

60' [1994] QB 198.

enabled the governor to interfere with privileged correspondence.

In determining that rule 33(3) was invalid, the Court of Appeal focused primarily on the fact that the rule was *ultra vires* the enabling statute. While the Court did not try to develop a substantive rule of privilege, its approach nonetheless echoed that adopted in *Solosky*. More interestingly, having regard to the way in which the Court examined the impact of rule 33(3) on a prisoner's civil rights, the decision has been hailed as a one which "delivers a highly effective common law bill of rights".[61] The Court's starting point was that a convicted prisoner retained all civil rights which were not taken away expressly or by necessary implication. Encouraged by the fact that it was not referred to any instance in which subordinate legislation had been employed to abolish common law privilege where the enabling legislation had similarly failed expressly to abolish it, the court was able to hold that because rule 33(3) conferred an unrestricted right on a governor to read potentially privileged correspondence, it was *ultra vires* section 47 of the enabling Act which did not itself authorise rules impeding communications between a prisoner and a solicitor.[62]

The result in *Leach (No 2)*, even if it evidences the progress made by the English Courts "towards the recognition of a general presumption in favour of fundamental rights",[63] does not, it is submitted, yet go so far as the Court in *Solosky* in treating privilege as a substantive right: in England, it is still first and foremost a rule of evidence temporally attached to the adducing of evidence in Court and which, divorced from that context, is dependent on statutory protection. However, as *Leach (No. 2)* (and the decision on similar facts of the European Court of Human Rights in *Silver* v *United Kingdom*[64]) shows, the climate may well be developing where privilege is, in certain circumstances, treated as a fundamental human right. In this regard, it will be interesting to see how the European Convention for the Protection of Human Rights[65] will impact on privilege as a substantive right once incorporated into domestic law (as now seems likely) in 1998.

61' See Murray Hunt, *Using Human Rights Law in English Courts* (1997), at 178–180.

62' However, the Court did approve the minimum interference rules developed in *Solosky*: see n. 52' above.

63' Hunt, *op. cit.* 180.

64' (1983) 5 EHRR 347.

65' (1953) Cmnd. 8969.

Chapter 2

LEGAL PROFESSIONAL PRIVILEGE: ADVICE PRIVILEGE

1. INTRODUCTION

This chapter examines the nature and the scope of the advice head of privilege, the focus of which is the protection of communications between a client and his lawyer. As well as examining the underlying principles which determine the application of this head of privilege, the chapter will also look at examples of the types of communications which are commonly within the scope of the privilege; as well as those which tend to fall outside it. The chapter includes a discussion of the important difference between advice privilege and litigation privilege (which is then considered in detail in Chapter 3).

2. ADVICE PRIVILEGE: THE ESSENTIAL ELEMENTS

In order to establish a successful claim to advice privilege, the following essential elements must be present:

- a communication, whether written or oral;
- made confidentially;
- between a client and his lawyer, acting in a professional capacity;
- made for the (dominant[1]) purpose of enabling the client to seek or the lawyer to give legal advice or assistance.[2-3]

These principles extend so as to protect other confidential communications made for the purpose of seeking or giving legal advice, namely:

---

1 It is still a matter of debate whether the purpose should be the "dominant" purpose: see the discussion on this in Section 3 below.
2–3 As discussed in Chap. 1, Section 7, this need not be English law advice.

- lawyer-to-lawyer communications made on behalf of the same client;
- communications between a client and lawyer made on their respective behalves by agents;
- communications between a client and lawyer in which related commercial advice or assistance is sought or given; and
- certain types of confidential documents which, strictly, are not communications but which are created by the lawyer or client and come into existence either to enable the legal (or related commercial) advice or assistance to be sought or given, or as a consequence of such legal advice or assistance having been sought or given, or to enable such legal advice or assistance to be carried into effect.

As should be apparent, what advice privilege does not protect is communications between a lawyer, or his client, and a third party. Subject to the vexed issue of communications with or through agents, which is considered in detail in Chapter 4, these fall within the exclusive ambit of litigation privilege.

3. ADVICE PRIVILEGE: LEGAL ADVICE AND ASSISTANCE

At one level, the characteristics summarised in Section 2 above enable most types of communications protected under this head of privilege to be identified without any real difficulty. So, assuming all the other requirements of the privilege are satisfied, any request by a client to his solicitor for legal advice on a particular issue will be privileged, as will the solicitor's advice. Similarly, the solicitor's instructions to a barrister on behalf of the client in relation to that same matter are also privileged.[4] On the other side of the coin, the mere fact that a professional relationship exists between a lawyer and a client does not mean that every communication between them will fall within the scope of advice privilege: casual social conversations not referable to the matter on which the lawyer has been retained to advise, and whether or not taking place at the lawyer's place of business, will not be privileged.[5] Similarly, a conversation between

---

4 See, *e.g.*, *Mostyn v West Mostyn Coal Co.* (1876) 34 LT 531.
5 See, *e.g.*, Lord Buckmaster in *Minter v Priest* [1930] AC 558 at 568. Note, however, that if during the course of such a conversation a solicitor learns information about his client, professional conduct rules require him to respect the confidentiality of the matters so

a solicitor and client about the subject matter of a former retainer between them may not fall within the privilege.[6] The real difficulty arises in attempting to determine what other communications between a client and legal adviser are protected under the advice head of privilege. Furthermore, while lawyers (including judges) routinely talk in terms of privileged "communications", it is clear that certain types of document which do not comprise communications[7] – in the sense, for example, of a letter – can nonetheless fall within the privilege: these too need to be identified.

The "purpose of advice" test

In the early nineteenth century, many such difficulties did not arise. Prior to the decision in *Greenough* v *Gaskell*[8] in 1833, legal professional privilege was confined to the seeking or provision of legal advice which related to contemplated or actual litigation, that is litigation privilege.[9] However, with Lord Brougham's famous judgment in *Greenough,* the requirement that privilege could only be claimed for qualifying communications which related to litigation was removed, since:

> "... the protection would be insufficient if it only included communications more or less connected with judicial proceedings; for a person often requires the aid of professional advice on the subject of his rights and liabilities, with no reference to any particular litigation...".[10]

Thus this judgment established advice privilege as a separate head of privilege which extended beyond legal advice sought or given in

---

imparted. Thus the seventh edition of *The Guide to the Professional Conduct of Solicitors* states in relation to a lawyer's general duty to keep his client's affairs confidential at para. 16.01 that "A solicitor is under a duty to keep confidential to his or her firm the affairs of clients and to ensure that the staff do the same". In expansion of this principle, commentary at p. 283 of the *Guide* emphasises that the duty in conduct, subject to specified recognised exceptions, "extends to all matters communicated to a solicitor by the client or on behalf of the client" and that "non-privileged communications remain subject to the solicitor's duty to keep the client's affairs confidential". As to the solicitor's duty of confidentiality at law, see the discussion of *Parry-Jones* v *Law Society* [1969] 1 Ch 1 in Chap. 1, Section 8.

6 See *Cobden* v *Kenrick,* 4 TR 431.

7 See Taylor, LJ in *Balabel* v *Air India* [1988] 1 Ch 317 at 330, quoted at p. 41 below.

8 (1833) 1 My & K 98.

9 See Taylor, LJ in *Balabel* v *Air India* [1988] 1 Ch 317 at 324. And no doubt this is why privilege is "sometimes ascribed to the exigencies of the adversary system of litigation under which a litigant is entitled within limits to refuse to disclose the nature of this case until the trial": per Lord Wilberforce in *Waugh* v *British Railways Board* [1980] AC 521 at 531.

10 *Op. cit.,* note 8 at 102.

connection with litigation.[11] But the question which the courts have continually grappled with since then is the extent to which advice privilege extends beyond the litigation context.[12]

In 1846, in *Carpmael* v *Powis*, Lord Lyndhurst, LC suggested that advice privilege was broad in scope:

> "I am of opinion that the privilege extends to all communications between a solicitor, as such, and his client, relating to matters within the ordinary scope of a solicitor's duty".[13]

Eighty years later, Greer, LJ in the Court of Appeal in *Minter* v *Priest*, spoke in similar terms when he said that legal professional privilege "... applies to communications between client and solicitor in respect of all matters which come within the ordinary scope of professional employment...".[14] When *Minter* v *Priest* was appealed to the House of Lords, Lord Atkin approved an arguably narrower test[15] to the effect that advice privilege covered "professional communications of a confidential character for the purpose of getting legal advice".[16]

Because of these various formulations, in 1988 the Court of Appeal in *Balabel* v *Air India*[17] was required to examine the scope of advice privilege in detail. The result is the leading modern judgment which has helped both to clarify this head of privilege and to place it in the modern commercial context in which many lawyers now operate.

Balabel concerned an action for specific performance arising from an alleged oral agreement between the parties for the grant of an underlease of business premises. There was a dispute as to whether an agreement had been reached. In an effort to try to obtain the necessary note or memorandum of agreement required under section 40, Law of Property Act 1925, the plaintiffs sought to probe the defendants' documentation. They accordingly sought discovery of various internal communications of both the defendants and their solicitors, as well as communications

---

11 Although this did not prevent attempts, even 40 years later, to confine privilege once more to communications which had a connection with litigation. All such doubts were finally put to rest by the 1873 decision in *Minet* v *Morgan* (1873) 8 Ch App 361, in which Lord Selborne, L.C., expressed his surprise that such arguments could be "revived". He approved Sir R.T. Kindersley's statement in *Lawrence* v *Campbell* 4 Drew 485 quoted at p. 43 below.

12 An excellent summary of the development of the advice head of privilege in the nineteenth century is to be found in Bray, *op. cit.*, pp. 368–371.

13 (1833) 1 My & K 98.

14 [1929] 1 KB 655 at 683–684.

15 Stated by Cotton, LJ in *Gardner* v *Irvin* (1878) 4 Ex D 49 at 53.

16 [1930] AC 558 at 581.

17 [1988] 1 Ch 317.

between them other than those by which legal advice was manifestly sought or given. Whilst the plaintiffs contended that it was only the latter communications which were privileged, the defendants argued that there should be a "blanket of privilege" over all of the documents in dispute since all steps, whether advisory or executive, taken by a solicitor in the course of negotiations for a lease would be within the scope of his ordinary business on behalf of his client and therefore privileged. The plaintiffs' contentions failed before the master but succeeded before the judge who held that the defendants were:

> "... entitled to withhold all communications which seek or convey advice, even though parts of them may contain narratives of facts or other statements which in themselves would not be protected. On the other hand, documents which simply record information or transactions, with or without instructions to carry them into execution, or which record meetings at which the plaintiffs were present, are not privileged".[18]

The judge's approach, which would have necessitated a selective exercise designed to distinguish those documents by which legal advice was sought or given (which could be withheld) from those which merely recorded information or events or merely gave instructions (which could not be withheld), was rejected by the Court of Appeal as being too restrictive.[19]

According to Taylor, LJ, who gave the court's judgment, the correct test for determining whether advice privilege applies to a particular document requires a court to ascertain:

> "... whether the communication or other document was made confidentially for the purposes of legal advice. Those purposes have to be construed broadly. Privilege obviously attaches to a document conveying legal advice from solicitor to client and to a specific request from the client for such advice. But it does not follow that all other communications between them lack privilege. In most solicitor and client relationships, especially where a transaction involves protracted dealings, advice may be required as appropriate on matters great or small at various stages. There will be a continuum of communication and meetings between the solicitor and client. The negotiations for a lease such as occurred in the present case are only one example. Where information is passed by the solicitor or client to the other as part of the continuum aimed at keeping both informed so that advice may be sought and given as required, privilege will attach. A letter from the client containing information may end with such words as "please advise me what I should do". But, even if it does not, there will usually be implied in the relationship an overall expectation that the solicitor will at each stage, whether asked specifically or not, tender appropriate advice. Moreover, legal

---

18 [1988] 1 Ch 317 at 323.
19 *Ibid.*, at 332.

advice is not confined to telling the client the law; it must include advice as to what should prudently and sensibly be done in the relevant legal context".[20]

The importance of this formulation is that it focuses on the purpose of the communication, as opposed merely to its specific contents, with the result that advice privilege extends beyond a client's bare request to his lawyer for legal advice and his lawyer's response. Indeed, as Taylor, LJ noted, the "purpose of legal advice" test will result in most communications between a solicitor and client in a conveyancing transaction being exempt from disclosure – so long as they are part of the continuum aimed at keeping both informed.[21] So, whilst communications between a solicitor and client which obviously seek or convey legal advice are privileged, the question whether those which do not are privileged depends:

> "on whether they are part of that necessary exchange of information of which the object is the giving of legal advice as and when appropriate".[22]

Purpose of the communication

The essence of advice privilege is a client–lawyer communication. As the law now stands, the subject matter of that communication is irrelevant to a claim to privilege under this head, so long as it is one which concerns the seeking or giving of legal advice or is otherwise part of "that necessary exchange of information" referred to in *Balabel*. Accordingly, advice privilege now properly encompasses client–lawyer communications which are concerned with litigation, whether pending or in progress. This is notwithstanding the fact that historically such communications were protected by litigation privilege.[23,24] However, the courts have for some time now emphasised that the historic link between privilege and litigation is no longer of relevance to these types of communications. Thus, in 1979 Lord Edmund-Davies, in *Waugh* v *British Railways Board,* the leading modern authority on litigation privilege, referred to a failure in some cases

---

20 *Ibid.,* at 330.
21 However, there are limits. The court in *Balabel* was concerned to ensure that its analysis was distinguished from dicta in the earlier cases which appeared "to extend privilege without limit to all solicitor and client communications on matters within the ordinary business of a solicitor and referrable to that relationship": see Taylor, LJ *ibid.,* at 331.
22 Taylor, LJ, *ibid.,* at 332.
23 For this reason, many of the decisions referred to in this chapter are concerned with advice given in relation to litigation.
24 It should be noted that some formulations of litigation privilege still encompass such communications, even though this is strictly unnecessary. In any case, the scope of the protection does not differ as between the two heads, though see n. 28 below.

"... to keep clear the distinction between (a) communication between client and legal adviser, and (b) communication between the client and third parties... in cases falling within (a), privilege from disclosure attaches to communications for the purpose of obtaining legal advice and it is immaterial whether or not the possibility of litigation were even contemplated... but in cases falling within (b) the position is quite otherwise. Litigation, apprehended or actual, is its hallmark".[25]

He pointed out that the law had recognised as much as early as 1859, when Sir R.T. Kindersley, VC in *Lawrence* v *Campbell* had noted that:

"... it is not now necessary as it formerly was, for the purpose of obtaining production, that the communications should be made either during or relating to an actual or even to an expected litigation. It is sufficient if they pass as professional communications in a professional capacity".[26]

In similar vein, Lord Denning, MR in *Buttes Oil & Gas Co v Hammer (No 3)* said:

"Privilege in aid of litigation can be divided into two distinct classes: the first is legal professional privilege properly so called. It extends to all communication between the client and his legal adviser for the purpose of obtaining advice. It exists whether litigation is anticipated or not...".[27]

More recently, Saville, J in *The "Good Luck"*,[28] dealt with a challenge to the plaintiffs' claim to privilege over documents containing information and advice from the plaintiffs' lawyers relating to proceedings brought against the defendants by the "Good Luck's" owners in these terms:

"The defendants submit that seeking and obtaining legal advice concerning litigation between other parties is not covered by legal professional privilege. I disagree. If the lawyer-client communication falls within the principles stated by Lord Justice Taylor [in *Balabel*] then it seems to me that ... the subject matter of the advice is an irrelevant consideration when deciding whether or not the communication is privileged".

Dominant Purpose?

That lawyer–client communications concerned with giving or seeking

---

25 [1980] AC 521 at 541–542. The distinction referred to by Lord Edmund-Davies is more or less made in the statutory definition of privilege contained in s. 10(1) Police and Criminal Evidence Act 1984, quoted at p. 235 below.

26 (1859) 4 Drew 485 at 490. (The All England report of *Waugh* in fact misquotes this extract, excluding the "not" in the first line: [1979] 2 All ER 1169 at 1181. Also, the report of *Lawrence* v *Campbell* refers to "production" when "protection" was clearly intended.)

27 [1981] 1 QB 223 at 243–244, cited as an "orthodox" summary of the law by Bingham, LJ in *Ventouris* v *Mountain* [1991] 1 WLR 607 at 617. See also Oliver, LJ in *Re Highgrade Traders* [1984] BCLC 151.

28 [1992] 2 Lloyd's Rep. 540 at 541.

advice in relation to litigation are now protected under the advice head of privilege does not affect the extent of the protection thereby afforded, as compared with litigation privilege: the benefits arising from legal professional privilege are the same, irrespective of which head of privilege is relied upon.[29] Nor in practice, subject to the point raised in the next paragraph, does the fact that the claim is made under the advice head affect the range of communications which is protected.

However, there remains one potential difficulty in applying the *Balabel* scope of advice test to all client–lawyer communications. This arises in relation to communications which comprise so-called "dual-purpose" communications, for example, documents prepared by a client both to enable legal advice to be sought from his lawyer in relation to litigation and to serve other purposes not directly related to that advice, such as an extraneous commercial purpose. In relation to litigation privilege, this problem has been solved by the dominant purpose test approved in *Waugh* and discussed in detail in Chapter 3. This only protects dual purpose communications which have come into existence with the dominant purpose inter alia of being used to seek legal advice in relation to litigation.

In relation to advice privilege, there has not yet been an English decision in which a court has had to grapple with the status of a client–lawyer communication which serves a dual purpose. No reference to the point was made in *Balabel,* although arguably the thrust of the "purpose of advice" test described in that decision achieves the same result in practice as the dominant purpose test. However, it could be argued that the dominant purpose test is in fact already an integral part of advice privilege given the House of Lord's approval in *Waugh* of the judgment of Barwick, CJ in the Australian decision of *Grant v Downs,*[30] and in particular his conclusion that a document produced "with the dominant purpose of its author... of using it or its contents in order to obtain legal advice..." is privileged.[31]

---

29 The courts occasionally deal with lawyer/client communications relating to litigation on the basis that they are subject to both litigation and advice privileges: see, *e.g. George Doland Ltd v Blackburn Robson Coates & Co* [1972] 3 All ER 959. As suggested in the text, this is strictly unnecessary, since no benefits or disadvantages accrue depending on whether such communications are properly susceptible to advice or litigation privileges. However, in *Doland* dual protection afforded by both privileges gave the litigant the ability to waive advice privilege, while allowing him to retain the benefits of litigation privilege which he was held not to have waived. The decision in relation to these waiver aspects is probably wrongly decided: see Chap. 7, Section 8.

30 (1976) 135 CLR 674 at 674: see further Chap. 3, Section 3.

31 *Grant v Downs* in the event established a "sole" purpose test, which the House of Lords in *Waugh* rejected as the appropriate English law test. It is clear from subsequent decisions that in Australia the "sole purpose" test applies to both the advice and litigation heads of privilege: see *Nickmar Pty Ltd v Preservatrice Skandia Insurance Ltd* (1985) 3 NSWLR 44.

In support of this view, one can point to sporadic references in subsequent case reports concerning the application to advice privilege of the dominant purpose test approved in *Waugh*. So, comments of Oliver, LJ in *Guinness Peat Properties Limited v Fitzroy Robinson Partnership*[32] appear to suggest that the dominant purpose test is relevant to both heads of privilege; and in *C.P.S. on behalf of D.P.P. for Australia v Holman Fenwick & Willan*,[33] Morland, J in the Divisional Court held that certain documents were not privileged because they had not come into existence "for the dominant purpose of giving legal advice".[34] On the other hand Gatehouse, J in *Re British & Commonwealth Holdings Plc*,[35] appeared to reject this view. The point arose in this case in relation to memoranda which were concerned with the question whether money should be lent to X. It was submitted that this was primarily a commercial decision. Accordingly, the memoranda could not be privileged, even though they referred to legal advice bearing on this issue, because their dominant purpose was not the obtaining or giving of advice. Gatehouse, J., disagreeing, did not think that "the principle of *Waugh*'s case applies to every document produced for dual purpose, in particular these memoranda".[36]

It is submitted that the logical solution to the dual purpose problem is to develop the *Balabel* principles by introducing the additional requirement of a "dominant purpose" test. Very recently, the courts moved towards this position, albeit in the event without needing to adopt it.

In *The Sagheera*,[37] a vessel blew up and sank in the Gulf of Oman. The owners and their war risk underwriters jointly instructed the same firm of London solicitors to investigate the cause of the explosion. The owners' hull and machinery ("H&M") underwriters were also notified. Litigation was anticipated at an early stage. In the event, the war risk underwriters paid the owners' claim, instructed their own solicitors, took an assignment of the owners' claim against the H&M underwriters and then sued them. In the litigation, the war risk underwriters' claim for privilege for communications between themselves and their solicitors "for the purpose of obtaining and giving legal advice and assistance" was challenged by the H&M underwriters. These communications related to the solicitors'

---

32 [1987] 1 WLR 1027 at 1039. The case is discussed in detail in Chap. 3, Section 7.
33 Unrep., 13 December 1993, transcript at p. 6.
34 The documents concerned are discussed in Section 5 below.
35 Unrep., 4 July, 1990.
36 *Ibid.*, Transcript at p. 3. The decision is considered further in Chap. 4.
37 *Hellenic Mutual Risks Association (Bermuda) Ltd v Harrison (The "Sagheera")* [1997] 1 Lloyd's Rep. 160.

investigation on the joint instructions of the owners and war risk underwriters. In relation to other categories of documents the war risk underwriters claimed privilege under the litigation head.

In relation to the client–lawyer communications, the defendants submitted that legal advice privilege was only available on a document-by-document basis, upon proof that each was brought into existence for the dominant purpose of obtaining or giving legal advice. The defendants apparently hoped to persuade the judge that because the solicitors had undertaken a factual investigation into the cause of the casualty, then he could not accept that the dominant purpose of the retainer as a whole was merely to give legal advice. On this basis, so it was hoped, many of the documents for which privilege was claimed would fall outside the scope of advice privilege.

The judge examined whether the dominant purpose test has any application to legal advice privilege and, noting the *Guinness Peat* case referred to above, as well as the judgment in *Balabel,* concluded that it did. However, he went on to note that for practical purposes its application differs as between the two heads of privilege. He said that, in relation to litigation:

> "... the focus is always very much upon the purpose for which a particular document was prepared, and that is readily understandable in the context of documents not passing directly between solicitors and their clients. In legal advice privilege, I would suggest, the practical emphasis is upon the purpose of the retainer. If the dominant purpose of the retainer is the obtaining and giving of legal advice, then, although it is in theory possible that individual documents may fall outside that purpose, in practice it is unlikely. If, however, the dominant purpose of the retainer is some business purpose, then the documents will not be privileged, unless exceptionally even in that context advice is requested or given, in which case the relevant documents probably are privileged".[38]

In the case before him, since the retainer was for the purpose of investigating and advising on the casualty, that meant the dominant purpose test was satisfied so that the claim for privilege was upheld.

Presumably the judge's intention in introducing the dominant purpose test in this way was to make it simpler in future to make and determine claims to privilege under the advice head, since he removed the necessity for a document-by-document examination. Does his test deal with the issue of dual-purpose documents? On one level, one could answer this question affirmatively, since on the basis of the judge's formulation, if a retainer can be identified for which the dominant purpose is the obtaining

---

38 *Ibid.,* at 168.

and giving of legal advice, then he appears to suggest that all documents passing between client and lawyer in relation to the retainer and which satisfy the *Balabel* scope of advice test will be within the privilege. To the extent that he suggested individual documents may fall outside it, no practical guidance is given as to what these might be, although his judgment does refer to Taylor, LJ's comments in this respect in *Balabel*. If this interpretation is right, then the *Balabel* test is potentially of wider application than the litigation privilege dominant purpose test, since advice privilege will now more readily catch dual-purpose documents than will the litigation head. In this one respect the decision is a disappointment since this formulation could arguably enable privilege to be claimed for dual-purpose documents whose dominant purpose was not the seeking of legal advice. No real difficulties arise in practice from a document-by-document claim to litigation privilege and it is not easy to see why the position should be any different in relation to advice privilege: after all, any lawyer worth his salt will scrutinise all documents individually before asserting his client's claim to privilege. It is, however, with this decision but a short step to apply this test to a dual-purpose document, and it is submitted that there can be no objection in principle to doing so.

4. ADVICE PRIVILEGE: WHAT IS COVERED

The following is an attempt to identify the more frequently encountered communications which form part of that "necessary exchange" between lawyer and client and for which advice privilege can be claimed in the light of the decision in *Balabel*:

- All communications, in whatever form, whereby a client expressly seeks legal advice or assistance, and a lawyer provides it, will be privileged. This applies as much to oral communications,[39] as well as to documentary communications. There is no limitation on the mode of communication which can qualify under either of the heads of privilege. Thus qualifying documents will include the full range from letter, memorandum, note, fax, telex through to modern forms of communication, such as electronic mail. Similarly, messages left on answering machines and the contents of computer disks can all, in appropriate circumstances, be within the privilege. Even an informal communication, such as a manuscript

---

39 See, *e.g.*, Cotton, LJ in *Kennedy v Lyell* (1883) 23 Ch D 387 at 403.

notation on a compliments slip, or on a copy document, can qualify for a claim to privilege.

- If the client's instructions are accompanied or supplemented by factual summaries, for example of background events, which he has prepared for the purpose of enabling his lawyer to advise him,[40] then these will be privileged since they will be part of the information exchange. This is not a new proposition. In 1876, in an oft-cited judgment, James, LJ remarked in a litigation context that:

> "... as you have no right to see your adversary's brief, you have no right to see that which comes into existence merely as the materials for the brief".[41]

However, generally speaking[42] such documents will not be privileged, even if passed to and used by the lawyer, if they already existed before the need to seek legal advice arose (unless covered by a pre-existing privilege). So, background or historic documents will not usually be privileged. In addition, difficult issues can arise where such information is procured or prepared by an agent or employee: these are considered separately in Chapter 4.

- Communications from a client in which he provides information, such as technical data, research notes, plans or maps which he has prepared, and which are needed by his lawyer to enable him to advise, will be privileged if prepared for the dominant purpose of the lawyer's retainer. In similar circumstances any notes he makes of information received from a third party, for example, during an interview will also be privileged;[43]

- A client's own note or minute of legal advice communicated to him orally, for example, over the telephone, by his solicitor will be privileged. There is no difference in principle between such a note and a formal, written communication from the solicitor;

- Generally, if the lawyer commits to paper during the course of his retainer matters which he knows only as a consequence of the professional relationship with his client then those papers will be

---

40 See Cotton, LJ in *Southwark Water Co v Quick* (1878) 3 QBD 315 at 322.

41 *Anderson v Bank of British Columbia* (1876) 2 Ch D 644 at 656. See also *e.g., Fenner v The London and South Eastern Railway Co* (1872) LR 7 QB 767 at 771 where Blackburn, J said, also in a litigation context, that "where it appears that the documents are substantially rough notes for case, to be laid before the legal adviser or to supply the proof ..." these should normally be treated as privileged.

42 There are some exceptions to this rule, applicable in a litigation context only, which are considered in Chap. 5.

43 See *Woolley v North London Railways* (1869) LR 4 CP 602. The communication from the third party will not be privileged unless made in relation to litigation: see Section 6 below.

privileged.[44] So, a lawyer's working papers such as his research notes, factual summaries and any notes which record or summarise information which he may have gathered (*e.g.* from textbooks or from third parties),[45] or which he needs to enable him to advise his client[46] will be privileged. This will include any internal communication with colleagues relating to the matter on which instructed, for example within his firm in the case of a solicitor,[47] as well as his diary notes.[48] Similarly with his notes of attendances on clients,[49] and drafts of any documents[50] he prepares as well as the final versions[51] *before* they are disclosed[52] to third parties (such as the purchaser where the solicitor acts for the vendor in a conveyancing transaction[53]). This would include pleadings prior to

---

44 Per Lord Brougham in *Greenough v Gaskell* (1833) 1 My & K 98 at 102. See also Stirling, J in *Ainsworth v Wilding* [1900] 2 Ch.315 at 323: "... notes or memoranda made by the solicitor are placed on the same footing as communications between the solicitor and the client". However, privilege may not be claimable where such notes include facts "patent to the senses": see Section 7 below.

45 See, *e.g.*, *Ward v Marshall* 3 TLR 578. As is discussed below, if the solicitor receives information directly from a third party then a communication relaying that information is not privileged unless it falls within the protection afforded to third party communications by litigation privilege: *Wheeler v Le Marchant* (1881) 17 Ch D 675. However, his own notes in which he describes or makes use of what he has received will be privileged if those notes are referrable to the provision of the legal advice sought by his client. See also *Re Sarah C Getty Trust* [1985] QB 956, discussed in Section 7 below.

46 See, *e.g.*, *Mostyn v West Mostyn Coal Co* 34 LT 531. But again, as noted at n. 44 above, if such information is provided by a third party, the communication containing such information is not privileged unless it falls within the scope of litigation privilege.

47 But see in relation to internal communications between lawyers employed by the Law Society, *R v Law Society, ex p. Rosen* (1990) *The Independent,* 12 February, discussed in Chap. 4.

48 *Ward v Marshall* (1887) 3 TLR 578.

49 As regards attendances notes of conversations with opposing solicitors during the course of litigation, see *Parry & Whelan v News Group Newspapers Ltd* [1990] 141 NLJ 1720 discussed in Section 7 below.

50 For example, pleadings, as in *Walsham v Stainton,* 2 H & M 1; and draft agreements as in *Reece v Trye* 9 Beav. 316. These documents need not be "legal" documents. In *Lowden v Blakey* (1889) 23 QBD 332, Denman J held that drafts of an advertisement (relating to the successful outcome of a trade-mark action) sent to counsel for approval, were privileged since the draft was a "communication to Counsel for the purpose of obtaining his advice". So, draft letters prepared or settled by counsel will be privileged.

51 In *The "Sagheera"* [1997] 1 Lloyd's Rep. 160, Rix, J noted, but did not have to determine, a submission that a solicitor's work product in the form of draft witness statements could be protected under the advice head of privilege, since the litigation protection only arose once the statements were adopted and signed by the witness.

52 At which point they may lose the essential element of confidentiality which the privilege requires.

53 But see the discussion on "Fruits of Advice" in Section 5 below.

service or filing.[54] This is evident from one of the categories of documents of which the plaintiff unsuccessfully sought discovery in *Balabel* which the court held to be privileged. These included "drafts, working papers, attendance notes and memoranda of the Defendants' solicitors relating to the proposed new underlease".[55] Further, it is not necessary that each such document contains a specific piece of legal advice to fall within the privilege.[56] In *CC Bottlers Ltd* v *Lion Nathan Ltd,* a New Zealand decision, the court held that a draft letter prepared for a client by his solicitor was "in effect advice, in a preparatory form".[57]

- When a solicitor has been instructed by a client, it is very likely that all of the solicitor's communications with other lawyers, whether counsel or lawyers qualified in other jurisdictions, will be privileged.[58] Thus instructions to counsel, counsel's advice, draft pleadings[59] and notes of conferences will all be privileged, as will written instructions to and advice from a foreign lawyer.[60] The communication of privileged documents of the types described above to counsel or another lawyer will not result in any loss of privilege. There is – or should be – no difference in principle between a solicitor's communications with counsel, and those with a foreign lawyer: provided, in the latter case, the *Balabel* purpose of advice test is met, the communication will be privileged irrespective of whether it relates to a litigation matter or not.

- Note, however, that correspondence between a client's current and former solicitors concerning the client's dissatisfaction with the former solicitor's conduct of his legal proceedings is not

---

54 *Walsham* v *Stainton.* 2 H. & M.1. If the effect of counsel's opinion is set out in pleadings which have been served then it is no longer privileged: *Mayor of Bristol* v *Cox* 26 Ch D 678.

55 Per Taylor, LJ in *Balabel, op. cit.* at 323. A barrister's papers will similarly be protected.

56 Per Taylor, LJ in *Balabel, op. cit.* at 332.

57 [1993] 2 NZLR 445 at 448. See also Master Kennedy-Grant in *Kupe Group Ltd* v *Seamar Holdings Ltd* [1993] 3 NZLR 209 at 213: "Drafts and other working papers are an essential part of the process of advising and being advised."

58 See Chap. 1, Section 7 as to the client's communication with foreign lawyers.

59 Including settled drafts of pleadings and other documents: *Vigneron-Dahl (British & Colonial) Ltd* v *Pettit* (1925) 69 SJ 693.

60 These propositions hardly require any authority in modern times. However, controversy surrounded these aspects in early times because of a House of Lords decision in *Radcliffe* v *Fursman* 2 Bro PC 514. Knight Bruce, V-C's decision in *Pearse* v *Pearse* 1 De G & Sm 12 put the law onto the right track. There are also a number of other older cases of interest which deal with privileged communications between town and country solicitors and overseas lawyers: *e.g. Hughes* v *Biddulph* 4 Rus 190 and *Bunbury* v *Bunbury* 2 Beav 173.

privileged.[61] It is submitted that such correspondence would be privileged if the present solicitors wrote to the ex-solicitors asking for information to enable them to act, whether in relation to the same or another matter: the ex-solicitors would, it is submitted, be writing as the party's agent. In contrast, there is the position where two parties have independently instructed the same solicitor. In litigation between them communications which occurred in relation to the earlier retainers will be privileged as against each other.[62] The position is different where the parties jointly instruct the same solicitor: then there is no privilege between them.[63]

Commercial advice

The decision in *Balabel* confirms that advice privilege can be claimed where the lawyer's advice goes beyond a consideration of purely legal matters to include advice on the commercial aspects of the transaction in which he is engaged on behalf of his client. According to Taylor, LJ:

> "... legal advice is not confined to telling the client the law; it must include advice as to what should prudently and sensibly be done in the relevant legal context.... [T]he range of assistance given by solicitors to their clients and of activities carried out on their behalf has greatly broadened in recent times and is still developing".[64]

Equally, a court will not recognise any privilege claimed for communications made in the course of a transaction in which a lawyer advises solely on the commercial aspects, without reference to any relevant legal considerations.[65] Thus there can be no claim to privilege where a lawyer who accepts appointment as director of a client company provides it with the benefit of his commercial wisdom at a board meeting.

A good example of the circumstances in which solicitors can provide their clients with commercial advice which attracts privilege is the decision in *Nederlandse Reassurantie Groep Holding NV v Bacon and Woodrow*.[66] The background to this decision was the plaintiff Dutch corporation's negotiations for the purchase of the share capital of three insurance companies. The plaintiff assembled a team of advisors comprising

---

61 See Jonathan Parker, J in *Hayes & Rowson v Dowding*. Unrep., 28 June 1996.

62 *Eadie v Addison* (1882) 52 LJ Ch 80, though see, *contra*, *MacFarlane v Rolt* (1872) LR 14 Eq. 580.

63 See Chap. 6.

64 [1988] 1 Ch 317 at 330 and 332.

65 See Rix, J.'s comments in *The "Sagheera"*, quoted at p. 46 above.

66 [1995] 1 All ER 976.

actuaries, accountants, bankers, corporate financiers and legal advisers (the latter from both the Netherlands and London). During the period leading up to the completion of the purchase there were numerous communications, both written and oral, between the Dutch clients and its various advisors, and between the advisers themselves.

The takeover of the insurance companies was unsuccessful and so negligence proceedings were brought, *inter alia*, against the accountants. In the course of discovery they received the plaintiffs' London solicitors' bills of costs[67] for their work in advising on the transaction. From these, it was apparent that the plaintiffs' legal advisors on the takeover transaction had provided not only legal advice but advice of a more general nature going to the commercial advisability of entering into the agreement at the price in question. This included drafting and discussing in detail the approach and contents of a crucial offer letter. Colman, J was therefore asked to determine which communications between the plaintiffs and its lawyers in relation to the takeover transaction were privileged.

Referring extensively to Taylor, LJ's judgment in *Balabel*, he noted that a solicitor's professional duty or function is frequently not exclusively related to the giving of advice on matters of law or, as in the case before him, on the drafting or construction of documents:

> "It not infrequently relates to the commercial wisdom of entering into a given transaction in relation to which legal advice is also sought".[68]

As to that, there was nothing whatever in the passages from the solicitors' bill of costs which suggested that those solicitors:

> "... gave any advice relating to this transaction which would not attract privilege because it was not professional advice given in their capacity as solicitors retained to give legal advice in relation to the proposed transaction".[69]

---

67 The decision is covered further in this respect in Section 5 below.
68 *Ibid,* at 983.
69 *Ibid,* at 983.

5. ADVICE PRIVILEGE:
WHAT IS NOT PROTECTED

No exhaustive list can be given of what documents are or are not covered by the *Balabel* principles in any given situation. However, the *Balabel* decision itself provides some indication of the restrictions on the scope of advice privilege. Thus communications between a lawyer and client which merely acknowledge receipt of a document or suggest a time or place for a meeting would not be within the privilege.[70] Other examples of communications between lawyer and client which are not referrable to the seeking or giving of legal advice are not so obvious. However, Taylor, LJ's approval of the decisions in *Smith-Bird* v *Blower*[71] and *Conlon* v *Conlons Ltd*[72] provides pointers albeit, perhaps, difficult ones.

The decision in *Smith-Bird* arose out of an oral agreement to sell a property from which the would-be vendor later tried to resile. At the trial of the would-be purchaser's action for specific performance, mention was made by the defendant vendor of a letter he had written to his solicitors which had not been disclosed because it was thought to be privileged. This letter, which was written in response to one received from his solicitors,[73] was short and stated:

> "... I beg to confirm that I gave to [the Plaintiff's agent] a note of authority to convey the above property to him for £510. I further note that you will let me know when you wish me to come over to complete."

The judge held that there had been a verbal agreement to sell the property but that the note of authority referred to in the defendant's letter to his solicitors was not a sufficient memorandum for the purposes of section 40 Law of Property Act 1925. However, the judge held that the defendant's letter to his solicitors was a sufficient memorandum. Further the plaintiff was entitled to rely on it because it was not privileged since it was written, not for the purpose of obtaining legal advice from his

---

70 Taylor, LJ thought that the purpose of legal advice test would isolate occasional letters or notes of this sort which could not be said to enjoy privilege but which would in any event almost certainly not be material or relevant and so not discoverable. Presumably, however, such documents would be relevant and therefore disclosable (since not privileged) if the question whether a meeting took place, and if so on what date, became an issue in subsequent litigation.

71 [1939] 2 All ER 406.

72 [1952] 2 All ER 462.

73 It is not apparent from the judgment of Luxmoore, LJ (sitting as an additional judge of the High Court) whether the letter from the solicitors to the vendor was treated (as perhaps it should have been) as privileged, his judgment merely stating that that letter was written "with regard to the matter": see 409.

solicitors, "but in answer to an enquiry by them and to inform them of the fact that he had agreed to sell the property in question".[74]

It is difficult to resist the comment that the conclusion in *Smith-Bird* was to some extent dictated by an understandable desire to find for the Plaintiff. Although the letter in question was characterised by Taylor, LJ in *Balabel*[75] as a client's letter written to his solicitor to inform him of "a fait accompli", it is not altogether easy to see why the letter was not characterised as a confirmation of the solicitors' instructions to act for the vendor in the proposed sale and to proceed with the preparation of the relevant documentation, and so form part of the necessary exchange of information between them.[76]

Evidently, there is, at times, a fine line to be drawn between what is and is not privileged under the advice head. It would be wrong to think that in every action for specific performance of a transaction in relation to real property in which one party lacks the necessary section 40 memorandum, he should seek his opponent's instructions to his solicitor to see if this will satisfy the statutory requirements: more often than not such instructions are likely, as well, to reveal the underlying legal advice which is sought or given and so will be privileged. Nonetheless, there are evidently opportunities here which the party in need of the section 40 memorandum can exploit – as indeed the plaintiff in *Balabel* attempted – in appropriate circumstances. The dangers, however remote, should be therefore appreciated.[77]

The issue in *Conlon* was whether terms of settlement offered by the plaintiff's solicitors to the defendants had been accepted. The plaintiff denied in his reply having made any agreement to compromise his claim and asserted that if any such agreement had been entered into it had been done by his solicitors without his authority. This provoked the defendants into serving interrogatories inquiring as to whether the plaintiff had authorised his solicitors to negotiate for the settlement of his claim and whether or not he had authorised them to offer terms of settlement. The Court of Appeal disallowed the plaintiff's objection to answering these questions which, he asserted, inquired into privileged communications passing between him and his solicitors.

---

74 *Op. cit.* at 410.

75 *Op. cit.* at 331.

76 Interestingly, the successful defendant in *Balabel* had contended that *Smith-Bird* was wrongly decided: see the report at 319.

77 Particularly as, in the light of the recent decision in *G.E. Capital Corporate Finance* v *Bankers Trust Co* [1995] 1 WLR 172, in certain circumstances, discussed in Chap. 9 below, a party may be required to give discovery of that part of a document which is not privileged even though other parts, which he can withhold by masking, are privileged.

In *Balabel,* Taylor, LJ[78] rationalised the court's decision in *Conlon* on the basis that the plaintiff's instructions were not given for the purpose of seeking legal advice and that "privilege was held not to extend to a communication from a client to his solicitor authorising him to offer terms of settlement". This statement does not, however, explain why privilege is not available in relation to such communications. The answer to that is found in the judgment of Morris, LJ in *Conlon,*[79] who said that "... these are not inquiries as to communications passing between the Plaintiff and his solicitor *confidentially*" (emphasis supplied). Both judges in *Conlon* justified their decision by focusing on the lack of confidentiality[80] in any communication made by the client to the solicitor to make a settlement offer which the solicitor is instructed to communicate to the other side.[81] However, the limits of the reasoning in *Conlon* should be appreciated. For while the court noted that a client could not claim privilege "in respect of that which he has said to his solicitor and at the same time has told his solicitor to communicate to the other side",[82] it is submitted that a court would not, without more, reach the same result if the client withdrew his instructions before his solicitors communicated with the other side: in that situation the confidentiality is not, at that stage, lost.

Furthermore, it is difficult to conceive that a court will order discovery of a letter written by a client to a solicitor which went beyond baldly asserting that a specific offer of settlement should be made to the other side. As was argued on behalf of the defendant in *Balabel,* it would surely not be permissible to order discovery of a letter giving instructions to settle a case on such terms as "the facts are such-and-such, settle for £X, if not, for £Y".[83] In any event, as Singleton, LJ noted in *Conlon,* the interrogatories put in that decision were capable of – and required no more than – simple "yes" or "no" answers. This suggests that this particular limitation on the advice head is a narrow one and that, in relation to instructions given to a solicitor, the Court will only permit the minimum information necessary to be disclosed. Such a proposition is supported by *Nicholl v Jones*[84] in which Sir W. Page Wood, V-C, said:

---

78 [1988] 1 Ch 317, at 331.
79 [1952] 2 All ER 462 at 466.
80 As to this generally in relation to privilege, see Section 8 below.
81 It should be noted that the courts would probably now hold that the contents of the plaintiff's reply was such as to "plead into relevance" his instructions to his solicitor and so waive any privilege over them and any related documents: see *Hayes and Rowson v Dowding,* unrep., 28 June 1996, discussed in Chap. 7, Section 5.
82 Singleton, LJ *ibid.* at 465.
83 See the summary of counsel's argument in *Balabel, op. cit.* at 321. The point did not arise for decision in *Balabel.*
84 2 H & M 588.

"If I were to direct the production of instructions [to Counsel] "to consent", I should in effect oblige him to disclose all the conditions which might have been imposed as a precedent to such consent... I cannot have questions of this sort raised which might lead to disclosure of that which would be admitted on all hands to be privileged".[85]

Further limitations on the scope of advice privilege can be seen from a hypothetical example put forward by counsel for the plaintiff in *Balabel* in which a client instructed his solicitor to collect rents from his tenants whilst absent on an extended holiday. If an issue subsequently arose as to whether the landlord had waived any right to forfeiture, the communication of those instructions to his solicitor would be disclosable and admissible because there would be no question of their being related to the obtaining of legal advice – presumably because the lawyer would be acting in a "business" capacity[86] and also because, in the same way as in *Conlon,* the landlord would have intended his instructions to be "communicated" to his tenant through his solicitor's action vis à vis the tenant.[87]

Lawyers' Feenotes

Most English case law proceeds on the basis that fee-notes – or bills of costs – are privileged from production. So, in 1866, in *Turton v Barber*[88] the Vice-Chancellor, Sir Charles Hall, upheld a witness's claim to privilege in the face of questioning about items on the bill of costs he had received from his solicitor. A hundred and twenty years later, in *IBM v Phoenix International (Computers Limited),*[89] Aldous, J was concerned with an application for an injunction restraining the plaintiffs from using information contained in documents which had been inadvertently disclosed by the defendants at the discovery stage of litigation. Some of the documents disclosed were the bills rendered to the defendants by their English solicitors in relation to which the judge said:

"The reasonable solicitor would have been in no doubt that the legal bills were privileged documents and therefore disclosure was made by mistake, unless a decision had been taken to waive that privilege. I cannot think of any logical reason why [the defendant] would decide to waive privilege in

---

85 *Ibid.,* at 596.
86 As to this, see Rix, J's comments in the extract from his judgment in *The "Sagheera"* quoted at p. 46 above.
87 This example is justified by a number of the older decisions such as *Walker v Wildman,* 6 Madd & G 47 and *Doe d Marriott v Hertford,* 19 LJ QB 526.
88 (1874) LR 17 Eq. See also *Chant v Brown* (1852) 9 Hare 790.
89 [1995] 1 All ER 413.

their legal bills and I do not envisage that the reasonable solicitor would arrive at a different conclusion".[90]

No reasons are given as to why it should have been thought that these particular bills were privileged.

In contrast, in *Nederlandse Reassurantie Groep Holding NV v Bacon & Woodrow*,[91] the discovery application the subject of this decision was initiated by the disclosure of the plaintiffs' lawyers' bills. The case appears to have proceeded on the basis that a solicitor's fee note or invoice is not susceptible to a claim for privilege: at least, it does not appear that such a claim was ever advanced.

It is submitted that a lawyer's fee-note is not necessarily a document which conveys legal advice, so as to satisfy a claim to privilege under the advice head. (Nor does it easily qualify for litigation privilege given that it is not prepared *e.g.* in contemplation of or for use in litigation). Even where rendered at frequent intervals, as a transaction progresses, a fee-note does not easily fall within the continuum of communications as described in *Balabel*. In New Zealand, it has been held that bills of costs and statements of account are not privileged by virtue of their nature.[92] In the same decision, it was recognised that passages in those bills could be subject to a proper claim to privilege, if, for example, in their detail they betrayed some of the legal advice or assistance received by the client.[93] This happened in *Ainsworth v Wilding*[94] where Stirling, J held that the defendant could cover up parts of a bill which described work undertaken in such a way as to reveal the advice given; however, another section consisted of "a simple statement of what took place in chambers" which was not privileged and had to be disclosed.[95]

"Fruits of advice"

Certain documents which can be regarded as the "fruits" of the legal advice given by a lawyer will not be privileged. So in *R. v Inner London Crown Court, ex p. Baines & Baines (a firm)*,[96] the Divisional Court held that "conveyancing matter", namely records of a conveyancing transaction (including the conveyance and the record of how the client financed it)

---

90 *Ibid.*, at 424. See also *X Corporation Ltd v Y (a firm)* (unrep.) 16 May 1997 which concerned, inter alia, a waiver of privilege over lawyers' invoices.
91 [1995] 1 All ER 976.
92 Per Master Kennedy-Grant in *Kupe Group Ltd v Seamar Holdings Ltd* [1993] 3 NZLR 209 at 212.
93 *Ibid.*, at 213. As for redacting in those circumstances, see Chap. 9, Section 5.
94 [1900] 2 Ch 315, at 325.
95 See further on this, Section 7 below.
96 [1988] QB 579.

conducted for a client by a solicitor were not "items subject to legal privilege" as that expression is defined in section 10 Police and Criminal Evidence Act 1984.[97] The court distinguished such documents from the solicitor's advice on the wisdom or otherwise of proceeding with a conveyancing transaction which is privileged. To similar effect is the decision in *Crown Prosecution Service (on behalf of DPP for Australia)* v *Holman Fenwick & Willan (a firm).*[98] This decision arose in the context of an application for discovery made under section 4 Criminal Justice (International) Co-operation Act 1990. The Divisional Court held that an agreement and a declaration of trust were not privileged. Morland, J noted comments made by Murphy, J in the High Court of Australia's decision in *Baker* v *Campbell:*

> "The privilege does not attach to documentation which constitute or evidence transactions[99] (such as contracts, conveyances, declarations of trust, offers or receipts) even if they are delivered to a solicitor or counsel for advice or for use in litigation.[1]"

The two English decisions considered here represent the common law position also, for section 10 Police and Criminal Evidence Act 1984 encapsulates the common-law rules as to privilege.[2]

6. ADVICE PRIVILEGE: THIRD PARTY COMMUNICATIONS[3]

Section 2 of this Chapter noted that advice privilege can only be claimed in respect of communications between a client and his lawyer.[4] Privilege cannot be claimed for a communication between either the client or a lawyer and a third party *unless* the communication is made in respect of litigation, in which case the communication is protected by litigation privilege (which is considered in detail in Chapter 3).[5] This follows from the

---

97 The decision was concerned with an application to quash an order made under s. 9 of the Act.
98 Unrep., 13 December 1993.
99 Unless these are in draft and are still confidential to the client.
1' [1983] 153 CLR 52 at 86.
2' Per Lord Goff in *R* v *Central Criminal Court, ex p. Francis and Francis* [1989] 1 AC 346 at 395.
3' The issues discussed here are considered in greater detail in Chap. 4.
4' And in appropriate cases their agents – as to which see Chap. 4.
5' In *The "Sagheera"* [1997] 1 Lloyd's Rep. 160 at 164, Rix, J commented: "It is, however, established law that third party documents, such as statements or experts reports, are only protected by litigation privilege, and not by advice privilege..." See also the comments of Lord Edmund-Davies in *Waugh* v *British Railways Board* [1980] AC 521 at 541–542, quoted at p. 43 above.

Court of Appeal's decision in *Wheeler* v *Le Marchant.*[6] This was an action for specific performance of an agreement under which the defendants were to grant a lease of land to the plaintiff upon his constructing certain buildings on the land. The defendants objected to producing documents which consisted of confidential correspondence between their solicitors and their current and former estate agents and surveyors. This correspondence took place at a time where no litigation was in progress or in contemplation, and related to the obtaining of information sought by the solicitors for enabling them the better to advise their clients.

In the Court of Appeal, Sir George Jessel, MR rejected the defendant's claim to privilege since it would have resulted in an extension of the protection afforded by the rule:

> "The solicitor, being consulted in a matter as to which no dispute has arisen, thinks he would like to know some further facts before giving his advice, and applies to a surveyor to tell him what the state of a given property is ... because it is desired or required by the solicitor in order to enable him the better to give legal advice. It appears to me that to give such protection would not only extend the rule beyond what has been previously laid down, but beyond what necessity warrants."[7]

It follows from this decision that if a client asks his solicitor to engage an expert valuer to advise him whether the asking price of a property which he is contemplating purchasing is a fair one his report will not be privileged. This has the result that the report will be discoverable in any subsequent related litigation.[8] But if he is engaged to value that same property in circumstances where a dispute has already arisen between the purchaser and the vendor, then his report, if prepared predominantly for use in that litigation, will be privileged.[9] This distinction is worth bearing in mind where, for example, banking or corporate finance solicitors engage external accountants to assist with an ongoing non-contentious transaction.

The decision in *Price Waterhouse* v *BCCI*[10] affords a recent illustration of this principle. Price Waterhouse partners were members of an investigating committee set up by the BCCI banking group in the months

---

6[1] (1881) 17 Ch D 675.

7[1] *Ibid.,* at 682.

8[1] Since its preparation will not satisfy the litigation privilege dominant purpose test: see Chap. 3.

9[1] *Plummers Ltd* v *Debenhams Plc* [1986] BCLC 447 is an example of (expert) accountants preparing a report for use by solicitors in anticipated litigation in which a challenge to the claim for privilege over the report was mounted. The challenge, which was unsuccessful, was based, *inter alia*, on a submission that the report did not satisfy the dominant purpose test.

10[1] [1992] BCLC 583.

before its collapse in order to report on the recoverability of various loans. The committee's terms of reference required it to report to BCCI's solicitors, to enable them to give legal advice to BCCI. The question arose as to whether the committee's reports were privileged in Price Waterhouse's hands. Millett, J held that they were not protected under the advice head: Price Waterhouse/the committee was producing material for BCCI and, at BCCI's direction, sending it to their solicitors. Millett, J held that Price Waterhouse's position was no different from that of the surveyors in *Wheeler* v *Le Marchant*[11].

7. PRIVILEGE: SOME DIFFICULTIES OF APPLICATION TO LAWYERS AND CLIENTS

The foregoing highlights that it is the communication between lawyer and client[12] – that is, what the one said or wrote to the other – which is protected by privilege. But the extent of the protection does not necessarily entitle a *client* to refuse to reveal to the court or to his opponent in litigation the *facts* which are contained in the privileged communication, for he can be interrogated, or examined in the witness box, as to facts which he knows at the time he consults his lawyer.[13]

The lawyer will learn about most if not all of the underlying facts only as a result of receiving a privileged communication from his client. Since the privilege belongs to the client, and not the lawyer, who must uphold and where necessary assert his client's privilege,[14] the consequence is that, with few exceptions, the lawyer is neither compellable nor free to give evidence of facts which he learns as a consequence of those communications. As will be seen, quite logically this prohibition does not extend to facts which the lawyer learns independently of the privileged communication.

---

11 *Ibid.*, at 589. In the result, the reports did not attract litigation privilege either: see Chap. 3, Section 3.

12 Or between lawyer or client and a third party in the case of litigation privilege.

13 See Cotton, LJ in *Southwark Water Co* v *Quick* (1878) 3 QBD 315 at 321. He can also be interrogated as to facts he is obliged to seek from an agent, even if obtained from the agent by a solicitor: *Pavitt* v *North Metropolitan Tramways Co* (1883) 48 LT 730 WN 83. Further, an inquiry by a client addressed to his solicitor in respect of factual, as opposed to legal, matters will not be privileged: see *Bramwell* v *Lineas*, 2 B & C 745. Though this decision has been doubted judicially as to whether the subject matter of that case was concerned with a matter of fact, the principle is not in doubt.

14 However, the lawyer cannot assert or hide behind the privilege if the client does not assert it: see *Re International Power Industries* [1985] BCLC 128 discussed in Chap. 7, Section 2.

In contrast, difficulties can arise, for both lawyer and client, where the lawyer learns from third party sources facts relevant to the advice he has been asked to provide to his client and which he communicates to his clients. In this situation some decisions appear to be authority[15] for the view that both can be compellable in relation to such facts where they are "patent to the senses". However, the contents of any qualifying client-lawyer communication will be privileged, even if it includes or refers to information acquired in non-privileged circumstances.[16]

These rules are not always easy to discern from the case-law. It is submitted however, that they are supported by the following decisions. So far as concerns the position of the client, Lord Brougham confirmed the general principle in 1833 in *Greenough* v *Gaskell*[17] that a client must discover all he knows and believes concerning his case. Similarly, Sir James Wigram, V.-C. in *Chant v Brown* noted that:

> "A party liable to give discovery at the suit of another cannot by communicating the matter of such discovery to his solicitor for the purpose of getting advice on the ground of that communication only excuse himself from giving discovery which he would otherwise have been bound to give".[18]

In contrast, anything the lawyer learns as a consequence of privileged communications with, or on behalf of, his client, and as consequence of his having been professionally instructed by the client, will not be discloseable.[19] As already discussed in Chapter 1, the extent of the protection is extensive so far as concerns information acquired in this way by the lawyer: "his mouth is shut forever".[20]

Ainsworth v *Wilding*[21] concerned protracted litigation in which a question arose in 1900 as to what had taken place during the course of a

---

15'Discussed at p. 66 below.

16'See *Lyell v Kennedy (No 3)* (1884) 27 Ch D 1. Further, as noted in Section 6, a discussion with a third party may well be privileged if it is referable to litigation on which the lawyer has been instructed, but will be unprivileged if held in relation to any other type of advice which he is called upon to provide.

17'1 My & K 98 at 101.

18'9 Hare 790, at 86. See also Sir RT Kindersley in *Manser v Dix* (1855) 1 K & J 451: "You can of course extract from the client everything that he knows: the circumstance that he has communicated to his solicitor is not a reason for refusing this kind of discovery".

19'See Lord Brougham, *Greenough v Gaskell, op.cit.* at 104–105.

20'See Lord Taylor, CJ, in *R v Derby Magistrates Court, ex p. B* [1996] 1 AC 487 at 505. There are numerous cases which illustrate this point. Thus, while a lawyer can be compelled to state who his client is (as to which see Section 8 below), he is very limited as regards what else he can disclose about matters relating to his instructions. He cannot, for example, disclose when documentation was provided to him, nor the reasons why it was (*Turquand v Knight*, 2 M & W 98); he cannot give evidence as to a document's contents if he comes into possession of it by virtue of his instructions *(Dwyer v Collins,* 7 Exch 639) and nor can he be forced to give discovery of it if prepared by the client for his use

chambers application in related litigation in 1878. In consequence, an application was made for the production of correspondence between one of the parties to the earlier action (who were also involved in the present action) and his solicitors, which contained statements as to what transpired in court over twenty years earlier.

Stirling, J accepted the general proposition[22] that a mere verbatim report, whether taken by a solicitor, his clerk, counsel or a short-hand writer,[23] of hostile proceedings in the presence of representatives of all sides could not be privileged. That proposition applies whether the note is taken of proceedings in open court,[24] chambers or of proceedings before an arbitrator,[25] and covers notes of the evidence given, as well as submissions made by counsel. Similarly, in *Nicholls* v *Jones*, the court ordered production of instructions to counsel, but only so far as they related to counsel's endorsement thereon which recorded the order made by the court.[26]

However, the position is not so straightforward where such a report is contained in a solicitor's letter to his client. Then, it is necessary for the Court to determine whether the letter goes beyond a mere recitation of the facts so as to fall within the advice umbrella. As to this, in *Ainsworth,* the judge had no reason to doubt statements in the resisting party's affidavit[27] to the effect that the correspondence of which production was sought comprised "professional communications of a confidential character, having been made solely for the purpose of enabling his solicitors to conduct the said litigation" in the related action. This persuaded the judge that the communications concerned did not comprise mere statements of fact. He accepted that they may well have been – and that he should so infer from the affidavit – "... made for the purpose of obtaining

---

(*Cleave* v *Jones,* 7 Exch 421 and *Moore* v *Terrell,* 4 B & Ad 870) unless already in existence and so not privileged in the clients' hands. Thus he cannot give evidence as to its condition and what markings it bears (*Wheatley* v *Williams,* 1 M & W 533) although he can give evidence as to the condition of a document produced in Court which he sees in his character as attorney and which is subsequently altered (*Brown* v *Foster* (1857) 1 H & N 736, discussed further in Section 8 below).

21'[1900] 2 Ch. 315.

22'Which was supported by, *e.g., North, J's judgment in Re Worswick* (1888) 38 Ch D 370.

23'In *Nicholls* v *Jones,* 2 H & M 588, privileged notes and observations on shorthand writers' notes which were disclosable were sealed up.

24'In *Lambert* v *Home* [1914] 3 KB 86, a majority in the Court of Appeal held that a transcript of a witness's evidence prepared for use in subsequent, related litigation was not protected under the litigation head.

25'As regards an arbitrator, see *Rawstone* v *Preston Corp.* (1885) 30 Ch D 116.

26'2 H & M 588. The court's order was expressly "confined to what took place in Court", so that the instructions themselves were not producible.

27'As will be seen in Chap. 9, such an affidavit is likely to be conclusive and unchallengeable.

information or instructions from the client necessary for the conduct of the action".

In contrast, whereas solicitor–client correspondence did not lose the protection of privilege merely because it contained statements of fact as regards proceedings in chambers in the presence of parties on both sides – statements which, standing alone, would not be privileged – Stirling, J went on to rule that extracts from notes or memoranda made by a solicitor which comprised entries in his bill of costs were discoverable since the affidavit evidence before him by which the claim to privilege was made was in fact consistent with those entries being mere notes of what had taken place in chambers. Such information could not be privileged.

To similar effect is the Court of Appeal's decision in *Parry & Whelan* v *News Group Newspapers Limited*,[28] which concerned a defamation action in relation to which the parties thought a concluded agreement had been reached following a telephone conversation between the plaintiffs' solicitor and the defendant newspaper's in-house legal manager. A disagreement arose as to the precise terms of the agreement, in consequence of which proceedings were commenced. Both parties disclosed on discovery the attendance notes which the lawyers had made of the disputed telephone conversation. The defendants argued that the plaintiff's attendance note was a privileged document[29] and that, since privilege in that document had been waived by its disclosure, it followed that the plaintiffs were bound to disclose all further, otherwise privileged, documentation relating to the disputed conversation. In particular, the plaintiffs were asked to produce all letters they had received from their solicitors reporting on that conversation together with attendance notes of the conversations between them thereafter on that subject.

The Court of Appeal, following *Ainsworth* v *Wilding*, held that the application was misconceived since the attendance note was not a privileged document. There was no distinction, in principle, between that document and attendance notes recording what took place in court or in chambers in the presence of the parties on both sides. Bingham, LJ[30] noted that there might have been some substance to the newspaper's application had the document disclosed by the plaintiffs formed part of a communication to them from their solicitor, or contained an analysis of or

---

28[1990] 141 NLJ 1720. See also *Hayes and Rowson* v *Dowding*, (unrep., 28 June 1996), transcript at p. 7.

29Even though they accepted before the court that verbal exchanges over the telephone between the lawyers which lead to the attendance notes were not privileged, no doubt in the light of the well-established principle (discussed in Section 8) that communications with opponents in litigation cannot be privileged.

30Transcript at p. 9.

views on the plaintiff's case. As it was, the memorandum was no more than a factual record, whether accurate or not, of what the plaintiff's solicitor believed to have passed on the telephone. Further, that it might have been a precis of what was discussed, the preparation of which involved a process of distillation or selection, made no difference:

> "... a bare record of what passed is... entitled to no legal professional privilege, whether it is a solicitor's memorandum, a transcript, or an exchange of letters....".[31]

On the other hand, a note of an attendance by a solicitor on his client (or vice versa) would be privileged.[32]

A further authority is *Re Sarah C Getty Trust*.[33] This concerned Californian litigation relating to the administration of the Getty family trusts, in the course of which an order of the court was made pursuant to a letter of request issued by the Californian Court requiring, *inter alia*, the examination of an English solicitor. During the course of his examination, objection was taken to twenty-three questions which related to conversations which the solicitor had had with his client, Paul Getty, who was involved in the Californian litigation.[34] The argument in the case centred on information which the solicitor had received from a third party. What the applicant wished to know was the extent to which the solicitor had passed that information on to his client during the course of meetings and telephone conversations between them.

Mervyn Davies, J held, following, *inter alia, Ainsworth* v *Wilding*, that the court could not encroach on communications which were "basically privileged" made by a solicitor acting in his professional capacity to his client with a view to hiving off the factual parts, which it was arguable were "separable from the main theme of the communicating, *i.e.* the giving

---

31'Although the decision is not mentioned in the judgments in *Parry*, Walton, J's decision in *Grant* v *Southwestern & Country Properties Ltd* [1975] 1 Ch 185, that a tape-recording of a conversation between the plaintiff and defendant was not privileged is to the same effect. Even though prepared for the use of one party's solicitor, the recording cannot thereby acquire a privilege when the contents are unprivileged.

32'Per Dillon, LJ in *Parry*, transcript at p. 7.

33'[1985] 2 All ER 809.

34'S. 3(1) of the Evidence (Proceedings in Other Jurisdictions) Act 1975, pursuant to which the order for the solicitor's examination was made, entitles the examinee to refuse to answer questions on the grounds that they encroach upon the solicitor–client privilege. This is so even if the communication for which privilege is claimed would not be privileged in the foreign proceedings for which it is sought: see Chap. 1 above. Section 3(1) provides:

> "A person shall not be compelled by virtue of an order under Section 2 above to give any evidence which he could not be compelled to give – (a) in civil proceedings in the part of the United Kingdom in which the court that made the order exercises jurisdiction ...".

and receiving of advice". The judge held that there was no basis for "allowing a solicitor to be questioned about what it is that he has conveyed to his client about information he may have received in a professional capacity from a third party".[35]

Clearly then communications between a solicitor and his client concerning the solicitor's discussions with a third party are privileged, if given in the course of giving legal advice and so long as they go beyond providing the client with a merely factual report. However, *Sarah Getty* must not be treated as an authority for the view that the solicitor would have been protected from questioning as to the mere fact of what he was told by the third party[36] unless a claim for litigation privilege could be made in relation to that conversation: this would follow from the decisions in *Wheeler* v *Le Marchant*[37] and in *Parry* v *News Group Newspapers Ltd.*[38] Arguably, the solicitor's conversation with the third party did fall within the ambit of litigation privilege given the pending proceedings in California. However, this is not made clear in the report, and indeed, some of the judge's comments suggest the contrary.[39]

Facts patent to the senses

To the extent *Re Sarah Getty* prevents attempts to probe into privileged solicitor–client communications which contain information communicated to the solicitor in circumstances which would not themselves be privileged, one must add some caveats. These arise from the case law relating to interrogatories[39a], and in particular the *Kennedy* v *Lyell* litigation of the late nineteenth century. Whilst the exact ambit of the decisions made in the course of this litigation is not particularly easy to decipher, there are some suggestions in decisions of both the Court of Appeal and the House of Lords in this litigation which would entitle a party to litigation to interrogate an opponent, or his lawyer, as to certain types of facts which

35'*Op. cit.* n. 33' at 816.

36'The third party, similarly, could not claim privilege if subpoenaed to give evidence of what he told the solicitor.

37'(1881) 17 Ch D 675, discussed in Section 6 above.

38'[1990] 141 NLJ 1720.

39'At p. 815, the Judge commented that, by analogy with *Ainsworth* v *Wilding*, "... one might say that there is privilege for [the solicitor's] oral report on facts not in themselves privileged (in that [the solicitor] is obliged to give evidence as to what the [third party] said)." However, having regard to the decision in *Ainsworth* v *Wilding,* the analogy is only correct if the solicitor's oral report is given in the context of giving legal advice or seeking instructions.

39a Privilege is a valid objection to answering an interrogatory. However, the abolition of the privilege relating solely to one's own case effected by s. 16(2) Civil Evidence Act 1968 relates only to documentary discovery and not to interrogatories.

either knows only as a consequence of a privileged communication, whether written or verbal, made between them.

Kennedy v *Lyell*[40] was the second action brought in the course of a dispute as to the ownership of property formerly belonging to one Anne Duncan who had died intestate. Lyell delivered a set of thirty-one interrogatories. A number of them went much further than asking simple questions of fact and instead involved a considerable amount of legal inference as regards the nature of the relationships of the various parties involved in the dispute. The plaintiff therefore gave answers to the effect that all his information had been provided to him by his solicitor, which information the solicitor had obtained as a result of his enquiries made in order to obtain materials for the purpose of the plaintiff's defence in other litigation also relating to the estate. The question arose therefore as to the extent to which a client is bound to state the effect of information received from his solicitor in the form of a privileged communication.

In the Court of Appeal, certain observations made by the court suggested that facts communicated in privileged circumstances by the lawyer to the client could be disclosed in the form of answers to interrogatories (and presumably also in oral testimony), if they were facts "patent to the senses" – that is, "anything which can be seen with the eyes or heard with the ears".[41] The Court recognised this was difficult territory and that the requirement this rule imposed on the client was very limited. Indeed, Cotton, LJ emphasised the "obvious" distinction between requiring a person to disclose his solicitor's reports as a whole, and requiring him to answer as to facts which he knows only from those reports.[42] Even so, in his view:

> "The information which a solicitor employed to obtain materials for his client's defence communicates to the client is privileged, if it is not merely the statement of a fact patent to the senses, but is the result of the solicitor's mind working upon and acting as professional advisor with reference to facts which he has seen or heard of."[43]

The Court gave illustrations of the distinction between a solicitor's communication of facts "patent to the senses", which might be disclosable, and those which are not. For example, if one interrogates as to whether or not there is a tomb bearing a particular inscription in a particular

---

40 '(1883) 23 Ch D 387, CA.

41 'Per Cotton, LJ, *ibid.*, at 407.

42 '*Ibid.*, at 404.

43 '*Ibid.*, at 407. The judgment of Baggallay, LJ, at 401–402 acknowledged the existence of a possible distinction between "a person being called on to answer as to matters of fact and being called on to answer as to matters of confidential communications".

churchyard, then both solicitor and client who know this information might be bound to answer no matter that one learnt it from the other; but where those questions go on to seek the probable results and inferences of and from such facts as might have been communicated in privileged circumstances, then this further information is privileged from disclosure. The court here contrasted the question "is there not a tombstone to the memory of the said George Duncan?", which goes too far (since it seeks to tie a particular tombstone with the George Duncan featuring in the action, a matter of legal inference), with the probably permissible question "is it not the fact that in the churchyard at Perth will be found a tombstone to the memory of George Duncan, stating that George Duncan died on a certain day" (a question merely as to fact). In the event, the interrogatories were disallowed, since they were of the second, impermissible kind.

In the House of Lords[44] the Court of Appeal's decision was upheld, albeit the speeches in the House did not adopt the "facts patent to the senses" formula.[45] Lord Watson noted that, in effect, the applicant, recognising he could not obtain production of the lawyer's communication, was seeking to get at its contents by probing the opinion the client had formed as a result of reading it. This presents enormous difficulties, because it is:

> "... quite impossible to separate belief in the mind of a client and litigant, which is derived from such materials as information from his [legal] agent... I cannot see upon what principle he can be called upon to state that belief whilst at the same time he is not under obligation to communicate or even to indicate one of the grounds on which it is founded".[46]

Both Lord Blackburn[47] and Lord Bramwell[48] appeared to acknowledge the distinction the Court of Appeal had sought to draw, but both saw the difficulties in its application. As Lord Bramwell noted, it is possible to conceive of a case where a litigant might be required to answer a simple factual question which related to information relayed to him as part of a confidential communication with his lawyer. Nonetheless, he had the greatest misgivings about the wisdom of drawing the distinction, apparently because of the risk of revealing the underlying privileged

---

44 'Sub nom *Lyell* v *Kennedy (No 2)*, 9 App Cas. 81.
45 'However Stirling, J in *Ainsworth* v *Wilding* [1900] 2 Ch 315 relied particularly on the judgment of Cotton, LJ in the Court of Appeal, especially at 401–402. See also *Brown* v *Foster*, 1 H & N 736, discussed in Section 8 below.
46 'Per Lord Watson, *ibid.*, at 92.
47 '*Ibid.*, at 87.
48 '*Ibid.*, at 93–94.

communication.[49] This is no doubt so in relation to oral communications, and would appear to justify the decision in *Re Sarah Getty* not to "hive off" the factual information which the solicitor obtained from the third parties. But in relation to written communications such unravelling is probably easier, as the discussion on this subject in Chapter 9 will consider.

8. PRIVILEGE: CONFIDENTIAL COMMUNICATIONS

In Chapter 1, the interplay between privilege and the duty of confidentiality which the lawyer owes to his client was briefly noted: it is essential that a communication for which privilege is claimed is made in confidential circumstances. This is true for both heads of privilege (so what follows applies equally to litigation privilege). However, this can on occasion be a difficult requirement to satisfy: not everything which the client communicates to his legal adviser will be treated by the law as within the duty of confidentiality; and sometimes the circumstances in which the communication is made are such that the confidentiality simply cannot arise.

Judicial statements tend to be unhelpful in trying to identify the precise nature of the confidentiality which the case law demands here. At first blush, the fact of confidentiality appears to follow from the existence of the professional relationship between lawyer and client and the passing of communications between them for the purposes of seeking legal advice. Thus in *Marsh* v *Keith*,[50] Sir R.T. Kindersley, V.-C. said:

> "... whatever passes between a solicitor and his client, as a matter of professional business, the Court will consider as confidential. But it must pass between them in the relative characters of solicitor and client: then it is confidential; and the interests of mankind require that it should be privileged."

---

[49]'The Court of Appeal in fact relied on this latter reason, in *Lyell* v *Kennedy (No 3)* (1884) 27 Ch D 1 when it refused an order for "... documents, perhaps *publici juris* in themselves, to be produced, because the very fact of the solicitor having got copies of certain burial certificates and other records, and having made copies of the inscriptions on certain tomb-stones, and having obtained photographs of certain houses might show what his view was as to the case of his client as regards the claim made against him", per Cotton, LJ at 26. See also *Walsham* v *Stainton,* 2 H & M 1. This issue is discussed further in Chap. 5.

[50]'1 Drew & Sm 342.

Eighty years later, Lord Atkin in *Minter v Priest*[51] echoed these sentiments when he said:

"It is I think apparent that if the communication passes for the purpose of getting legal advice it must be deemed confidential."

But these statements beg the question, "what is getting legal advice?". The enquiry has therefore to be broadened.

There is no doubt that, in one respect, the requirement for confidentiality means what it suggests, namely that in the course of a professional lawyer–client relationship in which legal advice is sought or given the information for which privilege is claimed must be of such a nature that disclosure of it by the lawyer to a third party would involve a breach of a duty of confidence owed to the client. Mervyn Davies, J touched on this aspect in his judgment in *Re Sarah C Getty Trust* when he remarked that

"... such communication [as] passed between [the respondents] was in confidence (*that is, in private*) ..." (emphasis supplied).[52]

So, the presence of a third party when the communications is made may mean that no claim to privilege can be maintained in the case of that communication. This is illustrated by the Australian case of *R v Braham & Mason*.[53] Here, the accused had just made a statement in a police station. He then telephoned his solicitor in the presence of a police inspector, seeking advice on whether to sign it. During the course of the conversation he admitted involvement in a criminal offence. When counsel for a co-defendant sought to cross-examine him on this conversation, he claimed privilege for it. Lush, J noted that:

"The fact of the presence of a third party should be examined to see whether that presence indicates that the communication was not intended to be confidential, or whether the presence of the third party was caused by some necessity or some circumstances which did not affect the primary nature of the communication as confidential".[54]

He found that "there is no real sign that Braham had any intention that this was to be a confidential conversation", and declined to allow the

---

51'[1930] AC 558, at 581.
52'[1985] QB 956 at 962. Lord Brougham in *Greenough v Gaskell* said there could be no privilege "where the matter communicated was not in its nature private and could in no sense be termed the subject of a confidential disclosure" (*ibid.* at 104). See also Whitford, J in *McGregor Clothing Company Ltd's Trade Mark* [1978] FSR 353 at 354: "If the advice is broadcast at large then no doubt the privilege claimed is bad."
53'[1976] VR 547.
54'*Ibid.*, at 552.

claim to privilege. In contrast is the New Zealand Court of Appeal's decision, *R v Uljee*.[55] Here an accused visited his solicitor's house for advice. While there, the police arrived to question him, but withdrew on being told the accused did not wish to speak to them. The accused and his solicitor then discussed the matter privately, but were overheard by a police officer who, in guarding the premises, had not intended to eavesdrop. The court held that the accused's conversation with his lawyer was clearly intended to be a private, or confidential, one and accordingly the privilege was not lost by reason of the accident of its being overheard.[56]

There can be no confidence (or privacy) in information communicated to a lawyer from those whose interests are opposed to his client's, or where the information comes from certain "collateral" – or non-client – quarters. This is so even where such information comes to the lawyer's attention as a consequence of his acting in a professional capacity for his client. So, in *Weeks v Argent*[57] an attorney objected to being called to give evidence for a defendant about an agreement reached between his client and the defendant in both his and the defendant's attorney's presence. The attorney objected on the ground that his knowledge of the facts which the defendant required him to give in evidence had been obtained in his character as an attorney and was therefore confidential. Parke, B held:

> "A mere bargain with the other side, in the presence of the opposite attorney, is not a confidential communication, within the rule of evidence".[58]

In *Spenceley v Schulenburgh*[59] Lord Ellenborough, CJ held that privilege could not apply to adverse proceedings communicated to an attorney in the cause by the opposite party. Thus he could be required to disclose, when called as a witness by the adverse party, the contents of a notice which he had received (which required him to produce a paper in the hands of his client) without breaching the duty of confidentiality which he owed to his client. The attorney did not acquire his knowledge of the contents of the document from his client and there could be no privilege in "communications from collateral quarters, although made to [the attorney] in consequence of his character of attorney". Similarly, in *Sawyer v Birchmore*,[60] the Court permitted the interrogation of a solicitor

55 '[1982] 1 NZLR 561. See also the Canadian decision *R v Choney* (1909) 13 CCC 289.
56 'The decision is discussed further in Chap. 7. See also *Feuerheerd v London General Omnibus Co Ltd* [1918] 2 KB 565, mentioned in Chap. 3, n. 68.
57 '16 M & W 817.
58 '*Ibid.*, at 821.
59 '7 East 357.
60 '3 My & K 572. Some care has to be taken with these cases, as Cotton, LJ pointed out in *Kennedy v Lyell* 23 Ch D 387 at 405, because reports obtained by a solicitor in contemplation of litigation from a person whom he employs to collect evidence are usually privileged under the litigation head: see further Chap. 3.

as regards letters he had received from a non-client; and in *Desborough* v *Rawlins*,[61] a communication by an insurer to an insurance agent in which he rejected the latter's proposal in respect of the life of an individual was made in the presence of the agent's solicitors. The court held that it was not a confidential communication so the solicitor could give evidence about it.[62]

Instructions given to a solicitor which are communicated to the adverse party may not be confidential, as in *Conlon* v *Conlons Ltd*,[63] considered in Section 5 above. However, instructions to Counsel, even if they are merely "to consent", will be privileged: *Nicholl* v *Jones*.[64]

Information incapable of being privileged

Even if a communication gets over the initial "privacy" hurdle, not everything so communicated will necessarily give rise to a claim to privilege. In *Bursil* v *Tanner*,[65] the Court of Appeal held that a solicitor could be required to state the names of the trustees set out in a deed of settlement which he had drafted for his trustee clients. The court held that disclosure of that information would not give rise to a breach of professional confidence. Cotton, LJ said:

> "It is not everything that solicitors learn in the course of their dealings with clients that is privileged from disclosure. ... The privilege extends only to confidential communications.... The mere fact who the trustees are cannot be said to be a matter communicated to the solicitor confidentially for the purpose of obtaining his professional advice, or at any rate, it is highly improbable that it should be so."[66]

Bursil v *Tanner* was followed in *Ex p. Campbell; In re Cathcart*[67] in which James, LJ held that a solicitor was obliged to disclose details of his client's place of residence, even though this knowledge only came to him in

---

61'3 My & CR 515

62'Note, however, the decision in *Minnesota Mining & Manufacturing Co* v *Rennicks (UK) Ltd* [1991] FSR 97 in which Hoffmann, J held that answers to interrogatories given in US proceedings were privileged, and so were not discoverable in UK proceedings. The short report does not make clear that the parties were the same in both sets of proceedings. While it does make clear that the answers were subject to confidentiality orders in the US proceedings, which would have justified Hoffmann, J's decision, that fact alone does not, it is submitted, entitle a claim to privilege to be made for them.

63'[1952] 2 All ER 462.

64'2 H & M 588.

65'(1885) 16 QBD 1. Similarly, a solicitor can be required to state what takes place at the execution of a deed: per Malins, V-C in *Crawcour* v *Salter* [1881] 18 Ch D 30.

66'*Ibid.*, n. 65 at 5.

67'(1870) 5 Ch App 703.

consequence of the professional business in which he was acting for his client:

> "The client's place of residence in such a case is a mere collateral fact, which the solicitor knows without anything like professional confidence ..."

Only if details of the residence have been communicated to the solicitor by way of a secret, perhaps because the client was in hiding, such that the solicitor was one of the few people in the world who knew the place of residence, could that fact then be brought within the scope of the professional confidence. *Re Arnott, ex p. Chief Official Receiver*,[68] in which Cave, J held that a client's address *was* privileged, appears to have been decided on this basis. In contrast, section 2(9) Criminal Justice Act 1987, which otherwise preserves a person's privilege in the face of the Serious Fraud Office's powers of compulsory document disclosure, excepts from that protection the name and address of a client, which a lawyer "may be required to furnish". This suggests a client's identity is a privileged matter at common law, so far as concerns requiring his solicitor to divulge it.

However, in *Gillard* v *Bates*,[69] it was held that the identity of the lawyer's client cannot form part of a privileged communication because that communication was not necessary "for the purpose of carrying on the proceeding in which the attorney was employed". More recently, the Court of Appeal in *Pascall* v *Galinski*[70] expressed the view that a solicitor could be compelled by subpoena to name his client if relevant to the proceedings in which he is called as witness. That there is a duty to divulge such information to the court was confirmed in *ICIC (Overseas)* v *Adham*,[71] where Harman, J ordered solicitors to divulge the names and addresses of two of their clients who were implicated in an international fraud. Harman, J expressed the view that he was exercising an "exceptional power" in exceptional circumstances.[72] Similarly, there is no confidence in a client's handwriting[73] or as regards whether he has secured a pleading.[74]

---

68 (1888) 60 LT 109.

69 6 M & W 547. Contrast this statement with Lord Macfadyen's in the Outer House of the Court of Session in *Conoco (UK) Ltd* v *The Commercial Law Partnership* (1996) *The Times*, 13 February: "A client was entitled to insist his solicitor keep confidential a fact communicated by him to his solicitor, even in circumstances in which the client, if asked, would be obliged to disclose it".

70 [1970] 1 QB 38.

71 (1997) *The Times,* 10 February.

72 Usually, such details will fall within a solicitor's professional duty of confidence: see n. 5 above.

73 *Dwyer* v *Collins,* 7 Ex 639.

74 *Greenough* v *Gaskell,* 1 My&K 98.

The law will not necessarily treat as confidential information which a lawyer acquires from non-client sources or which are "facts patent to the senses". So, in *Brown* v *Foster*,[75] counsel attended court with his client who had been charged with embezzling his employer's funds. In relation to this, a record was produced by the prosecution which it was alleged it was the accused's duty to keep. This purported to show that a sum of money for which the employee should have accounted to his employer had not been recorded. When the record was examined on a further occasion, the relevant entry was found to be there. The employee then brought an action for malicious prosecution in the course of which it was held that his counsel could give evidence as to whether the entry was in the book at the time of the first examination. The counsel was able to see these facts for himself and in any event he did not acquire them as a consequence of a communication from his client. Finally, in *Lewis* v *Pennington*[76] it was held that the mere fact of a client having made a confidential communication to his solicitor did not protect the solicitor from giving discovery if he acquired the same knowledge before or after from extraneous sources in relation to which no privilege could attach.

9. PRIVILEGE: THE LAWYER–CLIENT RELATIONSHIP

The case law is clear that a professional relationship must exist between a lawyer and his client to which the relevant communication between them must be referrable before a legitimate claim to privilege can be made.[77] To return once more to Lord Brougham's judgment in *Greenough* v *Gaskell*:

> "... no authority sanctioned the... violation of professional confidence ... which would be involved in compelling counsel or attorney or solicitors to disclose matters committed to them in their professional capacity and which, but for their employment as professional men, they would not have become possessed of".[78]

Once the requirement for a professional relationship is appreciated, then many apparent exceptions to the rule are more readily understood and in fact can be seen as generally consistent with this principle. Thus, as Lord Brougham explained in *Greenough* v *Gaskell*:

---

75 '1 H & N 736.
76 '29 LJ Ch 670.
77 'Again, this applies to litigation privilege as much as to advice privilege.
78 '(1833) 1 My & K 98 at 101.

"Those apparent exceptions are: where the communication was made before the attorney was employed as such or after his employment had ceased;[79] or where, though consulted by a friend because he was an attorney, yet he refused to act as such and was, therefore, only applied to as a friend; or where the thing disclosed had no reference to the professional employment, though disclosed while the relation of attorney and client subsisted...".[80]

As to the nature of this relationship, there are no formal requirements.[81] There is no necessity that the client should have agreed to pay fees (or else there would be no scope for acting on a *pro bono* basis); nor does there need to be a formal contract or retainer between them: formal engagement letters are by no means standard even in 1998. Further, a firm of solicitors should be able to advise itself in privileged circumstances, for example on health and safety legislation affecting its own workplace, without the need to employ external advisers.[82] In *Calley* v *Richards*[83] the necessary professional relationship was constituted even though the client was ignorant of the solicitor's removal from the Roll. In contrast, the decision in *R* v *Leeds Magistrates' Court, ex p. Dumbleton*[84] is predicated on the basis that the relationship between a dishonest client who is advised by a dishonest solicitor does not qualify for privilege.

The necessary professional relationship may be held to exist, albeit briefly, even though ultimately the solicitor refuses a prospective client's retainer. A good example of this is the House of Lords' decision in *Minter* v *Priest*.[85] Here, two prospective purchasers of a property approached the respondent solicitor, Mr Priest, to see if he would help both in raising the finance for the purchase[86] and also act as their solicitor in completing it. He refused to help or to act and in explaining his refusal allegedly slandered the vendor of the property, the appellant, with whom he had had previous dealings. When the appellant learnt of the slander from one

---

79'Though see the discussion of *Minter* v *Priest* [1930] AC 558 below.

80'*Op. cit.,* n. 78' at 104.

81'Though see Chap. 1, section 7.

82'But see Chap. 4 in relation to acting "in person".

83'19 Beav. 401.

84'[1993] Crim LR 866.

85'[1930] AC 558.

86'An approach to a solicitor to advance money to assist an individual to purchase a property will not of itself give rise to the necessary professional relationship in the context of which the privilege can be claimed. Thus Lord Warrington in *Minter* v *Priest, ibid.,* at 577–578 said:

"It cannot be denied that it is part of a solicitor's business to carry out contracts for sale and purchase of land and incidentally thereto to advance or procure the advance of money necessary for those purposes. But if the meaning of the remarks of the members of the [Court of Appeal] is that it is part of a solicitor's business to lend money independently of any professional employment, I must say ... that I do not agree ...".

of the prospective purchasers, he sued the solicitor for libel. The question arose as to whether the relationship of solicitor and client could exist between Mr Priest and the prospective purchasers, prior to the solicitor's acceptance of a retainer, but in the course of being interviewed in relation to such a retainer. If it did, then the slander was uttered in circumstances which rendered it a privileged communication.

In the House of Lords the nature of the professional lawyer–client relationship was examined in some detail. All the law lords were unanimously of the view that a solicitor does not need to be retained at the end of an interview to see whether or not he can act for a prospective client in order for the privilege to attach to qualifying communications. Lord Atkin said:[87]

> "If a person goes to a professional legal adviser for the purpose of seeing whether the professional person will give him professional advice, communications made for the purpose of indicating the advice required will be protected."

In the event, the House held that there was ample evidence to show that the solicitors' comments which were complained of by the appellant were uttered after the solicitor had refused to assist. From that moment on "any professional relation even in intention ceased, and words spoken thereafter would not be entitled to the privilege accorded to professional communications".[88]

---

87 *Ibid.*, at 584. See also Viscount Dunedi at 573.
88 Per Lord Warrington, *ibid.* at 577.

LEGAL PROFESSIONAL PRIVILEGE: LITIGATION PRIVILEGE

1. INTRODUCTION

Chapter 3 examines the nature and the scope of litigation privilege, the focus of which is the protection of communications between either (i) a client or (ii) his lawyer and a third party. As with the approach to advice privilege in Chapter 2, this chapter will first consider the underlying principles which determine the application of this head of privilege before examining some of the communications which commonly fall within its scope.

2. LITIGATION PRIVILEGE: THE ESSENTIAL ELEMENTS

It was argued in Chapter 2 that the *Balabel* "purpose of advice" test encompasses client–lawyer communications which otherwise contain the essential elements of a communication protected by litigation privilege. This conclusion is, it is submitted, supported by statements such as Lord Edmund-Davies' in *Waugh v British Railways Board*[1] quoted in Chapter 2, at page 43. Nonetheless, one can still find statements in textbooks, and indeed in decided cases,[2] which proceed on the basis that a lawyer–client communication which relates to litigation is protected by litigation privilege, or by both litigation and advice privileges. As argued in Chapter 2, the ability to protect such communications under the litigation head is of little, if any, relevance given that it adds nothing to the extent of the protection afforded under the advice head.[3] Accordingly, this Chapter will

---

1 [1980] AC 521 at 541–542.
2 Such as *George Doland Ltd v Blackburn Robson Coates & Co* [1972] 3 All ER 959.
3 To the extent the *George Doland* decision concludes otherwise, it will be suggested in Chap. 7, Section 8 that it was wrongly decided.

examine litigation privilege from the standpoint that its essence is a client or lawyer communication with a third party.

Having regard to the foregoing, the following essential elements must be present in order to establish a successful claim to litigation privilege:

- a communication, whether written or oral;
- made confidentially;
- between either (i) a client or (ii) his lawyer (who is acting in a professional capacity) and a third party;
- made for the dominant purpose of use in litigation, namely:
    (i) to enable legal advice to be sought or given; and/or
    (ii) to seek or provide information or evidence to be used in or in connection with litigation
  in which the client is or may become a party;
- which litigation is either proceeding or reasonably anticipated or in contemplation at the time when the communication is made.

As with advice privilege, litigation privilege can extend to cover:
- lawyer-to-lawyer communications made on behalf of the same client;
- communications between client or lawyer and the third party made on their respective behalves by agents;[4]
- certain types of confidential documents which, strictly, are not communications but which are created by the lawyer, client or third party and which come into existence to enable legal advice to be sought or given, or information or evidence to be prepared or gathered, in relation to the subject litigation.

The requirements of confidentiality and the need for a professional client–lawyer relationship, subject to the decision in *Minter v Priest*,[5] are the same for litigation privilege as under the advice head, and will not be discussed further in this chapter. It should be noted, however, that the client (but not the lawyer) can enter into privileged communications with a third party before any professional relationship arises.[6]

Like advice privilege, the precise ambit of litigation privilege has been the subject of considerable judicial debate. In terms of its practical application the greatest difficulty has been to specify with any precision the extent of the connection which is required between the preparation of a document and the anticipation of the litigation in relation to which it was

---

4 This issue is discussed in detail in Chap. 4.
5 [1930] AC 558, discussed in Chap. 2, Section 9.
6 See *Southwark Water Co. v Quick* (1878) 3 QBD 315.

made in order for it to be protected by litigation privilege.[7] Perhaps surprisingly, this issue was still unresolved in 1979 when what is now the leading modern authority on litigation privilege, *Waugh v British Railways Board*,[8] reached the House of Lords. Afforded a rare opportunity to opine on privilege,[9] and finding itself free to consider the issue on grounds of principle and convenience, unembarrassed by any previous authority,[10] the House of Lords firmly resolved all doubts when it unanimously adopted the "dominant purpose" test, which Lord Edmund-Davies there described as the "touchstone" of the privilege. The following sections examine the essential elements of litigation privilege, beginning with the important "dominant purpose" test.[11]

3 . LITIGATION PRIVILEGE: THE CONNECTION BETWEEN THE COMMUNICATION AND THE LITIGATION: THE "DOMINANT PURPOSE" TEST

In *Waugh*, the House of Lords decided that in order for a claim to litigation privilege to succeed, the claimant must show that the qualifying communication is made with the dominant purpose of being used in or in connection with litigation in which the maker of the document is or is likely to be a party. Use in such litigation need not be the sole purpose for which the communication was made: it can also be made for purposes other than the litigation. But where a document has other uses or purposes, its use in the litigation must be the dominant[12] purpose behind its preparation.

---

7 As will be seen from the "once privileged, always privileged" rules discussed in Chap. 6, the claim to privilege need not be made in the same litigation as that in relation to which the communication was made.

8 [1980] AC 521.

9 One of only seven reported occasions so far this century when the House of Lords has examined issues arising from legal professional privilege.

10 Per Lord Simon of Glaisdale, in *Waugh, ibid.,* at 534.

11 Given that this test was only adopted in 1979, care must be used when considering earlier authorities, especially those concerning claims to privilege over accident reports and the like, many of which were reviewed by Havers, J in *Seabrook v British Transport Commission* [1959] 1 WLR 509.

12 One is tempted to use alternative adjectives but this is dangerous. Obvious ones which spring to mind, such as "main", "substantial" or "primary", were canvassed and rejected in *Waugh. e.g.,* Lord Simon of Glaisdale felt that "mainly" was too "quantitative" (at 537). Lord Russell of Killowen felt that "... to select the standard of dominant purpose is not to impose a definition too difficult of measurement" (at 544).

The facts of *Waugh* were that a claim under the Fatal Accidents Acts 1846–1959 was brought by the widow of an employee of the board who was killed in an accident while working on their railways. A report on the cause of the accident was prepared two days afterwards by two of the board's officers. The report incorporated the statements of those who witnessed the accident, many of whom were potential witnesses in any ensuing litigation. The board refused to disclose the report in the action commenced by the widow. In resisting her application for discovery, its representative swore an affidavit from which it appeared that the report was made in accordance with longstanding board practice, and that its purpose was both to assist the board in establishing the cause of the accident and to enable its solicitors to advise on its legal liability and to conduct any proceedings arising from the accident. In the latter respect, the deponent asserted that the board "commonly anticipated" personal injury claims, either by employees or passengers, when railway accidents occurred. The board's deponent further asserted that these two purposes were of equal importance.

The facts therefore neatly encapsulated the competing policy considerations which underlie this privilege. According to Lord Wilberforce:

> "... while privilege may be required in order to induce candour in statements made for the purposes of litigation it is not required in relation to statements whose purpose is different – for example to enable a railway to operate safety.[13] It is clear that the due administration of justice strongly requires disclosure and production of this report: it was contemporary; it contained statements by witnesses on the spot; it would be not merely relevant evidence but almost certainly the best evidence as to the cause of the accident. If one accepts that this important public interest can be overridden in order that the defendant may properly prepare his case, how close must the connection be between the preparation of the document and the anticipation of litigation? On principle I would think that the purpose of preparing for litigation ought to be either the sole purpose or at least the dominant purpose of it: to carry the protection further into cases where that purpose was secondary or equal with another purpose would seem to be excessive, and unnecessary in the interest of encouraging truthful revelation".[14]

In the result, agreeing that the report had to be disclosed, he rejected the "sole" purpose test as being too strict a requirement and held that:

> "... unless the purpose of submission to the legal adviser in view of litigation is at least the dominant purpose for which the relevant document was

13   The report says "safety", but presumably Lord Wilberforce meant "safely".
14   [1990] AC 521 at 531–532.

prepared, the reasons which require privilege to be extended to it cannot apply".[15]

Lord Simon of Glaisdale, who also sought an "intermediate line"[16] between the competing policy considerations, similarly preferred the "dominant purpose" test. Lord Edmund-Davies, who felt that the public interest was "best served by rigidly confining within narrow limits the cases where material relevant to litigation may be lawfully withheld",[17] also allowed the appeal. He too favoured the "dominant purpose" test as the "touchstone" of privilege in cases where documents are prepared with a view to litigation and other purposes.[18]

It does not follow from the decision in *Waugh* that no accident report can be legally privileged. Although Lord Edmund-Davies commented in *Waugh* that "... the claims of humanity must surely make the dominant purpose of any report on an accident... that of discovering what happened and why it happened, so that measures to prevent its recurrence could be discussed and, if possible, advised",[19] a court will still need to examine in every case whether the report's use in view of litigation was the dominant purpose behind its creation, even though it may serve the secondary purpose of being used to ascertain the cause of an accident and measures to prevent its recurrence. To a considerable extent, this issue will turn in most cases on the claimant's ability to assert on oath that the dominant purpose test has been satisfied.[20] In *Waugh*, dominance was not claimed by the board, merely that the report's use in litigation was one of its principal purposes. However, in at least one Court of Appeal decision, "dominant purpose" has been successfully claimed for an accident report.[21]

---

15 *Ibid.,* at 533.

16 *Ibid.,* at 537.

17 Since privilege detracts from the fairness of the trial by denying a party access to relevant documents or subjecting him to surprise: *ibid.,* at 543.

18 All the speeches in *Waugh* adopted this test as originally formulated in the minority judgment of Barwick, CJ in *Grant v Downs,* 135 CLR 674 (quoted at p. 86 below), where the majority adopted a "sole" purpose test which is still the "touchstone" of litigation privilege in Australia.

19 *Op. cit.,* at 544.

20 As will be seen in Chap. 9, this then makes the claim to privilege extremely difficult to challenge in view of *Jones v Monte Video Gas Co* (1880)5 QBD 556 (although the Court does have a right to inspect, which it will on occasion exercise). Because of this decision, leading counsel for the plaintiff in *Waugh* accepted he could not challenge the Board's deponent's assertion that the subject report was prepared in anticipation of litigation arising out of Mr Waugh's death: [1980] AC 521 at 539.

21 The Court of Appeal in *Guinness Peat Properties Ltd v Fitzroy Robinson Partnership* [1987] 1 WLR 1027 referred to the unreported decision in *McAvan v London Transport Executive* (1983) 133 NLJ 1101) in which a claim for privilege for an accident report was upheld. The Court held on the particular facts that "the dominant purpose of the gathering of the information by [the accident reports in question] was to enable the Defendants to be advised on their prospects in relation to any claim" (per Fox, LJ).

Inevitably, there will on occasion be a fine dividing line between a "dominant purpose" document which is privileged and an "other purposes" document which is not. In any event, potential litigants should always be alive to the possibility of legitimately trying to use the cloak of privilege to carry out an investigation into problems which could give rise to litigation against them.[22] Despite the public policy considerations which point to the conclusion that accident reports and the like – especially those prepared in the immediate aftermath of a railway accident or a comparable incident – are unlikely to be privileged, it is suggested that careful observance of the rules of litigation privilege can enable a claim to protection properly – and justifiably – to be made for such documents in particular circumstances. Suppose, for example, a fraud is committed by a bank employee at one of the bank's branches which results in losses to the bank's customer. The bank's immediate reaction may well be to try to ascertain how the fraud occurred and to prevent it from happening again. A report to that effect would, in all likelihood, be unprivileged. But the bank, if well advised, will also want to give consideration to its position in any litigation which the customer may be minded to bring against it in consequence of the losses which he has suffered. There should be no insuperable objection to commissioning an internal report which investigates the background to the fraud and, for example, contains records of interviews of potential witnesses in such a way that its dominant purpose is to enable the bank to seek legal advice in relation to any claim for loss by the customer which it can reasonably anticipate at the time of its commission. In this way, if properly utilised, the law of privilege can enable the bank to carry out its enquiries candidly, while at the same time preserving its ability not to show its hand to the customer unless and until the bank is fully satisfied as to its legal responsibility to compensate that customer for the loss which he may have suffered. A secondary purpose of such a report might well be to examine how the loss actually occurred. Of course, such a strategy could only succeed so long as a bank representative could, in such circumstances, truthfully depose as to the report's dominant purpose.

A further angle to this, which is apparent from comments in the judgments in *Waugh,* is that it can be difficult to prove that a document which has been created in accordance with standing instructions or procedures was prepared for the dominant purpose of use in litigation, unless these are specifically geared to the creation of documents in so-called disaster scenarios which are predominantly intended for use in any

---

22 Though see the decision in *Price Waterhouse* v *BCCI Holdings (Luxembourg) SA* [1992] BCLC 583 discussed at p. 85 below.

resultant litigation, or to enable legal advice to be sought. As Lord Edmund-Davies commented in *Waugh* "... the test of dominance will ... be difficult to satisfy when enquiries are instituted or reports produced automatically whenever any mishap occurs, whatever its nature, its gravity, or even its triviality".[23] Thus a subordinate's report to a superior, sent in consequence of a general order to report, or in the ordinary course of his duty, will not normally be privileged, whether made before or after litigation began,[24] since the dominant purpose behind its creation was not use in the litigation.

The "dominant purpose" will be objectively ascertained by a consideration of all the relevant evidence.[25] So a claim to privilege will not be greatly advanced by the use of self-serving labels on a standard report form: the key issue is always, what was the dominant purpose for which the document was created?[26] In *Waugh* the accident report was headed: "For the information of the Board's solicitor: this form is to be used by every person reporting an occurrence when litigation by or against the B.R.B. is anticipated...". However, this heading was not in any way determinative of the appeal's outcome and was effectively ignored, since "words cannot alter the character of the report which is made by the employee for the purpose of informing his employers of the accident, and made at the time".[27] In any event, as Lord Wilberforce noted, despite the heading, the board's affidavit made clear the report was made for a dual-purpose, which brought the dominant purpose test into play.

Litigation privilege: dominant purpose post *Waugh*

There are a limited number of decisions which illustrate how the courts have applied the dominant purpose test following its formulation in 1979. Some of these are considered in the succeeding sections because they raise other issues as well. In other cases, no difficulties seem to arise. So, an

---

23 *Op. cit.*, at 544.

24 See *Woolley v North London Ry Co*, 4 CP 602 and *Fenner v The London & South Eastern Railway Co* (1872) LR 7 QB 767.

25 Per Millett, J in *Price Waterhouse v BCCI Holdings (Luxembourg) SA* [1992] BCLC 583 at 591.

26 In *Re Highgrade Traders Ltd* [1984] BCLC 151, discussed below, Oliver, LJ commented (at 175) that "... the Court is concerned to determine the actual intention of the party claiming privilege and, where it discerns a duality of purpose, to determine what is the dominant purpose... I would not want it to be thought the mere writing of such a letter by solicitors [i.e. written with a view to preclude further challenge to the privileged status of certain documents]... sometimes perhaps as a matter of drill, is in all cases necessarily going to be determinative".

27 Lord Strathclyde in *Whitehill v Glasgow Corporation*, 1915 SC 1015 at 1017, quoted by Lord Edmund-Davies in *Waugh, op. cit.*, at 539.

application for legal aid is regarded as privileged: see *R. v Snaresbrook Crown Court, ex p. DPP.*[28]

One case which should be considered here, because it also illustrates the "dual-purpose" document issue, is the Court of Appeal's decision in *Re Highgrade Traders Limited.*[29] Here, the stock and premises of a company were destroyed by fire shortly after a substantial increase in insurance cover had been taken out. The insurers suspected foul play and had several reports prepared into the cause of the fire by external investigators. From the time they received the first report, it was clear that any claim on the policy might be disputed. As a result, solicitors were instructed (*i.e.* after the insurers had received their first report) and, in due course, the insurers decided not to honour the policy. Shortly afterwards, the company entered into a members' voluntary liquidation. The only hope the creditors had of making any realistic recoveries was if the insurance claim was met. The liquidator attempted to negotiate a resolution with the insurers in the course of which he requested copies of their reports. These were withheld on the grounds of privilege, whereupon he applied for an examination under insolvency legislation of a responsible officer of the insurers coupled with an order for production of the reports.[30] These orders were made and the dispute was appealed to the Court of Appeal.

At first instance, Mervyn Davies, J held that the insurers' reports served a duality of purpose because the insurers wanted not only to obtain the advice of their solicitors, but also to ascertain the cause of the fire. The Court of Appeal found these two issues:

> "... quite inseparable. The insurers were not seeking the cause of the fire as a matter of academic interest in spontaneous combustion. Their purpose in instigating the enquiries can only be determined by asking why they needed to find out the cause of the fire. And the only reason that can be ascribed to them is that of ascertaining whether, as they suspected, it had been fraudulently started by the insured. It was entirely clear that, if the claim was persisted in and if it was resisted, litigation would inevitably follow ... It is ... entirely unrealistic to attribute to the insurers an intention to make up their minds, independently of the advice which they received from their solicitors, that the claim should or should not be resisted. Whether they paid or not

---

28 [1988] QB 532 at 536 per Glidewell, LJ See also *Descoteaux v Mierzwinski and A-G of Quebec* 171 DLR (3d) 590, discussed in Chap. 1, Section 10.

29 [1984] BCLC 151. Two Court of Appeal decisions which touch on the availability of litigation privilege in relation to police enquiry reports are *Neilson v Laugharne* [1981] 1 QB 736 and *Peach v Commissioner of Police of the Metropolis* [1986] 2 WLR 1080.

30 Note that there appears to be an argument, not canvassed in this decision, to the effect that privilege cannot be asserted to resist a liquidator's demands for documents made pursuant to his statutory powers (now contained in s.236 Insolvency Act 1986): see further, Chap. 1, Section 6.

depended on the legal advice which they received, and the reports were prepared in order to enable that advice to be given. The advice given was necessarily to determine their decision and ... whether the anticipated litigation would or would not take place".[31]

Accordingly, the reports were held to be privileged and the liquidator failed to gain access to them. To similar effect is Rix, J's rulings in *The "Sagheera"*.[32] Here, it had been argued that an investigation involving third-party communications into a vessel's sinking conducted by solicitors on the joint instructions of the vessel's owners and war-risk underwriters could not be subject to litigation privilege because it was possible that the purpose of such communications was merely background to advising joint clients on their general position short of litigation. This was rejected, Rix, J commenting:

> "... I do not think that it is possible to distinguish between the purpose of taking legal advice concerning one's rights or obligations, where that necessitates requiring information from third parties,[33] and the additional purpose of using that information in aid of litigation, should litigation be necessary, as long as litigation is reasonably in prospect. That is not... an example of a dual purpose which prevents the purpose of using information in aid of litigation from being dominant...".[34]

In contrast is the decision in *Price Waterhouse v BCCI Holdings (Luxembourg) S.A.*[35] The decision was considered in Chapter 2 in relation to an unsuccessful claim for advice privilege over the reports prepared by the investigation committee established by BCCI, of which the plaintiffs' partners were members. In the alternative, it was argued that the reports were protected by litigation privilege because they were prepared in order to obtain legal advice in connection with possible litigation for the recovery of outstanding loans. This much was conceded, but Millett, J refused to accept that this was the dominant purpose behind their preparation. Rather, this was to establish the facts necessary to enable BCCI's financial position to be determined: only then could a decision be taken to institute recovery proceedings. Here, the two purposes were "quite independent of each other".[36]

---

31 Per Oliver, LJ *op. cit.,* at 173. Strictly, then, this was not a "dual-purpose" case.
32 [1997] 1 Lloyd's Rep 160.
33 As to which, see Section 7 below.
34 *Ibid.,* at 166.
35 [1992] BCLC 583.
36 *Ibid.,* at 590.

4. LITIGATION PRIVILEGE:
WHAT PURPOSE?

Litigation privilege contemplates that a protected communication can be created for several different purposes, so long as such purposes include a dominant connection with the litigation process. In *Waugh*, Lord Edmund-Davies cited with approval Barwick, CJ's comments in *Grant* v *Downs* when he said

> "... a document which was produced or brought into existence either with the dominant purpose of its author, or of the person or authority under whose direction, whether particular or general, it was produced or brought into existence, of *using it or its contents in order to obtain legal advice or to conduct or to aid in the conduct of litigation,* at the time of its production in reasonable prospect, should be privileged and excluded from inspection"[37] (emphasis supplied).

This statement was in line with older authority. Thus in *Wheeler* v *Le Marchant,* in which the Court of Appeal refused to extend privilege to a solicitor's communications with a third party[38] in circumstances where no litigation was in contemplation, Cotton, LJ commented:

> "Hitherto such communications have only been protected when they have been in contemplation of some litigation, or for the purpose of giving advice or obtaining evidence with reference to it ... then the solicitor is preparing for the defence or for bringing the action ...".[39]

It is not essential that the solicitor or client should gather "evidence" in the strict sense of admissible materials: mere "information" obtained in reference to the litigation in which the client is concerned can be protected. In *In re Thomas Holloway*[40] Cotton, LJ suggested that where a solicitor received information pursuant to a public advertisement which promoted his client's case, that would be privileged information.[41]

In the *Highgrade* case[42] discussed above, the Court of Appeal rejected

---

37 (1976) 135 CLR 674 at 677.

38 As to which see further Section 6 below and Chap. 4.

39 (1881) 17 Ch D 675 at 684–685. See also Jessell MR's judgment at 682, and *Southwark Water Co* v *Quick* (1878) 3 QBD 315. Note as suggested in Chap. 2, Section 3, that Barwick, CJ's judgment is capable of being read as applying the dominant purpose test to legal advice privilege generally, and not just to advice sought in connection with the litigation process.

40 (1887) 12 PD 167. See also the numerous similar examples given in Bray, *op. cit.* Chap. 2, n. 12, at 405–406.

41 Contrast "information" with "opinion", for which no privilege will be available (unless the opinion is given in the form of expert evidence): *Bustros* v *White,* 1 QBD 423.

42 [1984] BCLC 151.

the judge's view that *Waugh* established that it was only if documents were brought into existence for the dominant purpose of actually being used as evidence in the anticipated proceedings that privilege could attach, such that the purpose of taking advice on whether or not to litigate was some separate purpose which did not qualify for privilege. That was to confine litigation privilege to too narrow bounds.[43] Holding that the reports were indeed privileged, Oliver, LJ concluded that:

> "The purpose was, and was only, to determine aye or no were they to litigate, and it was clearly in order to enable the solicitors to advise them on that matter that the relevant documents were obtained".[44]

Ultimately, privileged materials created for the purposes of litigation do not actually need to be used in connection with the anticipated litigation for which they were created. In *Southwark Water Co v Quick*,[45] it was held that a document prepared by a client which contained information *bona fide* procured for the purposes of consulting his solicitor in relation to litigation was privileged even though not ultimately sent to him. In such cases, the intention of the document's creator is examined, for the purpose of the privilege, at the time of creation.

Finally here, the decision of the Vice Chancellor, Sir Richard Scott, in *Re Barings plc*[45a] has expressed discomfort with the decision in *Re Highgrade Traders*[45b] and has suggested that the scope of litigation privilege should be linked to the question of whether disclosure of a document for which this privilege is claimed impinges on the inviolability of lawyer/client communications.

The decision concerned the status of a report prepared by solicitors to the administrators of Barings Group companies. Made pursuant to the administrator's duty contained in section 7(3) of the Company Directors Disqualification Act 1986, the report considered certain directors' fitness to be concerned with corporate management and was expressed to be prepared in compliance with the administrators' statutory duty to report

---

43 "... the proposition that privilege extends to documents coming into existence for the purpose of obtaining advice in connection with the prosecution or defence of a claim is supported by the judgment of Buckley, LJ in *Birmingham and Midland Motor Omnibus Co Ltd v London and North Western Rly* [1913] 3 KB 850 at 856, where he speaks of privilege extending to a document "procured as material upon which professional advice should be taken in proceedings pending, threatened or anticipated", per Oliver, LJ in *Highgrade,* at 174.

44 [1984] BCLC 151 at 174.

45 (1878) 3 QBD 315: A document created in order to be "laid before the solicitor... is not taken out of the privilege merely because afterwards it was not laid before the solicitor": per Brett, LJ at 330.

45a [1998] 1 All ER 673.

45b [1984] BCLC 151.

to the DTI. In reliance upon the report, disqualification proceedings were commenced in the course of which the Secretary of the State claimed that the report was protected from disclosure by litigation privilege. Examining the policy reasons behind litigation privilege, the Vice Chancellor concluded:

> "... documents brought into being by solicitors for the purposes of litigation are afforded privilege because of the light they might cast on the client's instructions to the solicitor or the solicitor's advice to the client regarding the conduct of the case or the client's prospects".

This meant, according to the Vice Chancellor:

> "There was no general privilege that attached to documents brought into existence for the purposes of litigation independent of the need to keep inviolate communications between the client and legal advisor. If documents in which privilege was sought did not relate in some fashion to communications between a client and legal advisor, there was no element of public interest that could override the ordinary rights of discovery and no privilege".[45c]

This is, it is suggested, a somewhat narrow view of the policy behind litigation privilege which, it is respectfully submitted, it is not a policy approach justified even by the authorities from which the Vice Chancellor sought comfort in his judgment.[45d] Only in December 1996 did Simon Brown LJ suggest in *Robert Hitchins Ltd* v *International Computers Ltd*[45e] that the policy objective underlying litigation privilege:

> "... must surely be to enable parties or prospective parties to prepare properly for litigation in the confidence that others thereafter will not be entitled to examine and perhaps profit from their preparatory documentation".

Nonetheless, in *Re Barings*, the Vice Chancellor objected to the Secretary of State's submissions that the only question she should ask herself is whether the administrator's solicitors' report was brought into existence for the sole and dominant purpose of being used in making a decision as to whether or not to commence disqualification proceedings. Recognising that *Re Highgrade Traders* was binding on him, the Vice Chancellor nonetheless noted that none of the authorities cited to him on behalf of the Secretary of State involved a statutory report. Accordingly, in his judgment:

> "... the question whether statutory reports provided to the Secretary of State

45c [1998] 1 All ER 673 at 681–682.
45d See as to this, the author's article on this decision in [1997] *New Law Journal* 1655.
45e Unrep., 10 December 1996. The decision is discussed in detail in Chap. 6 below.

under section 7(3) of the 1986 Act can be withheld from discovery on the grounds of legal professional privilege does not depend on the intentions or state of mind of the administrators who make the reports or on the nature of any communications between the Secretary of State's officials and the administrators that have preceded the preparation of the reports or on the intentions of the Secretary of State as to the use that will be made of the report... The question whether these statutory reports are privileged depends, in my judgment, on whether there is a public interest requiring protection from disclosure to be afforded to these reports that is sufficient to override the administration of justice, reasons that are reflected in the discovery rights given to litigants".[45f]

It is suggested that this judgment attempts to take litigation privilege on to a new, but more restricted, plane. It is unfortunate that the Court of Appeal had no opportunity to review this decision since the Secretary of State decided to hand over her report to the directors shortly before the Vice Chancellor delivered his judgment.

5. LITIGATION PRIVILEGE: THE LITIGATION

A document can only qualify for litigation privilege if its dominant purpose is use in litigation, in other words, judicial or quasi-judicial proceedings. Although these were broadly identified in Chapter 1, inevitably there will be certain types of "proceedings" in relation to which litigation privilege is simply not available.[46] This is not a problem for advice privilege since client–lawyer communications need not concern litigation in order to attract privilege: accordingly any uncertainties as to whether the proceedings are judicial in nature only give rise to privilege problems where the client or lawyer communicates with a third party. Two particular instances which require some care to be taken are where correspondence ensues with, for example, a government initiated enquiry (*e.g.* Lord Justice Bingham's enquiry in 1991–1992 into the collapse of the BCCI Banking Group), or with a professional's regulator (*e.g.* a solicitor with the Law Society, or an accountant with the ICAEW) who is enquiring into his conduct. In the case of the former type of proceeding there can be little doubt that client or lawyer communications with a third party will not be

---

45f [1998] 1 All ER 673 at 687–688.

46 See, *e.g.*, *W* v *Edgell* [1990] Ch 359, which could be read as suggesting that a claim for privilege asserted in respect of a doctor's report prepared for use in a mental health tribunal review failed because, according to the Court of Appeal, tribunal proceedings under the Mental Health Act 1959 are not adversarial in nature. Scott J appeared to take a different view at first instance.

privileged even though the subject matter of the correspondence may give rise to subsequent litigation involving those corresponding with the inquiry and a third party. In fact, that correspondence may well be discoverable in any subsequent litigation.[47]

A second possible problem area is in relation to inquiries by a regulator or professional body: when, if at all, do these become judicial proceedings? Although not a case concerning privilege, the Court of Appeal's decision in *R* v *Institute of Chartered Accountants of England and Wales, ex p. Brindle*[48] illustrates the difficulty. Here, accountants' conduct in relation to the collapse of a banking group caused the ICAEW to investigate it under its disciplinary scheme. The ICAEW confirmed that the accountants were not under enquiry in the first instance, at which stage it was only collecting information. Only later was the firm formally put under investigation, whereupon it could become subject to disciplinary sanctions. Presumably, by that stage at the latest the proceedings acquired a judicial character which made litigation privilege available.

It is not a requirement of the privilege that the litigation is already afoot for a communication to qualify for the privilege: communications in respect of litigation reasonably in anticipation at the time the communication is made will be protected. In *Fenner* v *London & South Eastern Railway Co*[49] the plaintiff's solicitors sent a letter to the defendant which referred to the deteriorated condition of the plaintiff's cattle carried on the defendant's railway. Though the letter contained no express statement that the plaintiff meant to commence an action if not compensated, Blackburn, J accepted that:

> "... it must be taken that on receipt of that letter, the [defendant's] manager would be aware that litigation would be very probable".[50]

More recently, in *Alfred Crompton Amusement Machines Ltd* v *Commissioners of Customs and Excise (No 2)*,[51] the House of Lords was concerned with a claim to privilege in the context of a dispute between the manufacturer of amusement machines and the Commissioners of Customs and Excise concerning the wholesale value of the machines by reference to which tax under the Purchase Tax Act 1963 was to be levied. From 1964, the manufacturers had paid tax pursuant to an agreed formula but, in 1967, having been advised by their accountant that that agreement was

---

47 Which is no doubt one of the reasons why professionals sometimes try to halt inquiries by their regulator until after the inclusion of the litigation.
48 [1994] BCC 297.
49 (1872) LR 7 QB 767.
50 (1872) LR 7 QB 767 at 769.
51 [1974] AC 405.

too favourable to the Commissioners, they wrote to dispute the amounts which should be paid and asked the Commissioners to prepare a formal opinion which they indicated they would then challenge in arbitration proceedings pursuant to the governing legislation. Strictly, the 1967 request for arbitration was premature in that all the appellants needed to do at that stage was to discontinue paying tax pursuant to the 1964 formula and to put in a return on what they thought was the correct basis. Only if no agreement on the point could be reached did they need to invite the commissioners to give a formal opinion which they could then challenge in arbitration proceedings. However, on receipt of their letter the Commissioners embarked on a prolonged investigation of the whole position during which they obtained documents and information from customers of the appellant.

In the event, the dispute went to arbitration where questions arose as to whether the Commissioners could claim privilege over certain categories of documents. The appellant argued that the Commissioners ought not to have anticipated litigation upon receipt of the 1967 letter so as to trigger a claim for litigation privilege. Lord Cross of Chelsea commented that there was no need for the appellants to have requested a reference to arbitration at that stage. However:

> "... whatever may have been in their minds it does not lie in their mouth to complain that the Commissioners on receipt of the letter formed the view that any value which they fixed would almost certainly be challenged and there was nothing in the subsequent correspondence to cause them to think otherwise. So even if the existence of privilege in respect of [such] documents depends on the reference to arbitration having been anticipated when they were written (which I doubt) I think that the Court of Appeal was right in holding that the claim was made out with regard to them ...".[52]

The potential dangers which can exist, then, are well illustrated by this decision: anticipate litigation prematurely and certain documents, especially third-party communications, may be outside the privilege; equally, threaten it unnecessarily and it may be possible for the party attacked to claim privilege in circumstances where it might not have been possible *but for* that threat. As the decision also demonstrates, it is not necessary for a complete cause of action to have accrued in order for the privilege to arise.

Some litigation has to be in contemplation in order to trigger the privilege. In certain situations, the court will more readily accept that

---

52 *Ibid.*, at 431. The documents concerned, being communications between the Commissioners and their internal solicitors sent or received for the purpose of obtaining or furnishing information or evidence to be used in the arbitration, would surely now be covered by the *Balabel* purpose of advice test.

litigation was in contemplation than in others. So an insured who suffers a motor accident expects by and large his claims to be paid:

> "The situation is, however, different where a major casualty occurs at sea, with the loss of the subject matter insured beneath the waves, in an area at any rate adjacent to a war zone where mines are sown, in circumstances where the question immediately arises whether the cause of loss is something for which one but not the other of two separate underwriters is responsible".[53]

In such situations, litigation is easily anticipated.

Where litigation is possible but it is decided not to litigate,[54] the privilege is no longer available, since litigation can no longer be said to be in anticipation. This is illustrated by the decision in the *Good Luck*[55] where a further category of documents for which the plaintiffs claimed privilege related to correspondence between their solicitors and the vessel owner's solicitors concerning the owners' actual or contemplated proceedings against the defendant insurers. In relation to these, Saville, J held that if the dominant purpose for which such documents came into existence was that of enabling the plaintiff to obtain legal advice on whether or not to join in the litigation started or contemplated by the owners, such documents would be protected by litigation privilege pursuant to the decision in *Waugh*. However:

> "...any such correspondence that took place after the plaintiffs had decided not to join in the owners' action against the defendants would not be privileged on this ground but only if the dominant purpose was to obtain legal advice on the plaintiffs' own contemplated proceedings against the defendants".[56]

While the client must have litigation in mind if he is to create documents subject to litigation privilege, he need not at that stage have decided to instruct a solicitor to make or resist a claim. The contrary submission was advanced in *Re Highgrade Traders Ltd* where Oliver, LJ said:

> "Such a proposition appears to me to be at variance with the decision of the House of Lords in *Waugh*'s case, from which it is, I think, clear that, if litigation is reasonably in prospect, documents brought into being for the purpose of enabling the solicitors to advise whether a claim shall be made or

---

53 Per Rix, J in *The "Sagheera"* [1997] 1 Lloyd's Rep 160 at 166.
54 Or, where the threat of litigation substantially recedes.
55 [1992] 2 Lloyd's Rep 540 at 542–543.
56 Although the plaintiffs can assert privilege over this correspondence, it is questionable whether the owners can: see *Schneider v Leigh* [1955] 2 QB 195 discussed in Chap. 7, Section 2.

resisted are protected by privilege, subject only to the caveat that that is the dominant purpose for their having been brought into being."[57]

As *Highgrade* further illustrates, the threat of litigation need not actually materialise. There, the litigation anticipated when the external reports were commissioned had not materialised by the time the matter reached the Court of Appeal.

Nor need a party warn his potential adversary that litigation between them is possible before he can avail himself of the privilege. In *Plummers Ltd v Debenhams plc*[58] the plaintiffs, who were indebted to the defendants, ran into financial difficulties which affected their ability to meet their loan repayments. The defendants, on the advice of solicitors, appointed accountants to investigate the plaintiff's position. The plaintiffs co-operated with the accountants, oblivious to the fact that, depending on what the accountants' report said, litigation was likely to ensue. The plaintiffs challenged the defendants claim to privilege over the accountants' report. Holding that "it is sufficient if litigation is contemplated by the party who seeks legal advice", Millett, J commented:

> "... the privilege ... must necessarily extend to documents obtained or brought into existence before that decision [i.e. to make a claim] is notified to the other side. I see no good reason in logic or principle for requiring a party to warn the other side that he is contemplating making a claim, or rejecting his demand, or for restricting the privilege to documents obtained or brought into existence only after such warning has been given .... There must be a real prospect of litigation. Where it is neither pending nor threatened, it must be in the active contemplation of the party seeking advice".[59]

A final example here of the principle that documents need to be prepared with a view to the litigation in which the privilege is to be asserted[60] if the claim to privilege is to be upheld is *The "World Era" (No 2)*.[61] Here, charterers sued the vessel owners for breach of a charter-party. The dispute was referred to arbitration. Charterers asserted they were agents for a disclosed principal from whom their solicitors took instructions in relation to the arbitration. Before its conclusion, charterers

---

57 [1984] BCLC 151 at 172. Oliver, LJ criticised a passage in the *Supreme Court Practise 1982* to the contrary effect which was based, inaccurately, on the House of Lords' judgment in the *Crompton* case. This criticism was repeated in *Guinness Peat Properties Ltd v Fitzroy Partnership* [1987] 1 WLR 1027 in respect of the 1985 White Book. The offending passage has been removed from later editions. But see also the discussion of *Re Barings plc* [1998] 1 All ER 673 at pp.87–89 above.

58 [1986] BCLC 447.

59 *Ibid.*, at 453–454.

60 Subject to the "once privileged always privileged" rules: see Chap. 6.

61 [1993] 1 Lloyd's Rep 363.

and their principals fell out and sued each other. The dispute concluded and the solicitors resumed taking instructions from both in the arbitration. The owners sought inspection of the documents generated in the action between charterers and principal who resisted on the grounds of common interest privilege.[62] Phillips, J was unable to conclude that the dominant purpose of those documents was use in the pending arbitration: the dominant object was to advance the principal's case in a dispute with the charterer and not in the arbitration. They could not therefore be privileged as against the owners on this ground.[63]

6. LITIGATION PRIVILEGE: WHOSE PURPOSE?

Barwick, CJ's judgment in *Grant* v *Downs*,[64] approved by Lord Edmund-Davies in *Waugh*[65] (see p. 86 above), demonstrates that it is not necessarily the maker or author of the privileged communication who must have litigation in mind when he makes that communication in order for the privilege to bite. It is sufficient if the communication is made at the behest of another who himself intends the document to be created for the dominant purpose of use in litigation. Indeed, in *Waugh*[66] the House of Lords was in reality examining the intentions of the British Railways Board in relation to the accident report, and not those of the two representatives who researched and wrote it. Similarly, in *Highgrade* it was the insurer's intentions which were key, and not those of the writers of the various reports in issue.[67] Thus it follows that witness and expert statements are privileged according to the intent of those who seek that evidence.[68]

Another type of document which is relevant to the "whose purpose"

---

62 As to which see Chap. 6.
63 In the event they were withheld on other grounds.
64 135 CLR 674 at 674.
65 [1980] AC 521 at 544.
66 [1980] AC 521.
67 See also *Price Waterhouse* v *BCCI* [1992] BCLC 583.
68 See *Feuerheerd* v *London General Omnibus Co Ltd* [1918] 2 KB 565. The Court of Appeal held here that a signed witness statement obtained by the defendant's representative from the plaintiff following an accident between a taxi carrying the plaintiff and the defendant's bus was privileged. The plaintiff thought the representative was from the solicitors she had consulted. This decision is difficult to justify, since none of the cases discussed in Chap. 2 concerning the unavailability of a claim to privilege for statements made in the presence of the opposing party was cited to the Court. See also *Britten* v *FH Pilcher & Sons* [1969] 1 All ER 491. *Feuerheerd* has been followed in Australia, albeit reluctantly: see p. 107 below.

enquiry is a communication with an insurer. In *Guinness Peat Properties Ltd v Fitzroy Robinson Partnership,*[69] the plaintiff building developers sued the defendant architects for breach of contract and negligence arising out of their design work on an atrium on an office site which the plaintiffs were developing. The plaintiffs wrote to the architects in June, 1984 to put them on notice of their intention to hold them responsible for the costs involved in curing the problems complained of. Consequent upon this notice, the architects immediately wrote to their professional indemnity insurers to make a formal notification of the plaintiff's claim as required by the terms of their policy. As well as enclosing copies of other relevant memoranda, that letter expressed the architects' views on the merits of the plaintiff's contention. In the litigation which subsequently ensued, the architects mistakenly included the notification letter in Part 1 of Schedule 1 of their list of documents, whereas they had intended to list it in Part 2 of Schedule 1 and claim privilege for it. Before this error was spotted, the plaintiff's solicitor was allowed to inspect and copy the letter. Once the error was appreciated the architects applied to restrain the plaintiffs from making any further use of the copy letter and requiring any copies they had made to be delivered up to them. A first issue was whether legal professional privilege attached to the notification letter at all.[70]

As to this, the plaintiffs submitted that the notification letter was written not for the dominant purpose of obtaining legal advice or assistance but to comply with the condition of the insurance policy which required notification of claims to be given. The Court of Appeal, accepting the proposition that the dominant purpose of a document does not necessarily fall to be ascertained by reference to the intention of its actual composer, disagreed. They preferred the architects' submissions that the notification letter came into existence on the requirement of the insurers who had the real interest in seeing that the claim was defended, since under the terms of the policy the defence of the plaintiff's claim against the architects would be conducted by the insurers' lawyers and not the insured's. Slade, LJ accepted that the dominant purpose of the notification letter:

> "... must be viewed objectively on the evidence, particularly by reference to the intentions of the insurers who procured its genesis .... I accept that, so viewed, the dominant purpose was to produce a letter of notification which

---

69 [1987] 1 WLR 1027. See the doubts expressed about the correctness of this decision in *Re Barings plc* [1998] 1 All ER 673.

70 The question of whether any privilege in the letter was waived by the inadvertent disclosure is discussed in Chap. 7.

would be used in order to obtain legal advice or to conduct or aid in the conduct of litigation which was at the time of its production in reasonable prospect".[71]

It should not be thought that assured–insurer communications will only be privileged in circumstances where the insured takes over the conduct of the insurer's defence by instructing his own solicitors. In the earlier Court of Appeal decision in *Westminster Airways Ltd v Kuwait Oil Co Ltd*,[72] decided on similar facts, Jenkins, LJ held:

> "... a communication between the assured and the insurance company, whether direct or through the assured's brokers, would be directed to the question whether the claim should be disputed or admitted, and if it was to be disputed, how best to conduct the defence. If the communications were of that character, then ... they would be well within the privileged area ...".[73]

Furthermore, where the insurer is subrogated to the rights of the assured then correspondence between the insurer and the assured's solicitors will be privileged even though no litigation is in contemplation, in other words, under the advice head. This the Court of Appeal held in *Standrin v Yenton Minster Homes Ltd.*[74]

There are, however, some grey areas here. First, in the *Standrin* decision, a claim for privilege over insurer/assured communications which pre-dated the insurer taking over the claim failed. The *Guinness Peat* and *Westminster Airways* decisions were not referred to in the court's judgments, so possibly the decision was decided *per incuriam*. And what of the position where the insurer seeks privileged information to enable him to advise on coverage issues? If he is merely considering this issue, so that litigation cannot be said to be in prospect, is the communication from the assured privileged nonetheless? In these circumstances, the court is now likely to hold that the "common interest" which subsists between insurer and assured – despite their potential for conflict – causes that communication to be privileged in both their hands.[75] This rule conveniently avoids any problems as regards who can assert the privilege. In *Guinness Peat*, Slade, LJ considered that the privilege in the notification letter was the insurer's since they had caused the document to come into existence;[76] whereas in *Svenska Handelsbanken v Sun Alliance & London*

---

71 *Ibid.*, at 1037.
72 [1951] 1 KB 134.
73 *Ibid.*, at 146–147. Curiously although the *Westminster* decision was cited to the Court in *Guinness Peat*, it was not referred to in the judgments.
74 (1991) *The Times*, 22 July.
75 See Chap. 6 and especially *Guinness Peat, op. cit., Svenska Handelsbanken v Sun Alliance & London Insurance Co* [1995] 2 Lloyd's Rep 84 and *Commercial Union Insurance Co v Mander* [1997] 1 Lloyd's Rep 84.

Insurance Co plc[77] the privilege in the insurer's communication to their reinsurers was the insurer's. In both cases, the application of common interest privilege entitled each entity to assert the privilege.

Finally, while the insured's original claim notification letter will usually be privileged – at least where litigation is contemplated – his formal claim on the policy, when he comes to submit this to the insurer, will be treated as an open communication which lacks the necessary confidence to give rise to any privilege.[78]

7. LITIGATION PRIVILEGE: COMMUNICATIONS WITH THIRD PARTIES

The ability of a client or his lawyer to engage in protected communications with a third party for the dominant purpose of litigation is the key feature which distinguishes the two heads of the privilege. This section illustrates some of the potential traps which can arise in relation to claims for privilege in respect of third party communications.

A good illustration of the difficulties which can arise in relation to such communications is the Court of Appeal's decision in *In re Thomas Holloway, Young v Holloway*.[79] Over the space of about two weeks each of the plaintiff, her solicitor and her counsel received unsolicited anonymous letters from a third party which concerned matters in dispute in an action which was already afoot and in which those lawyers represented the plaintiff. The Court of Appeal held that the letters received by the lawyers were privileged, whereas those received by the plaintiff were not and had to be disclosed to the defendant. The court held that the lawyers could only have received their letters in their character as legal advisers, so that the proper inference to draw was that these communications were made with reference to the action which was afoot; but there was nothing to show that the plaintiff received her letters for the purposes of being communicated to her solicitor in order to "forward" her litigation. Accordingly, no privilege could be claimed for them.[80] The

---

76 *Op. cit.,* at 1038.
77 [1995] 2 Lloyd's Rep 84
78 *The "Sagheera"* [1997] 1 Lloyd's Rep 160.
79 (1887) 12 PD 167.
80 It is surprising that the court was not prepared to treat the plaintiff as her lawyers' agent for the purposes of receiving these letters. Alternatively, it is a little difficult to appreciate why the plaintiff, in *receiving* information which could only have been sent to her in respect of the actual litigation then afoot was treated differently from the client who *collected* it himself in *Southwark Water* v *Quick* (1873) 3 QBD 315, where the privilege was upheld: see below.

decision therefore turned on the absence of any purpose on the part of the plaintiff to use them in her litigation. As for how the lawyers – whose letters were also unsolicited – came to possess a requisite purpose, Cotton, LJ[81] felt that the situation was the same as if the lawyers had actively procured the letters in the course of their employment.

The court's unwillingness to view the plaintiff's receipt of similar letters in the same light is not altogether convincing. However, had the plaintiff actively solicited the letters, they would have been privileged, so long as she had intended them for use in the litigation, or for passing to her solicitor for advice on the action. This is so whether or not the client obtains such documents on the instructions of his lawyer, or spontaneously on his own initiative. This is illustrated by the Court of Appeal's decision in *Southwark Water Company v Quick*.[82] Here the plaintiffs claimed privilege for (i) a transcript of the shorthand writer's notes of a conversation between a chimney sweep employed by the company and the company's engineer; (ii) transcripts of the shorthand writer's notes of interviews between the chairman of the plaintiff company and the engineer and certain inspectors of the company; and (iii) statements of facts drawn up by the chairman of the company. The company's deponent asserted that the purpose of the conversation contained in document (i) was to enable the engineer to obtain information which he could report to the company's directors who would then forward it to the company's solicitor for advice in relation to the intended action; whereas (ii) and (iii) had been sought with a view to submitting them to the company solicitor for advice in relation to the action.

When the claims for privilege over those documents were challenged in the Court of Appeal, the defendant argued that "communications spontaneously procured by the party from his agent to be submitted to a solicitor are not privileged".[83] These submissions were rejected. Holding that all three documents were privileged,[84] the court also held that it made no difference that the materials or information for which privilege was

---

81 *Op. cit.*, at 173.
82 (1878) 3 QBD 315.
83 See the submissions of Mr Matthew, *ibid.*, at 316, which were based in part on *Bustros v White*, 1 QBD 423.
84 The court felt some doubt about document (i) but took comfort from the language of the plaintiff's affidavit which was construed to mean that the transcript was made "in order that it might be furnished to the solicitor for his advice, although before passing on to him, it was to be laid before the board of directors ... in order that they might also see it. The object for which the notes were taken, and the transcript made, was that they might be furnished to the solicitor for his advice".

claimed had been obtained spontaneously and not at the request of a solicitor. Nor did it matter that document (i) had not in fact been submitted to the solicitor:

> "If at the time the document is brought into existence its purpose is that it should be laid before the solicitor, if that purpose is true and clearly appears upon the affidavit, it is not taken out of the privilege merely because afterwards it was not laid before the solicitor".[85]

One decision which needs to be treated with care here is *Anderson v Bank of British Columbia*[86] in which Jessel, MR delivered his famous judgment describing the underlying rationale of legal professional privilege.[87] Here, the manager of the defendant bank received a letter from the plaintiffs' solicitors which threatened legal proceedings in the event certain sums were not repaid. The bank's manager, appreciating that litigation against the bank was imminent, such that it was essential that the bank should have the benefit of legal advice, telegraphed the manager at the bank's Portland, Oregon branch, seeking full particulars of all the background facts and circumstances relating to the transactions likely to be in dispute. Following the commencement of litigation, the bank objected to producing the reports received from the Oregon branch manager in response to the London manager's request. Jessel, MR held that the response from Oregon was not privileged.

Even though his decision was upheld in the Court of Appeal (where James, LJ observed that this was one of the clearest cases that had ever come before the court), the reasoning is not convincing. Jessel, MR's decision appeared to turn on the lack of confidentiality in the communication between London and Oregon, and the failure of the affidavit claiming the privilege to demonstrate that the communications were made for the purpose of being submitted to the lawyer.[88] In the Court of Appeal, the decision was also justified by reference to agency law. So, James, LJ said that the:

> "... intelligible principle, that as you have no right to see your adversary's brief, you have no right to see that which comes into existence merely as the materials for the brief... [has]... no application whatever to a communication between a principal and his agent in the matter of the agency, giving information of the facts and circumstances of the very transaction which is

---

85 Per Brett, LJ (1878) 3 QBD 315 at 320.
86 (1876) 2 Ch D 644.
87 See Chap. 1, p. 3.
88 *Ibid.*, at 648.

the subject-matter of the litigation. Such a communication is, above all others, the very thing which ought to be produced".[89]

To modern eyes, the decision in *Anderson* is curious.[90] It is submitted it is unlikely to be followed today, as evidenced by Bingham, LJ's observations in *Ventouris* v *Mountain* when he said of the *Anderson* decision:

> "On modern principles (and unless the [deponent] was disbelieved, which was not stated) I think it plain that the representative's letter was privileged as a letter written (whether or not he knew it) for the purpose of laying before a solicitor to obtain legal advice".[91]

Another older decision which can still cause difficulties is the House of Lords' ruling in *Jones* v *Great Central Railway Co.*[92] This was concerned with a trade union's member who sought assistance from his union in the form of funding and the advice of the union's solicitor in order to pursue a claim of unjust dismissal against the railway company. The union rules required him to provide full particulars of the claim before it would sanction the engagement of a solicitor for which it would pay. Accordingly, certain letters passed between him and the union which contained information about the dispute with the employer. On the question of whether those documents were privileged from disclosure in the action which Jones eventually brought against the employers, Lord Loreburn, LC held that where a communication is made to a person who has himself to consider and act upon them, then there can be no privilege. The underlying rationale of this short judgment appears to have turned on the fact that a communication can only be privileged when it passes directly or indirectly between a person and his solicitor or between their respective agents. Here, "documents [were] in existence relating to the matter in dispute which were communicated to someone who was not a solicitor, nor the mere alter ego of a solicitor".[93] This led in this case, according to the House of Lords, to a wholesome result because it favoured "the placing before a court of justice of all material

---

89 *Ibid.*, at 656–657. Compare this decision with the earlier one in *Lafone* v *The Falkland Islands Co (No 1)*, 4 K & J 34 in which Page-Wood VC held that answers to inquiries made by the Defendants of their Falkland Islands' agent at the direction of their solicitor for the purpose of procuring evidence to support their position in London litigation were privileged.

90 In *Seabrook* v *British Transport Commission*, Havers, J commented that *Anderson* fairly represented "the high water mark to which the courts have gone in favour of those who seek inspection of documents of this character": [1959] 1 WLR 509 at 517.

91 [1991] 1 WLR 607 at 612.

92 [1910] AC 4.

93 *Ibid.*, at 6.

circumstances that may lead to a just decision".[94]

This decision is supportable on the basis that a third-party communication is only privileged if made for the dominant purpose of the litigation. This, evidently, was not the case in *Jones*.[95] It is difficult to see, however, that a court in 1998 would adopt the approach of the House of Lords in *Jones* which ruled out the privilege on account of the union having to "consider and act upon" the union member's letter.[96] Had *Jones* been able to depose that the only purpose for which he wrote to the union was to secure the funding necessary to enable him to employ solicitors then he might well have secured a different result in front of a modern court. Indeed, courts routinely treat applications for legal aid as privileged;[97] and the position in *Jones* is not easily distinguishable from the assured who notifies his professional indemnity insurer of a claim made against him so as to trigger defence costs funding clauses in the policy.[98] In the same way, it might also be possible to assert that the union and member had a common interest in the litigation, arising as a consequence of the union's costs exposure, which would enable both to assert the privilege.[99]

Nonetheless, the decision in *Jones* was followed by the House of Lords decision in *Alfred Crompton Amusement Machines Ltd* v *Commissioners of Customs and Excise No 2*[1] (the facts of which were considered at p. 89 above). Other documents in issue in that decision included those obtained from third parties. Legal professional privilege was claimed for them on the basis that they came into existence both to assist the valuation department of the Commissioners in fixing the wholesale value of the machines as well as to assist the legal department in upholding that valuation in the arbitration which was anticipated. The claim to privilege was not accepted because the documents were not obtained for the

---

94 *Ibid.*, at 6.

95 *Phipson on Evidence* (14 Edn.) at para. 20–30, n. 55, points out that the decision is a trap for the unwary because "in most such cases, in modern times, the dispensation of employed solicitors inaugurated by *Crompton*'s case [discussed in Chap. 4] will protect such communication". This is correct so long as the union employed solicitor acts for the member in his claim, or otherwise advises him. If the solicitor is merely processing the claim in an administrative capacity, the privilege will not arise.

96 [1910] AC 4 at 5.

97 See pp. 83–84 above. This is so, quite apart from the provision of s. 38 Legal Aid Act 1988.

98 See Section 6 above.

99 Common interest privilege is considered in Chap. 4. Further, a court might also refuse disclosure on the basis that it was not necessary for the purposes of saving costs that Jones' letter to the Union should be made available to the defendants: see RSC O.24, r.13 and *Robert Hitchins Ltd* v *International Computers Ltd*, (unrep.) 10 December 1996, CA.

1' [1974] AC 405.

purposes of litigation. Lord Cross, who gave the leading judgment, noted that the two purposes for which the documents in question were obtained or came into existence were parts of a single wider purpose, "namely the ascertainment of the wholesale value in the manner described by the Act". Thus it was an independent primary statutory duty, and not the litigation, which compelled the bringing into being of these documents. Lord Cross said:

> "... in this case just as much as in cases in which no arbitration was in fact anticipated the commissioners had to form their own opinion as to value on the evidence available to them, including these documents, before any arbitration could take place .... [In *Jones* this] House held that the letters in question were not the subject of legal professional privilege because the union authorities had themselves to consider them and act on them before the solicitor was employed to conduct the case. So here the commissioners had to form their own opinion as to value before the solicitor would use the documents for the purpose of defending their opinion in the anticipated arbitration".[2']

In the *Guinness Peat* decision,[3'] the Court of Appeal was also faced with a submission based on *Jones v Great Central Railway Co.* This was to the effect that, since the notification letter was written to the insurers, who were not solicitors, but independent third parties who would themselves have to consider and act on the letter, the claim for privilege was unsustainable. Slade, LJ held that the *Jones* case was distinguishable on its facts since the relationship between trade union and member was "by no means the equivalent of the relationship between insurers and insured in the present case, where the insurers will in all but name be effective Defendants to any proceedings".[4']

8. LITIGATION PRIVILEGE: EXPERT WITNESSES

Where a professional third party is engaged by or on behalf of a party to litigation, either with a view to assisting the litigant to understand, for example, the technical aspects of the claim or to provide expert evidence in court, litigation privilege will usually cover all communications between the litigant or his solicitors and the third party professional, so long as they are

---

2'   *Ibid.*, at 432. The decision in *Barings plc* [1997] All ER (D) 1, discussed at pp. 87–89 above, could, possibly, be justified on the basis of Lord Cross' reasoning.

3'   [1987] 1 WLR 1027 considered in Section 6 above.

4'   *Ibid.*, at 1036. As suggested above, the analogy between the two situations is surely closer than Slade, LJ was prepared to accept.

referrable to the litigation concerned and satisfy the dominant purpose test.[5] So, for example, the draft and final reports of the expert witness will be privileged in the hands of his client and their lawyers[6] until such time as they are exchanged, pursuant to the rules of court, with the other parties to the litigation.[7] Similarly, all communications between the expert's representatives – for example intra-firm communications relating to his instructions on behalf of the litigant – will similarly be protected. The rationale is the familiar one which, in relation to experts, was explained by Lord Denning, MR in *In re Saxton, decd* as follows:

> "... the expert should be allowed to give his report fully and frankly to the party[8] who employs him, with all its strength and weakness, and not be made to offer it beforehand as a hostage to the opponent".[9]

Once the report is exchanged or disclosed in accordance with RSC O38, rr.35–44, it loses all protection, even if not used at trial (*e.g.* because the action for which it was prepared settles beforehand). In such cases, experts' reports are different in nature from witness statements (as to which see Section 9 below) in that they are not subject to any form of implied undertaking to respect their confidentiality. Accordingly, the receiving party can use a report disclosed to him in accordance with those rules in any other litigation in which it is relevant.[10]

It is worth repeating that the foregoing is only applicable where the expert is instructed in relation to litigation, as the decision of the Court of

---

5[1] See *Walsham v Stainton*, 2 H & M 1, *Waugh v British Railways Board* [1980] AC 521, *In re Strachan* [1895] 1 Ch 439, *Worrall v Reich* [1955] 1 QB 296 and *Causton v Mann Egerton* [1974] 1 WLR 162. The position in other jurisdictions, but particularly in the USA, in relation to experts, can be quite different with the result that great care has to be exercised – and tailored local advice sought – in dealing with professional third parties if a claim for privilege in respect of communications with them are to be upheld before a foreign court.

6[1] However, in family proceedings involving children, regard must now be had to the House of Lord's decision in *Re L (a Minor), (Police Investigation: Privilege)* [1997] AC 16 discussed in Chap. 1, Section 6.

7[1] Experts' reports must be disclosed in advance of trial if reliance is to be placed on them at trial, see RSC O25 r.8 and Part IV of RSC O38.

8[1] In the present day, the emphasis is on the expert's over-riding duty to the court: see pp. 105–106 below.

9[1] [1962] 1 WLR 968 at p.972. See also Russell, LJ at p.974: "Documents such as proofs and reports of potential expert witnesses are privileged from production". In *Ventouris v Mountain* [1991] 1 WLR 607 at 612, Bingham, LJ thought the immunity from production of the expert witness proof was a right which had been "generously interpreted".

10[1] Or, indeed, for any purpose whatsoever. This is the effect of RSC O38 r. 42: see *Prudential Assurance Co v Fountain Page Limited* [1991] 1 WLR 756. If the expert's report is not disclosed to the opponent then it remains privileged for the purposes of any other litigation under the "once-privileged, always privileged" rules: see *Goldstone v Williams, Deacon & Co* [1899] 1 Ch 47 and generally Chap. 6, Section 5.

Appeal in *Wheeler* v *Le Marchant*[11] made clear.[12] Thus if a client asks his solicitor to engage an expert valuer to advise him whether the asking price of a property which he is contemplating purchasing is a fair one his report will not be privileged. This has the result that it will be discoverable in any subsequent related litigation, since its preparation will not satisfy the dominant purpose test. But if he is engaged to value that same property in circumstances where a dispute has already arisen between the purchaser and the vendor, then his report, if prepared predominantly for use in that litigation, will be privileged.[13] This distinction is worth bearing in mind where, for example, banking or corporate finance solicitors engage external accountants to assist with an ongoing non-contentious transaction, or where clients (or their solicitors) instruct environmental consultants on their exposure to environmental risks.

Just as a client can be compelled to give evidence of facts he knows, notwithstanding that a communication sent to his lawyer for the purpose of seeking legal advice which sets out those facts would be privileged, so an expert witness can be compelled to disclose the opinion he forms, notwithstanding that his opinion was formed on the instructions of another party to litigation. This is a difficult area which was considered by the Court of Appeal in *Harmony Shipping Co SA* v *Davis*.[14] Here, an handwriting expert was approached by the plaintiffs to advise on the authenticity of a document which was crucial to their case. Having advised informally that the document concerned was not genuine, the expert apparently forgot that he had given that advice and subsequently accepted instructions to advise the defendant. Fortunately, he advised in consistent fashion since the defendants were also told that the document was not genuine. When he later realised that he had inadvertently advised both sides, he told the defendant he could accept no further instructions from him. The defendant was keen for his evidence to be given to the court and so served a subpoena on the expert. The trial judge ruled that the expert was a compellable witness whose opinions on the genuineness of the document could be given to the court. The Court of Appeal dismissed the

---

11[1] (1881) 17 Ch D 675.

12[1] In *The "Sagheera"* Rix, J commented: "It is, however, established law that third party documents, such as statements or experts reports, are only protected by litigation privilege, and not by advice privilege...". [1997] 1 Lloyd's Rep 160 at 164. But see his further comment in n. 30[1] below.

13[1] *Plummers Ltd* v *Debenhams plc* [1986] BCLC 447 is an example of (expert) accountants preparing a report for use by solicitors in anticipated litigation in which a challenge to the claim for privilege over the report was mounted. The challenge, which was unsuccessful, was based, *inter alia*, on a submission that the report did not satisfy the dominant purpose test.

14[1] [1979] 1 WLR 1380.

plaintiff's appeal and in his judgment Lord Denning, MR said as follows:

> "Many of the communications between the solicitor and the expert witness will be privileged. ... They cannot be communicated to the court except with the consent of the party concerned. That means that a great deal of the communications between the expert witness and the lawyer cannot be given in evidence to the court. If questions were asked about it, then it would be the duty of the judge to protect the witness. ... Subject to that qualification, it seems to me that an expert witness falls into the same position as a witness of fact. The court is entitled, in order to ascertain the truth, to have the actual facts which he has observed adduced before it and to have his independent opinion on those facts ... In this particular case the court is entitled to have before it the documents in question and it is entitled to have the independent opinion of the expert witness on those documents and on those facts ...".[15]

The decision in Harmony Shipping was followed by the Court of Appeal in *R v King*, in which Dunn, LJ confirmed the general position that "privilege attaches to confidential communications between the solicitor and the expert".[16] He went on to comment that privilege "does not attach to the chattels or documents upon which the expert based his opinion". *King* was concerned with a document provided to a handwriting expert which was in existence before the proceedings commenced. It had not been brought into existence for the purpose of the proceedings themselves and therefore there can be no objection to the result which the court there reached. But since an expert opinion necessarily has to be based on facts, it will often be necessary for the expert to reveal the facts on which that opinion was based; and as Scott, J commented in *W v Edgell*,[17] it may be necessary, on occasion, to reveal facts revealed to him in a privileged communication. He said:

> "Legal professional privilege attaches to documents brought into existence for the purpose of legal proceedings; but if such a document is placed before an expert witness for his opinion, it becomes, in my judgment, part of the facts on which the opinion is based. The expert cannot be barred when giving evidence of his opinion from referring to the facts on which the opinion is based, including, if it be the case, documents which, in the hands of solicitors, would be covered by legal professional privilege".[18]

This statement does not represent the inroad into privilege that it might appear on first reading. Scott, J went on to recognise[19] the distinction to be

---

15' *Ibid.*, at 1385. See also Lord Nicholls in *In re L (A Minor)* [1997] AC 16 at 34.
16' [1983] 1 WLR 411 at 414.
17' [1990] Ch 359.
18' *Ibid.*, at 396.
19' *Ibid.*, at 396.

drawn between instructions given to an expert witness, which are privileged, and, the expert's opinion given pursuant to those instructions, which is not.[20]

The limits on Scott, J's comments in *W v Edgell* should be noted. In *Booth v Warrington Health Authority*,[21] Drake, J rejected a submission that an expert witness's reference in his report to a factual witness's statement warranted its disclosure, even though the statement was part of the material on which his opinion was based. This submission was founded on an alleged waiver of privilege over the factual statement.[22]

Harmony Shipping should not be seen as authority for the view that the expert can divulge the contents of, for example, his written opinion prepared for his client if this has not been exchanged pursuant to the rules. The expert's written opinion only loses its privilege once it is served pursuant to RSC O38.[23] If the expert is subpoenaed he can only give oral opinion evidence at trial.

Nonetheless, the result of the *Harmony Shipping* case is that there are dangers in instructing an expert and then dispensing with his services in the event he provides an unfavourable opinion. If the opponent becomes aware that an expert has been instructed whose report is not produced at the appropriate stage of the litigation, it may well give rise to the suspicion that he has provided an unfavourable opinion which he would like to have aired in court. In that situation there is evidently no objection to his being subpoenaed to give evidence in court at the trial as to the opinion he formed and the facts on which it was based. However, it does not appear that a litigant can test a mere suspicion that his opponent has dispensed with a witness whom the opponent might like to subpoena by cross-examining the opponent about any expert witnesses he may have instructed but did not call to give evidence at trial.[24]

The *Harmony Shipping* case was followed in a criminal context in *R v R*,[25] where privilege was applied to a substance, as opposed to a communication. The defendant had been convicted of a number of criminal charges following a trial in which the prosecution was permitted to allow representatives of the Crown Prosecution Service to interview a scientist who had carried out DNA tests at the request of the defence

---

20[1] Privilege issues barely featured when Scott J's decision was upheld by the Court of Appeal.
21[1] [1992] 1 PIQR 137.
22[1] See also *B v John Wyeth & Brother Ltd* [1992] 1 WLR 168 and *Robinson v Adelaide International Raceway Pty Ltd* (1993) 61 SALR 279.
23[1] *Derby v Weldon (No 9)* (1990) *The Times,* 9 November.
24[1] Per Rix, J in *The "Sagheera"* [1997] 1 WLR 160 at 171.
25[1] [1994] 1 WLR 758.

solicitors on a blood sample provided by the defendant to his general practitioner for the purpose of his defence. The trial judge ruled that the evidence of the scientist was admissible against the defendant who appealed against his conviction. There was no suggestion that the scientist gave any evidence at trial regarding communications between her and the defence solicitors.[26] The dispute centred on the fact that her evidence was based on a blood sample which the defendant had provided so that her advice could be obtained. The court had therefore to consider the status of the defendant's sample which had been made available for the purpose of obtaining her advice in connection with the pending charges.

Whilst recognising that it is usually documents and oral communications which are the subject of legal privilege, the court focused on the fact that section 9 of the Police and Criminal Evidence Act 1984 protects "items subject to legal privilege" from police powers of search and seizure.[27] Such items are defined in section 10 of the same Act. The court thus held that the statutory definition applies when the issue is whether the defendant can object to the object in question being produced in evidence, or to oral evidence or opinion based upon it. Since the blood sample was provided at the request of the solicitors for the purpose of the defence and was given in circumstances of confidence, the court held that the sample was an item which was subject to legal professional privilege made for the purposes of the criminal trial.[28] Historically, in civil proceedings, privilege has only applied to communications, which the blood sample evidently was not. Some commentators doubt that this decision could be applied outside the scope of the 1984 Act.

The role of the expert is likely to change considerably if the proposals which Lord Woolf in his Civil Justice Review has recommended in relation to experts are implemented. In particular, he has proposed that any communication between an expert and the client or his advisers "should no longer be the subject of legal privilege".[29] The intention behind this suggestion is to prevent the suppression of relevant opinions on factual material which do not support the case put forward by the party instructing the expert. Following lobbying by the profession, Lord Woolf has apparently accepted that it would not be realistic to make draft experts' reports discloseable, but he is pursuing his intention to remove

---

26' The fact of such communications having taken place, as distinct from their content, was not a privileged matter in any event.

27' See further on this section, Chap. 8, Section 5.

28' In the event, although the court held that the scientist's evidence should have been excluded, there was overwhelming evidence of his guilt quite apart from her inadmissible evidence.

29' Civil Justice Review, Interim Report, Chap. 27, para. 31.

privilege over the expert's instructions. This aim has not yet been carried through entirely into the Draft Civil Proceeding Rules produced in July 1996. These are still very much at the consultation stage. However, if implemented in current form they would require:

- where a single expert is instructed, that "parties must give instructions to a single expert" (r.32.6); and
- where parties instruct their own expert, they must give every other party notice of "the scope of the instruction to be given to him". (r.32.6)

If implemented, these will amount to radical changes. It is too early to predict whether they will come into force in anything like this form, how they will work in practice if they do, and the extent to which they will impact on the rules relating to privilege.

9. LITIGATION PRIVILEGE: WITNESS STATEMENTS

As with the reports of expert witnesses, so the statements of a factual witness and all communications with him in relation to the seeking, taking and finalisation of his statement will be privileged.[30] There can be no doubt that the privilege in the final statement is that of the party for whose benefit it has been obtained, and not the witness himself who has no independent right to assert or have the benefit of the privilege. This was decided by the Court of Appeal in *Schneider* v *Leigh*,[31] a case which is discussed in detail in Chapter 7. Furthermore, a proof of evidence will be privileged even if taken from an opponent in litigation who mistakenly believes the person taking the proof is her own solicitor: *Feuerheerd* v *London General Omnibus Co*.[32] It is difficult to see why the privilege attaches in these circumstances given the lack of confidentiality between the parties.[33] Nonetheless, the decision has largely continued to be followed, despite criticisms and disquiet.[34]

30[1] See, *e.g.,* Lord Wilberforce in *Waugh* v *British Railways Board* [1980] AC 521 at 531 and Bingham, LJ in *Ventouris* v *Mountain* [1991] 1 WLR 607 at 611–612. In *The "Sagheera"* [1997] 1 Lloyd's Rep 160 at 168, Rix, J was faced with a submission, on which he did not have to rule, to the effect that a solicitor's draft of a witness statement is protected by advice privilege, and only becomes capable of protection under the litigation head once adopted by the witness.

31[1] [1955] 2 QB 195. See also *Feuerheerd* v *London General Omnibus Company* [1918] 2 KB 565.

32[1] [1918] 2 KB 565.

33[1] As to which see further Chap. 2, Section 9.

34[1] See *Nickmar Pty Ltd* v *Preservatrice Skandia Ins Ltd* (1985) 3 NSWLR 44.

Provided all the requirements of the privilege are satisfied, a witness statement will be privileged not only where it has been given voluntarily but where it has been procured by, for example, utilising statutory powers to obtain evidence – as with a trustee in bankruptcy's or a liquidator's powers under insolvency legislation.[35]

In 1972, As Lord Wilberforce noted in his speech in *Waugh*[36] that the operation of privilege in relation to witness statements means that one side to litigation cannot ask to see the proofs of the other side's witnesses, nor even know which witnesses will be called: he has to wait until the card is played, he cannot see it in the hand. However, the practice changed markedly with the introduction in 1986 of the provisions for the exchange of witness statements before trial contained in RSC Order 38, rule 2A. As one commentator has put it, these "constituted a serious in-road into one of the time-honoured features of our adversarial system of civil litigation".[37] But do they make any in-road into the privilege which a party has in his witness statements once he has exchanged them in accordance with these provisions? This issue was first raised in an early but unsuccessful challenge to the legitimacy of the new rules. In *Comfort Hotels v Wembley Stadium*,[38] a defendant contended that he could not be forced to exchange his statements without his consent because to do so would infringe his privilege. Hoffmann, J's sensible response to this was

---

35' So in *Learoyd v Halifax Joint Stock Banking Company* [1893] 1 Ch 686, Stirling, J asked (at 693) "why should not a document obtained by a trustee in bankruptcy for his own information, in order to enable his solicitor to advise him as to future proceedings, be privileged?". Stirling, J was in no doubt that this principle applied equally to liquidators: as to which see the Court of Appeal in *North Australian Territory Company v Goldsborough* [1893] 2 Ch 381, decided by reference to s. 115 Companies Act 1862. More recently, see *Dubai Bank v Galadari* [1990] BCLC 90, decided by reference to s. 561 Companies Act 1985. Interestingly, none of these three cases has been referred to in the discussion on the current legislation – ss. 235 and 236 Insolvency Act 1986 – in any of the modern text books on company or insolvency law. The question of the extent to which information obtained by a liquidator pursuant to a s. 236 Insolvency Act 1986 examination can be disclosed or released to third parties has been considered in a number of recent decisions, including the House of Lords' decisions in *Re Arrows (No 4)* [1994] 3 WLR 656 and *R v Director of SFO ex p. Smith* [1993] AC 1. The privileged status of such information was not raised in any of these decisions (since this aspect was not in issue). This leads to the consideration that the underlying rationale of s.236 Insolvency Act 1986 may now be such that the nature of a formal examination by a liquidator does not permit of a claim to privilege over the resulting information. This appears unlikely, but it is curious that the issue is no longer canvassed in the recognised insolvency text books. See, however, the views of Style & Hollander, *Documentary Evidence* (6th Edn.) at p 300.

36' [1980] AC 521 at 531.

37' Ian Grainger in an excellent series of articles in the *New Law Journal* in June and July 1995 at pp. 961, 1000 and 1062.

38' [1988] 1 WLR 872.

that the rules did nothing more than require him to tell his opponent in advance of the trial the factual evidence he was going to lead: it was entirely up to him whether or not he complied with the practice. If he did not, he would not be allowed to lead evidence at the trial.[39] If, however, he did then it was apparent that his privilege in the statement would be lost.

This consequence was spelt out by Phillips, J in *Youell* v *Bland Welch (No 3)*:

> "There is no requirement under the rules to disclose a privileged document. There is simply a requirement that if a witness is to be called a written statement of what he is to say is to be served on the other party. It is up to the party who is considering calling the witness to decide whether to do so or not ... [but] once the statement is served any privilege attached to it goes".[40]

However, this statement requires some qualification, for the loss of the privilege upon service does not entitle the receiving party to put the witness statement to unlimited use. Unlike expert's reports, there is no provision in the rule 2A regime equivalent to RSC Order 38 rule 42.[41] This, coupled with what is now Order 38 rule 2A(6),[42] influenced Hobhouse, J in *Prudential Assurance Co* v *Fountage Page Ltd*[43] to hold that served witness statements are subject to restrictions as to use by the receiving party, despite the loss of privilege which occurs on service. Here, an action settled after exchange of statements but before trial. Since the statements were served voluntarily, and not under compulsion, they were not subject to an implied undertaking akin to that which applies to documents produced on discovery. Nonetheless, Hobhouse, J held that:

> "I infer that the receiving party is not to be allowed to put the statement in evidence save at the trial (if there is one) or[44] the action in which the statement has been served and then only if the serving party elects to call the relevant witness at that trial; and that, apart from this, the receiving party and his solicitor may not use the material nor allow it to be used for any purpose other than the proper conduct of that action on behalf of the

---

39[1] At the time of this decision, RSC O38 r. 2A(8) provided that "Nothing in this Rule shall deprive any party of his right to treat any communication as privileged or make admissible evidence otherwise admissible". The reference to privileged communications in O38 r. 2A(8) has since been removed.

40[1] [1991] 1 WLR 122, at 123. See also *Black & Decker* v *Flymo* [1991] 1 WLR 753, *Prudential Assurance Co* v *Fountain Page Ltd* [1991] 1 WLR 756 and *Balkanbank* v *Taher* (1994) (unrep., *The Times,* 19 Feb). *Fairfield-Mabey Ltd* v *Shell UK Ltd* [1989] 1 All ER 576 is the one authority which goes against this view.

41[1] Which enables the receiver to use a served expert's report. See p. 103 above.

42[1] Which provides that "Subject to paragraph (9), where the party receiving a statement under this rule does not call a witness to whose evidence it relates, no other party may put the statement in evidence at the trial".

43[1] [1991] 1 WLR 756.

44[1] Grainger, *op. cit.,* n. 37[1], p.100 suggests "or" is a misprint for "of", since otherwise the sentence is ungrammatical.

receiving party and may not use it or allow it to be used for any collateral or ulterior purpose. It follows from this that the solicitor and his client may not supply the material to any other person (until it has passed into the public domain and is covered by Order 24, r14A) save for the purposes of the action in which it was served and the serving party may ask the court to prevent any breach of this obligation".[45]

Since this decision,[46] Order 38, rule 2A(11) has introduced an express prohibition against the receiving party using a served witness statement "for any purpose other than the purpose of the proceedings in which it was served", save where the serving party consents or the statement has been put in evidence (in which case it is in the public domain). This rule does not, however, affect the decision in *Black & Decker* v *Flymo*,[47] where the receiving party was allowed to use a served witness statement to found an application for specific discovery in the proceedings in which it was served. Hoffmann, J refused to specify other types of interlocutory applications in which such statements might be used.[48]

Finally, it should be noted that if a witness statement which contains passages which consist of privileged communications is put in evidence at trial, this can result in the waiver of privilege attaching to related documents.[49]

45' *Op. cit.,* n. 43' at 773.

46' Which enabled Grainger, *op. cit.,* n. 37', to argue that there exists a new form of privilege, or collateral undertaking, in respect of served statements.

47' [1991] 1 WLR 753.

48' There is some uncertainty as to how served statements can be used at trial, *e.g.* in opening, before the particular witness has been called. See *Fairfield-Mabey Ltd* v *Shell UK Ltd* [1989] 1 All ER 576, *Balkanbank* v *Taher* (1994) (*The Times,* 19 February 1994) and Grainger, *op. cit.,* n. 37', esp. pp. 1064–1065.

49' See *Verity and Spindler* v *Lloyds Bank plc* [1996] Fam Law 213. This issue is discussed extensively in Chap. 7, Section 8.

Chapter 4

AGENTS AND THIRD PARTIES: FURTHER CONSIDERATIONS

1. INTRODUCTION

Chapters 2 and 3 refer to some of the difficulties which can arise in asserting a claim to privilege in respect of a communication involving a third party. If the claim is for advice privilege, then under English law[1] it will only succeed if the third party is an agent who is a medium of communication for either the client or lawyer. As a result, complications can arise where an employer communicates with, rather than through, a servant or agent, or communicates legal advice received within his organisation for the purposes of acting upon it. If the claim is for litigation privilege then, as we have seen, a communication with a third party – who need not be an agent – will only be privileged if the dominant purpose test is satisfied. This chapter examines each of these situations and then concludes with a brief examination of the position where a person seeks to advise himself.

2. AGENTS

A communication between a client and his legal adviser need not be made directly in order to qualify for advice privilege. Similarly, a communication with a third party need not be made directly by the client or lawyer if it is to be protected by litigation privilege. In both cases, the client and the adviser are entitled to make the communication through an agent, so long as their agent is merely a medium of communication. As Sir George Jessel, MR explained in *Anderson v British Bank of Columbia*, privilege goes:

---

1 But see in relation to Australian and (possibly) New Zealand law, Section 2 below.

"... not merely to a communication made to the professional agent[2] himself by the client directly, it goes to all communications made by the client to the solicitor through intermediate agents,[3] and he is not bound to write letters through the post, or to deliver himself personally to see the solicitor; he may employ a third person to write the letter, or he may send the letters through a messenger, or he may give a verbal message to a messenger, and ask him to deliver it to the solicitor, with a view to his prosecuting his claim, or of substantiating his defence".[4]

Similarly, as the same judge explained in the later Court of Appeal decision in *Wheeler* v *Le Marchant,* a qualifying communication by the client to the solicitor is:

"... equally protected ... whether it is made to the solicitor in person or to a clerk or subordinate of the solicitor who acts in his place and under his direction".[5]

Where an agent is employed in this way – and his employment need not be a matter of necessity[6] – it matters not whether the communication is made with a view to obtaining legal advice or in relation to pending or actual litigation: the agent must however be no more than the means of communication.[7]

So, if a client asks an agent to draw up instructions to his solicitor, that is a privileged communication, just as is a letter or other communication written on the client's behalf by a third person employed by him for that purpose. In order to identify an agent who is the medium of communication, the distinction needs to be borne in mind between an appointed channel of communication and one who is charged with the duty of bringing into existence material on which, for example, the lawyer bases his advice. This is illustrated by *Price Waterhouse* v *BCCI Holdings,*[8] the facts of which have been described in Chapter 2, Section 6. It will be recalled that advice privilege was claimed for reports prepared by an investigating committee (which included Price Waterhouse personnel). The committee was established to investigate certain problem loans made by

---

2 *i.e.,* the lawyer.
3 See also Millett, J in *Price Waterhouse (a firm)* v *BCCI Holdings (Luxembourg) SA* [1992] BCLC 583 at 588.
4 (1876) 2 Ch D 644 at 649.
5 (1881) 17 Ch D 675 at 682.
6 See *Reid* v *Langlois* 1 M & G 627.
7 A number of examples of this are considered by Sir George Jessel, MR in *Wheeler* v *Le Marchant, op. cit.,* at 651. The rule also applies where either the client or lawyer use a translator to effect a communication between them: see *Du Barré* v *Livette* (1791) Peake 77.
8 [1992] BCLC 583. See also *CC Bottlers Ltd* v *Lion Nathan* [1993] 2 NZLR 445, discussed at p. 120 below.

BCCI group companies. These reports were passed to the bank's legal advisers, Allen & Overy, to enable them to advise on recoverability issues. Following BCCI's collapse, the BCCI liquidators argued that since the investigating committee was an internal organ of BCCI, charged with reporting to the bank's legal advisers, it was merely the means of communication between BCCI and its lawyers. Following *Wheeler v Le Marchant*,[9] Millett, J rejected this claim as "untenable", and held that Price Waterhouse:

> "... was not merely an agent for communicating the material from BCCI to Allen & Overy; it was charged with the duty of bringing the material into existence. In so far as it reported to Allen & Overy (if indeed it did), it was not passing on a communication from BCCI; it was producing material for BCCI and, at BCCI's direction, forwarding it to Allen & Overy direct instead of to BCCI with a view of its being sent on to Allen & Overy".[10]

Where the third party is not the agent of communication then, as we have seen in the discussion of *Wheeler v Le Marchant*[11] in Chapter 3, the lawyer's communications with him will only be privileged if made in the context of pending or actual litigation. Here, the appellant had argued that what effectively the solicitors were doing in that case was to communicate with an agent or representative of the client. Cotton, LJ's response to this was as follows:

> "That is a fallacious use of the word 'representatives'. If the representative is a person employed as an agent on the part of the client to obtain the legal advice of the solicitor, of course he stands in exactly the same position as the client as regards protection, and his communications with the solicitor stand in the same position as the communications of his principal with the solicitor. But these persons were not representatives in that sense. They were representatives in this sense, that they were employed on behalf of the clients, the Defendants, to do certain work, but that work was not the communicating with the solicitor to obtain legal advice."[12]

The consequences of the decision in *Wheeler v Le Marchant* apply whether it is the client or the lawyer who communicates with a third party where no litigation is pending or in progress.[13]

A solicitor can also make privileged communications with his client

---

9 (1881) 17 Ch D 675.

10 *Op. cit.*, n. 8 at 589.

11 (1881) 17 Ch D 675.

12 *Ibid.*, at 684.

13 See Bray, *op. cit.*, p.399: "... *Wheeler v Le Marchant* having established that a report made by a third person to the solicitor at his request did not protect it unless in reference to litigation, it is difficult to see how a report made by a third person to the client, by the client's immediate direction, can be in any better position".

through third persons who act as his clerks or agents and who are, as Bray put it, "really pro hac vice the solicitor's clerk, or perhaps his confidential agent".[14] Thus, in a litigation context, the solicitor is not bound to collect information or testimony himself. He may employ his clerks or other agents to do it for him; and just as information he acquires directly is protected, so is the information acquired by a clerk or agent employed by him.

However, it should not be thought from this that the rule in *Wheeler* v *Le Marchant* can be circumvented by the solicitor having in his employment clerks or staff members who provide the sort of information which the court in that decision held could not be privileged when communicated by third parties. This is because the agent must be engaged in a communication of a type which privilege will protect. Thus, if a solicitor employs an accountant or surveyor who is able to provide information which the solicitor needs for the purposes of advising his client, it cannot be said that communications between the solicitor and his employee in relation to such information are privileged, if needed for the purposes of giving legal advice which has no reference to litigation. This is because the employee acting in that capacity is not truly the solicitor's clerk because he is not concerned with the giving of legal advice, rather the provision of facts or materials required to enable the legal advice to be formulated.[15]

A number of older decisions are concerned with the position where a client communicates with third parties at the request or under the direction of the solicitors. In such circumstances, the client becomes an agent or quasi-agent of the solicitor, for example, if he collects information or evidence which is needed by the solicitor for the purposes of litigation.[16] In this capacity the agent's communications are privileged so long as the dominant purpose test is satisfied. However, it is clear from the decision of the Court of Appeal in *Southwark Water Co* v *Quick*[16a] that a client can himself obtain privileged materials from a third party for use by his solicitor in relation to litigation *without* first being constituted the solicitor's agent. Despite this authority, some works still appear to suggest

14 *Ibid.*, p.402.
15 See the Law Reform Committee's Sixteenth Report (Privilege Civil Proceedings), Cmnd. 3472, para. 29, which equated "servants or agents of the client who are not employed in a professional legal capacity", with third parties.
16 See *Lafone* v *The Falkland Islands Co (No 1)* 4 K and J 36, where the client obtained information from his overseas agent at the request and under the direction of the solicitor. See also *Anderson op. cit.* at p. 560, where Jessel, MR gave the example of the solicitor who requests the client to obtain information in a foreign country where neither the solicitor, his clerk nor an ordinary agent can obtain it. Information so obtained by the client is "clearly within the rule of privilege".
16a (1873) 3 QBD 315.

that a client cannot engage in a privileged communication with a third party, even in relation to contemplated or actual litigation, unless he first becomes the solicitor's agent.[17]

These statements need to be treated with some care. It is quite clear, on the one hand, that where a client deals with a third party as principal then the underlying communications will not be privileged.[18] Thus, in *Jones* v *Great Central Railway Co*, Lord Loreburn, LC said:

> "Both client and solicitor may act through an agent, and therefore communications to or through the agent are within the privilege. But if communications are made to him as a person who has himself to consider and act upon them, then the privilege is gone; and this is because the principle which protects communications only between solicitor and client no longer applies. Here documents are in existence relating to the matter in dispute which were communicated to someone who was not a solicitor, nor the mere alter-ego of a solicitor."[19]

In contrast, where the client communicates with the third party and satisfies the dominant purpose test, the underlying communications will be privileged as in, for example, the House of Lords' decision in *Waugh* v *British Railways Board*[20] and the Court of Appeal's in *Re Highgrade Traders Ltd.*[21] Both cases could be rationalised on the basis that the client was, in effect, acting in a quasi-solicitor capacity, but in neither case was this the express basis of the decision.[22] Indeed, Lord Edmund-Davies in *Waugh* made it clear that his speech was concerned with the privilege available to communications between the client and third parties.[23]

Interestingly, although the judgments in *Anderson* v *British Bank of Columbia*[24] contain statements[25] which explain some of the principles relating to privileged communications through agents, the actual decision on this point is suspect. In the Court of Appeal, the judgments focused on

---

17 Thus Mathew and Malek in *Discovery* (para. 8.33) suggest that the client can make protected third party communications where he becomes "a kind of agent of the lawyer", for which authority the decision in *Anderson* is cited. But they go on to assert that "client–third party communications, even after litigation is contemplated, in which the client is not effectively the lawyers' agent, are not within this privilege". Further, the definition of litigation privilege in this work does not appear to contemplate communications between a client and a third party: see para. 8.26.

18 Unless a common interest privilege can be claimed: see Chap. 6.

19 [1910] AC 4 at 6. The decision is discussed in Chap. 3, Section 7.

20 [1980] AC 521.

21 [1984] BCLC 151.

22 Nor was it the basis of the Court of Appeal's decision in *Guinness Peat Properties Ltd* v *Fitzroy Robinson Partnership* [1987] 1 WLR 1027.

23 [1980] AC 521 at 541–542.

24 (1876) 2 Ch D 644.

25 See *e.g.* p. 114 above.

the fact that the Oregon agent's response to his London principal was based on information which the principal is deemed to know in law and which is discoverable.[26] The decision can be criticised on this point because it fails to make an appropriate distinction between discovery by production of documents which can be privileged, and discovery by means of interrogatories[27] where the "known" facts are most unlikely to be privileged.

A more recent decision which should be noted in this section is *McGregor Clothing Company Ltd's Trade Mark*.[28] This short decision of Whitford, J concerned a letter written by an American attorney who was advising the US intervenors in a UK trademark action. The letter, which was addressed to the client's UK trademark agents, was written in response to a question raised by the agents in relation to which the clients had asked their US attorneys for advice. They responded by way of a letter addressed directly to the trademark agents with a copy to the clients. It was accepted that if the advice had been contained in a letter addressed to the clients, then a claim to privilege for its contents would have been good. But, because it was addressed to the clients' professional agents, it was argued that the claim to privilege was bad. Whitford, J reached the conclusion that "it would really make nonsense of the claim to privilege if the mere communication of what was undoubtedly privileged advice as between [the American attorneys] and the American intervenors were to lose privilege by transmission for action to the agents of the American intervenors in this country".[29]

The decision can be criticised because it is not a true case of communication to an agent who is a mere medium of communication. Nonetheless, quite apart from the "nonsense" which Whitford, J identified, it is submitted that the decision can be justified on the ground that the letter came into existence for the dominant purpose of the litigation.

In Australia and New Zealand, the courts have taken a different stance in relation to advice privilege and third-party communications and are prepared to hold that communications between either a client or solicitor

26 Per Mellish, LJ, *ibid.*, at 659–660.
27 See Chap. 2, Section 7. Thus although a client can be required to give discovery of facts which are known to him (both personally and through agency) at the time the litigation arises, it does not necessarily follow, as Bray argued (*op. cit.*, pp. 416–417), that if those facts must be disclosed when required in answer to interrogatories, the document containing the same information in the form of a "dominant purpose" communication between agent and principal must also be produced. See also the views of Cotton, LJ in *Southwark Water Co v Quick*, 3 QBD 315 at 321.
28 [1978] FSR 353.
29 *Ibid.*, at 354.

and a third party can, in specified circumstances, be privileged even though litigation is not pending. In *Kupe Group Ltd v Seamar Holdings Ltd*,[30] Master Kennedy-Grant stated the effect of these authorities, as exemplified by the Australian decision in *Nickmar Pty Ltd v Preservatrice Skandia Ins. Ltd*,[31] as follows:

> "...if the third party has been appointed by the client, or by the solicitor on the client's explicit instructions, specifically to provide information to the solicitor on behalf of the client in relation to a particular matter then communications between the third party and the solicitor for the purpose of enabling the solicitor to give legal advice to the client are protected by the solicitor client privilege".[32]

Both the *Nickmar* and *Kupe* decisions assert that they are consistent with *Wheeler v Le Marchant*. This is, with respect, difficult to accept. In *Nickmar*, the Court appeared to accept that an insurer's agent, a loss adjuster, who was investigating an irrecoverable loss, could engage in privileged communications with the insurer's solicitors, notwithstanding that litigation was not contemplated. According to Wood, J, to hold otherwise would place undue emphasis on form and would be "to ignore the substance of the engagement of the expert as an agent by direction".[33] Although Henry, J in *CC Bottlers Ltd v Lion Nathan Ltd*[34] attempted to rationalise these principles, including *Nickmar,* as falling within the "intermediary" principles, as baldly stated in *Kupe Group* they appear to go much further than is the position in England.[35] In *CC Bottlers Ltd v Lion Nathan Ltd* Henry, J adopted the traditional view and held that communications between a solicitor and his client's financial adviser in which the latter made recommendations as to the client's future course of action were not protected even though their purpose was the provision of consequential legal advice.

---

30 [1993] 3 NZLR 209.
31 [1985] 3 NSWLR 44.
32 [1993] 3 NZLR 209 at 214.
33 [1985] 3 NSWLR 44 at 56.
34 [1993] 2 NZLR 445, a decision considered in Chap. 7.
35 Bray wrote *op. cit.,* p. 403: "There certainly does not seem to be any a priori reason why if privilege be allowed to documents containing information for the purpose of enabling the solicitor to advise as to the defence or prosecution of an action... the same privilege should not also be allowed to documents containing information obtained by the solicitor in order to enable him to give his client legal advice on matters not connected with litigation. However, such is the rule. See *Wheeler v Le Marchant*".

3. EMPLOYEES AND SERVANTS

One type of agent who provides some difficulties of analysis in relation to privilege is the employee. His position requires to be considered both from the standpoint of whether he can engage in privileged communications with his employer, or his employer's lawyer; and with regard to the use he can make of legal advice received by his employer.

So far as concerns employer/employee communications, one can find references in the reports to the fact that the employee is to be regarded as a third party whose communications with the employer (or the employer's lawyer) cannot be privileged unless they are made with reference to litigation and satisfy the dominant purpose test.[36] Thus, in *Price Waterhouse* v *BCCI Holdings*[37] Millett, J observed that he would still have refused to hold the investigating committee's reports as privileged under the advice head even if that committee had been an "internal organ" of BCCI. Such reports, he noted, could only be privileged if made in contemplation of litigation, as with the employees' reports prepared for the board's legal advisers in *Waugh* v *British Railways Board*.[38] Similarly, in *R* v *Law Society, ex p. Rosen*,[39] the Court of Appeal held that a party's communication to its in-house officials – in this case, the Law Society's in-house lawyers – were privileged if made once litigation has commenced. Mann, LJ emphasised that the success of the claim to privilege was dependent on the commencement of litigation.

So it appears that communications between an employer and employee stand on the same footing as communications between the employer and any other third party. However, this ignores the fact that business entities necessarily have to operate through the medium of human agents who initially will communicate with each other. Since privilege is essentially concerned with lawyer–client communications, these internal communications ought to be seen, ultimately, as part of the employer–client's chain of communications with the lawyer. So, a business entity should be entitled to claim privilege for internal communications which otherwise satisfy the scope of advice test and which are necessarily made to instruct or inform its lawyers. As will be seen, support for this view can

---

36 See, *e.g.*, The Law Reform Committee, Sixteenth Report, Cmnd. 3472, para. 29; Forbes, J in *Alfred Crompton Amusement Machines Ltd* v *Commissions of Customs and Excise (No 2)* [1972] 2 All ER 353 at 365 and Cooke, J in *Guardian Royal Exchange Assurance of New Zealand* v *Stuart* [1985] 1 NZLR 596 at 602.
37 [1992] BCLC 583.
38 [1980] AC 521.
39 *The Independent*, 12 February, 1990.

be gained from dicta of Gatehouse, J in *Re British & Commonwealth Holdings Plc*,[40] discussed at page 123 below.

However, some difficulties can still arise where an employee is involved in preparing his employer's formal instructions to his lawyer. Irrespective of whether those instructions relate to a litigious matter, communications made in order to prepare the instructions will be privileged since clearly the employee is acting as the agent, or medium of communication, on behalf of his (client) employer. On a practical level of course, a corporation necessarily must communicate through human agents in this way. The difficulty arises where the employee prepares documents or, for example, plans which accompany the formal instructions: if these are prepared with litigation in mind then they are privileged if within the dominant purpose test. But if only advice privilege is available, can they ever be protected? There are several considerations:

- the distinction between "discovery" of (unprivileged) facts by means of interrogatories (or testimony at trial) and discovery of (privileged) communications should be kept in mind;
- pre-existing communications between employer and employee will not, unless already privileged, become privileged merely because they are needed for the purposes of the employer seeking legal advice – see Chapter 5;
- if the document or plan is prepared expressly as part of the employer's instructions such that the employee is once more a "medium of communication" then it is privileged;
- however, in this situation the employee can only be treated as the agent of communication in relation to information he – and thereby his employer as principal – already knows or has to hand;
- so, when the employee obtains new information or produces new material, whether for his employer or the employer's lawyer (as in *Southwark Water Co v Quick*,[41] *Price Waterhouse v BCCI*[42] and *Waugh v British Railways Board*[43]), he may well be treated as a third party, with the result that the material so produced will not be privileged under the advice head: here the privilege can only be sustained under the litigation head.

---

40   Unrep., 4 July 1990.
41   (1878) 3 QBD 315.
42   [1992] BCLC 583.
43   [1980] AC 521.

Internal client communication

The extent to which an employer can safely disseminate to his employees the legal advice which he receives so that they can act upon it or implement it also gives rise to problems. In principle, it is submitted that a client should be able to disseminate the legal advice he receives to all employees who properly need to see it or know about it for the purpose of their employment without incurring any risk that he will thereby lose his privilege in respect of the advice received.

Before examining the English authorities which relate to those two issues, it is worth noting the approach adopted in parts of Australia and New Zealand. In *CC Bottlers* v *Lion Nathan Ltd,* Henry, J commented:

> "To the extent that some Australian authority (see for example *Vardas* v *South British Insurance Co Ltd*) may be read as suggesting that copies of privileged documents must be assessed as themselves having been created for the purpose of giving or receiving legal advice before they will be deemed privileged, I respectfully disagree. If the principal communication is privileged, copying it cannot in my view of itself destroy the privilege, and subsequent dissemination to a third party will only do so if the circumstances establish a waiver by the client".[44]

In other words, the privileged advice can be shown to others beyond the original client, provided it is done so in circumstances which do not cause the underlying confidentiality in the advice to be lost.[45-46] This would permit the advice being shown to an entity's officers and other relevant personnel who need to see it. Such an approach, which it is submitted has much to commend it, has not been unequivocally adopted in this country.

Indeed, some commentators have suggested, in line with the Australian authorities referred to by Henry, J, that each copy made of a privileged document must be considered individually, by reference to the purpose for which it was made, to see if it is privileged.[47] In the meantime, the English authorities have, fortunately, adopted a pragmatic stance which circumvents a number of these difficulties, albeit in a manner which

---

44 [1993] 2 NZLR 445 at 449.

45-46 As to this, see Chap. 7, Section 3. Adoption of this approach would solve certain difficulties identified by Style and Hollander in *Documentary Evidence* (6th Edn.) at 176–177. To take their example of copying legal advice to a company's PR department for use as a script in briefing journalists, the mere copying of that advice, all the while its confidentiality is maintained, will not destroy the privilege, whatever the intended use. It could only be the use of that document – in the form of publicly disclosing privileged information – which will destroy the privilege. For an example of this, see *Chandris Lines* v *Wilson & Horton Ltd* [1981] 2 NZLR 600, noted in Chap. 7, n. 27.

47 But note Rix, J's reference in *The "Sagheera"* to "the false premise that that which is communicated internally ceases to be confidential" [1997] 1 Lloyd's Rep 160 at 169.

arguably strains the underlying principles of privilege.

In *The "Good Luck"*,[48] the plaintiffs resisted an application for discovery of their internal documents which reflected information and advice obtained from their lawyers concerning the pending litigation between them and the defendant applicants. The defendants accepted that the actual advice received by the plaintiffs was privileged, as were their internal documents which came into existence for the purpose of considering or recording the advice tendered or to be sought. The challenge to the claim to privilege came in respect of those documents which came into existence to enable the plaintiffs as bankers to decide whether or not to continue to lend money to the owners of the subject vessel. Those documents, it was argued, were not part of that necessary exchange of information of which the object was the giving of legal advice as and when appropriate; nor as documents made confidentially for the purposes of legal advice. Saville, J rejected this argument because if the lawyer–client communication was privileged then:

> "... internal documents or parts of documents of the client (or indeed the lawyer) reproducing or otherwise revealing those communications are also covered by the same privilege, whatever the purpose or motive (short of fraud) for which the document comes into existence".[49]

The *"Good Luck"* was followed in *Re British & Commonwealth Holdings plc*,[50] where Gatehouse, J commented that Saville, J's decision "accorded with commonsense in today's world of commerce". Gatehouse, J had to deal with a discovery application involving documents disclosed by a merchant bank's credit committee which contained blanked out passages which recorded, summarised or revealed privileged communications between the bank and its internal and external lawyers. The documents were primarily concerned with commercial decisions relevant in the litigation, namely, whether money should be lent to an entity, Q. Refusing to order discovery of the redacted passages, Gatehouse, J held:

> "If, as is accepted, the original lawyer/client communication was plainly privileged, why should that privilege be lost because the advice is recorded or revealed in a document, the very purpose of which was to make use of that advice in reaching a commercial decision... it would frustrate the principle of legal professional privilege in virtually every commercial case if the argument were to be accepted."

---

48   Noted at [1992] 2 Lloyd's Rep 540.
49   *Ibid.*, at 540.
50   Unrep., 4 July 1990.

Style and Hollander criticise these two decisions as supporting a privilege against disclosing a document which is not a lawyer–client communication and which merely refers to or reveals legal advice received.[51] Notwithstanding these criticisms, Rix, J in *The "Sagheera"*[52] has also now followed *The "Good Luck"*. He was concerned with the question whether information "privileged within the organisation entitled to maintain its confidentiality loses that privilege because it is disseminated within that organisation in a document the primary purpose for preparing which may not be a protected purpose".[53] Rix, J held that it was "impossible" to say that a document had to be produced for inspection because "it may not have been brought into existence for the primary purpose of disseminating the advice, but for the purpose of taking a business decision in the light of such advice".[54] Rix, J went on to make clear his view that the "logic" of the *Good Luck* extended to the dissemination of information protected under either head of privilege.

These decisions represent a pragmatic and sensible solution. But their limits should be appreciated, since they only protect the advice in its disseminated or summarised form and the section of any document produced in consequence which reveals the advice. So a board minute recording action to be taken in the light of legal advice received but which does not reveal the advice will not be privileged. In *The "Sagheera"*, Rix, J thought there would be "difficult borderline" decisions in relation to documents which merely referred to the dates, provenance or authorship of privileged material.

Finally, it should be noted that an employer cannot assert any privilege in a document disseminated to an employee with whom he subsequently engages in litigation.[55]

4. IN-HOUSE LAWYERS

A particular type of employee who merits consideration is the in-house or salaried legal adviser. The modern phenomenon by which many large business organisations have legal departments of their own, staffed by

---

51 *Op. cit.*, at 170. Although the decisions in *The "Good Luck"* and *British & Commonwealth* were approved by the Court of Appeal in *GE Capital Corporate Finance* v *Bankers Trust Co* [1995] 1 WLR 172 this was only on the subject of redacting partly privileged documents, and not in relation to the internal dissemination issues.
52 [1997] 1 Lloyd's Rep. 160.
53 *Ibid.*, at 171.
54 *Ibid.*, at 171.
55 See *Derby* v *Weldon (No 10)* [1991] 1 WLR 660 discussed in Chap. 7, Section 3.

qualified solicitors and barristers, was probably unknown when the Courts began to establish legal professional privilege.[56]

Whatever, in 1972, Forbes, J ruled in *Alfred Crompton Amusement Machines Ltd* v *Customs & Excise Communications (No 2)*[57] that advice privilege was not available to protect communications between an employer and members of his internal legal department. In the Court of Appeal, this suggestion was quickly scotched. Lord Denning, MR said that salaried legal advisors are:

> "... regarded by the law as in every respect in the same position as those who practise on their own account. The only difference is that they act for one client only, and not several clients.... I have always proceeded on the footing that the communications between the legal advisers and their employer (who is their client) are the subject of legal professional privilege. ... I speak, of course, of their communications in the capacity of legal advisers. It does sometimes happen that such a legal adviser does work for his employer in another capacity, perhaps of an executive nature. Their communications in that capacity would not be the subject of legal professional privilege.[58]

In most instances, the dividing line between the in-house lawyer's privileged and non-privileged communications with his employer is easy to spot. So, for example, where the in-house lawyer provides legal advice to his client employer, represents him in litigation or acts as a conduit with his employer's external legal advisers, the privilege is available. However, where he acts in an executive capacity, for example, in advising on company strategy[59] or as company secretary, relevant communications are unlikely to qualify for privilege unless they also involve the giving of legal advice. There is no one test which would enable all situations to be classified as falling on one side of the line or another. Two helpful benchmarks, however, might well be first, whether the communication involves the use of skills for which an external lawyer could be employed and claim privilege; and secondly, whether the lawyer is engaged on a matter in which he has to seek instructions before concluding a matter. If

---

56 As the Law Reform Committee noted in its 16th Report "Privilege in Civil Proceedings", December 1967, Cmnd. 3742, at para. 27. Note, however that both Lord Denning and Orr, L.J in the Court of Appeal in 1972 in the *Crompton* case, discussed in Section 4 below, spoke in terms of in-house lawyers having long been in existence.

57 [1972] 2 QB 102.

58 [1972] 2 QB 102 at 129 The Court of Appeal's judgment was not appealed on this point when the matter subsequently went to the House of Lords: see Lord Cross of Chelsea's judgment at [1974] AC 405 at 430–436.

59 Unless this falls within "commercial advice" in the sense described by Colman, J in the *Nederlandse* [1995] 1 All ER 976 decision discussed in Chap. 2, Section 4. Note, however, that the US Courts are taking a strict line in relation to in-house lawyers who act as negotiators making business judgments: see the report in the *Law Society Gazette*, 9 October 1996.

so, his communication may well be privileged. If not, this may well suggest he is acting in non-legal or executive capacity. Communications between in-house lawyers are also, in principle, likely to be privileged, just in the same way as intra-solicitors' firm communications.[60]

One increasingly problematic "grey" area involving communications with the employer is where these are made by compliance officers employed by, for example, a bank or other financial institution. Quite clearly, the compliance officer can only engage in privileged communications with his employers/client in which he tenders legal advice if he is a lawyer and then only if employed in that capacity.[61] Communications relating to his compliance function are unlikely to fall within the scope of legal advice in any event, unless they are concerned with a legal interpretation point. Where the compliance officer is involved in an investigation, in which new information is generated or materials are produced, his reports, etc. will only be privileged if they satisfy the various requirements of litigation privilege, including the condition that they are made in respect of litigation. As suggested in Chapter 1, not all investigations conducted by SRO's will amount to litigation for these purposes. Finally, in relation to such an investigation can the compliance officer take statements which will be privileged? So long as they are prepared predominantly for litigation, the answer ought to be "yes": see *Southwark Water Co v Quick*.[62] However, the safest course is for this task to be carried out by a lawyer employed for that purpose.

The ability of an in-house lawyer to make privileged communications with his employer is subject to an important exception which arises in an European law context. In *AM & S Europe Ltd v Commission of the European Communities*,[63] the European Court of Justice was asked to consider the entitlement of the European Commission to require AM&S, in the course of an investigation conducted pursuant to Article 14 of Council Regulation (EEC) Number 17/62 and charged with verifying whether or not there had been an infringement of Articles 85 and 86 of the Treaty of Rome, to produce documents for which AM&S claimed legal professional privilege. The Court held that AM&S could not withhold from the Commission privileged communications made with its in-house lawyers since such a privilege was not recognised under Community law. On the face of it, though potentially very inconvenient for employers of

---

60   The claims to privilege in such cases should not be dependant on the existence of
     litigation, as was suggested in the *Rosen* decision mentioned at p. 120 above.
61   Or, possibly, if he works in a legal department under supervision. See Chap. 1, Section
     10.
62   (1878) 3 QBD 315.
63   [1983] QB 878.

legal services, this is a relatively small exception to the general rule since it is usually regarded as being limited to competition law investigations by the Commission. However, while the Commission's powers of document seizure are presently limited to such investigations, the court's reasoning deserves closer analysis because the implications of this case could apply in any new, analogous situations.

The European Court acknowledged in *AM&S* that all Member States recognise principles which are akin to legal professional privilege. These are not identical but they have common criteria in as much as they protect, in similar circumstances, the confidentiality of written communications between lawyer and client. However, the effectiveness of such principles in a European context is such that they are subject to two conditions, namely that on the one hand such communications must be made for the purposes and in the interests of the client's rights of defence and, on the other, they emanate from independent lawyers, that is, *not* in-house lawyers.

In the event, the court was able to interpret the Council Regulation in issue on the basis that it primarily recognised as protected by privilege all written communications which were exchanged *after* the commencement of the competition policy investigation, but only so long as these were written by external lawyers. Further, it only recognised the privilege in earlier written communications to the extent that they had a relationship with the subject matter of that investigation. The decision therefore appears to enable the court to require the production of privileged materials which do not obviously relate to the subject matter of the investigation.

In the latter respect, the court in *AM&S* at least gave a generous interpretation as regards which communications have a relationship to the subject matter of the investigation: the court allowed a claim to privilege to be upheld in connection with legal opinions obtained by AM&S towards the end of 1972 and during the first half of 1973, when in fact the Commission's investigation started in 1978. It appears that the 1972/73 communications arose during the period preceding and immediately following the UK's accession to the European Community and they were principally concerned with how AM&S might avoid conflict with the community authorities on its position with regard to Community laws on competition.[64]

There are other points of detail arising from the *AM&S* decision which

---

64 However, see *Are your internal communications protected?* Josephine Carr, *European Counsel*, September 1996, p. 27, which discusses the adverse consequences of the Commission's frequent willingness to seize privileged documents in the course of competition law investigations.

suggest the need for some care in considering privilege in the context of European competition law issues. Thus, for example, the judgment is expressed to apply only to written communications. This introduces an element of uncertainty in relation to oral communications, as where an independent lawyer advises his client who makes a written record of the advice communicated orally. Arguably, the note of that legal advice would not be privileged as it is not, strictly, a written communication from the independent lawyer. Similarly, if the client were to abstract from written advice received from the lawyer in order to prepare his own internal memorandum, that, too, is not obviously privileged on the basis of *AM&S*. Nor does the judgment appear to cover communications between the independent lawyer and a third party (apart from another independent lawyer acting for the same client).

Although the European Commission can require the production of privileged materials, such production does not result in a whole-sale loss of the underlying confidentiality in the communications concerned. In *Hilti AG v EC Commission*[65] the Court of First Instance of the European Communities would not allow intervenors in an investigation into breaches of Article 86 access to certain privileged documents belongong to the party under investigation. These included a letter received from an external lawyer, the privilege in which had been waived vis-à-vis the Commission; and internal notes reporting on the content of advice received from external lawyers. The court held, in line with *AM&S*, that the "principle" of the protection of written communications between lawyer and client may not be frustrated on the sole ground that the content of that legal advice was reported in documents internal to the undertaking.

5. ACTING IN PERSON

As we have seen in Chapter 1, the justification for legal professional privilege is the need for a client to be able to consult a lawyer in absolute confidence given, *inter alia*, the complexity and difficulty of our law. Since the advice head of privilege applies to communications between a client and a lawyer, it appears that the "client" who advises himself cannot claim advice privilege for the product of his own efforts since there is no communication on which it can "bite". In this respect, Cotton, LJ's comments in *Lyell* v *Kennedy* that:

---

65 [1990] 4 CMLR 602.

"if a man does not employ a solicitor he cannot protect that which, if he had employed a solicitor, would be protected",[66]

are generally accepted as representative of the law.[67]

There are, however, qualifications to this bald proposition. It would, surely, be absurd if a lawyer who advised himself could not claim privilege for the product of his efforts. Thus, a solicitor firm's employment lawyers who advise their colleagues as to the impact on their working practices of employment-related legislation (such as the Disability Discrimination Act 1995) must surely be able to claim privilege for that advice even though the "client–lawyer" relationship is an internal one not dependant upon the existence of a formal retainer or solicitor–client relationship.

The position in relation to litigation privilege is probably more favourable. Recently, Bingham, LJ in *Ventouris v Mountain* appeared to recognise the availability to a litigant in person of litigation privilege. He commented that:

"The expression 'legal professional privilege' ... also suggests, surely wrongly, that a litigant in person is denied, in preparing his litigation, the protection of secrecy which is enjoyed by a litigant who instructs a lawyer".[68]

In principle there can be no obvious objection to this rule. It is evidently consistent with a head of privilege described by Bray[69] as "the protection attaching to materials for evidence", which concerned the obtaining of evidence for the purposes of litigation. Such a head of privilege has some support in nineteenth-century case law;[70] and the Law Reform Committee also recognised in its 1967 Report the entitlement to privilege for communications between a litigant in person and third parties "if made for the purpose of obtaining factual information for the preparation of his case in pending or contemplated litigation".[71]

Arguably, reliance in the present day on the "materials for evidence" head is unnecessary (and, possibly, difficult to justify since the discussion of this head in the older authorities was not concerned specifically with the litigant in person).[72] In any event, given that a client can claim privilege for

---

66 (1884) 27 Ch D 1 at 18.

67 Though see *O'Rourke v Darbishire* [1920] AC 581.

68 [1991] 1 WLR 607 at 611.

69 *Op. cit.,* pp. 406–408.

70 Particularly in *Kennedy v Lyell* (1883) 23 Ch D 387 at 404.

71 *Op. cit.,* para. 17.

72 There is a very full discussion of the "materials for evidence" head in *Discovery,* Matthews & Malek, paras 8.44–8.9. In para. 8.47, the authors refer to notes on this subject which appeared in the Annual Practice up until 1962 which probably originated with Bray. In these, he referred to the materials for evidence privilege in terms of its being available "where a party is conducting his own case".

materials which he obtains or collects himself for the purposes of using them in litigation in which he intends to be legally represented – as in *Southwark Water* v *Quick, Waugh* v *British Railways Board* and *Re Highgrade Traders* – an obvious extension of the litigation privilege principles to the litigant in person would be justified in these circumstances. If that is not right, then it is difficult to disagree with the submission made by Matthews and Malek to the effect that the materials for evidence privilege is justifiable in favour of the litigant in person, so long as it is confined to:

> "... communications made by or to, or materials prepared by or on behalf of, a litigant for the purpose of either:
> (a)   deciding whether to prosecute or defend legal proceedings; or
> (b)   prosecuting or defending such proceedings".[73]

---

73 *Discovery* at para. 8.49.

Chapter 5

PRE-EXISTING
DOCUMENTS

1 . INTRODUCTION

This chapter considers whether a documentary communication which was not made in privileged circumstances can nonetheless be treated as subject to legal professional privilege by virtue of its being subsequently required in connection with the giving or seeking of legal advice, or for use in connection with litigation. As a matter of principle, one would have thought that there could be no question of a "pre-existing" document acquiring the benefits of legal professional privilege merely because it is needed to enable a lawyer to advise his client or to prosecute or defend a legal action. As Sir Balliol Brett, MR remarked in an oft-approved judgment:

> "I do not think that, where documents are already in existence aliunde, the mere fact of their being handed to a solicitor for the purposes of the conduct of the action can create a privilege; but, where documents are brought into existence by a solicitor[1]... for the purposes of consultation with such solicitor, with a view to his giving professional advice or to the conduct of an action, these are in the nature of professional communications, and are as such privileged".[2]

Unfortunately, these rules have not been consistently followed, with the result that, in relation to copies of pre-existing documents acquired by a solicitor as part of the evidence-gathering process for litigation, the Court of Appeal has held[3] that privilege can in certain circumstances be asserted in the litigation for which they were acquired. Such decisions, though they evidently represent the law, cannot be supported as a matter of principle. Indeed, in more recent times, the courts have indicated their discomfort

---

1   Or by the client: see *Southwark Water v Quick* (1878) 3 QBD 315, discussed in Chap. 3.

2   *Pearce v Foster* 15 QBD 114 at 118–119. This statement has been referred to with apparent approval by, *inter alia*, Lord Denning, MR in *Buttes Gas & Oil Co v Hammer (No 3)* [1981] QB 223, at 244, Dillon, LJ in *Dubai Bank v Galadari* [1990] Ch 98 at 104–105 and Bingham, LJ in *Ventouris v Mountain* [1991] 1 WLR 607 at 616.

3   See *"The Palermo"* (1883) 9 PD 6 and *Watson v Cammell Laird & Co (Ship Builders & Engineers) Ltd* [1959] 1 WLR 702, discussed in Section 3 below.

with them and have expressed a preference for the general rule described by Sir Balliol Brett, MR quoted above.[4]

Regrettably, as these later decisions have recognised, that preference cannot be given effect to until the earlier ones are overruled by the House of Lords. That has not, however, prevented subsequent courts which have had to consider the question of pre-existing documents straining to distinguish the earlier authorities. The consequence of this ongoing debate has been to leave this area riddled with confusing and often fine, not to say ridiculous, distinctions which no practitioner should have to grapple with.

2. PRE-EXISTING DOCUMENTS: A SUMMARY

Having regard to the authorities which are discussed in Section 3 below, it is suggested that the following summarises the present state of the law as regards how a court will treat a claim to privilege made in respect of a pre-existing document. As noted in the introduction, this is a controversial (and fluid) area of the law. In all cases it is assumed that the pre-existing documents are not already privileged.[4a]

1. Subject to what is said in 7 below, a pre-existing document, whether a copy or in original form, obtained by a solicitor *from his client* will not, without more, be privileged from production in litigation in which it is relevant.[5]

2. Where the solicitor obtains a pre-existing *original* document *from a third party,* that is, a non-party to the action, his client is not entitled to claim privilege for it.[6]

3. Where the solicitor obtains a *copy* of a pre-existing document from a third party it may well be privileged.[7] However, where copy documents

---

4   See *e.g.* Bingham, LJ in *Ventouris v Mountain* [1991] 1 WLR 607 at 616 who referred to various authorities which he thought suggested a general rule that "... non-privileged documents do not, without more, acquire privilege simply because they are copied by a solicitor for purposes of an action".

4a   Where the document which is acquired is already privileged, different considerations apply, as in *Lee v South West Thames Regional Health Authority* [1985] 1 WLR 845, and *Robert Hitchins Ltd v International Computers Ltd* (unrep.) 10 December 1996. See further Chap. 7, Section 2.

5   The decision to the contrary effect by the Divisional Court in *R v Board of Inland Revenue, ex p. Goldberg* [1989] QB 267 must be treated as having been wrongly decided: see *Dubai Bank v Galadari* [1990] Ch 98.

6   *Ventouris v Mountain* [1991] 1 WLR 607.

7   See *The "Palermo"* (1883) 9 PD 6 and *Watson v Cammell Laird & Co (Ship Builders and Engineers) Ltd* [1959] 1 WLR 702.

obtained from the third party are *publici juris* (as in depositions on a court file), privilege is unlikely to be available for them.[8]

4. Where the solicitor obtains *copy documents* from a third party in order to *replace* unprivileged original or copy documentation which his client has lost (and which, but for the loss, would have been unprivileged and admissible in evidence against him), the replacement copies so obtained from the third party will not be privileged.[9]

5. Where a *client* receives a *document* from a *third party* which is not privileged, a copy of that document made for litigious purposes either by the client or the solicitor will likewise not be privileged.[10]

6. *A fortiori,* copies of documents prepared by a client for his solicitors for the purposes of use in litigation are not privileged as against an opponent who has copies of the documents concerned (but who cannot, *e.g.*, make use of them because of protective orders made in other jurisdictions).[11]

7. However, where *copy documents* obtained by a solicitor for the purposes of litigation consist of *a selection of documents* which, if produced to the opponent in litigation, would betray the trend of the advice which he is giving his client, those documents may be privileged from production, at least in the format as selected. This conclusion appears to apply not only to copy documents obtained from third-party sources,[12] but also where the copies (and presumably the originals) are supplied to the solicitor by the client himself.[13]

3. PRE-EXISTING DOCUMENTS: ANALYSIS

As noted in the introduction, the general rule is that documents which are not privileged do not become privileged simply because they are handed to a solicitor by a client for the purposes of seeking advice or for use in

---

8   See *Goldstone v Williams, Deacon & Co* [1899] 1 Ch 47.
9   See *Chadwick v Bowman* and *Land Corp of Canada v Puleston* [1884] WN 1.
10 *Dubai Bank v Galadari* [1990] Ch 98. See Bingham, LJ's statement of the ratio of this decision in *Ventouris v Mountain* [1991] 1 WLR 607 at 619.
11 *The Lubrizol Corporation v Esso Petroleum Company Ltd* [1993] FSR 64.
12 See *Lyell v Kennedy (No 3)* (1884) 27 Ch D 1 and *Walsham v Stainton* (1863) 2 Hem & M 1.
13 *Dubai Bank Ltd v Galadari (No 7)* [1992] 1 WLR 106.

litigation then in contemplation.[14] However, a refinement to this rule was introduced by the Court of Appeal in *"The Palermo"*.[15] This was a vessel collision action in which the "Rivoli's" owners sued the "Palermo's". The defendant vessel owners sought copies of depositions taken by the Board of Trade from the master and crew of the "Rivoli" under section 432 Merchant Shipping Act 1854. The Board of Trade had supplied copies of the depositions to the plaintiffs (whose vessel was British) but refused to supply copies to the defendants (whose vessel was foreign). The "Palermo's" owners therefore sought discovery of the copies which had been made available to the plaintiffs. In a very short judgment, Butt, J dismissed the application, *inter alia*, on the basis that the plaintiff's copies had been obtained for the purposes of the collision action. The report then merely noted that the Court of Appeal dismissed the "Palermo's" owners' appeal without calling on the plaintiff's counsel in reply.[16] Thus, with this decision was established the rule that pre-existing copy documents obtained by a solicitor from a third party for the purposes of litigation are privileged from production even though the originals are not privileged.

The decision reached in *The "Palermo"* is surprising given that one of the Court of Appeal's members was Brett, MR whose views in *Pearce* v *Foster* (quoted in the introduction to this chapter above) appear to contradict the decision in this case. Furthermore, Lord Blackburn in *Lyell* v *Kennedy (No 2)* had already commented that:

> "I do not mean to state... that a man has a privilege to say, 'I have a deed, which you are entitled to see in the ordinary course of things, but I claim a privilege for that deed, because it was obtained for me by my attorney in getting up a defence to an action,' or 'in the course of litigation'. That would be no privilege at all".[17]

Nonetheless, *The "Palermo"* was followed nearly 70 years later by the Court of Appeal in *Watson* v *Cammell Laird & Co*.[18] This was a personal injury action in which the plaintiff claimed privilege for their copies of the original case notes prepared by the hospital which treated him at the time

---

14 *Pearce* v *Foster,* 15 QBD 114. See also *R* v *Peterborough Justices, ex p. Hicks* [1977] 1 WLR 1371. Comments made by Swanwick, J. in the earlier decision of *Frank Truman Export Ltd* v *Metropolitan Police Commissioner* [1977] 3 All ER 431 suggested that, for the purposes of criminal proceedings at least, privilege extends to pre-existing documents entrusted to a solicitor for advice, even though those documents did not come into existence for that purpose. These comments were doubted by the Court of Appeal's decision in *R* v *King* [1983] 1 All ER 929 and are surely wrong in the light of the *Peterborough Justice* decision.

15 (1883) 9 PD 6.

16 The Court of Appeal consisted of Brett, MR, and Baggally, and Bowen, LJJ.

17 (1883) 9 App Cas 81 at 87.

18 [1959] 1 WLR 702.

his injury was sustained. The plaintiff's legal advisors had made the copies from the hospital's originals for the purposes of advising him in the making of his claim. Although it was accepted that the notes would be relevant to the defence, the Court of Appeal held that they were privileged since they had come into existence for the purposes of the litigation. It rejected the defendants' contention that the privilege should not be available in respect of "a mere verbatim copy of a document not itself the subject of privilege, the making of which involved no exercise of skill by the solicitor". To this, Lord Evershed, MR said:

> "The question of privilege does not really have any significance in regard to the original: that is a document which is not, and never has been, in the possession or power of the plaintiff. It is a document which is in the possession of a third party; and undoubtedly by the appropriate means it can be produced at the trial. But that fact seems to me to have very little to do with the question whether this document ... did or did not come into existence... by being obtained by the solicitor for the purpose of advising his client in regard to the litigation".[19]

In reaching its decision, the court distinguished *Chadwick v Bowman*,[20] a decision which appeared to refuse to follow *The "Palermo"*.[21] Here, an action for the price of goods sold and work done depended upon the terms of correspondence which the defendant had had with certain third parties. The defendant had not kept this correspondence, but his solicitor managed to obtain copies from the originals and copies held by the third parties concerned. The defendant contended that the copies his solicitor had obtained were privileged, having come into existence for the purposes of his defence. In two very short judgments, Denman and Mathew, JJ rejected the claim to privilege. Denman, J, noting that the originals once held by the defendant would have been admissible in evidence against him, could see "nothing in the circumstances under which the copies came into existence to render them privileged against inspection".[22]

Chadwick v Bowman was distinguished in *Watson* on the basis that the claim for privilege was in respect of copies procured from the third parties of original documents which, had the defendant retained them, would undoubtedly have had to be produced by him. In *Watson*, according to Lord Evershed, the solicitor had at least exercised his professional skill in

---

19 *Ibid.*, at 704.
20 (1886) 16 QBD 561. See also *Land Corp of Canada v Puleston* [1884] WN 1.
21 In the sense that *The "Palermo"* was cited to the court, but not referred to in its judgments.

assisting his client to go to the hospital to obtain the copies of the case notes.[22]

In reaching its decision, the court in *Watson* did not have cited to it the earlier Court of Appeal decision in *Lambert v Home*,[23] a decision which has largely been ignored in this context. Here, a majority in the Court of Appeal held that a shorthand note of earlier, related county court proceedings, and a transcript thereof which the defendant had caused to be made in anticipation of the present action were not privileged, even though relevant to the later action. Cozens-Hardy, MR held:

> "A defendant who has obtained at his own cost a copy of a document, not in his possession, which is not itself privileged, cannot decline to produce the copy, although he obtained it in anticipation of future litigation. So here a mere production in a physical form of material which was publici juris cannot ... be privileged".[24]

In similar vein, Buckley, LJ commented:

> "This is privilege based upon reproduction by writing. In my opinion, no such privilege exists. If it did a copy of a document as distinguished from the original would be privileged".[25]

The decisions in *The "Palermo"* and in *Watson v Cammell Laird* have in recent years been heavily criticised by subsequent Courts of Appeal and therefore must be regarded as suspect decisions. Necessarily, only the House of Lords can overrule them, but in the interim the Courts are distinguishing their effect wherever it is possible to do so. These decisions first came under criticism by Lord Denning, MR in *Buttes Gas and Oil Co v Hammer (No 3)*[26] in which he expressed the view, *obiter,* that if an original was not privileged then any copy made of it similarly could not be privileged, even if made by a solicitor for the purposes of litigation. For this proposition he relied on *Chadwick v Bowman*.[27] He suggested that

---

22 The decision in *Watson* would have been justifiable had the exercise of the solicitors' professional skill resulted in a note of extracted, pertinent material, as opposed to a complete copy of the documents he required.

23 [1914] 3 KB 86.

24 *Ibid.,* at 91.

25 *Ibid.,* at 91. In *Goldstone v Williams, Deacon Co* [1899] 1 Ch 47, Stirling, J refused a claim for privilege in respect of depositions made in an action following an examination by an examiner. The depositions were on the Court file and so could be inspected by those who had "proper grounds" for doing so. Some reliance in support of the claim to privilege was placed on *The "Palermo"*. The judge rejected the claim and distinguished *The "Palermo"* on the basis it was concerned with private depositions, whereas the depositions in issue before him had become *publici juris:* "that which has become public is to be produced".

26 [1981] QB 223. Lord Denning noted criticisms in the Law Reform Commission's 1967 Report.

27 (1886) 16 QBD 561.

both decisions were "suspect" and that it was open to the Court of Appeal to reconsider them.[28] One compelling reason he gave for not following these cases was that the original documents in the hands of the third parties of which copies had been obtained by one party but not the other, and for which privilege was claimed in the hands of the party which had obtained the copies, would in any event be producible at trial upon service of a subpoena duces tecum. Given the accelerated subpoena procedure introduced by the decision in *Khanna* v *Lovell White Durrant*,[29] this reasoning is all the more convincing.

Further criticism of these decisions was made by the Court of Appeal in *Dubai Bank Ltd* v *Galadari*,[30] a decision which supports guideline no. 5 above. Here, the defendants appealed against an order permitting the plaintiff's solicitors to inspect a copy affidavit in the possession of their solicitors. That affidavit had been sent to the solicitors to enable them to advise in respect of claims which the deponent, a former employee of the defendants, was then bringing against their company in unrelated proceedings for wrongful dismissal. The Court was able to hold, having regard to the affidavit evidence before it, that on the facts the claim to privilege was not made out: since it was not clear that the copy sent to their solicitors had been made by or on behalf of the defendants, that copy could equally well have been the copy supplied by the deponent to the defendants, which could not have been privileged on any basis.[31] Accordingly, the claim to privilege was not made out.[32]

The Court went on to demonstrate that the claim to privilege advanced by the defendants was in any event unsound as a matter of law. Although the Court accepted that *The "Palermo"* and *Watson* v *Cammell Laird* were binding on it, Dillon, LJ distinguished both decisions on the grounds that they did not warrant the conclusion that by making a photocopy of a document which in the hands of the maker of the photocopy is not privileged, and then sending the photocopy to a solicitor for the purposes

---

28 Both Watkins, LJ in *R* v *Board of Inland Revenue, ex p. Goldberg* [1989] QB 267 at 277, and Dillon, LJ in *Dubai Bank* v *Galadari* [1990] Ch 98 at 105 acknowledged that the Divisional Court and the Court of Appeal remain bound by *The "Palermo"* and *Watson* v *Cammell Laird*.

29 [1995] 1 WLR 121.

30 [1990] Ch 98.

31 To support this proposition, Dillon, LJ referred to *Pearce* v *Foster* and the comments of Sir Balliol Brett, MR quoted in the introduction to this chapter.

32 See Dillon, LJ at [1990] 1 Ch 98, 104. In response to the plaintiffs' submission that, if the photocopy sent to the solicitors had been made by the defendants or at their direction in order to get advice, then it would be privileged, whereas if the defendants had merely forwarded the copy received from the deponent it would not, Dillon, LJ commented "It seems to me incredible that the law of privilege should depend on such a fine distinction".

of obtaining advice, privilege is thereby cast upon the copy sent to the solicitor.[33] Instead, the Court held that *Chadwick v Bowman* was "closely in point" in as much as the affidavit was already in existence and the copy of it when first received by the defendants was not privileged. Although, according to Dillon, LJ, that copy was no longer in the possession of the defendants,[34] to produce a further copy, albeit for the purposes of obtaining advice, was closely parallel to obtaining further copies for the purposes of litigation when the original was not privileged.

In the process of reaching their conclusions in *Galadari,* the Court indicated that they thought the Divisional Court's decision in *R v Board of Inland Revenue, ex p. Goldberg,*[35] which had purported to follow *The "Palermo"* and *Watson,* was wrongly decided. In *Goldberg,* leading counsel had been instructed to give tax advice for which purposes his clients' solicitors supplied him with copy documents which were not privileged in the hands the client. The Revenue, which had been investigating his lay client (who had ensured the original documents from which counsel's copies were made were out of the jurisdiction), served notices on counsel under section 20(3) Taxes Management Act 1970, requiring him to produce copies of some of these documents.[36] Section 20B(8) of that Act entitled him to withhold, subject to client consent, any document for which a claim for professional privilege could be maintained. The Court held that the copy documents which the solicitor had prepared for the purposes of enabling counsel to advise were privileged. Dillon, LJ in *Galadari* felt that the Divisional Court had gone too far in that respect since the copies were not made as part of the evidence-gathering process; and because the client in that case would have been obliged to produce the originals to the Revenue, since they were not privileged.[37]

In *Ventouris v Mountain,*[38] the Court of Appeal cast further doubt on the correctness of the decisions in *Watson v Cammell Laird* and *The "Palermo".* The defendants claimed privilege for original documents which were obtained for them by their solicitors for the purposes of the

---

33 *Ibid.,* Dillon, LJ at 106.

34 It has to be said that it is not at all clear from the recital of the facts given in his judgment as to how he was able to reach this particular conclusion.

35 [1989] QB 267.

36 See further Chap. 1, Section 6.

37 Note however that Farquarhson, LJ in *Galadari,* [1990] Ch 98 at 109 felt that the decision in *Goldberg* could be supported, following *Lyell v Kennedy (No 3)* (1884) 27 Ch D 1, since the documents presented to Counsel by the solicitor had been prepared "by a process of selection and sifting". *Lyell v Kennedy* could not apply in the *Galadari* case for reasons discussed in Section 4 below.

38 [1991] 1 WLR 607.

claim brought by the plaintiff. Thus, the issue before the court was whether privilege could be claimed for original documents not previously in the possession, custody or power of a party to actual or contemplated litigation, which had not come into existence for the purposes of that litigation, but which have been obtained by the solicitors of that party for that purpose. In support of the claim to privilege, the cases concerning copy documents were prayed in aid.

In dealing with this issue, Bingham, LJ conducted a wide-ranging review of the development of legal professional privilege. For him, the guiding principle was that the courts must not in any way encroach on the right of a litigant to seek and obtain legal advice on his prospects and the conduct of proceedings under the seal of confidence or on his right to prepare for and conduct his case without revealing the effect of that advice. However:

> "... it is hard to see how these rights are infringed if a party is obliged to produce an original document which was in existence before litigation was in the air, and which a litigant or his legal adviser have obtained from a third party for the purposes of the litigation, but which the third party could himself be compelled to produce at the trial without any possible ground for objection".[39]

Although that question had never "fallen squarely" for decision, he held that authority supported that "in principle" conclusion. Accordingly, he held that there was:

> "... no reason in principle why a pre-existing document obtained by a solicitor for purposes of litigation should be privileged from production and inspection, save perhaps in the *Lyell v Kennedy (No 3)* ... situation which, in an age of indiscriminate photocopying, cannot often occur".[40]

Accordingly, the documents in question, although supplied to the solicitors for the purposes of the litigation, were not protected by legal professional privilege.

Since this decision was concerned with original documents supplied to the solicitors, the cases on copies were not strictly relevant. Nonetheless, in an authoritative review of the case law, Bingham, LJ described the decision in *The "Palermo"* as "questionable",[41] given that the original depositions were entitled to no privilege in the hands of the Board of Trade; and that *Watson v Cammell Laird* seemed "ripe for authoritative reconsideration".[42] Clearly, it was not open to the Court of Appeal to overrule these decisions which, however suspect, presumably still represent the law in relation to

39 *Ibid.*, at 612.
40 *Ibid.*, at 621. *Lyell v Kennedy (No 3)* is discussed in Section 4 below.
41 *Ibid.*, at 614.
42 *Ibid.*, at 617.

copies obtained from third parties. The distinction between copies and originals obtained from third parties is of course absurd. It is submitted that the House of Lords must overrule the cases on copies in due course and that reliance on them would be inadvisable. In the meantime, the courts will continue to distinguish *The "Palermo"* and *Watson* wherever possible.[42a]

Thus in the *Lubrizol Corporation* v *Esso Petroleum Co Ltd*,[43] Aldous, J was concerned with a patent action which reflected parallel proceedings between the same or related parties in Canada and the USA. In the English action, the defendants claimed protection for unexpurgated versions of affidavits sworn by the plaintiffs' witnesses in the Canadian proceedings. Much of the discovery, including the affidavits, given in the Canadian proceedings was covered by protective orders which confined inspection to persons who were part of a "confidentiality club". For reasons which are not explained in the judgment, the protective orders prevented the plaintiffs from disclosing the unexpurgated affidavits to anyone not in the confidentiality club, whereas the defendants could disclose them to whomsoever they pleased. The defendants submitted that because their copies had been made for the purposes of the English litigation and because they would not have been able to disclose the originals – because they had never had them – then their copies were privileged. They relied on *Watson* v *Cammell Laird* and the *Goldberg* decision. Commenting that the defendants' submissions were "incredible"; and that they would lead to "a stupid result", the judge noted that they were based on decisions where the party seeking inspection does not have the documents in question. Those cases did not decide whether a copy made for the purposes of consideration by a party's legal adviser was privileged when the document is in the possession of the other party. In the event he held:

> "I cannot believe that legal professional privilege attaches to documents which are in the possession of both parties unless the documents would tend to indicate either the advice that might be sought or the advice that was given".[44]

42a Though Peter Gibson, LJ in *Robert Hitchins Ltd* v *International Computers Ltd* (unrep.) 10 December 1996 was "reluctant to hold today that where a document for which a party could not claim privilege was photocopied, the mere making of the photocopy for the purposes of litigation was sufficient to create the privilege in the party causing that photocopy to be made".

43 [1993] FSR 64.

44 See also the Divisional Court's decision in *CPS on behalf of DPP for Australia* v *Holman Fenwick & William (a firm)* (unrep., 13 December 1993). But compare these decisions with the Australian decision in *Cole* v *Elders Finance & Investments Co Ltd* [1993] 2 VR 356.

4. THE TREND OF ADVICE

One rather more supportable exception to the general rule described above concerns the assembling of copy documents which betray the trend of the advice which the client is seeking or receiving. This situation was first recognised by the Court of Appeal's decision in *Lyell v Kennedy (No 3)*.[45] This was, in part, concerned with an application for the production of documents comprising copies of entries in registers and public records and photographs of tombstones and houses, all of which were made for the purposes of the litigation. The Court dismissed the application because the way in which this evidence had been collected together would possibly give an insight into the advice which the respondent was receiving, something the court would not permit. In relation to such documents, Cotton, LJ held:

> "... they were obtained for the purpose of his defence, and it would be to deprive a solicitor of the means afforded for enabling him to fully investigate a case for the purpose of instructing counsel if we required documents, although perhaps *publici juris* in themselves, to be produced, because the very fact of the solicitor having got copies of certain burial certificates and other records ... might shew what his view was as to the case of his client as regards the claim made against him".[46]

This reasoning is potentially open to abuse. Surprisingly, it has featured very rarely in the case reports. It appeared to receive modern approval in *Ventouris v Mountain,* where Bingham, LJ described the ratio of that decision as being:

> "... that where the selection of documents which a solicitor has copied or assembled betrays the trend of the advice which he is giving the client the documents are privileged ... If the ratio I have given is correct, [*Lyell v Kennedy (No 3)*] is consistent with the fundamental principle underlying the privilege".[47]

Bingham, LJ also commented that this type of claim to privilege should not occur often in the "age of indiscriminate photocopying". Similarly, Dillon, LJ in *Dubai Bank v Galadari* noted that such a claim to privilege could not apply in relation to a single document.[48]

One recent decision in which a "trend of advice" claim to privilege has been upheld is *Dubai Bank v Galadari (No 7)*.[49] This concerned an order

---

45 (1884) 27 Ch D 1.
46 *Ibid.,* at 27.
47 [1991] 1 WLR 607, at 615.
48 Note that in *Galadari* the Court indicated that the decision in *Goldberg* could possibly be justified on the basis of *Lyell v Kennedy (No 3)*.
49 [1992] 1 WLR 106.

requiring the defendants to give discovery of a category of documents which were copy documents in the UK of original or original copy documents which were situated abroad, and which in that form were unprivileged. Nonetheless, Morritt, J acceded to the defendant's submission that a quantity of the copies in the UK were privileged from production on the grounds that their disclosure would betray the trend of the advice which the Galadaris were receiving from their solicitors. In reaching this decision, the judge accepted that, as a matter of principle, the selection of own-client documents was just as likely to portray the trend of advice as a selection of documents obtained from a third party.[50] And presumably, in an appropriate case, there is no reason why the same reasoning cannot apply to original documents.

Finally, the Australian Supreme Court's decision in *Nickmar Pty Ltd* v *Preservatrice Skandia Insurance Ltd*[51] should be noted. Here, Wood, J. stated that, as a general proposition, it was incorrect to state that:

> "...a copy of an unprivileged document becomes privileged so long as it is obtained by a party, or his solicitor, for the... purpose of advice or use in litigation. I think that the result in any such case depends on the manner in which the copy or extract is made or obtained. If it involves a selective copying or results from the research, or the exercise of skill and knowledge on the part a solicitor, then I consider privilege should apply (*Lyell's* case). Otherwise, I see no reason in principle why disclosure should be refused of copies of documents which can be obtained elsewhere...".[52]

---

50 It should not be thought that this decision relieved the defendants of their obligation to give discovery of the documents concerned, for subsequently the originals or original copies were disclosed to the plaintiffs, albeit in a manner which did not portray the trend of the advice they were receiving. It should also be added that it is unlikely that the trend of advice cases, exemplified by this decision, would prevent an application for discovery of documents specifically identified in such an application, as opposed to categories of documents, from succeeding.

51 (1985) 3 NSWLR 44.

52 *Ibid.,* at 61–62.

Chapter 6

COMMON INTERESTS: SHARING PRIVILEGED INFORMATION

1. INTRODUCTION

Where the subject matter of a client's privileged communication is one in which another can show a joint or common interest then several possible consequences follow:

- first, if the client's privileged communication is provided to that other party, then the protection conferred by the privilege is not necessarily lost, in which case the recipient may be entitled to assert the client's privilege as against the rest of the world;
- secondly, it may not be possible for the client to assert his privilege in litigation with that other party in respect of the privileged communication: in other words, his opponent may be able to establish a right of access to the client's privileged information which obliges the client to make disclosure to him whether or not he wants to.

This chapter considers the various joint interests which the law requires before either of these consequences will occur. The chapter concludes with a brief look at the so-called "once privileged, always privileged" rules which are also concerned with the sharing of another's privilege.

2. JOINT RETAINERS AND COMMON INTERESTS

Broadly speaking, all of the situations considered in this chapter are ones in which a client who makes or receives a privileged communication can share the information contained in the communication with another who enjoys a common interest with him in that information, without running the risk that the privileged status of that communication will be lost as against others who do not share that same interest. However, a clear distinction needs to be made between circumstances in which the other party can establish a right to obtain access in legal proceedings to the client's privileged documents by reason of a common interest in their subject matter which existed at the time the privileged documents came into existence;[1] and one in which the nature of the relationship between them is merely such that the client is entitled, but not obliged, to communicate those privileged documents to him without there being a resultant loss of privilege. The latter situation has given rise to the concept of "common interest privilege", which has been developed in modern times by the Court of Appeal's decision in *Buttes Gas & Oil Co v Hammer (No 3)*.[2] The former situation has long been known to the law and will be considered before common interest privilege.

Joint retainers

One obvious situation in which a joint interest can be identified is where there is a joint retainer. When a lawyer is retained by more than one client, then all the clients who instruct him pursuant to that retainer are entitled to enjoy the benefit of any privileged communications made in the course of that retainer, irrespective of whether, for example, an advice from their lawyer was addressed to one or all of them. The consequences of a joint retainer so far as concerns privileged information were succinctly described by Rix, J in *The "Sagheera"*:[3]

> "Parties who grant a joint retainer to solicitors of course retain no confidence as against one another: if they subsequently fall out and sue one another, they cannot claim privilege. But against all the rest of the world, they can maintain a claim to privilege for documents otherwise within the ambit of legal professional privilege; and because their privilege is a joint one, it can only be waived jointly, and not by one party alone".[4]

In *The "Sagheera"*, it was held that vessel owners and their war risk underwriters who jointly retained a firm of solicitors to investigate the circumstances in which the insured vessel sank could both enjoy the benefits of advice and litigation privileges attaching to qualifying communications made during the course of that firm's acting for them

---

1 Per Moore-Bick, J in *Commercial Union Assurance Company Plc v Mander* [1996] 2 Lloyd's Rep 640 at 649.
2 [1981] QB 223.
3 [1997] 1 Lloyd's Rep 160 at 165–166.
4 See also *Minter v Priest* [1930] AC 558. Waiver of privilege is covered in Chap. 7.

both. Consequently, both could assert the privileges attaching to such communication in subsequent litigation with the vessel's hull and machinery underwriters. Another common example of a joint retainer is where a husband and wife jointly instruct a solicitor in relation to a property transaction: while there is no privilege between them, such that in proceedings between them they are entitled to adduce in evidence privileged information, in litigation with third parties both can assert the privilege over communications made to one or other or both of them by their solicitor.[5]

Joint interests

The consequences are similar where a third party can establish a common or joint interest in the subject matter of a privileged communication which has been made in the course of a client–lawyer relationship to which he is not party. If a joint interest in the privileged communication can be established, then not only can the third party assert the client's privilege against others if the privileged communication is voluntarily copied to him by the client; more importantly, in litigation with the client he may have a right of access to that communication, assuming it is relevant to an issue in the action notwithstanding.

In this area, there are a number of recognised "joint interest" relationships to which these principles apply. They have to some extent been developed in line with a number of decisions involving legal advice sought by trustees, decisions which also demonstrate the limits of the right of access to another's privileged information. Thus, in *Talbot* v *Marshfield*,[6] the question arose whether, in litigation between beneficiaries and the trustees of a will, the beneficiaries were entitled to see two confidential opinions which the trustees had obtained from counsel. The answer depended on whether there was an identity of interest between the parties at the time the opinions were taken.[7] As to the first opinion, this

---

5   See *Re Konigsberg (a bankrupt), ex p. the Trustee* v *Konigsberg and Others* [1989] 1 WLR 1257. No doubt the situation is the same where the solicitor is jointly instructed by co-habitees.

6   2 Drew & Sm 549. The extent of the general principle which it is submitted can be derived from this decision and which is discussed in the text now requires to be considered, in a trustee–beneficiary context, in the light of the Court of Appeal's decision in *In re Londonderry's Settlement* [1965] 1 Ch 918.

7   In *Commercial Union & Assurance Co* v *Mander* [1996] 2 Lloyd's Rep 640 at 648, Moore-Bick, J held that the party who applies for discovery of his opponent's privileged materials: "... must be able to establish a right to obtain access to them by reason of a common interest in their subject matter which existed at the time the advice was sought or the documents were obtained." The decision is discussed further below.

concerned the exercise of a testamentary power vested in the trustees in favour of certain beneficiaries only. This opinion was taken before the litigation brought by the other beneficiaries, who sought to restrain the exercise of that power, had been threatened. So, it was taken in relation to the trust, and not the litigation. Accordingly, Sir R.T. Kindersley, V-C held that all the beneficiaries had a right to see that opinion. As for the second opinion, which was taken after the action had commenced, its purpose was not to guide the trustees in the execution of the trust, but to advise them how to defeat the proceedings. This was therefore privileged as against the beneficiaries who had brought the proceedings against them.[8]

The principles established in this case only apply where there is litigation between the beneficiary and trustee. Where the beneficiary seeks "trust" documents "in the air", the position is quite different, being governed by the Court of Appeal's subsequent decision in *In re Londonderry's Settlement*.[9] However, as Salmon, LJ commented in that decision, once beneficiaries sue their trustees, then on discovery the trustees must disclose relevant documents, whether or not they are trust documents, including ones which, as against non-beneficiaries, would be privileged:

> "In some instances ... the fact that they are trust documents may nullify the privilege that would otherwise exist, as for example if the document consists of counsel's opinion taken before the issue of the writ, clearly the beneficiary is entitled to see any opinion taken on behalf of the trust".[10]

Similar principles apply in litigation between other recognised joint interest relationships, such as a company and its shareholder (*e.g.* in relation to the interpretation of a company's articles of association[11]); also, where legal advice is sought by one partner in relation to partnership

---

8   The Vice-Chancellor also held that the beneficiaries had a right to see the first opinion because it had been properly paid for out of the trust estate. Had the beneficiaries been able to show that the trustees could pay for the second opinion out of trust funds, the Vice-Chancellor appeared to suggest that they might have had the right to see it. This does not reflect modern practice where a trustee would seek to protect his costs position by obtaining a Beddoe's order (following *Re Beddoe* [1893] 1 Ch 547) pursuant to which privileged information is filed before the court. The beneficiaries would not expect to see this: see *Re Moritz* [1960] Ch 251. Similarly, in relation to shareholder–company litigation, a legal opinion paid for out of company funds which relates to the company's position in the litigation would not be discloseable to the shareholder: see *Woodhouse & Co (Ltd) v Woodhouse* (1914) 30 TLR 559, followed in *W. Dennis & Sons Ltd v West Norfolk Farmers' Manure and Chemical Co-op Ltd* [1943] and *Re Hydroson Ltd* [1991] BCLC 418.

9   [1965] Ch 918.

10 *Ibid.*, at 938.

11 See *W. Dennis & Sons Ltd v West Norfolk Farmers' Manure and Chemical Co-operative Co Ltd* [1943] Ch 220.

affairs, that advice will not be privileged as against any other partner because of the existence of the joint interest between them.[12] In *Mayor of Bristol v Cox*,[13] Pearson, J indicated that in an action by a ratepayer against the City Corporation with regard to the raising or spending of the city rates, it might be possible to argue that the ratepayer was in a position analogous to that of a beneficiary such that he would be entitled to see the corporation's legal advice obtained at ratepayers' expense in relation to such matters.[14]

In more recent times, the courts have recognised the existence of joint interests in commercial relationships which carry with them the right in litigation of one party to that relationship to obtain disclosure of the other's privileged documents. The right to obtain such disclosure is based on such documents having been created or obtained by one party in furtherance of the joint interest and, in that sense, on behalf of all those who share it.[15]

In *CIA Barca de Panama SA v George Wimpey & Co Limited*,[16] the parties each held a 50% holding in a joint venture company. When they terminated these arrangements, Wimpey bought out Barca's interest on terms that when the joint venture company's final losses were ascertained Barca should pay Wimpey its share of the losses, if any. At this point, the joint venture company was engaged in proceedings with a third party which meant that finalisation of the financial results would have to await the conclusion of the litigation, which was now conducted by Wimpey alone. In the event, it settled. In subsequent litigation between them, in which Barca disputed Wimpey's entitlement to settle without its prior approval, Barca sought discovery of documents relating to the settled dispute which Wimpey attempted to withhold because they were subject to legal professional privilege. The Court of Appeal upheld the claim to production. Stephenson, LJ thought the relevant principles were those which governed the position where a person had a joint interest with the client in the subject matter of his privileged communications with his

---

12 See *Pearse v Pearse* 1 De G & Sm 12 and *In re Pickering* 25 Ch D 247. Though where a majority of partners seeks a legal opinion which is paid for out of partnership funds and which concerns their rights or position as against other partners with whom they are in dispute, it is at least arguable that those other partners can see the majority's legal opinion: see n. 8 above.

13 26 Ch D 678.

14 But see Nourse, LJ's comment in *St Alban's City and District Council v International Computers Ltd* [1996] 4 All ER 481 "... it would be incorrect, except in a broad sense, to describe a local authority as a trustee for the inhabitants of its area..." (at 489).

15 Per Moore-Bick, J in *Commercial Union Assurance Co plc v Mander* [1996] 2 Lloyd's Rep 640 at 645–646.

16 [1980] 1 Lloyd's Rep 598.

lawyer, as with partners, a company and its shareholders and a trustee and beneficiary.[17] Here, the litigation with the third party which Wimpey had been conducting had been pursued for the joint benefit of both parties who had a common interest in the claim which arose out of their contractual relationship.[18]

The decision in *Formica Limited* v *Secretary of State (acting by the Export Credits Guarantee Department)*[19] also illustrates how a contractual relationship can create the type of joint interest which overcomes a claim to privilege. The facts were that the plaintiffs had agreed to supply goods to a Swedish company under a contract supported by an ECGD guarantee. This obliged the ECGD to pay the plaintiffs 90% of any loss they sustained on that contract. The ECGD's guarantee was subject to a number of conditions which included requiring the plaintiffs (i) at all times promptly to disclose all facts in any way affecting the risks guaranteed, and (ii) to take all practicable measures to prevent or minimise any loss recoverable under the guarantee. The plaintiffs' customer went into liquidation owing them large sums of money. The ECGD resisted the plaintiffs' call on the guarantee, claiming that the plaintiffs failed to keep them fully informed, *inter alia*, in relation to litigation abroad in which they had tried to recover some of the monies owing to them. The judge held that the plaintiffs' contractual disclosure obligations were wide enough to oblige them to provide ECGD with timely information, including privileged information, about their attempts to recover their losses. That information was not privileged as against ECGD, who had been contractually entitled to see it at the time by virtue of their rights under the guarantee. Although it was too late for ECGD now to obtain disclosure of the information by this route (the operation of the guarantee having ceased), nonetheless it was not open to the plaintiffs to raise or claim privilege against them.[20]

Although the decision turned to an extent on the contractual disclosure obligations, Colman, J was evidently of the view that the contractual relationship between the parties was such that both parties had an interest in recovering the outstanding indebtedness from the plaintiff's customer.[21]

---

17 *Ibid.*, 614. Bridge, LJ stated the relevant principles (at 615) as follows: "If A and B have a common interest in litigation against C and if at that point there is no dispute between A and B, then if subsequently A and B fall out and litigate between themselves and the litigation against C is relevant to the disputes between A and B, then in the litigation between A and B neither A nor B can claim legal professional privilege for documents which came into existence in relation to the earlier litigation against C".

18 Per Moore-Bick, J in *Commercial Union Assurance Co Plc* v *Mander* [1996] 2 Lloyd's Rep at 646.

19 [1995] 1 Lloyd's Rep 692.

20 *Ibid.*, at 702.

21 *Ibid.*, at 701.

One other commercial relationship which is now generally treated as creating a community of interest similar in nature to the one which featured in the *Barca* decision is that which exists between insurer and reinsurer under a contract of insurance which contains a "follow settlements" clause. In *Commercial Union Assurance Co* v *Mander*,[22] Moore-Bick, J held that:

> "... insurers cannot withhold from the reinsurers on the ground of privilege documents brought into being *for the purpose of handling the original claim*, even if they would be subject to legal professional privilege as against a third party".[23]

Termination of the joint interest

As the decision in *Talbot* v *Marshfield*[24] illustrates, the right of the parties who share the joint interest to obtain access to each other's privileged documents does not extend to privileged communications which relate to the subject matter of any dispute between them and which are made *after* the dispute is anticipated. Thus, in *Cox*,[25] Pearson, J was concerned with an action brought by the Mayor and other dignitaries against Mr Cox in which Bristol City Corporation was defending the interests of ratepayers against a defendant who it was alleged was injuring those interests. As their interests were at odds, there was no basis upon which the defendant could have access to the plaintiffs' privileged communications with their legal advisers concerning the action.

In *Woodhouse & Co (Ltd)* v *Woodhouse*,[26] the Court of Appeal, whilst recognising the principle that a shareholder enjoys a common interest in company property such that he would be entitled to see a legal opinion paid for out of company funds, nonetheless held that that principle does not apply "where the parties were sundered by litigation",[27] since that would make it impossible for a company in litigation with a shareholder to obtain confidential advice.[28] Similarly, where partners are potentially in

---

22 [1996] 2 Lloyd's Rep 640.

23 Judge's emphasis (*ibid.*, 646). See also Colman, J in the *Formica* case, *op. cit.* at 699.

24 2 Drew & Sm 549.

25 26 Ch D 678.

26 (1914) 30 TLR 559.

27 Per Phillimore, LJ at 560.

28 See also *Gourand* v *Edison Gower Bell Telephone Co Ltd* (1888) 57 LJ (Ch) 498. Here, Chitty, J allowed a shareholder who was seeking to set aside an agreement allegedly entered into in fraud of his rights as shareholder to see communications between the company and its lawyers which related to the agreement the subject of the action. However, that right appears to have been limited to documents which pre-dated the shareholder's writ.

dispute with each other, legal advice sought in relation to their individual interests ought to be held privileged as against the other partners to the potential litigation.[28a]

Similarly, in the *Commercial Union* decision, Moore-Bick, J noted that the fact that a dispute subsequently arises between the parties[29] so that their interests are in conflict at a later stage does not affect the accrued entitlement to the other's privileged documents:

> "In a case where the documents contain legal advice, that joint interest must exist at the time the advice is sought, and if it exists at that time, it is not lost simply because the parties subsequently fall out: see, for example, *CIA Barca v Wimpey*. The fact that the interests of two parties are potentially in conflict does not in my view prevent their having a sufficient joint interest in the subject matter of the advice at the time it is sought to bring this principle into operation".[30]

In relation to companies, sometimes difficulties can arise in trying to determine what are "adverse" proceedings. In *Re Hydroson*,[31] Harman, J held that a contributories' petition for a just and equitable winding up of a company under section 485 Companies Act 1985 was not "adverse" litigation as classified by the Court of Appeal in *Woodhouse & Co (Ltd) v Woodhouse*,[32] even though it produces "severe results" for the company if it succeeds.[33] However, the petitioners were not entitled to see certain privileged documents relating to a rights issue proposed by the company in a circular issued in May 1989:

> "Down to that date the documents are within the general rule... that all documents concerning the administration of the company, being advice by solicitors to the company about its affairs, are discloseable to the shareholders; after that date litigation against the company in the true sense... was in contemplation...".[34]

Co-plaintiffs and co-defendants

One further category of "shared" interests which should be mentioned here but which does not fit easily into the examples described above arises from what has been described as the principle that protects confidential

---

28a Though see n. 8 above.
29 See also *The "World Era" (No 2)* [1993] 1 Lloyd's Rep 363, discussed at p. 152 below.
30 [1996] 2 Lloyd's Rep 640 at 646.
31 [1991] BCLC 418.
32 (1914) 30 TLR 559.
33 Per Harman, J, [1991] BCLC 418 at 422. However, discovery of privileged documents would not include anything relating to unfair or wrongful dismissal proceedings brought by the contributories against the company.
34 *Ibid.,* 423.

communications between co-plaintiffs or co-defendants for the purposes of an action. This "principle" needs to be considered with some care since the decision in *Jenkyns* v *Bushby*,[35] which is sometimes cited as authority for this principle,[36] concerned a letter written by a defendant to his co-defendant with instructions to send it to their joint solicitor, in which case it is not too surprising that it was protected by privilege. As Bray points out,[37] there have been a number of decisions in this area which are not altogether easy to reconcile; but in any event communications between co-defendants and co-plaintiffs should be subject to the same general rules as those governing communications between, say, a defendant and a third person. Thus, such communications should only be regarded as privileged where they satisfy the requirements of litigation privilege, especially its dominant purpose element, or otherwise fall within the "common interest" principles discussed in the next section.

The difficulties which can arise where parties to litigation try to assist each other against a common opponent are to an extent illustrated by the Court of Appeal's unreported decision in *Robert Hitchins Ltd* v *International Computers Ltd*.[37a] Here, A sued B for breach of contract arising out of the supply of an integrated software system. A's complaints were primarily directed at the system's software which B had obtained from its sub-contractor C whom B sued as a third party, alleging that if B was in breach of contract with A, then C was in breach of the sub-contract with B. The main and third party actions were due to be heard together, but the third party proceedings settled shortly before the deadline set for exchanging witness statements. As a result, only A and B exchanged statements. At the same time, C supplied B with copies of the draft statements which had been prepared for each of its nine proposed witnesses. A applied for discovery of the draft witness statements held by B.[37b] This application gave rise to the difficult issue of whether or not C's draft witness statements continued to be privileged in B's hands. The privilege was undoubtedly C's and not B's. Further, the court recognised that C intended to waive its privilege in the draft as against B only but not

---

35 LR 2 Eq 547.

36 See Brightman, LJ in *Buttes Gas & Oil Co* v *Hammer (No 3)* [1981] QB 223 at 267, discussed in Section 3 below.

37 *Op. cit.*, Chap. 2, n. 12, at 422–423.

37a 10 December 1996

37b A also applied for discovery of the settlement agreement entered into between B and C. This was clearly not a privileged document. However, the Court of Appeal had no difficulty rejecting the application for discovery of this document on the grounds of its irrelevance: see *O* v *M* [1996] 2 Lloyd's Rep 347.

as against any other party including A.[37c] Thus privilege would still have been a good answer to the service by A on C of a *subpoena duces tecum* seeking production of the drafts in C's hands. The question for the Court of Appeal was whether B could, in effect, assert in the face of A's application, C's privilege. The Court of Appeal answered this question in the affirmative but reached its conclusion by different routes. Simon Brown, LJ dealt with this issue by reference to the policy objective underlying litigation privilege, which "must surely be to enable parties or prospective parties to prepare properly for litigation in the confidence that others thereafter will not be entitled to examine and perhaps profit from their preparatory documentation".

Since C had not waived privilege in the statements as against A at any stage and had consistently refused to assist A, C ought therefore to be free to communicate its statements to B without surrendering their privileged character. Although B was not a successor in title to C[37d] that was not fatal to B's right to assert the same privilege as C, had it remained a party to the proceedings, would unarguably have been entitled to invoke. Accordingly,

> "... a finding here that the documents continue to enjoy a privileged status in [B's] hands would accord entirely with the common sense and justice of the case. All agree that there can be no question of [B's] being entitled to see the equivalent trial statements prepared for [A's] witnesses. All agree that had the third party proceedings stood up there would be no question of [A] seeing these draft statements. All agree that had [C] also been a co-defendant in the main action they could then have exchanged draft statements with B without either being at risk of having to produce them to [A] on discovery."[37e]

Hobhouse LJ also held that the draft statements supplied by C to B remained privileged in B's hands. He based his decision on the more pragmatic one that the policy of the law should clearly encourage the sharing of material between litigants, thus resulting in a saving of costs. To reach any other conclusion would mean that problems would arise whenever material is shared between parties in litigation, whether as between co-defendants or defendant and third party.

37c See also *Gotha City v Sotheby's* [1998] 1 WLR 114. This case is discussed in Chapter 7, Section 3.

37d See Section 4 below.

37e Simon Brown LJ's conclusion that B was entitled to assert C's interest appears to have been based upon the existence of a common interest between them. Common interest privilege is discussed in the next section. Peter Gibson LJ could not accept that a common interest can exist in respect of documents – the draft statements – prepared at a time when B and C were engaged in hostile litigation against each other.

3. COMMON INTEREST PRIVILEGE

Common interest privilege is a recently developed concept which differs from the "joint interest" situations discussed in Section 2 above in that it is "concerned with the effect of the confidential communication of a privileged document to a person who has a common interest in its subject matter or in litigation in connection with which the document was brought into being".[38] So, while in many cases the relationship between two parties which supports a claim to common interest privilege will also be one which gives rise to a right to obtain disclosure of the other's relevant privileged materials, this will not be so in every case.[39] Consequently, its importance derives from the client's ability voluntarily to share privileged information with those with whom he shares a sufficient identity of interest in the subject matter of the information without there being a resultant waiver or loss of the privilege. Furthermore, the recipients of such information are also entitled to assert his privilege as against the rest of the world.

As originally developed, common interest privilege was seen as an aid to litigation. Indeed, as one judge has described it, it is an extension of the principles relating to communications between co-plaintiffs or co-defendants for the purposes of an action.[40] As common interest privilege has developed, such analogies can be misleading as it is probably now available in a non-contentious context. Additionally, recent case law has developed a more convincing explanation for the privilege which focuses on the existence of a duty of confidentiality owed by the receiver of the privileged information to the original beneficiary of the privilege.[41]

Common interest privilege: the principles

Common interest privilege came to prominence with the judgments of the Court of Appeal in *Buttes Gas & Oil Co v Hammer (No 3)*.[42] The privilege was described there by Lord Denning, MR as:

> "... a privilege in aid of anticipated litigation in which several persons have a common interest. It often happens in litigation that a plaintiff or defendant has other persons standing alongside him – who have the self-same interest as he – and who have consulted lawyers on the self-same points as he – but

---

38 Per Moore-Bick, J in *Commercial Union* [1996] 2 Lloyd's Rep 640 at 645.

39 Per Moore-Bick, J in *Commercial Union, ibid.,* at 647.

40 See n. 37 above.

41 See Colman, J In *Formica Ltd v Secretary of State (acting by the Export Credits Guarantee Department)* [1995] 1 Lloyd's Rep 692, discussed at p. 157 below.

42 [1981] QB 223.

these others have not been made parties to the action. Maybe for economy or simplicity ... [all] exchange counsel's opinions. All collect information for the purpose of litigation. All make copies. All await the outcome with the same anxious anticipation – because it affects each as much as it does the others.... All are the subject of the privilege in aid of anticipated litigation, even though it should transpire that, when the litigation is afterwards commenced, only one of them is made a party to it".[43]

The effect of this privilege was described by Brightman, LJ in the same decision. He commented that where two parties:

"... exchange information for the dominant purpose of informing each other of the facts, or the issues, or advice received, or of obtaining legal advice in respect of contemplated or pending litigation, the documents or copies containing that information are privileged from production in the hands of each".[44]

Lord Denning in *Buttes Gas* offered a number of examples of situations where he thought a common interest privilege could arise. He suggested that the owners of adjoining houses who complained of a nuisance which affected them equally and who took legal advice and exchanged relevant documents could both avail themselves of the privilege in aid of litigation, even though one only of them commenced legal proceedings to try to prevent the nuisance. Similarly, where an author who wrote a book which after publication was found to contain a libel or to infringe a copyright, then if both author and publisher took legal advice and exchanged documents but only one of them was made a defendant to the complainant's action, nonetheless both could avail themselves of the other's privilege. A further example given by Donaldson, LJ was that of the landlord who took proceedings against a particular tenant resident in a block of flats concerning a term of the lease which was common to all the tenancies. In his view, the tenant would be entitled to circulate all other tenants in confidence with a copy of his counsel's opinion as to their rights under the lease. If the landlord were then to join another tenant as an additional defendant, Donaldson, LJ did not think that he would be able to obtain production of the copy of the opinion passed to him by the first tenant.[45]

The Court of Appeal was prepared to recognise a common interest privilege on the facts of the *Buttes Gas* case. Here, two rival American oil companies claimed oil drilling rights at the same location in the Arab Gulf,

---

43 *Ibid.*, at 243.
44 *Ibid.*, at 267.
45 Presumably such a tenant could assert the privilege in response to a subpoena duces tecum served on him by the landlord.

each claiming under mandates conferred by rival local rulers. The plaintiff's concession had been granted by reference to the territorial waters of Sharjah, whose ruler subsequently publicised a decree which asserted a twelve-mile nautical limit for his territorial waters which covered the disputed location. The defendant oil company asserted that the decree had been fraudulently backdated. These issues all featured in an action for slander in which the defendants made a discovery application for documents held by the plaintiffs and which had come into their hands either directly or indirectly from the ruler of Sharjah. Lord Denning, MR and Brightman, LJ were prepared to recognise these documents as being privileged in the hands of Buttes Oil (to the extent that they were privileged in the hands of the ruler of Sharjah). Buttes Oil and the ruler had identical interests in that both wanted to make sure that the oil fields of Sharjah were as extensive as possible, and they had exchanged documents in the context of possible litigation arising in respect of the disputed drilling rights.

As to the underlying principles which would assist a court to recognise a common interest which would support the privilege, Lord Denning spoke in terms of two or more parties having "the self same interest" so that the courts should, for the purposes of discovery, treat all the interested parties "as if they were partners in a single firm or departments in a single company".[46] Donaldson and Brightman, LJJ[47] both spoke in terms of the need for the parties claiming the privilege to share not only a common interest but also a common solicitor.[48] The requirement for a common solicitor was considered further by Saville, J in The "Good Luck",[49] who slightly refined the principle. He did not regard it as an essential prerequisite for claiming common interest privilege that the parties actually shared a common solicitor; however, he did regard it as necessary that they could, had they so chosen, have used the same lawyer. In The "Good Luck" Saville, J was concerned with the defendants' challenge to the plaintiff bank's claim to privilege in respect of documents which contained or revealed details of the legal advice which the owners of the "Good Luck" had received from their lawyers about the owners' own claim against the defendants. The owners had shared this legal advice with the plaintiff and their lawyers. Saville, J did not regard the lack of a

---

46 *Ibid.,* at 243.

47 *Ibid.,* at 252 and 267.

48 Only from about 6 months after the date on which the court in *Buttes Gas* determined that litigation could first be contemplated did the ruler and Buttes instruct the same solicitor. Lord Denning thought it did not matter that there was a period of six months when the parties had had different solicitors.

49 [1992] 2 Lloyd's Rep 540. This decision is also discussed extensively in Chaps. 2 and 3.

common solicitor as a bar to a claim of common interest privilege. Instead, he identified the requirement for:

> "an identity of interest so close that the parties concerned could (had they chosen to do so) have used the same solicitor or other lawyer".[50]

Indeed, he interpreted the *Buttes Gas* decision, particularly the judgment of Lord Denning, as envisaging common interest privilege arising only in cases where the interests of the parties were so close that they could properly be regarded (for discovery purposes) as one and the same. In the case before him, such identity of interests did not in fact exist even though the plaintiffs had the greatest possible interest in the owners' action against the defendants. Since the plaintiffs were creditors of the owners and their interest was to recover any fruits of the owners' actions so as to reduce or at least service that indebtedness, whereas the owners' interests were to prosecute the litigation with a view to reducing their indebtedness to the Plaintiff bank, their respective interests could not have been dealt with by the same solicitor.

However, subsequent decisions, all at first instance, indicate that the ability to instruct the same solicitor is no longer an essential requirement. As Rix, J commented in *Svenska Handelsbanken v Sun Alliance and London Insurance plc*:

> "... it is clear that the fact that differences may arise between parties of whatever closeness of interest, such as prevent them from at all times using the same lawyers, or such as may indeed even cause them to find themselves ultimately on opposite sides of litigation, does not necessarily mean they cannot be parties with a common interest for the purpose of this concept ...".[51-52]

This is well illustrated by the decision in the *"World Era" (No 2)*,[53] where the parties who shared the requisite common interest engaged in a short dispute between themselves. The facts were that charterers claimed damages from vessel owners in circumstances where they contended they had made the charter party as agents for principals. The charterers' solicitors, with their clients' consent, also accepted instructions from their principals in relation to the conduct of the arbitration. However, before it was concluded, a dispute broke out between them concerning the conduct of the arbitration which led to the principals issuing a writ and seeking an injunction against the charterers. That dispute duly settled, whereupon the charterers' solicitors resumed taking instructions from the principals in

---

50 *Ibid.*, at 542.
51–52 [1995] 2 Lloyd's Rep 84.
53 *Leif Hoegh & Co A/S v Petroleum Inc* [1993] 1 Lloyd's Rep. 363.

relation to the arbitration. Phillips, J held that the charterers and their principals had at all times a common interest in the claim being advanced by the charterers in the arbitration, and that that common interest did not come to an end simply because a dispute arose between them as to who should have the conduct of the proceedings. On this point, Phillips, J endorsed the arbitrators' comments:

> "The relationship between parties with a common interest in proceedings is not always harmonious: they may quite legitimately hold different views about who is to conduct the litigation and how. Such views may be strongly held and vigorously expressed. But the mere existence of such disagreements does not necessarily entail the conclusion that the parties no longer have a 'common interest' in the proceedings themselves".[54]

In *Formica Limited* v *Secretary of State (acting by the ECGD)*[55] Colman, J noted that Lord Denning's analysis in *Buttes Gas* of partners in a single firm or a department in a single company, and Saville, J's yard stick in *The "Good Luck"* of the common solicitor, were both useful ways of testing for the existence of an interest common to both parties so as to allow both to assert the same privilege. In his view, however, the real rationale for this privilege is a sharing of information in which there is not only a common interest but also a particular type of relationship which gives rise to a duty of confidence which the law will protect. As Colman, J put it:

> "The protection by common interest privilege of documents in the hands of someone other than the client must pre-suppose that such third party has a relationship with the client and the transaction in question which, in relation to the advice or other communications, brings that third party within that ambit of confidence which would prevail between the legal adviser and his immediate client.... [T]he essential question in each case is whether the nature of their mutual interest in the context of their relationship is such that the party to which the documents are passed receives them subject to a duty of confidence which the law will protect in the interests of justice".[56]

These comments were deployed in the *Commercial Union* case to advance submissions to the effect that a party could seek disclosure of privileged documents on the grounds of common interest if he is a person in whose hands the documents would have been privileged if they had in fact been disclosed to him. Doubting that that was the intended effect of Colman, J's judgment in *Formica*, Moore-Bick, J held that the applicant

---

54 *Ibid.,* at 366. The common interest privilege was not apt to protect from production upon the owners' discovery application the writ and affidavit relating to the injunction proceedings see Phillips, J, *ibid.,* at 386. However, see further on this Chap. 7, Section 4.
55 [1995] 1 Lloyd's Rep. 692.
56 *Ibid.,* at 699.

had to establish a right to disclosure which existed at the time the privileged communication occurred.[57] It is difficult to articulate a formula for determining which type of common interest creates disclosure rights and which does not. Less difficult is to provide specific examples. So, Moore-Bick, J in *Commercial Union* suggested, correctly it is submitted, that the sharing tenants in Donaldson, LJ's example in *Buttes Gas* (see p. 154 above) had no basis for insisting on seeing the first tenant's advice had he chosen not to disclose it. And while his decision was concerned specifically with reinsurance contracts containing "follow settlement" clauses, the tenor of the judgment in *Commercial Union* suggests that the "joint interest" right to disclosure will exist under most reinsurance contracts, quite apart from common interest privilege.[58]

In this regard, the *Svenska*[59] decision is relevant. Here, the plaintiffs had taken out commercial mortgage indemnity insurance with Sun Alliance, the defendants. The plaintiffs claimed under one such policy. In the course of the litigation they sought discovery of documents which included the legal advice Sun Alliance had obtained from their solicitors regarding the issues in dispute in the action and which Sun Alliance had communicated to their reinsurers. One of the grounds on which the application was resisted was that the advice fell within the doctrine of common interest privilege, with the result that disclosure to the reinsurers did not amount to a waiver of privilege. The plaintiffs argued that there was an insufficient community of interest between Sun Alliance and their reinsurers; and that there was some evidence there might even be conflict between Sun Alliance and one or two of their reinsurers as to whether the reinsurance in question was binding. Rix, J held:

> "... it does seem to me that there is a very close community of interest between an insurer and a reinsurer in general. No particular contractual provision is relied upon by [the defendant's deponent], rather she says that Sun Alliance felt obliged to communicate the relevant advice to their reinsurers. In my judgment that is something which I can accept as being the circumstance under which, and the purpose for which that advice was communicated. It is, in effect, a recognition of de facto obligations in

---

57 [1996] 2 Lloyd's Rep. 640 at 648.
58 Ultimately the reinsurers' application for access to Commercial Union's privileged documents failed. Since the reinsurers had pleaded that the contract of reinsurance had been avoided, they sought to place the parties in the same position as if it had never been made. As the reinsurers could not therefore rely upon the contract in order to found the basis for seeking disclosure, they were unable to establish any other relationship with the insurers which was capable of supporting a common interest in the subject matter of the documents they sought.
59 [1995] 2 Lloyd's Rep 84.

circumstances where, in the absence of policies, the precise legal obligation may not have been clear".[60]

Otherwise, generally the courts will readily recognise common interest for the purpose of the privilege in relation to certain types of insurance matters.[61] Thus, in *Guinness Peat Properties Ltd* v *Fitzroy Robinson Partnership*[62] an issue arose as to whether architects could resist the application for discovery of a copy of their claim notification letter to their professional indemnity insurers. The architects asserted that this was a privileged communication, even though it had been brought into existence at the behest of the insurers who were not parties to the action. Applying *Buttes Gas*,[63] the Court of Appeal held that the communication was protected by a common interest privilege which they were entitled to assert.

Legal advice

The *Svenska* decision noted above is also important because it extends common interest privilege beyond the original "aid in litigation" concept to cover the situation where there is a sharing of legal advice with a third party who is not, and is not likely to be, a party to litigation to which the advice relates. The plaintiffs had argued that it needed to be shown that the documents containing the advice which the insurers disclosed to their reinsurers were brought into existence for the dominant purpose of being used in pending or contemplated litigation. The defendants made no attempt to establish that the documents came within litigation privilege: they relied on advice privilege alone. Rix, J held:[64]

> "Ultimately, this question has to be dealt with as a matter of first principle. Where parties can properly be considered as having such community of

---

60   *Ibid.*, at 87. Although this was a case in which the insurers volunteered documents to the reinsurers, the judge also commented that "… where there is, either under legal compulsion or in practical terms, a need for legal advice to be shared confidentially with parties with a community of interest, then the law should not be astute to find distinctions between, for instance in this case a reinsurer and the reinsured on the one hand, and an assured and his legal liability insurers on the other".

61   *Lee v South West Thames Regional Health Authority* [1985] 1 WLR 845 is an example, in a non-insurance context, of a claim to common interest privilege failing. See also *Robert Hitchins Ltd v International Computers Ltd* (unrep.) 10 December 1996, in which members of the Court of Appeal disagreed as to whether a third party who supplied privileged documents to the defendant with whom he had just settled had a common interest in their subject matter which entitled the defendant to assert the third party's privilege against the plaintiff: See the discussion of this case at p. 151 above.

62   [1987] 1 WLR 1027, discussed in detail in Chap. 3 at Section 6.

63   [1981] QB 223.

64   *Op. cit.*, at 88.

interest that they can be regarded, if necessary putting it at the highest, as being in effect one and the same person, then it should make no difference whatsoever whether one is dealing with [litigation privilege] or [advice privilege]".[65]

As a matter of principle this decision is clearly right. It is a welcome extension and it ought to provide comfort to lawyers who act for separate clients who have an identity of interest and who share legal advice in a situation where no litigation can be contemplated. Thus supposing two companies, each separately advised, join forces to make a joint takeover bid. It is inevitable that they and their respective lawyers will share information and advice and it can only be right that such materials so exchanged should – all other conditions of the privilege being satisfied – be the subject of common interest privilege maintainable against the outside world. Even here, though, there are limitations. In *The "Sagheera"*[65a], two parties had jointly instructed one firm of solicitors to investigate a vessel's demise. One of them, H&M underwriters, then instructed separate solicitors to negotiate an assignment of the owners' cause of action against their war risk underwriters. Rix, J held there was no common interest privilege in their respective solicitors' correspondence since this was inter partes correspondence which was non-confidential and was designed to protect each of them in the perfection of the assignment.

4. SUCCESSORS IN TITLE

Two other situations in which the client's privilege can be asserted by another are where that other claims under or in the same interest as the client; and also where he is a successor in title to the client. In the latter case, the death of a client, for example, does not destroy his privilege since this can be asserted by his heirs;[66] and as will be seen, similar principles apply in a corporate context.

The first decision to establish clearly that the privilege of a predecessor in title can be asserted by his successor was *Minet v Morgan*,[67] where the defendants sought orders for production of documents in the possession of the plaintiff. The plaintiff claimed privilege for some of them, which included "correspondence between himself and his family solicitors and his present solicitors", and "letters between his mother and her solicitors with reference to questions connected with the matters in dispute in this cause".

---

65 See also Colman, J in the *Formica* case, *op. cit.*, at 699.
65a [1997] 1 Lloyd's Rep. 160.
66 Per Lord Lindley in *Bullivant v AG for Victoria* [1901] AC 196 at 206.
67 (1873) 8 Ch App. 361

These claims to privilege were upheld, the Lord Chancellor, Lord Selborne, making it clear[68] that the only issue was whether the plaintiff had sufficiently claimed protection for these confidential letters.[69]

This issue arose again in the Court of Appeal's decision in *Calcraft* v *Guest*.[70] One of the questions dealt with here concerned the privileged status of certain relevant documents which had come into existence in relation to Mr Calcraft's forebear in an action which had taken place over 110 years previously. Once again, there appears to have been no challenge to the principle that a successor in title can assert and maintain his predecessor's privilege.[71]

Consistent with the principles which have been discussed in this chapter, where more than one person claims under or in respect of the interests of the original beneficiary of the privilege, none can assert that privilege as against any other claimants. Thus in *In re Pickering*[72] a partner in a two-man partnership died and his surviving partner was one of his several executors. His children were the residuary legatees. In an action by one child, an order was made for the taking of the accounts of the partnership as between the surviving partner and the testator's estate. The Court of Appeal refused to allow the surviving partner the usual liberty to seal up entries in the partnership documents which did not relate to matters in dispute. The child, in effect as beneficiary under the estate, was entitled to access to the partnership books. Though a decision primarily concerned with irrelevant entries, it is clear from the Court's judgment that any privileged communications between one of the partners (before his death) and his lawyer relating to partnership matters could not have been withheld in litigation against a legatee.

Similarly, in *Russell* v *Jackson*,[73] it was held that in proceedings brought by the next of kin of the deceased against his executors, no privilege could be asserted as against any of them arising in respect of professional communications between the testator and his solicitor. However, where that same solicitor acted for the executors, then in relation to

---

68 *Ibid.*, at 366.

69 In *Crescent Farm (Sidcup) Sports Ltd* v *Sterling Offices Ltd* [1972] Ch 553 (discussed below), Goff, J commented, at 562, that *Minet* v *Morgan* was the first case which clearly settled that the legal professional privilege of a predecessor in title enures for the benefit of his successor. He noted that this was unequivocally expressed in the second part of the head note of this case although "the judgment does not say so quite specifically but ... when analysed the case clearly so decided".

70 [1898] 1 QB 759. The decision is further considered in Chap. 7.

71 For a more recent authority, see *Kershaw* v *Whelan* [1996] 1 WLR 358 at 364.

72 25 Ch D 247.

73 9 Hare 387.

communications between them, the privilege could be asserted as against the next of kin.[74]

But it is not only upon the death of an individual that these issues arise. A liquidator can enjoy and assert the company's privilege in any qualifying communications made before the date upon which the liquidation occurred.[75] Similarly, a trustee in bankruptcy inherits any privilege previously enjoyed by the bankrupt. This is illustrated by the decision in *Re Konigsberg*,[76] in which a husband and wife jointly instructed a solicitor in relation to a property transaction. The husband subsequently became bankrupt, whereupon his trustee in bankruptcy sought to set the transaction aside. The wife swore an affidavit asserting that the transaction had been made for a valuable consideration. The solicitor who had acted for them both swore an affidavit which contradicted that assertion. The wife applied to exclude the solicitors' affidavit from use at the hearing of the trustee's motion in so far as it trespassed, *inter alia*, on communications between the solicitor and both the husband and wife.

Peter Gibson, J rejected the submission that the trustee was a third party against whom Mrs Konigsberg, one of two joint clients, could insist on the maintenance of her privilege (even if the solicitor's other joint client was prepared to waive it). As to this, the judge ruled:

> "Important and desirable though I recognise it is to maintain the principle of legal professional privilege I can see no sufficient reason to treat the trustee as a third party for that purpose. The rule recognises that joint clients cannot maintain privilege against each other and as the privilege of the bankrupt has devolved onto the trustee who is entitled to obtain the privileged information from the bankrupt, in my judgment it is appropriate to treat the trustee as being in the shoes of the bankrupt for the purpose of privilege in proceedings against the joint client".[77]

This successor in title principle also operates where the privilege is an incidence of a title to property. This aspect featured in the decision in *Crescent Farm Sports* v *Sterling Offices*.[78] The plaintiff and first defendant were purchasers and sub-purchasers under a 1959 conveyance of land which granted the plaintiffs a first option over any of that land which the first defendant wished to sell. The first defendants agreed to sell the land to the second defendant, subject to obtaining a release of the plaintiff's pre-emptive rights under the 1959 conveyance. In the event, the plaintiffs

---

74 See also *Curtis v Beaney* [1911] P 181.
75 See *e.g.*, *Re International Power Industries Ltd* [1985] BCLC 128 and *Re Brook Martin & Co (Nominees) Ltd* [1993] BCLC 328.
76 [1989] 3 All ER 289.
77 *Ibid.*, at 297–298.
78 [1972] Ch 553.

decided to exercise their right to purchase but there was a difficulty in working out the arrangements by which the sale price should be agreed. The first defendant then sold the land to the second defendant whereupon the plaintiff sued for breach of contract and conspiracy. A preliminary issue arose as to the plaintiffs' entitlement to production of counsel's opinion obtained by the first defendant which they sent to the second defendants prior to the conveyance of the land to the second defendant.

It was accepted that the opinion was privileged in the hands of the first defendant, but it was argued that since it had been sent to the second defendant in circumstances where there was no litigation contemplated or pending, then that could not be a privileged communication. The defendants met this argument by asserting that the opinion was a document which was a matter of title: since the second defendant was the successor in title to the first defendant then it was entitled to the first defendant's privileges, even though the second defendants received the opinion before completion, that is before they succeeded to the first defendant's title. Goff, J held that it was impossible to say:

> "... that the second defendants did not receive the documents as successors in title, and whether or not they could have called for them at any stage is in my judgment irrelevant. They were prospective purchasers. They had actually entered into a conditional contract and the documents were sent to them with a view to persuading them to complete ...".[79]

5. THE DURATION OF THE PRIVILEGE

Intertwined with the successor of title issues raised in some of the cases considered in Section 4 above is the issue of the duration of the privilege, particularly litigation privilege. If privileged materials are created for the purposes of one action, can the holder of the privilege also assert privilege for them – whether as a party or a mere witness – in a subsequent action? The courts have answered this question in the affirmative, in the process adopting the shorthand rule of "once privileged always privileged".

One of the earliest cases in which this issue was considered was *Bullock & Co v Corry & Co.*[80] The plaintiffs sued the defendants for their failure to accept delivery of a cargo of rice, after they had been successfully sued by the ship owners for their failure to discharge the cargo according to the terms of the charter party. The defendants claimed that they were entitled

79 *Ibid.,* at 564.
80 (1878) 3 QBD 356.

to inspect correspondence passing between the plaintiffs and their solicitors in relation to the ship owners' action. The plaintiffs argued that there was no reason why their privilege "should be limited to an existing suit" and in a short judgment Cockburn, CJ agreed:

> "The privilege which attaches by the invariable practice of our courts to communications between solicitor and client ought to be carefully preserved. In my opinion the rule is, once privileged, always privileged. This will apply, a fortiori, where the succeeding action is substantially the same as that in which the documents were used".[81]

Any arguments as to the scope of the once privileged rule were finally put to rest by the Court of Appeal's decision in *The "Aegis Blaze"*[82] in which the facts were as follows. The defendant vessel owners instructed surveyors to carry out an inspection in the light of threatened proceedings for damages by cargo owners. Several months later, other cargo carried on the same vessel was also damaged with the result that separate proceedings were commenced by different cargo owners against the owners. The plaintiffs became aware of the earlier survey report because of a reference to it in a letter disclosed by the owners upon discovery. The owners asserted that this report was a privileged document which had come into existence in the wake of the first set of contemplated proceedings (which in the event took place in Greece, not England). At first instance, Sheen, J, following an Irish decision in *Kerry County Council v Liverpool Salvage Association*,[83] held that a document does not retain its privilege in subsequent proceedings concerning different parties and different subject matters.

In the Court of Appeal, Parker, LJ reviewed the authorities[84] and concluded that:

> "Unless the party claiming the privilege or his successor is a party to the subsequent action, no question of a claim to privilege will arise. That is established by *Schneider v Leigh*.[85] If, however, the party claiming privilege

---

81 At 358. See also *Pearce v Foster* (1885) 15 QBD 114, where Brett, MR commented at page 119 that Cockburn, CJ's judgment in *Bullock v Corry* laid down "a most valuable principle on this subject". The "once privileged, always privileged" rule was also applied by the Court of Appeal in *Calcraft v Guest* [1898] 1 QB 759 (a case discussed in detail in Chap. 7), which Lord Lindley, MR there described as "a general rule", a comment adopted by Stirling, J in *Goldstone v Williams, Deacon & Co* [1899] 1 Ch 47.

82 [1986] Lloyd's Rep 203. See also *R v Derby Magistrates' Court, ex p. B* [1996] 1 AC 487, at 506 per Lord Taylor, LCJ.

83 (1905) 38 ILT 7.

84 Including *Calcraft v Guest* [1898] 1 QB 759, where he noted (*op. cit.* at 207) that the parties in that action were entirely different and the only connection of subject matter which he could ascertain from the report was that there were successors in title in the two actions concerned

85 [1955] 2 QB 195. This decision is discussed in detail in Chap. 7.

in the second action is the person entitled to privilege in the first action, but there is no connection of subject matter whatever, it is most improbable that the question will arise, for in such circumstances the document will not be relevant and will not therefore be disclosable, and there will therefore be no question of production. If, however, there is a sufficient connection for the document to be relevant, then it is, in my view, right that the party entitled to the privilege should be able to assert it in the second action. I accept, of course, that that may mean that the Court trying the second action is deprived of full information, but so would the Court have been in the first action, and so also may it be in any case where privilege is asserted".[86]

In the same case, Croom-Johnson, LJ, in a short concurring judgment, also rejected a submission advanced on behalf of the cargo interests to the effect that where the privilege is claimed in subsequent litigation, the rule "once privileged always privileged" is no more than a general rule in applying which the court must balance the conflicting public policy considerations, namely that of the completeness of the evidence before the court and that of the legal professional privilege. In his view:

> "... that balancing act should not be done in any circumstances where legal professional privilege attaches. The balancing act has already been done by the making of the rule of legal professional privilege; and to do what Counsel for the respondents submitted should be done in subsequent litigation would be to deny, in effect, the existence of that rule. Certainly it could not be done in view of the authority of *Calcraft* v *Guest* and of the other authorities to which [Parker, LJ] has referred".[87]

For the sake of completeness, reference should be made once more to the House of Lords' decision in *R* v *Derby Magistrates Court ex p. B*[88] in which Lord Taylor CJ's review of the long history of the development of legal professional privilege referred approvingly to the "once privileged always privileged" rules. Although the House of Lords' decision was, strictly, concerned with the application of section 97 Magistrates Court Act 1980, such that its observations on privilege were obiter, the importance of the "once privileged, always privileged" rule is underlined by Lord Taylor's explanation of the rationale of privilege; and the views expressed on the inappropriateness of the "spent privilege" argument canvassed in that decision.[89]

---

86 [1986] 2 Lloyd's Rep 203, at 209.
87 *Ibid.,* at 211.
88 [1996] 1 AC 487.
89 See Chap. 1, sections 2 and 3.

Chapter 7

LOSING PRIVILEGE

1. INTRODUCTION

The rights conferred by privilege can be lost or waived. The consequence, in either case, is that the beneficiary of the privilege can no longer refuse to disclose during the course of litigation the communications to which the privilege attaches.[1] There are, generally speaking, three sets of circumstances in which loss of privilege can occur:

- Where the conditions necessary for a claim to privilege no longer apply, as where the underlying confidentiality in a privileged document is lost. This can occur as a result of the disclosure of privileged information during the course of – as well as outside of – the litigation process. In such cases, the privilege is normally expressly, or deliberately, waived by the beneficiary, as where he discloses privileged information to the opposing party in legal proceedings, for example, because he wishes to adduce it in evidence. Difficult issues can arise as to the extent or nature of the disclosure which must occur before confidentiality can be said to be lost.

- Where the beneficiary will be deemed to have waived his privilege. Such implied waiver will occur even though the beneficiary did not intend or wish to lose his privilege, as where privileged documents are inadvertently put in evidence at trial, or where he sues his legal adviser.

- Where an opponent is able to adduce secondary evidence of the contents of a privileged communication, as where he steals a copy of a privileged document or obtains it from the beneficiary's legal adviser (usually in breach of the adviser's duty of confidentiality to his client). Although not strictly an instance of waiver of privilege,

---

1 Similarly, he can no longer, *e.g.,* resist on the grounds of privilege a search warrant issued under ss. 8 or 9 Police and Criminal Act 1984: see generally as to search warrants and privilege Chap. 8, Section 5.

nonetheless the privilege can be lost as it is, in effect, circumvented or out-flanked.

Where an inadvertent disclosure of privileged material occurs, or an opponent attempts to adduce secondary evidence of it, the beneficiary is not necessarily powerless to take steps to protect his position. In these circumstances, the courts may well be prepared to grant an injunction in aid of the privilege which prevents the use of the disclosed materials or of the secondary evidence. The court's jurisdiction to grant such an injunction does not derive directly from the privilege, since the rules as to privilege, being mere evidential rules, only entitle the beneficiary to resist compulsory disclosure of privileged communications: they do not as yet confer a right to prevent their use against the beneficiary's wishes. Rather, the jurisdiction is an equitable one which derives from the court's willingness to restrain the publication or use of confidential information improperly obtained or disclosed in circumstances where it ought not to have been divulged.

2. PRELIMINARY CONSIDERATIONS

A preliminary question which needs to be considered is: "who can waive a client's privilege?" One might have expected the answer to this to be "the client": after all, the privilege belongs to the client and not to his legal adviser. So, a legal adviser cannot be compelled to answer questions or to produce documents which would involve the disclosure of his client's privileged information.[2] Nonetheless, the implied authority of both solicitors and counsel to conduct litigation on behalf of their client extends to a waiver of the privilege. This can be seen from Lord Denning, MR's judgment in *Causton* v *Mann Egerton Limited,* a decision examining the disclosure of medical reports:

> "here there was an understanding which amounted to a waiver of the privilege. It was suggested that the solicitor could not waive the privilege on behalf of his client. To this there is a short answer: a solicitor, like counsel, has complete authority over the suit, the mode of conducting it and all that is incident to it. Unless his client has expressly withdrawn that authority or any

---

2 See, *e.g., R* v *Derby Magistrates Court, ex p. B* [1996] 1 AC 487. Where the legal adviser holds documents which are not privileged and, at best, confidential only, he can be compelled to disclose them. In such cases, the clients in whom the benefits of the confidence rest will usually be given an opportunity to intervene to argue against the disclosure of the confidential information: see *e.g. CHC Software Care Ltd* v *Hopkins & Wood* [1993] FSR 241.

part of it, the other party is entitled to assume that he is acting within his authority.[3] This is certainly the case when he enters into an agreement to compromise the action itself ... a fortiori when he makes a reasonable agreement to disclose medical reports, thereby waiving any privilege in respect of it."[4]

The Court of Appeal's decision in *Great Atlantic Insurance Co v Home Insurance Co*[5] provides a striking example of a lawyer's ability to waive his client's privilege without the client's express consent. Here, two paragraphs of a document were read out in open court by leading counsel for the plaintiff who did not appreciate that he was reading an extract from a longer document which was privileged. It was not apparent from the extract alone that he was about to trespass onto his client's privilege. Though the client did not consent to the waiver and counsel did not intend to waive his client's privilege, counsel's action nonetheless had that consequence. Similarly, as with the cases considered in Section 7 below, concerning inadvertent disclosure of privileged materials at the discovery stage of an action, it is the mistakes of the solicitors, undertaken without the express consent of their clients, which give rise to the waiver issues.[6]

If the client does decide to waive privilege, then it is not open to the adviser to claim it or to try to hide behind it. In *Re International Power Industries*,[7] letters rogatory were issued to the High Court in England in connection with bankruptcy proceedings in the USA requiring the English solicitors who had acted for the company subject to those proceedings to produce certain documents. The solicitors applied to discharge the order of the English court which gave effect to the letters rogatory, arguing, *inter alia*, that it required them to disclose information in the form of privileged legal advice. However, the court held that since the privilege belonged to the company, its US trustee in bankruptcy was entitled to waive it, thereby preventing the solicitors from taking advantage of it and from relying on it in order to resist the order.[8]

An expert witness who has provided privileged evidence to a party to

---

3   This sentence prompts the thought that the problems which arise with inadvertent disclosure at the discovery stage of litigation (discussed in Section 7 below) could be prevented by the solicitors informing their opponents at the outset of the litigation that they have no authority to waive their client's privilege.

4   [1974] 1 WLR 162 at 167.

5   [1981] 1 WLR 529.

6   Note, however, Singleton, LJ's comment in his dissenting judgment in *Schneider v Leigh* [1955] 2 QB 195 that "... the mere recital by solicitors to the solicitors on the other side of a part of a [privileged] report does not mean that their clients had authorised them to waive the question of privilege" (at 200).

7   [1985] BCLC 128.

8   In the result, the order was overturned on other grounds.

litigation has no right to assert that privilege on his own behalf in separate proceedings to which he, and not his client, is party.[9] Nor is he, in those circumstances, under any duty to his client to assert or protect the client's privilege. In *Schneider v Leigh*,[10] a doctor who was acting as an expert witness for a plaintiff company in a personal injury action (which had not concluded) was sued for libel in separate proceedings by the defendant in the personal injury action. The claim for libel arose out of some statements which the doctor had made in his expert report. The company's solicitors had quoted those statements to the defendant's in an effort to procure a settlement of the personal injury action. Instead, the defendant's reaction was to sue Dr Leigh for libel and in the libel action he sought from Dr Leigh production of the whole report. Dr Leigh, who had a copy in his possession, argued that as it was a privileged document he need not disclose it. By a majority, the Court of Appeal rejected Dr Leigh's contentions. According to Hodson, LJ:

> "What is being sought here is, in effect, to extend the umbrella of the protection which the privilege gives the company [in the original action] to [Dr Leigh], who is, on the hypothesis that he is the author of the libel, to be looked at for the purpose of this application as a proposed witness on behalf of the company. In this capacity not only has he no privilege of his own, but he is under no duty to assert the right of the company to resist the production of any documents."[11]

In similar vein, Romer, LJ said:

> "The privilege which exists in the first action is, in my opinion, that of the company and of no one else; and the company can at any time waive the privilege without the defendant's consent and, indeed, without any reference to him at all."[12]

The limits of this decision need to be appreciated. First, it involved an unusual situation in which the defendant in the first action was able to assert a cause of action against Dr Leigh in a separate action in which privileged documents prepared for use in the original action were relevant. But for that, it is improbable that any question of discovery against Dr Leigh could have arisen (certainly, the defendant could not have subpoenaed him to produce his report in the first action if, *e.g.*, the

---

9 The same principle applies to a non-expert witness's witness statement, and in relation to any third party who engages in privileged communications with a litigant or his solicitor: see *Lee v South West Thames RHA* [1985] 2 All ER 385, discussed at p. 168 below.

10 [1955] 2 QB 195.

11 *Ibid.*, at 203.

12 *Ibid.*, at 205.

plaintiff had chosen not to use it[13]). Secondly, had the libellous statement been made in a report prepared by the company's solicitors, it is difficult to see that a discovery order would be made against them since, unlike Dr Leigh, they have a positive duty as his fiduciary agent to assert their client's privilege.[14] Thirdly, it is not at all clear from the judgments how the Court would have reacted had the company sought to protect its privilege by seeking to restrain the disclosure of its confidential information to Dr Leigh. This would have presented the Court with a difficult issue which is considered further in Section 7 below.

Finally, the decision does not conflict with a principle enunciated by Lord Donaldson, MR in *Lee v South West Thames RHA* to the effect that:

> "... a defendant or potential defendant[15] shall be free to seek evidence without being obliged to disclose the result of his researches to his opponent".[16]

The plaintiff in *Lee* was a young boy who was treated at two hospitals run by different health authorities and transported between them in an ambulance provided by a third, the defendant. He was put on a respirator at one hospital and was on a respirator when transported in the defendant's ambulance. He suffered brain damage caused by lack of oxygen, possibly caused by a kink in a respirator. His mother sought pre-action discovery against all three health authorities. One, Hillingdon, revealed that it held the original of a report obtained from the defendant's ambulance crew which Hillingdon had sought to enable it to obtain legal advice as to its potential liability to the boy. The original was clearly privileged. The defendant authority, which did not anticipate litigation against it at the time its crew provided the report, retained a copy which it refused to disclose to the mother. In effect, it advanced Hillingdon's claim to privilege. Hillingdon had not waived its privilege (though had it done so the defendants could not have resisted the application). The Court of Appeal upheld the defendant's stance. In doing so, it distinguished *Schneider v Leigh* on the basis that the cause of action now being asserted against the defendants was not a wholly independent cause of action but one arising out of the same incident as that which rendered Hillingdon a likely defendant. The defendants and its employees (the ambulance crew)

---

13 Though see *Harmony Shipping Co SA v Saudi Europe Line Ltd* [1979] 1 WLR 1380 and the discussion on the compellability of an expert's opinion in Chap. 3, Section 8.

14 Unless it could be said that the disclosure of the extracts waived the privilege in the whole. Only the dissenting judge, Singleton, LJ, addressed this aspect and he was clear that there had been no waiver of privilege. See also his comment quoted at n. 6 above.

15 And, presumably, a plaintiff or potential plaintiff.

16 [1985] 1 WLR 845 at 850.

had no rights as witnesses but because both authorities would inevitably have to be sued together, there was no other way of protecting Hillingdon's rights as defendants.[17]

The principle annunciated in *Lee* (and quoted above) does not serve to protect a party's privilege where there is no risk of that party becoming involved in litigation in relation to which a document protected by litigation privilege was prepared. Thus the decision in *Lee* did not assist a claim to privilege being mounted by a defendant in respect of a third party's privileged draft witness statements which had been supplied to him by the third party to assist his continuing defence against the plaintiff. So said the Court of Appeal in *Robert Hitchins Ltd* v *International Computers Ltd*[17a] in which it was held that there was no real risk of the plaintiff suing the third party as a defendant. However, as explained in Chapter 6, the third party's draft statements were nonetheless held to be privileged in the hands of B inter alia because the policy of the law encourages the sharing of material (and thereby the saving of costs) between parties to the litigation.

3 . LOSS OF CONFIDENTIALITY

General principles

For privilege to be claimed, the relevant communication must be a confidential one. If the confidentiality requirement cannot be satisfied, then no claim to privilege can be made. As was discussed in Chapter 3, the presence of an adversary, or even of a third party, during the making of a communication, may well (but not inevitably) destroy any confidentiality. So a statement made by a suspect in police custody to his lawyer in the presence of a police inspector was held not to have been a confidential conversation;[18] notes of *inter partes* proceedings in chambers will not be confidential;[19] and neither will an attendance note prepared by a solicitor recording a conversation between himself and the solicitor acting for the other parties.[20] In each case, there could not be said to be any confidentiality in the record of the meeting, telephone call or court

---

17   Per Lord Donaldson, MR *ibid.*, at 389.

17a   (Unreported) 10 December 1996

18   *R* v *Braham and Mason* [1976] VR 547. In similar circumstances, Friedmann, J in
Euroshipping of Monrovia v *Ministry of Agriculture and Economies* [1979] (1) SA
(CPD) 637 at 648 suggested the lawyer's note might be. This decision is not in line with
the case mentioned in n. 20 below.

19   *Ainsworth* v *Wilding* [1900] 2 Ch 315.

20   *Parry and Whelan* v *News Group Newspapers* [1990] 140 New LJ 1719 (judgment
dated 16 November 1990).

proceedings, and as a result privilege could not be claimed. In contrast, is the New Zealand Court of Appeal's decision in *R v Uljee*.[21] Here, a privileged communication between a solicitor and his client who was later charged with attempted murder was overheard by a policeman. The communication occurred at the solicitor's home where the policeman was posted in case the accused tried to leave the premises. The question arose as to whether the policeman's account of what he heard was admissible at his trial. Contrasting this case with *R v Braham & Mason*,[22] which he said was a case in which the true inference was that the communication was not intended to be confidential, Cooke, J held:

> "... once it is found that confidentiality was intended, that should be enough and it would be beside the point to embark on an inquiry into whether the client and the adviser took all due precautions... the law should not shrink from the fair and natural consequence. A third party who has overheard such a communication, if oral, or come into possession of it, or a copy of it, if written, should not be allowed to give evidence of it unless the client waives the privilege".[23]

But what of the situation where an otherwise proper claim to privilege is challenged because of a disclosure of the privileged communication made to third parties: does such disclosure undermine the confidentiality? The answer appears to be that confidentiality is not necessarily lost with every disclosure beyond the client and legal adviser. Perhaps unhelpfully, the converse position is that every disclosure of privileged information to a third party carries with it some risk that privilege can no longer be claimed, or at least that a challenge to the privilege/confidentiality might be mounted.[24]

In this regard, the general law of confidentiality provides some assistance. So, for these purposes, communications which contain information which is in the public domain, as where "the information in question is so generally accessible that, in all the circumstances, it cannot be regarded as confidential",[25] are unlikely to be the subject of a sustainable claim to privilege. Documentation read out in open court will therefore lose any confidentiality. Conversely,

> "... a claim that the disclosure of some information would be a breach of
> confidence is not defeated simply by proving that there are other people in
> the world who know the facts in question besides the man as to whom it is

---

21 [1982] 1 NZLR 561.
22 [1976] VR 547.
23 At 552.
24 See *e.g. Goldberg v Ng* [1994] 33 NSWLR 639 discussed at p. 180 below.
25 Per Lord Goff in the "Spycatcher" litigation, *Attorney-General v Guardian Newspapers Ltd (No 2)* [1990] 1 AC 109 at 282.

said that this disclosure would be a breach of confidence and those to whom he has disclosed".[26]

Consistent with these general principles, Bray[27] nearly a hundred years earlier, stated how these considerations might apply to privilege:

> "The mere gratuitous production or communication of privileged matter in the shape of a copy or otherwise to some other person (not the adversary) cannot it is conceived have the effect of depriving the client of his right to refuse discovery of it, unless the production or communication is such as altogether to deprive it of its confidential character..."

How does this apply in practice? Necessarily, at one end of the scale, publication of privileged information to the general public will deprive the information of any privilege which previously existed. So any press release which makes use of privileged information will almost certainly result in a waiver of that privilege.[28]

At the other end of the scale, where the client is a large corporation, privileged information may be widely disseminated within the client. This may cause problems at a later stage so far as concerns asserting the privilege, for example in future proceedings between the company and a former employee who has had legitimate access to the privileged material. In that situation, there can be no confidentiality in that information as against the employee, even though it would be open to the company to assert privilege against its adversaries who had not had access to it.[29] In *Derby* v *Weldon (No 10)*[30] a claim to privilege in respect of memoranda produced by in-house legal counsel on the measures necessary for regulatory compliance in the USA was defeated because copies of the memoranda had at the time been circulated to Mr Weldon, then an executive with the plaintiff company, and now one of the defendants to the company's action. In similar vein, board directors who have considered legal advice obtained for the company could defeat a claim to privilege in respect of that advice in any proceedings brought against them by the company or its liquidators, even though that privilege could be asserted

---

26 Per Cross, J in *Franchi* v *Franchi* [1967] RPC 149 at 152–153. See also Lord Donaldson, MR in *Attorney-General* v *Guardian Newspapers Ltd (and others) (No 2)* [1988] 3 All ER 545 at 595.

27 *The Principles and Practice of Discovery,* at 366.

28 An extreme example of this is *Chandris Lines* v *Wilson & Horton Ltd* [1981] 2 NZLR 600. Here, a newspaper sued for defamation published a "follow-up" article which gave details of an analyst's report commissioned by the newspaper for the purposes of the litigation. Hardly surprisingly, an attempt later in the proceedings to withhold production of the report on the grounds that it was privileged failed.

29 As to the effect on privilege of the dissemination of legal advice within a corporation see Chap. 4, Section 3.

30 [1991] 1 WLR 660.

against other adversaries. This appears from Vinelott, J's comments in the *Derby* case when he said:

> "[Counsel] submitted that privilege is not lost merely because a document is communicated by a company to an officer or employee. That is no doubt true where the question arises in litigation between the company and a third party. But it does not follow that the company can rely on the privilege attaching to, for instance, instructions and advice passing between the company and its solicitors, copies of which have been supplied to the director, if there is subsequently litigation between the company and the director and the advice or instructions are material to an issue raised in the litigation."[31]

The risk of losing confidentiality is necessarily greater where the contents of a privileged document are disclosed beyond the client. As the passage from Bray suggests, disclosure to the adversary will normally be fatal.[32,33] But what about disclosure to others, where the protected information does not come into the public domain? Such disclosure will not always result in a loss of privilege, though it will frequently make it arguable that this is so. In some instances, disclosing privileged advice beyond a client may be unavoidable. A classic example is where the lawyers advising the client are working as members of a multi-disciplinary team advising on a large corporate transaction. It will frequently be necessary for the legal advice to be copied to other members of the team. Does this amount to a waiver of privilege? So long as the disclosure is made on confidential terms, then the answer ought to be "no", for, as Hobhouse, J pointed out in *Prudential Assurance Co v Fountain Page Ltd*:

> "There is no conceptual difficulty about the reservation of rights of confidentiality or privilege notwithstanding that a document or piece of information has been communicated to another".[34]

---

31 *Ibid.*, at 670.

32 But see the cases involving mistaken disclosure on discovery discussed in Section 7; and also p. 178 *et seq* below. It is also possible to agree arrangements preserving the confidentiality of documents disclosed in litigation: see *The Lubrizol Corporation v Esso Petroleum Company Limited (No 2)* [1993] FSR 53; and the Court can also make orders to like effect pursuant to RSC O24 r. 14A.

33 However, as the rules on exchange of witness statements show, not every disclosure of a privileged document to an adversary will result in loss of the privilege. In *Prudential Assurance Co v Fountain Page Ltd* [1991] 1 WLR 756, at 776, Hobhouse, J held that when a statement is served pursuant to a direction given under RSC O38 r. 2A and the witness to whose evidence that statement relates is never called by the serving party to give evidence, that statement remains a privileged document. So, the serving party cannot be compelled to disclose the statement to any other person and is entitled to prevent any other person using that statement without his consent. The position in relation to expert's reports is different: see generally Chap. 3, Sections 8 and 9 and p. 190 below.

34 [1991] 1 WLR 756 at 770. See also Goff, J in *Crescent Farm (Sidcup) Sports Ltd v Sterling Offices Ltd* [1972] Ch 553 at 564.

This issue was partly examined in *Nederlandse Reassurantie Groep Holding NV ("NRG") v Bacon & Woodrow.*[35] The decision concerned a negligence action brought by NRG against actuarial advisors, accountants and bankers who had been part of a team, including lawyers, assembled to advise NRG on the acquisition of an insurance group which had not gone as planned. The accountants sought the production of all legal advice received by NRG during the course of the transaction. That argument was advanced on the grounds that, since some of it had already been supplied to them as members of the team advising NRG on the acquisition, as against them *all* such advice lacked any confidentiality. Colman, J accepted that where solicitors provide legal advice to a client on a transaction involving other professionals, their duty of confidentiality is qualified, thus permitting the disclosure of their advice to other advisers where the solicitors consider it necessary to discharge their duties.

However, he held that this did not justify the further submission that *all* legal advice given during the acquisition – including that which the non-lawyers had not seen – could not be privileged as against the defendants. Where documents had not been disclosed to the non-legal advisers, Colman, J noted that the reason must have been that the legal advisers did not consider such disclosure necessary. For this reason, the documents could not have fallen within the implied qualification to their duty of confidence and so remained confidential as between NRG and its legal advisers. Accordingly, privilege attached to them in the proceedings brought against the non-legal advisers.

What *NRG v Bacon & Woodrow* does not examine is whether documents which have been properly disclosed to the non-legal members of the team can still be said to be privileged as against the rest of the world. As all the advisers who receive copies of privileged documents during such a transaction would owe a duty of confidentiality to the client in respect of all information they receive (other than in respect of that which is in the public domain) there appears to be no reason in principle why the client should not still be able to assert his legal professional privilege to withhold the document from any party outside the "ring of confidence" which all the advisers must maintain. So much appears as a matter of general principle, and having regard to Hobhouse, J's comments quoted at page 175 above.

This was the conclusion the Court of Appeal reached in *Gotha City v Sotheby's.*[36] Here, Sotheby's were in possession of legal advice given to their co-defendant, and minutes of a meeting between the co-defendant and their solicitors at which Sotheby's were present. The deputy judge made an order

---

35 [1995] 1 All ER 976, discussed in detail in Chap. 2, p. 51.
36 [1998] 1 WLR 114.

for their disclosure against the co-defendant (the disclosing party) on the grounds that the disclosure to Sotheby's amounted to a waiver of the co-defendant's privilege as against the whole world. The Court of Appeal disagreed, holding that the real issue was whether the documents and information were disclosed to Sotheby's in confidence. Although their disclosure was not expressly agreed to have been made on a confidential basis, Staughton, LJ held that there was "a plain inference that those communications were intended to be confidential".[37]

This issue has also been examined in the New Zealand decision, *CC Bottlers Ltd* v *Lion Nathan Ltd*.[38] This case arose out of the purchase by the plaintiffs of all the shares in the defendants. The defendants applied for an order for production of documents which included draft letters of advice prepared by the lawyers for the client, and copies of past advice to the client, both of which were sent by the plaintiffs' lawyers to the financial advisers in the course of the transaction. The judge noted that there was no doubt that they were created for the purpose of providing confidential legal advice to the client. The question was whether privilege had been waived by their disclosure to the financial advisers. Henry, J referred to his earlier decision in *Harbour Inn Seafoods* v *Switzerland General Insurance Co* where he had said:

> "...the fact of disclosure of a document when confined to a particular non-party does not necessarily constitute a waiver of privilege available to a party seeking production. In principle, it seems to me that disclosure, for example by a plaintiff to an associate or confidant unconnected with the proceeding of written legal advice on a claim against the defendant, in ordinary circumstances would not and should not constitute a waiver as against the defendant".[39]

Noting that a waiver can occur where disclosure is made to a third party who can be said to be the agent or representative of the party seeking the production, such that this amounts to disclosure to the opponent, Henry, J held in *CC Bottlers* that there was no such connection between the plaintiff's financial advisers and the defendants. In consequence, the documents could not be said to have been publicly disclosed and the defendant's application for production was dismissed.

---

37 The Court emphasised that no disclosure order had been made against Sotheby's. It is now apparent from the Court of Appeal's unreported decision in *Robert Hitchins Ltd* v *International Computers Ltd*, 10 December 1996, that Sothebys could have resisted a disclosure order either by asserting the co-defendant's privilege or on the grounds that disclosure was not necessary within the meaning of RSC O24 r.7. See the discussion of *Robert Hitchins* in Chap. 6. See further Section 7 below.

38 [1993] 2 NZLR 445.

39 [1990] 2 NZLR 381 at 384.

In other circumstances, disclosure to third parties will not result in a waiver of privilege either because the courts can find a common interest[40] between the disclosing and receiving party – as in the case of insured and insurer – which permits the sharing of the privileged information without their being a loss of confidentiality; or for the pragmatic reasons adopted in *Robert Hitchins Ltd* v *International Computers Ltd*[40a] (discussed in Chap. 6) or because – as in the case of disclosure to the "authorities" – pragmatic rules have been developed which are designed to prevent loss of confidentiality. For some situations, the position is less clear, as with disclosures to auditors. The position relating to insurers has been considered in chapter 3. The position relating to the authorities and to auditors is discussed next.

In *British Coal Corporation* v *Dennis Rye Ltd (No 2)*,[41] the plaintiffs had investigated overcharging by one of their suppliers with a view to taking legal proceedings against them. Copies of the privileged reports and other material which resulted from their investigation were made available to the police, who were also investigating the defendant's conduct. In the resultant prosecution, some of the material supplied by British Coal was disclosed by the police to the defendants under the Attorney General's Guidelines on Disclosure of Information to the defence. Some of the remaining material supplied by British Coal to the police was disclosed to the defendants during the course of the criminal trial pursuant to orders made by the judge.

When the criminal proceedings concluded, British Coal instituted civil proceedings against the defendants and applied for the return of all their privileged materials in the hands of the defendants. The defendants argued that any privilege in the documents had been lost since the documents came into their hands quite properly and in circumstances in which the plaintiffs either approved or acquiesced in their disclosure to the defendants. In the Court of Appeal, Neill, LJ said:

> "...it is clear that the plaintiff made the documents available for a limited purpose only, namely to assist in the conduct first of a criminal investigation and then of a criminal trial. This action of the plaintiff, looked at objectively as it must be, cannot be construed as a waiver of any rights available to them in the present civil action for the purpose of which the privilege exists... the action of the plaintiff in making documents available for the purpose of the criminal trial did not constitute a waiver of the privilege to which it was entitled in the present civil proceedings".[42]

---

40 In which case, the recipient will also be able to assert the discloser's privilege: see Chap. 4, Section 3.

40a (Unrep.) 10 December 1996.

41 [1988] 1 WLR 1113.

42 *Ibid.*, at 1121–1122.

The decision is, surely, a pragmatic one, designed to encourage those with relevant knowledge to assist the criminal justice authorities in circumstances where those authorities could not use their compulsory powers of disclosure (*e.g.* under s.2 Criminal Justice Act, 1987) to obtain such information, since such powers do not cover the disclosure of privileged information.[43] Indeed, Neill, LJ expressly referred to the plaintiff's disclosure to the police as being "in accordance with its duty to assist in the conduct of criminal proceedings".[44] Further, it would, in his view, be contrary to public policy if a person who assisted the police in this way were subsequently to find his privilege was lost for the purposes of civil proceedings.

It is difficult, though, to justify this decision on principle, since the confidentiality in the disclosed documents had as against the defendants undoubtedly been lost in circumstances in which the defendants were *entitled* to access to the information concerned. This contrasts with the examples discussed in Section 7 below, in which injunctions were obtained to procure the return of confidential documentation and to restrain its use,[45] where the defendants had no such entitlement. It is suggested that had any of the privileged material in *British Coal* been deployed in court then the plaintiffs in the civil action could not have succeeded in maintaining a claim to privilege in respect of that material in the later civil action.

Neill, LJ's comments quoted above have caused the decision in *British Coal* to be cited as authority for the broad proposition that it is possible to waive privilege for a specific purpose and in a specific context. This happened in *Goldman v Hesper*,[46] which concerned an application by a party for a review of a taxation on the ground that he was entitled to see the privileged documents which had been lodged with the taxing master by the other side. In the Court of Appeal, Taylor, LJ noted that a taxation inevitably involves some inroads into privilege because of the obligation to disclose privileged material to the taxing master pursuant to RSC Order 62, rule 29(7). He accepted that there might be some instances in which the taxing master would need to disclose part of a privileged document to the other side. He noted that:

> "Any disclosure of privileged material which does have to be made in the exercise of the taxing master's discretion would in my judgment be only for the purposes of the taxation. That it is possible to waive privilege for a specific purpose and in a specific context only is well illustrated by the

---

43 See Chap. 1, Section 5.
44 *Op. cit.* at 1121–1122.
45 Although Neill, LJ was ably to rely on certain of these cases in reaching his decision in *British Coal.*
46 [1988] 1 WLR 1238.

decision of this court in *British Coal Corporation* v *Dennis Rye Limited (No 2)*."[47]

However, this may be to give the case a wider application than it will bear. The result in *British Coal* appears to have depended on the purpose for which the disclosure was made, namely to assist the police in a criminal investigation, and the public interest in encouraging such assistance. It is not clear that the result would have been the same if this public interest had not existed, and the case may well be limited to its own facts. Certainly, in the absence of any such public interest a party should be well advised of the potential risks involved in waiving his privilege for a specific or limited purpose.

British Coal should be contrasted with the Australian decision in *Goldberg* v *Ng*.[48] Two clients of Mr Goldberg, a solicitor, sued him for damages. As well, they complained to the Law Society of New South Wales, leading the Law Society to ask Mr Goldberg various questions, and to request various documents. The documents were privileged,[49] so Mr Goldberg produced them subject to an express reservation of that privilege and in return for an assurance from the Law Society that their confidentiality would be respected.[50] The Ngs subpoenaed the Law Society for the production of the documents. They argued that in producing them to the Law Society, Goldberg had waived any privilege he had in the documents. The Law Society and Goldberg argued, *inter alia*, that, even if there had been a waiver of privilege, it was a waiver for a limited purpose, and did not affect his right to rely on the documents in the current proceedings. The New South Wales Court of Appeal rejected this argument, and in the process held that *British Coal* was authority only for the proposition that the plaintiff's actions in providing the documents to the prosecuting authorities and complying with the order of the trial judge did not constitute an express or implied waiver of its rights in its own civil litigation. It declined to hold that the case had any wider application, and did not follow *Goldman* v *Hesper*.[51] Instead the court asked whether it was

---

47   *Ibid.*, at 1244.

48   [1994] 33 NSWLR 639.

49   They had been produced by Goldberg in the course of obtaining advice from his own solicitors in connection with his defence of the Ngs' claim.

50   The defendant in *British Coal* appears to have accepted that had the plaintiffs made a reservation of their privilege when making their documents available to the police no question of waiver would have arisen.

51   Clarke, JA noted:

"...*British Coal Corporation* v *Dennis Rye Ltd (No 2)* stands as authority for the proposition that the particular conduct of the plaintiff did not constitute a waiver of the privilege which the plaintiff enjoyed in the relevant documents and simply demonstrates the fact that there is no universal rule that the disclosure of documents produced for the sole purpose of seeking legal advice on litigation to a stranger to that litigation constitutes a waiver of the privilege in that document."

"fair" to allow Goldberg to rely on his privilege after he had disclosed the material to the Law Society, and found that it was not.[52]

Ultimately, in civil litigation, disclosure of privileged information to a third party will always bring with it a risk of challenge by an adversary to the privilege. This is so even though such disclosure might be made on a confidential basis. In such situations, the notion of "fairness" could be employed, as in *Goldberg*,[53] to determine whether the disclosure amounts to a more general waiver. As ever, the result may be pragmatically just, but not entirely logical. The disclosed material remained confidential having regard to the manner in which and terms on which it was shown to the Law Society.[54]

Having regard to these authorities, there must be some uncertainty as to whether, for example, a financial institution could safely disclose privileged information to its regulator in order to assist it with an investigation. As discussed in Chapter 1, financial services regulators tend not to have powers of compulsory disclosure of privileged information, so such disclosure would have to be made voluntarily by the regulated body.[54a] On the authority of the *British Coal* decision, such disclosure could be made without running the risk of losing privilege, provided there was no intention to waive privilege, there was a public interest in the disclosure and the court was prepared to accept an analogy between a criminal investigation by the police and one for example into financial services irregularities by one of the main regulating bodies. Would these arguments succeed? *Goldberg*, assuming the English courts would follow it, in terms of its actual decision, is an authority against. It is submitted that the real issue is the existing

---

52 The Court noted, *e.g.*, that Goldberg was using the documents to his advantage in showing them to the Law Society to counter a complaint by the Ngs, and that had he not done so, he would have been obliged to provide the Law Society with a written statement which would not have been privileged, and so would have been discoverable in the action. Kirby, P delivered a dissenting judgment which did find *British Coal* persuasive authority for the propositions for which Goldberg argued.

53 And see also *R v Uljee* [1982] NZLR 561, discussed at p. 173 above.

54 But see Kirk and Woodcock, *Serious Fraud: Investigation and Trial* (1992) which refers at p. 38 to a ruling by Mackinnon, J in *R v NatWest Investment Bank & Others*, 23 January 1991, in which he held that the release of documents under a limited waiver of privilege to inspectors appointed by the Secretary of State for the Department of Trade & Industry could not be subject to a claim for privilege in criminal proceedings. Mackinnon, J ruled that the waiver to the inspectors could not be limited to the immediate purposes of their inspection under s. 432 Companies Act 1985. The ruling appears to have been based on the fact that the scheme of Part XIV of the Companies Act 1985 entitled the inspectors to pass documents to the Secretary of State who could pass them to the prosecuting authorities.

54a In the limited circumstances under sections 39, 41 and 42 Banking Act 1987 in which the Bank of England can compel production of privileged documents, it cannot be said that there has been a voluntary confidential disclosure entitling the discloser to assert privilege over those documents as against others.

confidentiality in the disclosed materials. Provided the information is supplied on confidential terms and remains confidential to the disclosing party and the recipient, it is submitted the privilege should be maintainable.[55]

Communications with auditors

Solicitors are frequently asked to report in writing to a client's auditors on pending litigation or other liability issues involving the client for the purposes of the statutory audit. Unless the report is covered by legal professional privilege, there arises the risk that the client's adversary could, in litigation in which it is arguably relevant, seek disclosure of the report either from the client or from the auditors pursuant to a subpoena.[56] The mere existence of this risk dictates that the solicitor should take care in the drafting of the report, so as to minimise the chances of damaging information being disclosed.

Is the report privileged? This question has given rise to conflicting views.[57] It is submitted that the report is not privileged, for these reasons:

- First, the report does not qualify under the litigation head since it is called into existence by the extraneous needs of the auditors dictated by the statutory audit process. It is not brought into being for the purposes of the litigation, rather it is written as a consequence of the litigation. Thus it does not satisfy the dominant purpose test. If any authority were needed to support this view, the analysis is, it is submitted, comparable to that adopted in *Jones* v *Great Central Railway*.[58]
- Nor does it qualify, on first blush, under the advice head, since it is not advice given to the auditor as client of the solicitor: the solicitor's client is the entity being audited.

Does the analysis change if the auditor is, in fact, the agent of the client? Strictly, the answer is "no", since unless litigation privilege is available – an option ruled out above – then a privileged communication

---

55   However, there remains the risk that the receiving party could be sub-poenaed for these materials. On the authority of *Schneider* v *Leigh* [1955] 2 QB 195 the recipient could not assert the discloser's privilege. Against this, see *Robert Hitchins Ltd* v *International Computers Ltd* (Unrep.) 10 December 1996. See further Section 7 below.

56   As to whether the auditors would be obliged to comply with a subpoena aimed at material in their possession which would, in their client's hands, be covered by privilege, see the discussion in Section 7 below.

57   See Matthews and Malek, *Discovery* at para. 8.23, which concludes there is no privilege; and Style and Hollander, *Documentary Evidence* (6th Edn.), pp.178–180, which appears to conclude that such reports may be privileged (albeit recognising that "the legal analysis is not free from doubt").

58   [1910] AC 4. The decision is discussed in Chaps. 3 and 4.

to an agent can only be made to him as a medium of communication which clearly, in the case of the auditor, it is not. In this respect, the analogy is closer to the situation in *Price Waterhouse v BCCI*,[57] in that the communication is made to the auditors for their benefit (*i.e.* to enable them to discharge their statutory responsibilities), and not so that they can pass the advice on to their clients.

However, it is unlikely in any case that the statutory auditor stands in the position of a true agent of the client. This question was considered by the Court of Appeal in *Chantrey Martin v Martin*.[60] This decision was concerned with an attempt by a company's accountants to say that their working papers, generated in connection with an audit, were not discoverable as they were the company's property and were only in the possession of the accountants as auditors of the company.[61] The Court of Appeal rejected the argument that the accountants were therefore merely agents of the company, and held that the relationship between auditors and their client is that of client and professional man and not that of principal and agent. In *Chantrey Martin,* the working papers were, in consequence, held to be the plaintiffs' own property.[62]

It is clearly unsatisfactory for there to be a risk that these reports could be discoverable if, as argued, they are not privileged. In most cases, however, it ought to be possible to argue that they are not relevant to the litigation, and so not discloseable. As Style and Hollander put it,[63] statements by lawyers containing their opinion as to the client's prospects of success in litigation are not obviously relevant. However, if the report goes beyond providing a report on the merits of the litigation to setting out the facts on which the lawyer's advice is based, that argument may not be accepted. In *Svenska Handelsbanken v Sun Alliance*,[64] an action between an insured and their insurer, it was argued on an application for the production of, *inter alia*, an opinion on the merits of the action provided by solicitors for the insurers to the reinsurers, that it was irrelevant to the action. The judge refused to accept this argument as it was not clear from

---

59 [1992] BCLC 583.

60 [1953] 2 QB 286.

61 Under the present RSC O24, the papers would now be discoverable by virtue of their being in the accountants' possession, irrespective of ownership. Under the rules prevailing in 1953, namely RSC O31 r. 14, mere physical possession of documents did not make them discoverable.

62 It is of interest to note that the court also rejected the further argument that the working papers should not be disclosed because they: "embodied information which was the subject of professional confidence as between the plaintiffs and the client company and their production, and the consequent disclosure of their contents would be a breach by the plaintiffs of their duty to the client company."

63 See n. 56 above.

64 [1995] 2 Lloyd's Rep 84, discussed in Chap. 6 above.

the affidavit sworn by the insurers's solicitor that the opinion did not deal with the "factual basis upon which the advice was tendered".[65]

The threat of potential disclosure of the solicitor's report prompts the suggestion that this risk could be avoided by addressing the report to the client, and either copying it to the auditor or merely letting him have sight of it. Assuming the auditor would accept such arrangements,[66] what is the analysis?[67] Still the report cannot qualify for litigation privilege (for the reasons suggested above), but it may qualify for advice privilege.[68] If so, does disclosure to the auditor undermine the privilege? No firm answer can be given since the point has yet to be judicially considered. Adopting earlier analysis, the privilege is lost if the confidentiality in the document is lost. However, where there has only been restricted and controlled communication of the document to a specified third party on terms, as between them, that the privilege has not been waived and that the contents remains confidential,[69] it should be possible to argue, albeit with some caution, that the privilege in the information communicated to the auditors has *not* been lost or waived. In this respect, it is suggested that the New Zealand decision, *CC Bottlers Ltd* v *Lion Nathan Ltd*,[70] considered above, supports this analysis.

One alternative solution to the risk, such as it may be, to an auditor being subpoened to produce communications from their client's lawyers which convey privileged information is to consider the applicability of the common interest privilege principles discussed in detail in Chapter 6.[71] Whilst there is no decided authority which yet determines whether common interest privilege could arise, it is evident that the principles discussed in the various cases considered in Chapter 6 could provide protection for both the client and the auditor. As Colman, J commented in *Formica Limited* v *The*

---

65 In the event, the advice was held to be privileged on the basis of common interest privilege.

66 In this respect, the ICAEW has recognised the problem in its October 1995 Audit Faculty Technical Release No. 2/95 entitled: "The Ascertainment and Confirmation of Contingent Liabilities arising from Pending Legal Matters (Handbook statement 3-903)". This suggests that auditors could make file notes of the information they need for audit purposes, rather than receive a solicitor's letter. Arguably, the file note could be sought by service of a subpoena.

67 Obviously, the lack of a copy in his hands remove the threat of his being subpoenaed for a copy, although he could always be required to testify as to its contents. In any case, he is very likely to make a note of what he sees if only to protect his own position, and that note will not be privileged.

68 There must be a risk that a court would hold the arrangements as a device; and that the report is not truly "advice" so as to qualify for privilege.

69 But what if the auditors have to refer to the report, or its contents, in their audit report?

70 [1993] 2 NZLR 445.

71 The author is extremely grateful to Anthony Vernon, legal adviser to Price Waterhouse, for sharing his thoughts on this topic.

Secretary of State Act (acting by the Export Credit's Guarantee Department):

> "The protection by common interest privilege of documents in the hands of someone other than the client must pre-suppose that such third party has a relationship with the client and the transaction in question which, in relation to the advice or other communications, brings that third party within that ambit of confidence which would prevail between a legal adviser and his immediate client".[72]

4. Express waiver: legal proceedings

Privilege can be lost when a qualifying communication is deliberately used during the course of legal proceedings, or as a by-product of taking a particular step in the proceedings which involves the use of privileged materials. However, not every use of privileged material during the course of legal proceedings will result in a loss of privilege. These issues most commonly occur in the following circumstances:

(i)   by inclusion of privileged information in a pleading;
(ii) by inclusion of privileged information in an affidavit;
(iii) by disclosure of privileged information in inter-solicitor correspondence;
(iv) by the inclusion of privileged documents in the wrong part of a list of documents which the opposing party is allowed to inspect;
(v)   by the exchange of witness statements or expert reports;
(vi) by the deployment of privileged information in evidence during a trial or in an interlocutory application.

Pleadings

Where a privileged document is referred to in a pleading, whether or not the privilege has thereby been waived will depend on the extent of the reference, and whether or not the pleading party intends to rely on it at trial or at a hearing. So, a mere reference to a privileged document in a pleading will not usually amount to a waiver of privilege. For, though the opposing party is entitled to seek the production of that document under RSC Order 24 rule 10(1) and (2), it is open to the pleader to object to production under Order 24 rule 11(1)(a). However, a more substantial reference to the

---

72 [1995] 1 Lloyds' Rep 692 at 699.

document, such as an extensive quotation from it, would make it more likely that privilege had been waived.[73]

The issue arose for consideration in *Buttes Gas & Oil Co v Hammer (No 3)*,[74] where an application was made for production of certain privileged documents referred to in Buttes' reply and defence to counterclaim. On the question of waiver, Donaldson, LJ had this to say:

> "It must be right that a bare reference to a document in a pleading does not waive any privilege attaching to it as otherwise there would be no scope for taking objection under R.S.C. Ord. 24 r. 11(1). ... If, on the other hand, a document is reproduced in full in the pleading, its confidentiality is gone and no question of privilege could arise. Where the line is drawn between these two extremes may be a matter of some nicety ...".[75]

If the pleader maintains his reference to a privileged document because he intends to rely on it, then he will have to forego his client's privilege. Otherwise, the pleading should be amended to remove the offending reference. In *Buttes*, Brightman, LJ felt (*obiter*) that if the pleader "sat on the fence" until trial he would risk an adjournment if he disclosed the pleaded documents at that late stage; alternatively, it was open to his opponent to seek to strike out the offending passages.[76]

As will be seen in Section 5 below, raising particular issues (as opposed to privileged documents) in pleadings can give rise to waiver issue: see *Hayes and Rowson v Dowding*.[77]

Affidavits

A reference to a privileged communication in an affidavit will not amount to a waiver unless the reference is to the substance of the communication. In *Government Trading Corporation v Tate & Lyle Industries Ltd*,[78] the advice of an Iranian lawyer was referred to in an affidavit filed in interlocutory proceedings. One of the issues in the action was whether the liabilities of an Iranian company set up under the Shah would have devolved on to a new government-owned entity. The affidavit set out

---

73 In New Zealand, the court's approach is to determine whether the reference in the pleadings is so extensive that it would be unfair to the opponent to allow only selected aspects of the document to be used as evidence in court: per Henry, J in *CC Bottlers v Lion Nathan Ltd* [1993] 2 NZLR 445 at 448, citing *Equiticorp Ind. Group Ltd v Hawkins* [1990] 2 NZLR 175.

74 [1981] QB 223, a case discussed in Chap. 6, Section 3. See also Cotton, LJ in *Roberts v Oppenheim* (1884) 26 Ch D 724.

75 [1981] 1 QB 223 at 252. See also Lord Denning, MR at 246, and Bingham, LJ at 268.

76 *Ibid.*, at 268.

77 Unrep., 28 June 1996.

78 Court of Appeal, unrep., 24 October 1984.

information as to the formation of the new entity, quoted from the law pursuant to which the entity was created, and then identified a firm of Iranian lawyers as the source of the information. The reference was limited to the fact that the lawyer had given advice to a particular effect, and did not set out the substance of the advice or the scope of the instructions given to the lawyer. The Court of Appeal held that there had been no waiver of privilege.

Similarly, in *Marubeni Corporation* v *Alafouzos*,[79] an affidavit sworn on behalf of the plaintiffs contained the paragraph:

> "The plaintiffs have obtained outside Japanese legal advice which categorically states that this agreement does not render performance of the sale contract illegal in any way whatsoever."

It was argued before the Court of Appeal that this was a reference to a document and that the advice should therefore be produced under Order 24 rule 10. Although the Court of Appeal could not agree on this issue it did agree that the reference was not sufficient to waive privilege in respect of the advice given. Both Lawton and Lloyd, LJJ drew attention to the real difference between a reference to the *effect* of a document and a reference to the *contents* of a document, and noted that this case was an example of a reference to the effect of a document, so that privilege was not waived. Lawton, LJ held:

> "All that the deponent was doing was saying: 'Well, I am asking the court to allow service out of the jurisdiction. I am being frank with the court. I have received certain information from Japan and I believe it provides no defence to the defendants.' In other words, he was not relying on the contents of the document: he was relying on the effect of the document. He had to refer to the Japanese lawyers because he was under a duty to give the source of his information and he could only do so by referring to what they had told him."

The distinction between a "mere" reference to privileged information, or a reference to the effects of that information, and a reference to the contents or the substance of the information, can be a difficult one to draw. The Court of Appeal in both cases was influenced by the fact that references must frequently be made in affidavits to privileged advice (as on an application for summary judgment which is supported by affidavit evidence that the deponent has been advised there is no defence to his claim).[80] Similarly, it is obligatory, generally, to set out the sources of any statement of information or belief made in an affidavit, which may necessarily require some reference to privileged information. Where the

---

79 Court of Appeal, unrep., 6 November 1986, CA transcript 996 of 1986.
80 See also *T Bonzel* v *Intervention Ltd (No 2)* [1991] RPC 231.

reference to privileged information goes beyond what is necessary for such purposes, then the greater the risk that the court will hold that there has been a waiver of the privilege.

However, not every reference to the contents of privileged information in an affidavit will result in the waiver of the privilege. This is illustrated by the somewhat unusual facts of *The World Era*.[81] Two parties M and P, who had a common interest in the outcome of an arbitration with a third party, L, which they were conducting through the same solicitors, fell out and sued each other. One party applied ex-parte for an injunction, *inter alia*, restraining the other from interfering with the arbitration. The supporting affidavit exhibited opinions from counsel and solicitors. The action was settled and the two parties began to co-operate once more in the conduct of the arbitration. L, the other side in the arbitration, sought discovery of the opinions exhibited to the affidavit sworn in the injunction proceedings. The court rejected their submission that the documents had been brought into the public domain, thereby waiving any privilege:

> "The affidavit evidence in the ex parte proceedings was not in the public domain and neither [M] nor [P] waived any rights that they had to assert against third parties a claim for privilege in respect of such documents".[82]

The decision was evidently based on the fact that the exhibited opinions had retained their confidentiality as against L, which was a party to the arbitration but not the injunction proceedings. The position would have been otherwise had the affidavit been used in open court or had L been a party to the action who had received the privileged documents.[83]

Inter-solicitor correspondence

Just as the effect of a legal advice is occasionally referred to in affidavits so, perhaps even more frequently, it is referred to in open inter-solicitor

---

81 *Leif Hoegh & Co A/S* v *Petrolsea Inc* [1993] 1 Lloyd's Rep 363, a decision discussed in Chap. 6.

82 Per Phillips, J at 367.

83 See *ITC Film Distributors Ltd* v *Video Exchange Ltd* [1982] Ch 436 discussed in Section 7 below. In *Derby & Co* v *Weldon (No 2) (The Times*, 20 October 1988), Browne-Wilkinson, V-C held that a party's "privacy" in respect of documents or information contained in or exhibited to an affidavit sworn "voluntarily" in support of interlocutory proceedings is voluntarily "destroyed". It does not fall within the scope of the usual implied undertaking so that the receiving party is free to disclose or make use of the information even though it has not been read out or referred to in open court. See also *Lubrizol Corporation* v *Esso Petroleum Co Ltd (No 2)* [1993] FSR 53, *Prudential Assurance* v *Fountain Page* [1991] 1 WLR 756 and *Eagle Star Insurance Co Ltd* v *Arab Bank plc* (unrep., 25 February 1991).

correspondence,[84] as where one side, in the hope that his opponent will back down, frequently asserts the compelling effect of his own researches or of counsel's advice. While there is no authority which canvasses the issue of waiver in respect of such letters, logically it would seem that the court would deal with the issue in line with the principles enunciated above. Nonetheless, the practice carries the risk of challenge, in which case the prudent solicitor will make clear that his references to the effect (as opposed to the contents) of privileged advice given to his client do not amount to a waiver of privilege. It should be noted that an agreement to waive privilege can be revoked before any action is taken on the agreement.[85]

List of documents

Where in High Court proceedings a party includes privileged documents in Part 1 of Schedule I of his list of documents served pursuant to RSC Order 24, *prima facie* the other party has a right to inspect those documents under Order 24, rule 9. It is open to the party serving the list to correct the mistake by serving an amended list, or otherwise notifying the other party of the mistake and giving notice of an intention to claim privilege.[86] However, unless this is corrected before inspection takes place, or steps are taken to invoke the equitable jurisdiction of the court by seeking an injunction for the return of the privileged material and an order preventing their use,[87] the mistake may lead to an irrevocable waiver of privilege. So, in *Re Briamore Manufacturing Ltd,*[88] inspection was given of privileged documents listed in Part 1 of Schedule 1 of the liquidators' list of documents. Before the liquidators' solicitors realised their mistake, the inspecting party was allowed to take notes of the privileged documents and, in one case, to take a photocopy of a document for which privileged could have been claimed. When, subsequently, the liquidators tried to correct the error, the court held that it was too late to do so since the other party was in a position to give secondary evidence of the privileged information. Hoffman, J held that:

> "It would seem to me illogical that having carried out the inspection, but not

---

84 If written on a without prejudice basis, a separate privilege would protect the communication: see Chap. 10. See also n. 6 above.
85 *Goldman* v *Hesper* [1988] 1 WLR 1238.
86 See Slade, LJ in *Guinness Peat* v *Fitzroy Robinson* [1987] 1 WLR 1027 at 1045–1046 and Hoffmann, J in *Minnesota Mining & Manufacturing Co* v *Rennicks (UK) Ltd* [1991] FSR 97.
87 See Section 7 below.
88 [1986] 1 WLR 1429.

gone through the physical process of making copies at the time, [the inspecting solicitor] should now be disentitled from obtaining the best evidence of the documents which he has seen. Accordingly, on this very narrow point, namely, whether the process can be put into reverse between the moment of inspection and the request for copies of the documents inspected, I would respectfully disagree with the registrar and hold that once inspection has taken place it is too late to correct the mistake and that the respondent is entitled to his copies".[89]

It should be noted that Hoffman, J's decision was the first in a series of decisions in the late 1980s on the issue of inadvertent disclosure by solicitors of their clients' privileged documents. Arguably, that decision, though since approved as correct,[90] might well be decided differently under the principles subsequently developed by the courts. These are considered in more detail in Section 7 below.

Witness statements and expert reports

Witness statements remain privileged even after exchange with the opposing party. Privilege over such documents is only lost or waived when the serving party puts them in evidence at trial.[91] In contrast, an expert's report loses its privilege once it is exchanged pursuant to an Order of Court made under RSC Order 38.[92] Note that in *Webster* v *James Chapman & Co (a firm)*[93] it was held, in the circumstances of that case, that where an expert's report was inadvertently sent to the opposing party's solicitors in draft and before formal service under RSC Order 38, the privilege was lost. Scott, J refused to exercise the court's equitable jurisdiction to order its return. The decision has since been criticised and would probably be decided differently in the light of the more recent case law considered in Section 7 below.

Production in evidence

The use of a privileged document in evidence whether at trial or in interlocutory proceedings[94] will result in a waiver of privilege. So, Stirling, J noted in *Goldstone* v *Williams, Deacon & Co*[95] that privileged depositions

---

89 *Ibid.*, at 1432.
90 See Slade, LJ in *Guinness Peat* v *Fitzroy Robinson* [1987] 1 WLR 1027 at 1045–1046.
91 See *Prudential Assurance Co* v *Fountain Page Ltd* [1991] 1 WLR 756.
92 See generally, Chap. 3, Section 8.
93 [1989] 3 All ER 939.
94 See, *e.g., Re Konigsberg (a bankrupt)* [1989] 3 All ER 289 and *ITC Film Distributors Ltd* v *Video Exchange Ltd* [1982] Ch 436. Against this, note *Def American* v *Phonogram Ltd* (unrep., 29 July 1994), discussed in Section 7 below.
95 [1899] 1 Ch 47.

obtained before an examiner are frequently produced in open court, whereupon their privilege is taken to have been waived. In the case before him the proceedings were compromised before the depositions had become part of the record: accordingly, since the document had never effectually been made public, the use made of it did not amount to a waiver of privilege.

However, not every privileged document produced in court proceedings loses its privilege. In *Minnesota Mining & Manufacturing Co v Rennicks (UK) Ltd*,[96] Hoffman, J held that answers to certain interrogatories,[97] administered in proceedings before the International Trade Commission in Washington, did not lose their privilege by their use in those proceedings. This was because they were subject in the US proceedings to a protective order, whereby their circulation was limited within the proceedings themselves and could not after the proceedings be disclosed to anyone without the consent of both parties.[98]

Further, a party can seek the Court's assistance so as to prevent a loss of his privilege arising from the use of privileged documents in Court proceedings. So, in *T Bonzel v Intervention Ltd (No 2)*,[99] Bonzel applied to amend its patent. In doing so, it filed affidavit evidence which referred to privileged information. Bonzel did not wish to waive its privilege for fear that the privileged information would be used against it in proceedings in other jurisdictions.[1] Bonzel were first granted an order by Hoffman, J[2] under RSC Order 24 rule 14A restraining the defendants from making any use of the affidavit or its exhibits, or any information contained in it, in any proceedings in any jurisdiction other than England and Wales. The order was expressed to last until the plaintiffs read and relied on the affidavit in court. Bonzel therefore applied for an order that the affidavit be referred to in camera, so as to avoid the loss of the privilege by having it made public. Aldous, J held that it was in the public interest that patentees should not be deterred from disclosing the full position in relation to their patents, and granted the order sought. This decision also illustrates a more general point, namely that loss of the privilege by production in one set of proceedings is likely[3] to result in waiver for the purposes of proceedings in other jurisdictions:

---

96 [1991] FSR 97.

97 Which he held were privileged since they were called into existence for the purpose of US litigation. With respect, this seems a questionable basis for the privilege since they came into existence pursuant to Court order.

98 See also *The Lubrizol Corp v Esso Petroleum Company Ltd (No 2)* [1993] RPC 53.

99 [1991] RPC 231.

1' They were involved in litigation relating to equivalent patents in both the USA and Germany.

2' This decision was followed in *Lubrizol*, n. 98 above.

3' Though, ultimately, this will depend on the *lex fori*.

"...if they are referred to, then the privilege can be lost both in this country and in other jurisdictions. Furthermore, in the United States reference to one document in open court can mean that the privilege is lost in respect of other documents of the same class, even though they are not referred to in this country".[4]

Making use of privileged information during a trial, for example by introducing it in oral evidence either in examination in chief or in cross-examination, or by counsel reading it in opening or closing speeches, will result in the loss of the privilege. The waiver will occur irrespective of whether the parties or their legal advisers intended to waive the privilege. The decision in *Great Atlantic Insurance* v *Home Insurance*[5] discussed in Section 2 above, is an example of an unintentional waiver, while *General Accident Corporation* v *Tanter*,[6] discussed below, is an example of a deliberate waiver.

In *Banque Keyser Ullman SA* v *Skandia (UK) Insurance Company*[7] an important issue was the identity of the person referred to in a manuscript note made by one of the witnesses for the defendants. At trial, the witness gave two conflicting explanations of the note. Under cross-examination, he referred to the fact that in a (privileged) statement given to the solicitors for the defendants he had given an explanation consistent with his second explanation to the court. The trial was adjourned and he was given the opportunity to check his witness statement. On re-examination, he was asked whether he had done so, on what date the statement was made and who he had identified in that statement. The court held that this had introduced part of the statement into the evidence, thereby waiving privilege in respect of the whole document. Kerr, LJ said:

"Once the contents of a document, whether it be a witness's proof or some other document for which privilege can properly be claimed, are referred to as such as the result of counsel's questions and conduct of the case, in order to have some effect upon the oral evidence which has been given – whether to support or challenge what a witness may have said in evidence – then the whole of the document becomes admissible, because the waiver of privilege resulting from the introduction of the document into the witness's testimony applies to the whole document and not merely to one or more selected parts of it".[8]

As with affidavits, the Courts will draw a distinction between referring

4' [1991] RPC 231 at 237.
5' [1981] 1 WLR 529.
6' [1984] 1 WLR 100.
7' [1986] 1 Lloyd's Rep. 336.
8' See also *Burnell* v *British Transport Commission* [1956] 1 QB 187 and, generally, Section 8 below.

in evidence to the effect of legal advice received, and referring to the actual advice tendered. In *R v Condron*[9] Stuart-Smith, LJ observed that if an accused person gives as a reason for not answering questions that he has been advised by his solicitor not to do so, the mere reference to that advice does not amount to a waiver of privilege. However, since the accused would have to state the reasons for that advice to avoid any adverse inference being drawn from his silence under section 35 Criminal Justice and Public Order Act 1994, so doing "may well amount to a waiver of privilege, so that the accused, or if his solicitor is also called, the solicitor, can be asked whether there were any other reasons for the advice and the nature of the advice given, so as to explore whether the advice may also have been given for tactical reasons".[10]

5. IMPLIED WAIVER: PROCEEDINGS BY CLIENT AGAINST SOLICITOR

A client who brings civil proceedings against his solicitor impliedly waives privilege in respect of all matters which are relevant to the claim he pursues.[11] The waiver will extend to all matters relevant both to the cause of action brought by the plaintiff, such as the issue of the solicitor's negligence, and to any defence the solicitor may have such as questions of causation of loss. A claim brought by the client against his solicitor which relates only to one retainer may also result in matters relevant to other retainers, whether or not with the same solicitors, also becoming relevant to the issues raised in the action, in which case the waiver of privilege will extend to those other retainers. These principles have now been extended so that waiver in these situations can occur in respect of retainers with solicitors who are not a party to the client's action. In summary, the danger of waiver now exists whenever the client decides to plead issues which provoke necessary enquiry into privileged communications with his solicitors past and present.

In *Lillicrap v Nalder (a firm)*,[12] the plaintiffs sued their solicitors for negligence arising out of a conveyancing matter, alleging that they had failed to advise their clients as to the lack of a right of way to part of the property purchased. The solicitors had acted for the clients on a number of similar transactions. They conceded they had acted negligently but

---

9[1] [1997] 1 WLR 827.
10[1] Transcript of judgment, pp. 22–23.
11[1] *Lillicrap v Nalder (a firm)* [1993] 1 WLR 94, per Russell, LJ at 101.
12[1] [1993] 1 WLR 94.

defended the claim on the basis that even if the clients had been properly advised they would have proceeded with the transaction. They applied to amend their defence to refer to six earlier transactions in which the clients had proceeded with conveyancing transactions despite being advised by the solicitors of the risks or that the timescale required did not leave sufficient time to make proper enquiries. The plaintiffs applied for the return of their papers, an application which May, J granted. Although the Court of Appeal allowed the solicitors' appeal, Dillon, LJ approved May, J's formulation of the scope of the implied waiver:

> "A client who sues his solicitor invites the court to adjudicate the dispute and thereby ... waives privilege and confidence to the extent that it is necessary to enable the court to do so fully and fairly in accordance with the law ...".[13]

However, there are limitations. There is:

> "... no waiver for a roving search into anything else in which the solicitor or any other solicitor may have happened to have acted for the clients. But the waiver must go far enough not merely to entitle the plaintiff to establish his cause of action, but to enable the defendant to establish a defence to the cause of action if he has one".[14]

In *Lillicrap,* the court held the solicitors were entitled to rely on the earlier transactions in their amended defence (though the court expressly left to the trial judge issues as to the relevance of the evidence sought to be adduced).

In *Kershaw* v *Whelan*[15] the implied waiver was taken a step further when Ebsworth, J held that files of the plaintiff's former solicitors then in the hands of his current solicitors were subject to the implied waiver and so discoverable in his action against a further firm of solicitors. The action arose out of the distribution of part of the plaintiff's father's estate which occurred on the advice of the defendant solicitors given in a letter written in 1979. The plaintiff commenced several abortive actions in the 1980s through various firms of solicitors. He then sued the defendant in respect of the 1979 letter. The defendant denied he ever acted for the plaintiff and claimed the action was statute barred; whereupon the plaintiff relied on section 32(1)(b) Limitation Act 1980 and advanced a plea of deliberate concealment of the 1979 letter.

13' *Ibid.,* at 99.

14' *Ibid.,* at 99.

15' [1996] 1 WLR 358.

16' *Ibid.,* at 370. It should not, it is submitted, be crucial to this decision that the present solicitors physically held the previous solicitors' files. If the latter still possessed them, they would still be discoverable by the plaintiff.

To meet this, the defendant sought discovery of privileged documents (including advices) in the files of the plaintiff's solicitors who acted in earlier and separate proceedings relating to the father's estate, with the aim of showing the plaintiff in fact knew of the 1979 letter. Ebsworth, J granted the application. The plea of deliberate concealment had the effect of waiving the plaintiff's privilege in respect of such documents as went to that issue. Noting that in *Lillicrap* the material was held in files of the same solicitors in respect of discrete transactions, Ebsworth, J could see "no difference in principle where his present solicitors hold files of the clients' earlier solicitors in relation to discrete but essentially related factual matters".[16]

The implied waiver principles were further extended by Jonathan Parker, J's decision in *Hayes and Rowson v Dowding*.[17] Of particular interest was his interpretation of the *Lillicrap* decision as authority for the proposition that:

> "... it is not a necessary condition of an implied waiver of privilege by a plaintiff that the privilege should arise out of the professional relationship between the plaintiff and the defendant... the principles expressed by the Court of Appeal in [*Lillicrap*] are applicable to privileged communications between a plaintiff and a third party".[17]

So it is not essential that the plaintiff sues his solicitor before the implied waiver comes into operation. In *Hayes* two shareholders sued a third for having fraudulently induced them to compromise an earlier action between them. The defendant denied these charges and alleged that in any case the settlement arose from his acceptance of an open offer made on the plaintiffs' behalf by their former solicitors. The defendant followed this pleading up by seeking discovery of documentation relating to the solicitors' authority and their instructions to compromise the earlier action.

Holding that the issue of inducement had been "pleaded into relevance",[19] the judge held that by:

> "inviting the court to adjudicate on, inter alia, the inducement issue, the plaintiffs... must be taken to have waived privilege in such documentary material as is relevant to the determination of that issue.".

Whilst one can appreciate Jonathan Parker, J's reasoning, it does render

---

17' Unrep., 28 June 1996.

18' Transcript, p.17. One of the justifications given for this view was that "the Court must have access to all the evidential material which is required to enable it to do [justice] fully and fairly".

19' A phrase used by Henry, J in *Data Access Corp v Powerflex*, cited by Derrington, J in *Waldrope v Dunne* [1996] 1 Queensland Reports 224.

a little uncertain the decision in NRG v *Bacon Woodrow*.[20] Colman, J's decision in this case was to the effect that a client's action against his non-legal professional advisers did not involve a waiver of privilege over any evidentially relevant communications between the client and his lawyers to which the defendants wanted access for the purposes of their defence. Colman, J expressly refused to follow the American decision in *Hearn* v *Rhay*[21] which, in his view, necessitated that waiver of privilege would operate where it could be established that privileged communications were likely to be evidentially relevant to an issue and it would be unfair for a defendant not to have access to them. Jonathan Parker J's decision appears to take the opposite view, albeit it adopts the test of "pleaded into relevance", as opposed to "evidential relevance". The distinction between them, it is submitted, is that in *NRG* it was merely desirable that the defendants had access to the privileged materials; whereas in *Hayes* they had actually been "pleaded" into relevance by the beneficiary of the privilege.

This distinction was recognised in *X Corporation Limited* v *Y (a firm)*[21a] in which Moore-Bick, J held that:

> "... the principle underlying all these decisions is that if a Plaintiff himself invites the Court to examine the relationship which gives rise to the privilege he cannot at the same time insist on withholding from disclosure documents which are relevant to that relationship since it would be unfair for him to be allowed to do so and thereby present a partial picture to the Court ... `where a party himself puts the confidential relationship between himself and his lawyer in issue he will waive privilege in respect of documents passing between them which are relevant to the issue in the proceedings."

Extent of implied waiver

One related issue on which there is, as yet, no authority, is the extent of the waiver in terms of the parties who are entitled to discovery of the privileged materials. Suppose that, in the *NRG* case, the plaintiffs had sued their solicitors as well as their other professional advisers. Would the non-legal advisers have been entitled to discovery of privileged materials in relation to which the implied waiver rule came into operation as a result of the claim against the solicitors? If those materials were relevant to an issue pleaded into relevance as against the non-legal advisers, then *Hayes* would be an authority in their favour. But supposing the pleadings did not assist in this way. Would the non-lawyers be entitled, from the stand-point of co-

---

20[1] [1995] 1 All ER 976, discussed in Section 3 above.
21[1] (1975) 68 FRD 574.
21a (Unrep.) 16 May 1997. The facts of the decision are discussed in Section 6 below.

defendants in the action, to the materials in relation to which, as between the plaintiffs and the defendant lawyers, privilege is waived pursuant to the principles enunciated in *Lillicrap?* Or would privilege be waived selectively, that is, as against the lawyers only? It is submitted that, once the privilege is waived, then there can be no justification for holding that it is still maintainable as against other defendants in relation to whom the evidence is relevant. As May, J pointed out in *Lillicrap,* in a passage approved by Dillon, LJ in the Court of Appeal,[22] the bringing of a claim in relation to a particular retainer will normally be a waiver of privilege and confidence. There is no obvious justification for restricting the waiver to the claim as between plaintiffs and solicitors.

Wasted costs and client fraud

The implied waiver will only arise where the client sues his solicitor,[23] or otherwise pleads privileged material into relevance in an action against a third party. A lawyer faced with an application for a wasted costs order made under RSC Order 62 rule 11 and section 51(6) Supreme Court Act 1981 cannot, in defending himself, make use of privileged materials without his client's consent. This seems a little inconsistent with the line of decisions beginning with *Lillicrap v Nalder* discussed above, but possibly is a consequence of the wasted costs application being made not as a consequence of an act by the client,[24] but one on the part of the lawyer. In view of this restriction, the Court of Appeal in *Ridehalgh v Horsefield and Isherwood*[25] noted the "grave disadvantage" which "this potential source of injustice" could cause respondent lawyers. Judges have therefore to make full allowance for a lawyer's inability to tell the whole story[26] in trying to resist such an application.

The position in relation to wasted costs would appear to suggest that lawyers cannot use privileged materials to defend themselves in other contexts where the charge or complaint is not brought at the instance of the client, for example disciplinary proceedings.[27]

22' [1993] 1 WLR 94 at 99.

23' Though presumably a client who tries to sue an expert witness for negligence will similarly be taken to have waived any privilege. See also *Schneider v Leigh* [1955] 2 QB 195, considered in Section 2 above.

24' See generally Toulson and Phipps, *Confidentiality,* Chap. XVII.

25' [1994] Ch 205 at 237: the leading authority on wasted costs.

26' See also *Orchard v South Eastern Electricity Board* [1987] QB 565. Sir Richard Scott, V-C's decision in *Walter v Neville Eckley & Co* (unrep., 10 October 1996) is a rare example of the client waiving his privilege.

27' See Toulson and Phipps, *Confidence,* at p. 190 where the authors point out that Law Society guidance on this subject (at p. 333 of the 1996 *Guide to Professional Conduct*) on the use of confidential information to establish a defence overlooks the issue of privilege.

However, the solicitor can "tear aside" the client's privilege where he suspects the client of fraud. In *Finers v Miro*,[28] London solicitors were engaged to set up a series of companies and trusts to hold substantial client assets which were ultimately in the solicitors' control through the companies and trusts. Suspecting that the assets were the proceeds of the defendants' fraud, they applied to the court for directions. The Court of Appeal held that the solicitors could disclose details of the suspected fraud to the victim to enable him to decide whether to claim the assets. As to the issue that it was the client's own solicitor, and not a hostile third party, who wished to breach the client's privilege, Dillon, LJ said:

> "... the privilege does not require the court to compel the solicitor to continue, at his own personal risk, to aid and abet the apparently fraudulent ends of the defendant in covering up the original fraud of which there is such a prima facie case".[29]

The decision is no doubt justified on the basis that this was a clear case in which the crime/fraud exception would come into play,[30] the court concluding that there was a probability that the solicitors were unwittingly stifling a fraud. Other cases are likely to be less clear, with the result that there could be dangers here for the lawyer who makes a wrong judgment call as to the applicability of the exception. The safest course of action in such situations is to seek directions as Finers did.

6. LIMITATION ISSUES AND SETTLEMENTS

The Court of Appeal has held that pleading certain types of limitation issues can waive privilege to a limited extent. So, by section 2D Limitation Act 1939, as amended by the Limitation Act 1975, the court may allow an action to proceed notwithstanding the fact that the relevant limitation period has expired if "it appears to the court that it would be equitable" to do so. In deciding this question, the court is directed to have regard to all the circumstances of the case and in particular to:

> "The steps, if any, taken by the plaintiff to obtain medical, legal or other expert advice and the nature of any such advice he may have received".

The effect of this provision was examined in *Jones v G.D. Searle & Co.*[31] The defendants were manufacturers of a contraceptive taken by the

28' [1991] 1 WLR 35.
29' *Ibid.*, at 41.
30' See Chap. 8.
31' [1979] 1 WLR 101.

plaintiff between 1966 and 1969, which the plaintiff alleged had caused her to develop venous thrombosis in her leg in 1969. She commenced proceedings for negligence in June 1976. Since this was well outside the limitation period, reliance was placed on section 2D. In response, the defendants served a number of interrogatories on the plaintiff. Two of these asked whether she had received legal advice from counsel before the issue of proceedings, when the advice had been given and whether junior or leading counsel had been consulted. The defendants then asked whether the advice received was favourable or unfavourable to the plaintiff's prospects of success in an action against the defendants. The plaintiff refused to answer on the grounds that to do so would infringe her legal professional privilege.

The Court of Appeal accepted that in the ordinary case the rules relating to privilege meant that a party to litigation could not be made to answer an interrogatory directed to finding out the nature of any legal advice previously given. However, section 2D Limitation Act 1939 required the court to have regard to the nature of any legal or medical advice received by the plaintiff. Roskill, LJ noted[32] that when the court has regard to the nature of the legal advice:

> "...it has to consider its characteristics in so far as they bear upon the question whether or not the plaintiff has been guilty of unreasonable delay once he or she became aware of the information which might give rise to a cause of action against the defendant."

He refused to define what was meant by the "nature of the advice" with any greater precision, noting that it would depend on the facts of each case. He held that it was right that the plaintiff should be required to state generally the nature of the advice received. However, Roskill, LJ expressly left open the question whether section 2D of the Limitation Act 1939 could oblige the plaintiff to give discovery of the opinions which had been given by counsel. Eveleigh, LJ noted in the same decision that the "court must be in a position to demand evidence as to what the nature of the advice was",[33] but it is not clear whether this would require a plaintiff ultimately to produce the advice, even to just the Court alone.

However, the *Supreme Court Practice* (1997)[34] asserts that the decision in *Jones* supports the proposition that:

> "Legal professional privilege does not protect from production documents by which legal advice is sought or given, if the question whether, and in what

32' At 105.
33' At 106.
34' At para. 24/5/6.

terms, advice was sought, and the nature of such advice, are themselves material facts, as, e.g. upon an application under the Limitation Act 1936, section 2D, as added by the Limitation Act 1975 (see now 1980 Act)".

This possibly goes too far, for the Court of Appeal in *Jones* expressed concern at the encroachment on legal professional privilege, and decided that the interrogatories must be answered only because of the particular wording of the Act in question. The Court did not decide that the opinions referred to in the interrogatories were no longer protected by legal professional privilege. Accordingly, *Jones* itself is not authority for the proposition that where legal advice received is itself a material fact in the proceedings, legal professional privilege can no longer be claimed in respect of that advice. However, this may now be an arguable proposition having regard to the cases cited in Section 5 above.

Pleading Settlements

Two later cases which have examined the proposition quoted from the *Supreme Court Practice* (1997) above are the *Society of Lloyd's* v *Kitsons Environmental Services Ltd (and Others)*[35] and *DSL Group Ltd* v *Unisys International Services Ltd*.[36] Both were concerned with the discovery implications for privileged documents in litigation where an earlier settlement was in issue. *Lloyd's* v *Kitsons* resulted from the construction of the Lloyd's building. Lloyds incurred substantial liability to the main contractors working on the project for the additional expense and time taken in completing it. Lloyd's settled this liability, and then sued the defendants (specialist asbestos removers, architects and engineers on the project) in respect of their loss. The statement of claim included the assertion that the settlement was reasonable. This was denied by the defendants, who claimed to be entitled to inspect documents relating to the reasonableness or otherwise of the settlement, including any of the plaintiff's internal memoranda which explained the rationale behind the settlement, as well as the views of their experts and any letters of advice from solicitors and counsel. The judge, Richard Havery QC, suggested that it was plain from the reasoning of the Court of Appeal in *Jones* v *Searle:*

> "...that a plaintiff whose claim for damages involves proof of the existence and nature of legal or ...technical advice he has received loses his privilege in relation to the relevant documents".

Since the plaintiffs' pleadings allowed them to support their case by reference to the advice they had received in respect of the settlement, this

35' (1994) 67 BLR 102.
36' (1994) 67 BLR 117.

was an admission that the existence, terms and nature of the advice was a material fact. This "admission" was, the judge held, a waiver of privilege in relation to the documents in question, and the plaintiffs were ordered to give further discovery. This decision is perhaps surprising since the Court in *Jones* v *Searle* only took away "a well-established privilege" because it saw a "positive indication that the legislature so intended".[37]

However, when the same question was examined in *DSL Group* v *Unisys International Services Ltd* a contrary decision was reached. Again the plaintiff was seeking to claim from the defendant the amount which had been paid out in settlement to a third party. The defendants applied for discovery of correspondence between the plaintiffs and their solicitors in relation to the settlement and other, clearly privileged, material and they relied on *Lloyd's* v *Kitson*. Judge Hicks, QC was unwilling to proceed on the basis of there being a general ground for the loss of privilege. Instead, he noted that the converse of the rule stated by Judge Havery was that:

> "If the plaintiff's claim does not require proof of the existence and nature of any legal advice received the privilege is not lost by reason of any general principle; any claim to override [the privilege] must be brought within a specific recognised category."

He examined whether the facts required the proof of the legal advice received.

A review of the authorities on the relevance of a settlement with a third party to the issue of damages[38] led him to conclude that where a defendant was liable for the cost to the plaintiff of meeting a claim by a third party settled by the plaintiff, the plaintiff can recover as damages the amount paid out under the settlement on showing that the settlement was a reasonable one – not by showing that he acted reasonably. In consequence the question what advice the plaintiff acted on in entering into the settlement was irrelevant. At most the fact that the plaintiff acted under advice might be relevant, but Judge Hicks held that there should be no enquiry into the content of that advice, and declined to make the order requested by the defendant.[39]

Moore-Bick, J reached a similar conclusion in *X Corporation Ltd* v *Y (a firm)*,[39a] although it is not apparent from the transcript of his decision that

---

37['] Per Eveleigh, LJ [1979] 1 WLR 101 at 106.
38['] Notably *Biggin & Co Ltd* v *Permanite Ltd* [1951] 2 KB 314.
39['] [1979] (1) SA (CPD) 637. A similar result was reached in the South African decision in *Euroshipping Corp. of Monrovia* v *Minister of Agriculture* [1979] (1) SA (CPD) 637. Friedmann, J held that to plead that a settlement was a reasonable one, so as to make this an issue in the case, neither expressly nor impliedly waives privilege attaching to documents relating to the settled claim.
39a (Unrep.) 16 May 1997.

either the *Lloyd's* or *DSL* decisions were cited to him. Here, the plaintiff sued its former solicitors for negligence and included in their claim for damages the costs which they incurred by bringing legal proceedings in a number of countries by means of which they attempted, unsuccessfully, to recoup (or mitigate) their losses.

In their points of claim, the plaintiffs expressly alleged that they commenced and prosecuted the various proceedings "acting reasonably in mitigating [their] losses". They produced for inspection the court documents generated in the course of the different actions and the inter partes correspondence, but not the correspondence and documents passing between themselves, their English solicitors and the foreign lawyers whom they instructed. The defendants challenged their claim for privilege over the latter category of documents. They argued that it was relevant to examine the advice the plaintiffs received concerning their prospects of success in the various proceedings. Only then could the court determine whether they acted reasonably in taking the steps they did. Despite an initial attraction to this argument, Moore-Bick, J dismissed the defendants' application:

> "Although the plaintiff's conduct is to be judged by reference to the circumstances as they presented themselves...at the time, the test in my view is essentially an objective one and does not depend on the advice which the plaintiff was receiving from his lawyers".[39b]

Moore-Bick, J also held that the line of decisions beginning with *Lillicrap* v *Nalder & Sons* [1993] 1 WLR 94 (discussed in Section 5 above) similarly did not assist the defendants' challenge to the plaintiff's claim of privilege. The judge held that if the reasonableness of the plaintiffs' conduct in bringing proceedings fell to be judged simply by reference to their own assessment of the position rather than by objective standards, it would be of great importance to know what advice they had received from their lawyers in connection with those proceedings. However, the judge held that that was not the correct approach so that the test of whether the plaintiffs had acted reasonably was an objective one in relation to which their lawyers' advice was not relevant.

39b Transcript, at Page 7. The Judge went on to observe that "the plaintiff ought to be entitled to recover the cost of taking steps which can in fact be shown to have been reasonable, even though his advisers had advised him to the contrary. In my judgment, although the burden of showing that he acted reasonably in mitigation may not be an unduly onerous one, it is for the plaintiff ... to put before the Court sufficient evidence to show that the steps he took were reasonable in the circumstances."

7. REASSERTING PRIVILEGE AFTER INADVERTENT DISCLOSURE

The general rule discussed above is that if privileged information is disclosed to a third party, including an adversary, in circumstances where that information can no longer be said to be confidential, then the privilege is lost. But on occasions the loss of confidentiality is unintended – perhaps the result of a mistake by a legal adviser, or a trick by the adversary or his agents – in which case injunctive relief can be granted to restrain the use of the information by a third party. In such cases, it is not the privilege which entitles the applicant to this relief, for this is a mere evidential rule; rather, it is the court's equitable jurisdiction to restrain the publication of confidential information improperly obtained or otherwise wrongly divulged which comes to the aid of the privilege.

This area of the law has been bedevilled by two apparently conflicting Court of Appeal decisions in *Calcraft* v *Guest*[40] and *Ashburton* v *Pape*[41] which have to be examined in this context, not least because subsequent decisions have spent much time trying to rationalise them. In summary, whilst not consistently applying the usual principles relating to the unauthorised use of confidential information,[42] the position which the law has now reached is that, in most cases, the following conditions need to be satisfied in order to restrain the use of privileged (and therefore confidential) information which has got into the hands of third parties:

- the disclosure must have been inadvertent, in the sense that there was no intention to waive privilege, and either was procured through fraud or was the result of an obvious mistake; and
- the application is made to recover the privileged information before it is deployed in evidence at trial.[43]

What these principles do not deal with is the *Schneider* v *Leigh* scenario discussed in Section 3 above. This will be considered separately below.

Calcraft v *Guest* and *Ashburton* v *Pape*

These decisions are examples of "two independent and free-standing principles of jurisprudence".[44] The former case was concerned with

---

40[1] [1898] 1 QB 759.
41[1] [1913] 2 Ch 469.
42[1] As to this, see Toulson and Phipps, *Confidentiality*, Chap. XX, which also contains an exhaustive discussion of *Calcraft* v *Guest*, *Ashburton* v *Pape* and subsequent decisions.
43[1] The position in relation to interlocutory proceedings is discussed below.
44[1] Per Scott, J in *Webster* v *James Chapman & Co* [1989] All ER 939 at 943.

privileged documents and the scope of the protection provided by legal privilege. The latter case was concerned with confidential documents and the protection that equity will provide to such documents. The consequence of the decision in *Calcraft v Guest* is that, *prima facie*, a party who obtains another's privileged document, or a copy of it, can deploy it in evidence against the original beneficiary of the privilege, whose privilege is thereby effectively lost. This is so whether the receiving party steals such a document,[45] sees it (so that he can give secondary evidence of it[46]), is inadvertently given a copy of a privileged document by the beneficiary's solicitor,[47] overhears a privileged conversation[48] or where, as in *Calcraft v Guest*, the document comes into another party's hands by accident.

The facts of *Calcraft v Guest* were that the defendant had obtained copies of privileged documents prepared for litigation a hundred years earlier on behalf of the plaintiff's predecessor in title. The predecessor's solicitor's descendent – also a solicitor – allowed the defendant to take copies (for they were relevant to the subsequent action) before returning the originals to the plaintiff. The Court of Appeal held that the originals were still privileged under the "once privileged always privileged" rules,[49] despite their disclosure to the defendant, but that the defendant was not precluded from giving secondary evidence of them in the form of the copies he had been – wrongfully – allowed to take. The Court followed *Lloyd v Mostyn*[50] where Parke, B had said:

> "Where an attorney intrusted confidentially with a document communicates the contents of it, or suffers another to take a copy, surely the secondary evidence so obtained may be produced. Suppose the instrument were even stolen, and a correct copy taken, would it not be reasonable to admit it?"

Fortunately, the effect of *Calcraft v Guest* has been greatly alleviated by the second principle described above which depends on a line of authority which begins with *Lord Ashburton v Pape*.[51] This case arose out of bankruptcy proceedings in which copies of letters written by the plaintiff to his solicitor were obtained by the defendant through the collusion of a clerk to the plaintiff's solicitors. The plaintiff started separate proceedings

---

45' *Lloyd v Mostyn* (1842) 10 M & W 478, and see *ITC Film Distributors Ltd v Video Exchange Ltd* [1982] Ch 436.

46' As in *Mills v Oddy* (1834) 6 C & P 728.

47' *Butler v Board of Trade* [1971] Ch 680.

48' See *e.g. Cleave v Jones* (1852) 21 LJ Ex 105 and also cases cited by Heydon, "Legal Professional Privilege and Third Parties", (1974) MLR 601. But see *R v Uljee* [1982] 1 NZLR 561.

49' See Chap. 6.

50' (1842) 10 M&W 478. This decision is critically analysed in *R v Uljee* [1982] 1 NZLR 561.

51' [1913] 2 Ch 469.

for their return. The defendant was prepared to return the original documents, but argued that he should be permitted to keep the copies which had been made so that he could use them as secondary evidence of the privileged information in the bankruptcy proceedings. The Court of Appeal rejected this argument.[52] It distinguished *Calcraft v Guest* by noting that it simply referred to the rule of evidence that secondary evidence can be given of privileged information regardless of how that evidence was obtained. Thus Cozens-Hardy, MR[53] said:

> "The rule of evidence as explained in *Calcraft v Guest* ... merely amounts to this, that if a litigant wants to prove a particular document which by reason of privilege or some circumstance he cannot furnish by the production of the original, he may produce a copy as secondary evidence although that copy has been obtained by improper means, and even, it may be, by criminal means. The Court in such an action is not really trying the circumstances under which the document was produced ... that does not seem to me to have any bearing upon a case where the whole subject-matter of the action is the right to retain the originals or copies of certain documents which are privileged".[54]

Thus, so long as application is made to restrain the use of privileged materials before they are deployed in evidence by the adversary, so that the court *is* seised of the circumstances by which the adversary came to obtain them, then the harsh effects of *Calcraft v Guest* are avoided. The basis of the court's jurisdiction to intervene in such cases was explained by Swinfen Eady, LJ who noted that:

> "The principle upon which the Court of Chancery has acted for many years has been to restrain the publication of confidential information improperly or surreptitiously obtained or of information imparted in confidence which ought not to be divulged...".[55]

In reality, the litigation process will usually alert one party to the fact that an opponent has gained access to his privileged materials before they are deployed in evidence against him. Provided he acts in timely fashion to prevent such use, by seeking an *Ashburton v Pape* injunction, his privilege will be preserved. This suggests that in practice the production of

---

52' Though at first instance Neville, J was prepared to allow the defendant to use copies in the bankruptcy proceedings.

53' Much is made of the fact that the Master of the Rolls was the successful leading counsel in *Calcraft* who cannot have intended to undermine that decision. The apparent conflict between the two decisions is not helped by textual differences in the various reports of this decision: see Tapper, "Privilege and Confidence", (1972) MLR 83. See also the New Zealand Court of Appeal's critical examination of the basis of the Court's reasoning in *Calcraft* in *R v Uljee* [1982] 1 NZLR 561.

54' [1913] 2 Ch. 469 at 473.

55' *Ibid*, at 475–476.

secondary evidence of privileged material is only likely to occur in cases where the privilege does not belong to one of the parties to the litigation.[56] However, the courts have taken some time to work out this position, as they have strived to reconcile the decisions in *Calcraft* v *Guest* and *Ashburton* v *Pape*. In general, the approach taken in *Ashburton* v *Pape* has been preferred, while there have been calls for the House of Lords to overrule *Calcraft* v *Guest*.[57]

Subsequent authorities

In *Goddard* v *Nationwide Building Society*,[58] the same solicitors acted for both parties in respect of a mortgage transaction. A privileged document (an attendance note of conversations between the plaintiffs and their solicitors) was supplied to the defendants by the solicitors. The plaintiffs sought its return. The leading judgment was given by May, LJ who considered that *Calcraft* v *Guest* and *Ashburton* v *Pape* were authority for the following propositions:

> "If a litigant has in his possession copies of documents to which legal professional privilege attaches he may nevertheless use such copies as secondary evidence in his litigation: however, if he has not yet used the documents in that way, the mere fact that he intends to do so is no answer to a claim against him by the person in whom the privilege is vested for delivery up of the copies or to restrain him from disclosing or making use of any information contained in them".[59]

Accordingly, the court granted the relief sought by the plaintiffs.

The same approach was followed in *English and American Insurance Company* v *Herbert Smith*[59] where because of an error by counsel's clerk the papers for one party in the action were delivered to the other party's solicitor. Herbert Smith realised when the bundles were opened that they contained privileged information which they had received by mistake. They read the papers (on their client's instructions) and made notes of them before returning them to the other side, who promptly issued an *Ashburton* v *Pape* application for relief. Browne-Wilkinson, V-C noted that:

> "The position therefore depends, following the decision in the *Nationwide* case, on whether proceedings [to recover the privileged information] are taken before the information is tendered in evidence or not".[60]

56['] See the discussion on this below.
57['] See for example, Browne-Wilkinson, V-C in *English & American Insurance Co Ltd* v *Herbert Smith* [1988] FSR 232.
58['] [1987] QB 670.
59['] At 683.
60['] [1988] FSR 232.

Here, proceedings had been taken in time and the relief sought was granted. It was irrelevant to the exercise of the Court's equitable jurisdiction that Herbert Smith were not implicated in the obtaining of their opponent's papers.

Shortly afterwards the Court of Appeal adopted a more stringent approach to the requirements which have to be satisfied before *Asburton v Pape* relief can be granted. In *Guinness Peat Ltd v Fitzroy Robinson*,[61] privileged documents were in error included in Part 1 of Schedule 1 of the defendants' list of documents. Copies were supplied to the plaintiffs after their solicitors had inspected them. Slade, LJ accepted the plaintiff's argument that the decisions in *Ashburton*, *Goddard* and *Herbert Smith* could be distinguished, as they had not dealt with a loss of privilege occurring as a result of a step taken in the litigation by the party entitled to the privilege. He commented that:

> "Ordinarily ... a party to litigation who sees a particular document referred to in the other side's list, without privilege being claimed, and is subsequently permitted inspection of that document, is fully entitled to assume that any privilege which might otherwise have been claimed for it has been waived."

However, he also stressed that the court was entitled to intervene if the circumstances warranted it. As to this he set out certain principles which he "broadly" stated as follows:

> "(1) Where solicitors for one party to litigation have, on discovery, mistakenly included a document for which they could properly have claimed privilege in Part 1 of Schedule 1 of a list of documents without claiming privilege, the court will ordinarily permit them to amend the list under R.S.C. Ord. 20, r. 8 at any time before inspection of the document has taken place;
>
> (2) However, once in such circumstances the other party has inspected the document in pursuance of the rights conferred on him by R.S.C. Ord. 24, r. 9, the general rule is that it is too late for the party who seeks to claim privilege to attempt to correct the error by applying for injunctive relief. Subject to what is said in (3) below, the *Briamore*[63] decision is good law;
>
> (3) If however ... the other party or his solicitor either (a) has procured inspection of the relevant document by fraud, or (b) on inspection, realises that he has been permitted to see the document only by reason of an obvious mistake, the court has the power to intervene for the protection of the mistaken party by the grant of an injunction in exercise of the equitable jurisdiction illustrated by the *Ashburton*, *Goddard* and *Herbert Smith* cases. Furthermore, in my view it should ordinarily

---

61' [1987] 1 WLR 1027.
62' [1987] 1 WLR 1027, also discussed in Chaps 3 and 6.
63' Discussed in Section 4 above.

intervene in such cases, unless the case is one where the injunction can properly be refused on the general principles affecting the grant of a discretionary remedy...".[64,65]

Pizzey v *Ford Motor Co Ltd,*[66] has helped to clarify when a mistake is "obvious". Here, in response to an order for discovery, the plaintiff's solicitor mistakenly sent the defendants an expert's report which was adverse to the plaintiff's case. When the plaintiff sought an injunction restraining the defendant from making any use of the report, the Court of Appeal, applying Slade, LJ's principles, held that cases of mistake, in which an injunction would be granted, were stringently confined to those which are obvious, that is those which were "evident" to the recipient of the document. In *Pizzey,* the court interpreted this to refer to a reasonable person with the qualities of the recipient. Here, the recipient's relevant quality was that she was a solicitor whose assertion on oath that she had thought her opponent was waiving privilege in the course of "simple" discovery was accepted by the court.

It is clear that the courts adopt the stance that cases involving the inadvertent disclosure of privileged materials at the discovery stage of litigation are subject to a "special consideration".[67] This has the result, as subsequent decisions show, that the court's ability to grant an injunction "in aid of the privilege"[68] does not depend exactly on the type of balancing exercise usually carried out when deciding to restrain the unauthorised use of confidential information. Such an exercise was conducted by Scott, J in *Webster* v *James Chapman & Co*[69] in which he refused an injunction for the return of a draft expert's report sent to an opponent in error (in circumstances where the conclusions expressed in the draft differed considerably from those in the final version). That approach was impliedly disapproved by the Court of Appeal in *Derby* v *Weldon (No 8);*[70] and expressly disapproved by Mann, LJ in *Pizzey* v *Ford Motor Co Ltd.* In *Derby* v *Weldon (No 8)*, Dillon, LJ, said:[71]

"The court does not ... weigh the privilege and consider whether the privilege should outweigh the importance that the document should be before the

---

64' *Ibid.,* at 1045–1046.
65' Such as inordinate delay: see Nourse, LJ in *Goddard* v *Nationwide Building Society* [1980] QB 677 at 685.
66' (1993) *The Times*, 8 March.
67' Per Mann, LJ in *Pizzey* v *Ford Motor Co Ltd, (1993) The Times,* 8 March.
68' Per Nourse, LJ in *Goddard, op.cit.* at 685.
69' [1989] 3 All ER 939.
70' [1991] 1 WLR 73.
71' *Ibid.,* at 99.

court at the trial, or the importance that possession of the document and the ability to use it might have for the advocate ..."

The concept of the reasonable recipient was also applied in *IBM* v *Phoenix International*.[72] Here, the defendants' privileged documents were mistakenly copied to the other side after they had been inspected by the plaintiffs at the discovery stage of the litigation. No claim for privilege had been made in respect of these documents in the list of documents. The discovery in the case was extremely extensive (some 100,000 pages were provided) and it was apparent that the discovery had been completed under considerable time pressure. In granting the defendants an injunction Aldous, J noted that when fraud is not established, the general rule is that no injunction will granted after inspection, unless (a) the document is privileged, and (b) disclosure has occurred as a result of an obvious mistake.

He held that the circumstances in which discovery was given would have led the reasonable solicitor to conclude that a mistake had been made. The reasonable solicitor who concluded that there had been no proper review of documents would not be surprised to find mistakes. So:

> "The reasonable solicitor would have been in no doubt that the legal bills were privileged documents[73] and therefore disclosure was made by mistake, unless a decision had been taken to waive privilege. I cannot think of any logical reason why Phoenix would decide to waive privilege in their legal bills and I do not envisage that the reasonable solicitor would arrive at a different conclusion".[74]

To suggest that unless a solicitor can think of a logical reason for privilege having been waived in the disclosed document he must assume that a mistake has been made seems to ignore the importance of being able to rely on the discovery provided by the other side in litigation, a factor stressed in *Pizzey* v *Ford*. It also suggests that a solicitor who has attempted a careful and thorough discovery exercise is at a disadvantage compared with the solicitor who has conducted a brief review, for it will thereby be more difficult to prove that an unintended disclosure of a privileged document was due to an "obvious" mistake.

The *IBM* decision can be contrasted with *Derby* v *Weldon (No 10)*,[75] where a number of privileged documents were mistakenly included in trial

---

72[1] [1995] 1 All ER 413.

73[1] It should not follow that the reasonable solicitor will be free from doubt in every case, for legal bills are not always privileged: see Chap. 2 Section 5. See also the *NRG* decision discussed in Section 3 above in which it was the disclosure of lawyers' invoices which led to the various discovery applications in that case.

74[1] *Ibid.*, at 424.

75[1] [1991] 1 WLR 660. This decision was not cited to the court in *IBM*.

bundles. The plaintiffs argued that the defendants were not thereby entitled to assume that privilege had been waived. To the contrary, because of the time pressures under which the bundles had been prepared, they should have been alert to the fact that a mistake might have been made. This submission was rejected. Vinelott, J noted that the bundles were reviewed by experienced solicitors and counsel to ensure that privileged material was excluded. He held (with some hesitation) that the defendants were entitled to assume that the documents included in the bundles were documents on which the plaintiffs proposed to rely, privileged or not.

Another recent decision which is worth noting is *Def American Inc v Phonogram Ltd.*[76] The plaintiffs in a Chancery action had obtained a copy of a tape recording of a conversation between the defendants and, *inter alia*, their American attorney. It was conceded that the contents of the tape were privileged. The plaintiffs made a transcript of the tape which they exhibited to an affidavit sworn on their behalf; and they quoted from the transcript in the body of the affidavit. The affidavit had been sworn in advance of the hearing of two substantial motions. When the defendants applied in separate proceedings to restrain the use of their privileged material, they were met with the argument that there could no longer be any confidentiality in the transcript. This argument was based on the fact that part of the transcript had already been mentioned in open court before the motions judge. This occurred when the defendant's counsel sought to explore, without any notice of motion before the court, certain issues in relation to the use of the transcript by the plaintiffs. The motions judge asked to see the affidavit and certain passages were read to him. In the result, Lindsay, J held that these amounted to very sparing references, of the order of 2 or 3% of the entirety of the transcript. Further, the references were made to enable the defendants to express their concerns in relation to the use of the transcript by the plaintiffs. Having reviewed a transcript of the proceedings in the motions court, Lindsay, J held that the defendants had not deployed the material in evidence because it was (mostly) not referred to verbatim.

He also distinguished the decision in *Great Atlantic*[77] (where the reading at trial of two paragraphs of a longer document was sufficient to waive privilege) by noting that in that case the privileged material had been read out at trial, whereas in the instant case the court was concerned with interlocutory proceedings. He justified the distinction between trial and interlocutory proceedings by reference to the earlier cases and the fact that

---

76' Unrep., 29 July 1994. It does not appear from the transcript of judgment that *Guinness Peat Properties v Fitzroy Robinson Partnership* was cited to Lindsay, J.

77' [1981] 1 WLR 529.

this distinction was essential to the reconciliation of *Ashburton* v *Pape* and *Calcraft* v *Guest*:

> "It may be unsatisfactory to distinguish between use at trial and use at interlocutory stages but not only is that distinction vital to the manner in which *Calcraft -v- Guest* and *Lord Ashburton -v- Pape* can both stand together, but also in this area of the law *Great Atlantic* itself and other cases have recognised the possibility of such a distinction by emphasising use at trial or in speaking of adducing evidence to the *trial judge*".[78]

His second, and more important, reason for distinguishing *Great Atlantic* was that the reasons given in that case as to why waiver of part of a document had to be taken to be waiver of the whole of the document did not apply where the party resisting the claim to privilege had himself seen the whole document and sought to use it in whole in evidence. This was not a case where it was the beneficiary of the privilege who was attempting to *use* a part of a privileged document: here that party, was *resisting* its use *in toto*.

It is submitted that the result in *Def American* can be justified only on the grounds that the use of privileged material at the interlocutory stage was *de minimis* and then in the course of an attempt to restrain its use by an opponent. Had there been more extensive use of the transcript, for example, for the purposes of other applications, then the fact of it being an interlocutory application should have been irrelevant.

In this respect, the *Def American* decision can be contrasted with *ITC Film Distributors Ltd* v *Video Exchange Ltd*.[79] Following an interlocutory hearing, some of the plaintiffs' privileged documents which had been in court awaiting collection ended up in the hands of the second defendant as the result of a trick he perpetrated on the plaintiffs' representatives.[80] The plaintiff's motion for *Ashburton* v *Pape* relief was heard after the second defendant's own motions, in support of which he had sworn an affidavit exhibiting the privileged documents. Some of these documents were read in camera by Warner, J who was referred to them in the course of the defendant's argument and during his cross-examination of the plaintiffs' witness. When the judge came to hear the plaintiffs' motion, he indicated that he would have granted *Ashburton* v *Pape* relief had this been sought *before* the date (1 October) on which the defendant's affidavit had been sworn. Delivering judgment eleven days later in respect of motions which had been heard in the interim, he indicated there were certain "difficulties"

78' Transcript, at 31, Lindsay, J's emphasis.
79' [1982] Ch 436.
80' As regards the unauthorised removal of photographs from Counsel's papers, see *In the matter of Paul Griffin* (1996) *The Times*, 6 November.

in his way, presumably because the affidavit (but not all the exhibits) had been put in evidence. In the event, following *Riddick* v *Thames Board Mills Ltd*,[81] Warner, J, held that a party who took possession by stealth or by a trick of an opponent's documents within the precincts of the court should not be allowed to put such documents in evidence. However, from his order he excluded the documents he had already read because, though not formally put in evidence, they had nonetheless been used by the court.

Where a party obtains by inadvertence his opponent's privileged materials, he not only faces the risk that he will be injuncted for their return, but also that he will lose the services of his solicitor who reads that material. In *Ablitt* v *Mills and Reeve*,[82] the defendant solicitors received in error privileged papers emanating from a counsel who was acting for the plaintiff in an action in which they represented the defendants. On their clients' instructions,[83] the solicitors read counsel's papers after having warned them there was, as happened, a real risk that they would face injunction proceedings. However, the plaintiff went further and asked the Court to restrain Mills and Reeve from acting altogether, notwithstanding the inconvenience and expense to their own clients. Influenced by comments in *Ridehalgh* v *Horsefield and Isherood*[84] on the importance of the "cloak of confidence" thrown over client-lawyer communications, Blackburne, J granted this relief.[85]

Inevitably, there are cases where the court will not grant *Ashburton* v *Pape* type relief to the unfortunate party who has disclosed privileged materials by mistake. One important general exception was established in *Butler* v *Board of Trade*.[86] Here, the Official Receiver (a department of the Board of Trade) collected a number of papers relating to the affairs of a company in compulsory liquidation from its solicitors. A copy of a letter written by the solicitors to the plaintiff, a former director, was in error

---

81' [1977] QB 881.

82' *The Times*, (1995) 26 October.

83' Given pursuant to guidance contained in the *Guide to the Professional Conduct of Solicitors*. This guidance was changed for the current edition (7th Edn., at para. 16.06) as a result of criticisms made in this case.

84' [1994] Ch 205 at 224.

85' Nor would the judge permit the construction of a "Chinese wall", so as to enable Mills & Reeve to continue acting, albeit through new personnel.

86' [1971] Ch 680. See also *R* v *Tompkins* (1977) 67 Cr App R 181. The decision in *Butler* caused considerable interest in academic circles at the time. Not only did it see the revival of *Ashburton* v *Pape,* but Goff, J's comments on the extent of the equitable jurisdiction to restrain the unauthorised use of confidential information were used despite the narrowness of the actual decision to argue that this could give rise to a "privilege" in respect of communications to doctors, priests and the like: see Tapper, *op. cit.,* n. 52, and Heydon, *op. cit.,* n. 47.

included in the papers taken.[87] The plaintiff sought a declaration from the court that the Board of Trade were not entitled to make any use of that letter in subsequent criminal proceedings brought against him under section 332(3) of the Companies Act 1948. The Court acknowledged the existence of the equitable jurisdiction exercised in *Ashburton* v *Pape*. However, Goff, J held that:

> "*Ashburton* v *Pape* does differ from the present case in an important particular, namely, that the defendants are a department of the Crown and intend to use the copy letter in a public prosecution brought by them. ... In my judgment it would not be a right or permissible exercise of the equitable jurisdiction in confidence to make a declaration at the suit of the accused in a public prosecution in effect restraining the Crown from adducing admissible evidence relevant to the crime with which he is charged".[88]

This decision is not universally popular. Noting that it had not been followed in the New Zealand Court of Appeal's decision in *R* v *Uljee*,[89] Nourse, LJ commented in the *Goddard* decision that:

> "The practical result of [*Uljee*] would seem to me to leave the spirit of *Ashburton* -v- *Pape*... supreme in both civil and criminal proceedings in that jurisdiction, a supremacy for which in my respectful opinion there is much to be said".[90]

One situation which has yet to be considered judicially is whether a litigant in the position of Dr Leigh in *Schneider* v *Leigh*[91] discussed in Section 2 above could have been restrained by injunction by the plaintiff company in the original action from disclosing his expert's report in the subsequent action in which the company was not a party. Similarly, what about the auditor who is given a privileged litigation status report in lieu of the usual (unprivileged) disclosure letter? It will be recalled that Dr Leigh had no right to assert for his own benefit in the second action the privilege in his expert report prepared for the company for use in the first

---

87' Goff, J assumed that the original was privileged, but referred to the copy only as "confidential". The copy was undoubtedly privileged as well, but as has been discussed in this chapter, it is only the document's confidentiality which gives to any remedy to restrain its unauthorised use.

88' [1970] 3 WLR 822 at 829. In fact, in stating that the public interest in prosecuting offenders outweighed any interest the plaintiff had in the confidentiality of the document, Goff, J did not examine whether the fact that the document was not only confidential but privileged should have entitled the plaintiff to protection even though the plaintiff would have been entitled to withhold the document from the authorities, but for the inadvertent disclosure. This should be contrasted with Dillon, LJ's observation in a civil context made in *Derby* v *Weldon (No 8)* [1991] 1 WLR 73 quoted in the text above.

89' [1982] 1 NZLR 561, discussed in Section 3 above.

90' [1987] QB 670 at 686.

91' [1955] 2 QB 195.

action.[92] The reports of the decision do not establish whether the company attempted to prevent disclosure by Dr Leigh in the second action, although the court did order that disclosure to Schneider had to await the conclusion of the original action. But what if the company had sought to intervene? The difficulty would have been that Dr Leigh was legitimately in possession of his report. Further, there had been no disclosure consequent upon a mistake or induced by fraud, which would suggest that the *Guinness Peat* principles would not obviously assist.

One particular difficulty, as the Court of Appeal pointed out in *Lee v South West Thames RHA*,[93] is the unique one that Dr Schneider was a defendant in a separate action where the cause of action arose out of a communication which was privileged in the first action.[94] Without the privileged document the court would not have the full picture before it. Although this is the usual consequence when privilege is asserted, in such a case, the court might nonetheless be prepared to determine an application restraining the use of the statement according to usual equitable principles and without the predisposition – evident in the *Goddard* and *Derby v Weldon (No 8)* decisions, for example – to grant an injunction in aid of the privilege which, unless and until waived, is regarded as absolute.[95] It may be that, in the case of expert witnesses, whose opinion evidence is in any event compellable,[96] a court may be swayed to allow his opinion to be made available in the public interest, notwithstanding his client's privilege, as in *W v Edgell*.[97]

In other cases, such as with the auditor, it is submitted that the answer should be that the beneficiary can restrain disclosure to a third party. Assuming the auditor's possession of the report did not involve any express or implied waiver of the privilege as against the whole world; and given that he owes obligations of confidentiality to the client, then there should be no balancing exercise to perform.[98] On that basis, the Court ought to be willing to preserve the client's privilege.[99]

92' Similarly, the auditor will not be able to assert his client's privilege (unless he can establish a common interest privilege); although he will be able to argue that disclosure is not "necessary": see RSC O24 r. 7 and the use which Peter Gibson, LJ made of this rule in *Robert Hitchins Ltd v International Computers Ltd* (unrep.) 10 December 1996, CA.

93' [1985] 2 All ER 385 discussed in Section 2 above.

94' Hobhouse, J qualified his remarks in the *Prudential Assurance* case quoted at p. 171 above by noting that the beneficiary of the privilege can prevent his statements being used without his consent particularly where it is sought to be used in evidence against him.

95' See Nourse, LJ in *Goddard* [1987] QB 670 at 685.

96' See *Harmony Shipping Co SA v Saudi Europe Line* [1979] 1 WLR 1380.

97' [1990] Ch 359.

98' *Derby & Co v Weldon (No 8)* [1991] 1 WLR 73, discussed above.

99' Some support for this view can be found in Phillips, J's judgment in *Leif Hoegh & Co v Petrolsea Inc* [1993] 1 Lloyd's Rep. 363 at 367–378.

8 . WAIVER:

THE KNOCK-ON CONSEQUENCES

A party is entitled at any time expressly – that is, deliberately – to waive his privilege over particular documents. As a general rule, he can waive privilege selectively, so long as it is waived in respect of the entirety of a privileged communication. Cotton, LJ's comments in *Lyell v Kennedy*[1] are often cited with approval:

> "There was this contention raised ...: that the Defendant had waived his privilege, and therefore could not claim it at all. That, in my opinion, was entirely fallacious. He had done this, he had said, 'Whether I am entitled to protect them or not I will produce certain of the documents for which I had previously claimed privilege – I will waive that and I will produce them,' but that did not prevent him relying on such protection with regard to others which he did not like to produce."

However, the rule is not absolute, for waiver of privilege over document A can, in limited circumstances, result in a waiver of privilege over document B. In addition, the courts will not permit a party to put *in evidence* part only of a privileged communication.[2] Such use will be treated as a waiver of privilege in respect of the whole document, unless the *Great Atlantic* separate subject matter test[3] can be satisfied. If not, then the deployment in evidence of the non-privileged part of a document, the remainder of which is privileged, will result in a waiver of privilege over the whole document.[4]

The guiding principle which the courts apply when a party waives privilege is a concern to ensure that that party is not acting unfairly by only disclosing privileged information which is favourable to his case, while maintaining a claim to privilege in respect of anything which is unfavourable. As Mustill, J pointed out in *Nea Karteria Maritime Co Ltd v Atlantic and Great Lakes Steamship Corp:*[5]

> "... where a party deploys in Court material which would otherwise be privileged, the opposite party in the Court must have an opportunity of satisfying themselves that what the party has chosen to release from privilege represents the whole of the material relevant to the issue in question. To

---

1[*]   (1884) 27 Ch D 1 at 24.

2[*]   Cotton, LJ contrasted the position in his comments qutoed above by saying "it is not like the case of a man who gives part of a conversation and then claims protection for the remainder...".

3[*]   Described in Chap. 9.

4[*]   See Section 2 above.

5[*]   [1981] Comm LR 138.

allow an individual item to be plucked out of context would be to risk injustice through its real weight or meaning, being misunderstood."

In assessing the extent of any further waiver of privilege which occurs when privileged material is deployed in evidence or voluntarily disclosed to an opponent in advance of trial, the Court will usually look to see that everything has been disclosed in respect of the transaction or issue to which the originally disclosed material is judged to be relevant. This misleadingly suggests that the consequences could be extensive, but in fact they tend to be limited. As the recent Divisional Court decision in *R v Secretary of State for Transport and Factortame Ltd*[6] noted, nearly all of the reported cases on this subject relate to a single "transaction", involving a single document or a number of documents relevant to the same issue. Auld, LJ noted that in such cases the question for the Court is whether the matters in issue and the documents in respect of which partial disclosure has been made are respectively severable so that the partially disclosed material clearly does not bear on matters in issue in respect of which privileged material is withheld. So:

> "... the more confined the issue, for example as to the content of a single document or conversation, the more difficult it is likely to be to withhold, by severance, part of the document or other documents relevant to the document or conversation".[7]

However, where the issue is broad or there are several related issues, partial disclosure which is clearly confined in its impact to one aspect of the case may well not require the all or nothing approach evident in the "single transaction" decisions. The broad issue approach can be seen in the Divisional Court's decision in *Factortame*. This arose out of the passing of the Merchant Shipping Act 1988 which excluded from the British Register of Shipping fishing vessels which were owned or managed by non-nationals and by persons who were not resident or domiciled in this country. The Act was passed so as to prevent so-called "quota hoppers" obtaining the benefit of the UK's fishing entitlement under the EC's Common Fisheries Policy. In the main, the Act was aimed at Spanish

---

[6] (1997) *The Times,* 11 September. In *Derby & Co Ltd v Weldon (No 10)* [1991] 1 WLR 660, Vinelott, J at 669 suggested it is "easier to conclude that fairness does not require the disclosure of the whole of a document... than to conclude that fairness does not require the disclosure of the whole of a conversation which... is a seamless whole". And in *Sills v Tilbury Cargo Handling Ltd (and others),* (unrep., 2 November 1994), Clarke, J held that parts of Counsel's opinion relating to interlocutory issues which had been deliberately exhibited to an affidavit did not warrant disclosure of the remainder, which were plainly separate and distinct parts, which related to the merits of the action.

[7] Per Auld, LJ. The extracts in this Section from Auld, LJ's judgment in *Factortame* are taken from an unrevised transcript.

fishing interests. Those interests challenged the operation of the Act in judicial review proceedings which resulted in three references to the European Court of Justice. These led to the suspension of the nationality, residence and domicile conditions contained in the Act and declarations to the effect that those conditions infringed Community Law. Its third judgment dealt with the question whether such infringements give rise to private law rights against the UK Government. As to this, the Court held, in summary, that such breaches could confer a right of reparation on an individual where the national court was of the view that certain conditions were satisfied, including one which required the breach to be "sufficiently serious". In determining this issue the decisive test would be whether the Member State had "manifestly and gravely" disregarded the limits on its discretion taking into account a number of factors, including whether the infringement of community law and the damage thereby caused was intentional or involuntary. Thus armed, the applicants set out to prove that the UK Government had committed a "sufficiently serious" breach of community law which they asserted was carried out intentionally or recklessly since, *inter alia*, the government was on notice of the Act's possible unlawfulness.

In readiness for a hearing in respect of these issues, an order for discovery was made. In complying with this, the Secretary of State waived privilege in respect of legal advice which he had received in connection with his "formulation of policy" in relation to this legislation. However, the waiver was limited to legal advice received before 29 October 1987, which was the date upon which the Merchant Shipping Bill was first introduced to Parliament. The applicants challenged his entitlement to limit his waiver in this way. They argued that having decided to waive some of his privilege, fairness dictated that he waive it for the period of the Bill's passage through Parliament to its enactment on 1 December 1988; its taking effect on 1 April 1989 and up to the European Court's second ruling in the same litigation on 25 July 1991 which held that the legislation contravened community law.

The difficulty with this argument was that the materials sought by the applicants encompassed a long period and different stages of the introduction and implementation of the offending legislation; further, it was broad in nature in that it sought legal advice covering not only policy matters over several years, but also associated legal advice, some of which encompassed the present and other proceedings. Auld, LJ's approach to this was to consider whether the partially disclosed matter had any bearing on matters in issue in respect of which privileged material was withheld. Taking comfort from the Secretary of State's indication that he would not suggest at trial that his conduct after 29 October 1987 in relation to the enactment and implementation of the Merchant Shipping Act 1988 was governed by the disclosed legal advice that he had received before that date, he held that this was therefore:

> "... not a case of partial disclosure in relation to his conduct throughout the period in issue, but one of clear severability of two periods within it and of the disclosed and undisclosed documents relating respectively to each period. If the Secretary of State keeps to [counsel's] word I can see no unfairness to the applicants".

In "single transaction" cases, the "knock-on" consequences of the voluntary waiver will not extend to *every* document or communication relevant to the subject matter of the disclosed material, merely those which bear on the relevant transaction or issue. However, determining the relevant transaction in relation to which further waiver is deemed to have occurred can sometimes be a difficult task, as the decision in *Nea Kateria Maritime Co Ltd* v *Atlantic & Great Lakes Steamship Corp* illustrates.[8] Here, a witness gave evidence at trial about his interview with Greek lawyers who had been given a list of questions to put to him by the plaintiff's English solicitors. The witness's answers were incorporated into a document which was used at trial. His oral evidence at trial conflicted with the written answers. In response, the plaintiffs called the Greek lawyers who had conducted the interviews, whereupon the defendants sought production of the list of questions which formed the basis of the interview. Having regard to the purpose for which the plaintiffs deployed the Greek lawyer's evidence, namely whether the seaman accepted the truth of an account of events which was different to ones he put forward on other occasions, necessarily the circumstances surrounding that account were relevant. Accordingly, the court held that it needed all available information on the meeting with the Greek lawyer. This required that the waiver of privilege – arising from the use of the witness's answers – extended to the list of questions used at the meeting with the Greek lawyer. The extent of the "knock-on" waiver in this case was limited, as Hobhouse, J explained in *General Accident Corporation* v *Tanter*,[9] where he said that Mustill, J was looking

> "... to see what is the issue in relation which to the material has been deployed. He held that the issue was what was said at the meeting between the lawyer and the [witness], and the correct evaluation of that meeting. But he did not accept that it extended to other matters which did not form part

---

8[1]   [1981] Comm LR 138.
9[1]   [1984] 1 WLR 100.

of that transaction. He did not treat the transaction as being the facts of the subject matter of the conversation at the meeting".[10]

General Accident Corporation v *Tanter*[11] was an action for damages for breach of a reinsurance contract. One of the issues was what was said by a broker to the reinsurance underwriters at the time the reinsurance slip was written. Before trial the brokers' solicitors served a Civil Evidence Act 1968 notice in respect of a privileged memorandum written by a Mr Baxter (one of the brokers) to his solicitor in which he provided details of a number of conversations between the brokers and the defendant underwriters on 6 October 1981 and earlier. The memorandum was extensively used in cross-examination by counsel for the brokers, both as a summary of the evidence which Mr Baxter was due to give, and in an attempt to impress the witness with what had been said on 6 October 1981. That use caused the underwriters to argue that the brokers had thereby waived privilege in all documents which dealt with the subject matter of the conversations described in the memorandum including instructions to counsel and witness statements. Hobhouse, J rejected this submission as being of "astonishing breadth". In relation to issues of waiver, he held:

> "... by adducing evidence at a trial one does get involved in potential further waiver. The underlying principle is one of fairness in the conduct of the trial and does not go further than that ... [I]f the evidence is adduced then the extent of the waiver relates to the transaction to which that evidence goes. The extent of the transaction has to be examined and where it is what somebody said on a particular occasion, then that is the transaction. It is not the subject matter of those conversations. It does not extend to all matters relating to the subject matter of those conversations."[12]

In reaching this decision, Hobhouse, J in *General Accident* declined to follow *George Doland Ltd* v *Blackburn, Robson Coates & Co*[13] in which Geoffrey Lane, J held that once a solicitor had given oral evidence at trial of his instructions in relation to a certain matter, then the opposing party was entitled to see any documents relating to the facts so revealed. However, this did not entitle the opponents to see instructions to counsel and proofs of evidence because:

> "The mere fact that the plaintiffs may have waived the professional privilege which exists between client and solicitor does not ... also result in the waiver

---

10[2] Per Hobhouse, J, *ibid.*, at 113.
11[2] [1984] 1 WLR 100.
12[2] At 114–115.
13[2] [1972] 1 WLR 1338.

of the further privilege which protects documents brought into existence for the purpose of litigation...".[14]

This decision was referred to without criticism in both *Great Atlantic*[15] and *Nea Karteria*.[16] Hobhouse, J thought the decision on the extent of the further waiver was, at best, justifiable on its own facts. As for the distinction between the two privileges he did not regard it as a valid one to apply in all cases.[17]

That each case is likely, ultimately, to turn on its own facts, was a point made by Peter Gibson, J in *Re Konigsberg (a bankrupt)*.[18] This concerned an application by Mr Konigsberg's trustee in bankruptcy to set aside the transfer of his home to his wife as being a transfer otherwise than in good faith and for valuable consideration. In resisting the application, Mrs Konigsberg swore an affidavit exhibiting a letter from the solicitors who represented her and her husband as joint clients. The solicitor then swore an affidavit on behalf of the trustee which contradicted the wife's evidence and which exhibited further correspondence and attendance notes made by him in connection with the transfer. Some of the exhibits concerned privileged communications between the solicitor and the couple as joint clients.

Mrs Konigsberg sought to prevent these being used on the hearing of the trustee's application. She conceded that to the extent her affidavit was in evidence then she had waived privilege. However, she argued that the waiver should be limited to a conversation with the solicitor, described in her affidavit, and the letter she exhibited, concerning whether the transfer was a sale or a gift. The judge rejected this argument. The issue before him was whether the transfer was for no consideration or for valuable consideration. There was a risk of injustice if an individual item were plucked out of context. Mrs Konigsberg, by her evidence, had chosen to lift the veil of privilege in part and fairness required that it should be lifted in whole. This meant that privilege was waived in respect of three further documents which went to the same point.

Timing Issues

Until the Divisional Court's decision in *Factortame*, it had been thought that the "knock on" waiver would only occur once the privileged materials had been deployed in court, whether at trial or in the course of an

14[2] Per Geoffrey Lane, J, *ibid.*, at 1341.
15[2] [1981] 1 WLR 529.
16[2] [1981] Comm LR 138.
17[2] [1984] 1 WLR 100 at 116.
18[2] [1989] 3 All ER 289, discussed in detail in Chap. 4.

interlocutory hearing.[19] However, *Phipson on Evidence* (14th Edn., 1990 at 527), has long argued that the necessity to deploy the evidence in court before there can be a knock-on waiver was illogical: "a party is not entitled to show his hand in part". Notwithstanding, Clarke, J ruled in *Balkanbank* v *Taher*[20] that

> "... the mere disclosure of a document which is privileged does not have the effect of waiving privilege for connected documents. In my judgment the statement to the contrary effect in paragraph 20-37 of Phipson is wrong".

In *Factortame*, Auld, LJ agreed with the views expressed in Phipson and rejected the Secretary of State's argument that the application was premature given that the disclosed legal advice had yet to be deployed in evidence. His reasons for disagreeing with the decisions in *General Accident* and *Balkanbank* are pragmatic. He held that if a party does intend to adduce in evidence material over which privilege has been waived, then:

> "There is an obvious advantage in both parties knowing where they stand before trial. It enables each of them to determine whether and how to proceed with the litigation and to avoid costly adjournments for further discovery and consequential work which otherwise would occur if the point had to be determined at trial".

19[1] See Hobhouse, J in *General Accident Corporation* v *Tanter* [1984] 1 WLR 100 at 114.

20[1] (1994) *The Times*, 19 February, thereby agreeing with Hobhouse, J in *General Accident* v *Tanter*. The decision in *Balkenbank* to the effect that mere service of a witness statement does not waive any privilege so as to give rise to "knock-on" waiver issues is still correct.

Chapter 8

THE CRIME/FRAUD EXCEPTION

1. INTRODUCTION

An important exception to the usual rules of legal professional privilege is the so-called crime/fraud exception. This shorthand description refers to the line of authority which usually starts with the decision in *R v Cox and Railton*[1] in 1884 in which it was first authoritatively decided that communications between a client and his legal adviser would not qualify for privilege (and so can be admissible in evidence against the client) where they seek or give legal advice which is required by the client to facilitate or to guide him in the commission of a crime or a fraud. Since then, the exception has been extended to cover equivalent communications between a third party and his lawyer where the third party is the innocent tool of another's criminal or fraudulent purpose.

At first blush, this exception has the potential seriously to undermine the privilege. In practice it is "only in very exceptional circumstances that the privilege can be displaced".[2] This chapter looks at the general principles underlying the crime/fraud exception, the extent of its applicability in civil law proceedings (as well as in criminal proceedings) and the grounds on which it can be invoked.

The crime/fraud exception also features sometimes in the context of the police's powers to seize documentary evidence. Accordingly, the chapter concludes with a brief look at those powers and how the exception is relevant to their exercise.

2. BASIC PRINCIPLES

Stephen, J's judgment in *R v Cox and Railton*[3] is the usual starting point for a study of the scope of the crime/fraud exception. Cox and Railton were

---

1 (1884) 14 QBD 153.
2 Per Vinelott, J in *Derby & Co Ltd v Weldon (No 7)* [1990] 1 WLR 1156 at 1159.
3 (1884) 14 QBD 153.

partners who had been convicted upon a charge of conspiring to defraud one Munster, who had obtained judgment in a libel action against Railton. The libel appeared in a newspaper of which the partners were proprietors. Cox was not sued. In order to frustrate the execution of the judgment against him, Railton executed a bill of sale in favour of Cox in respect of the partnership's assets. The prosecution alleged that the bill of a sale was a fraudulent one, executed while the two were still partners. As evidence of the fraud, the prosecution alleged that a memorandum of dissolution of the partnership, indorsed on the original partnership deed, had been backdated so as to pre-date the commencement of the libel action. The prosecution sought to prove this by calling as a witness a solicitor who had acted for them in the preparation of the deed of partnership and whom the partners had consulted shortly after the libel judgment had been entered against Railton. At that consultation, the partners had discussed with the solicitor what steps they could take to prevent property being seized upon execution of the judgment. The Recorder of London, before whom the defendants were tried, allowed this evidence to be admitted. The jury found the defendants guilty but the court reserved judgment until the Court for Crown Cases Reserved had ruled on whether the solicitor's evidence had been properly admitted.

The court agreed that it had been and the convictions were affirmed. However, because of the importance attached to the principle involved,[4] the court, acknowledging that the law on this subject had never been wholly free from doubt, endeavoured to define the relevant principles "with clearness to act as a guide in future cases".[5] In so doing, the court examined the underlying rationale for legal professional privilege and concluded that this did not justify allowing the partners to withhold their communications from the court. This was because privilege could not:

> "... include the case of communications, criminal in themselves, or intended to further any criminal purpose, for the protection of such communications cannot possibly be otherwise than injurious to the interests of justice, and to those of the administration of justice. Nor do such communications fall within the terms of the rule. A communication in furtherance of a criminal purpose does not 'come into the ordinary scope of professional employment'."[6]

---

4 Attested to by the fact that the case was first argued before a court of 4 judges and subsequently before a court of ten. In all, a total of eleven judges heard the matter: see Stephen J's judgment *ibid.*, at 164.

5 Per Grove, J, at 163, in his short judgment delivered at the conclusion of argument some six months before Stephen, J delivered the full judgment of the court.

6 Per Stephen, J, *ibid.*, at 167. However, in a criminal law context, such a communication may constitute "special procedure" material under the Police and Criminal Evidence Act 1984: see Section 5 below.

So much for the general principles of the crime/fraud exception. What are the detailed considerations?

Innocent legal adviser

First, the exception can be invoked notwithstanding that the legal advisor who is consulted acts in good faith and is unaware of the illegal purpose for which his advice is sought and given. In *Cox and Railton,* the court noted that the conduct of the solicitor whom the defendants consulted appeared to have been unobjectionable. This principle has been applied by the courts without question ever since.[7]

Innocent client

Secondly, it is now settled that the crime/fraud exception can extend beyond communications, for example between a fraudster and his legal adviser, to those between an innocent client and the client's legal adviser. Such communications can become discloseable in circumstances where the client is an innocent "tool" who is being used by the fraudster for the purpose of effecting his criminal intentions. This appears from the speeches of the majority in the House of Lords in *R v Central Criminal Court, ex p. Francis & Francis (a firm).*[8] This decision was concerned with section 10 of the Police and Criminal Evidence Act 1984 (which reflects the common law rules of legal professional privilege) and, in particular, the proper interpretation of section 10(2), which contains the statutory version of the crime/fraud exception.[9] Here, the applicant solicitors had sought judicial review of an order made under section 27 Drug Trafficking Offences Act 1986 which required them to produce files in their possession relating to the purchase of various properties undertaken on behalf of one of their clients. The client was a relative of a person suspected by the police of large-scale drug trafficking. The police suspected that person of salting away the proceeds of the drug trafficking in property purchased by members of his family, who included the solicitors' client whose files were the subject of the order. The family member concerned was, so the court was asked to assume,[10] apparently unaware that drug money was being

---

7   See also, *e.g.,* Hoffman, J in *Chandler* v *Church* (1987) 137 NLJ 451.

8   [1989] 1 AC 346.

9   Lord Griffiths, *e.g.,* commented that s. 10(1) corresponded "closely with the established common law principles that govern the existence of legal privilege" (at 382). See also Lord Goff, at 395. These provisions are discussed further in Section 5 below where s. 10(1) is set out in full.

10 Which Lord Griffiths found unlikely: *ibid.,* at 381.

used to assist in the purchase of the property. The particular question which arose was whether the solicitor's files were "items subject to legal privilege" within the meaning of section 10(1) Police and Criminal Evidence Act 1984 (as applied by s.29(2) Drug Trafficking Offences Act 1986), or whether, as was advanced on behalf of the police, they fell within section 10(2) of the 1984 Act. This provides that:

> "Items held with the intention of furthering a criminal purpose are not items subject to legal privilege".

Adopting a pragmatic interpretation of section 10(2),[11] the majority construed it as effectively mirroring the scope and extent of the crime/fraud exception as exemplified in *R v Cox and Railton*. Indeed, by reference to the underlying rationale of this decision, there being no other authority directly in point, Lord Goff observed as follows:

> "... when I have regard both to the purpose which has long been understood to underline the principle of legal professional privilege, and to the reason why communications passing between a client with a criminal purpose and a solicitor who is innocent of any such purpose are held not to be protected by such privilege, it appears to me to be immaterial to that exception whether it is the client himself, or a third party who is using the client as his innocent tool, who has the criminal intention.... I would hold that the criminal intention of the third party will, in the circumstances under consideration, exclude the application of the principle of legal professional privilege at common law, even though the privilege, if it attached, would be the privilege of the client and not of the third party".[12]

At first sight, this decision appears to be a major incursion into a client's ability to communicate openly and freely with his legal adviser under a cloak of confidentiality. The incursion appears all the more serious given that the client is the innocent tool of another whose criminal objectives are thereby being furthered. However, as Lord Goff went on to point out, the client's privilege is excluded only "... in so far as it relates to communications ... made with the [fraudster's] intention of furthering a criminal purpose".[13] To this limited extent the incursion is justifiable, since not only will such cases be exceptional, but also the disclosure of the fraudster's iniquity must, in the interests of justice, prevail over the privilege of the client, however innocent he may be.

---

11 Albeit, it has to be said, one which strains the natural meaning of the language of the sub-section.

12 *Ibid.*, at 396.

13 *Ibid.*, at 397.

Interlocutory applications

A third consideration is that the crime/fraud exception is not restricted to situations concerning the giving of oral evidence at trial, as in *Cox and Railton*. Application for access to privileged materials can be made at a much earlier stage. As *Francis & Francis* demonstrates, the police can use the exception to obtain access to otherwise privileged material at an early stage of their investigation.[14] Similarly, as is discussed in Section 3 below, the issue can arise at the discovery stage of civil actions,[15] in the context of a taxation of costs[16] and in relation to the taking of evidence on commission.[17]

The criminal purpose

Fourthly, the crime/fraud exception is not limited to materials, otherwise privileged, which relate to steps preparatory to the commission of a criminal offence, as in *Cox and Railton*. In *Francis & Francis*, Lord Goff expressed the view that the statutory version of the crime/fraud exception in section 10(2) Police and Criminal Evidence Act 1984 should not be read as being limited to materials relating to "furthering the commission of a criminal offence". He felt that so to read it would exclude those cases where the criminal offence has been committed and the purpose of the criminal is to salt away, for his own benefit, the proceeds of his crime:

> "The purpose of a bank robber is not just to rob a bank: it is to obtain the money for his own benefit. His criminal purpose is still being furthered when he is concealing the money which he has stolen, or otherwise salted it away".[18]

It followed in *Francis & Francis* that no difficulty arose from the fact that at the relevant time the drug trafficker had completed the commission of the offence of trafficking in drugs and that the materials the police sought related to the subsequent laundering of the proceeds of their sale. Nor should there be any difficulty, since disposal or laundering of the proceeds of crime is likely anyway to constitute, in most cases, the commission of a further crime. Once more there is no reason to think that similar considerations would not apply in relation to the common law

---

14 As to this, see further Section 5 below.
15 See *e.g.* *O'Rourke* v *Darbishire* [1920] AC 581, *Derby & Co* v *Weldon (No 7)* [1990] 1 WLR 1156 and *Dubai Bank* v *Galadari (No 6)* (1991) *The Times*, 22 April.
16 See *Skuse* v *Granada Television Ltd* [1994] 1 WLR 1156.
17 See *Bullivant* v *Attorney-General for Victoria* [1901] AC 196.
18 [1989] AC 346 at 394. See also Vinelott, J in *Derby & Co Ltd* v *Weldon (No 7)* [1990] 1 WLR 1156 at 1174, quoted at p. 234 below.

version of the exception. So, in this regard, the decision in *R* v *Orton*[19] is also pertinent. Here the court allowed into evidence the defendant's instructions to his solicitor to draw up a will disposing of certain estates which he was in the process of fraudulently obtaining. In relation to this, Cockburn, CJ said that "if the client had a dishonest purpose in view of the communication he makes to his attorney with the view of making the attorney the innocent instrument of carrying out fraud, it deprives the communication of the privilege". The instructions were therefore disclosed.

Timing

As to the time at which the exception applies, Lord Goff in *Francis & Francis*[20] indicated that, at least for the purposes of section 10(2) Police and Criminal Evidence Act 1984, this would be when the relevant communication is made. This would be on delivery to the solicitor of the client's communication or when the solicitor's communication to his client is written or spoken.

Limitations

Naturally, the crime/fraud exception has its limits. As Morritt, J commented in *Dubai Bank* v *Galadari (No 6)*[21] the original fraud or crime will not by itself displace litigation privilege. So it does not apply in relation to the legal advice sought once the crime has been committed and advice by way of a defence is needed. Otherwise, as Lord Denning, MR observed:

> "No person faced with an allegation of fraud could safely ask for legal advice".[22]

As Lord Sumner explained in *O'Rourke* v *Darbishire*:[23]

> "To consult a solicitor about an intended course of action, in order to be advised whether it is legitimate or not,[24] or to lay before a solicitor the facts relating to a charge of fraud, actually made or anticipated, and make a clean breast of it with the object of being advised about the best way in which to

---

19 Shorthand Notes vol. iii. p. 9381. The judgments in this decision were quoted in full with approval by Stephen, J in *Cox and Railton*, (1884) 14 QBD 153 at 170–172.
20 *Ibid.*, at 392.
21 (1991) *The Times*, 22 April.
22 *Buttes Gas & Oil Co* v *Hammer (No 3)* [1981] QB 223 at 246.
23 [1920] AC 581 at 613.
24 But see *Barclays Bank plc* v *Eustice* [1995] 1 WLR 1238, discussed in Section 3 below.

meet it, is a very different thing from consulting him in order to learn how to plan, execute or stifle an actual fraud".[25]

This aspect is given practical recognition in the terms of the orders made when the crime/fraud exception is successfully invoked. Thus in both *Derby & Co v Weldon (No 7)*[26] and *Barclays Bank plc v Eustice*[27] (both discussed in Section 3 below) the court limited the extent of the disclosure ordered by excluding from its ambit any document which consisted of legal advice obtained and documents coming into existence for the dominant purpose of being used in pending or contemplated proceedings. In practice, therefore, the crime/fraud exception will tend to operate against legal advice privilege, rather than litigation privilege. However, as Morritt, J indicated in *Dubai Bank v Galadari (No 6)*,[28] the rationale behind the exception is "as applicable to communications after proceedings had been brought as to those which took place before". It appears from the short report of this decision that Morritt, J held that the privilege over communications to their solicitors whereby clients put forward a bogus defence will be displaced where they are in furtherance of the antecedent crime. On the other hand, Hoffmann, J refused disclosure in *Chandler v Church*[29] of what a client had told his solicitors to enable them to defend him against a fraud charge, notwithstanding the fact the client might be using his solicitors to put forward a bogus defence.

Nor is a court likely to invoke the exception to order disclosure of a legal aid application form. This appears to follow from the Divisional Court's decision in *R v Snaresbrook Crown Court, ex p. DPP*.[30] Here, an accused complained that his nose had been broken when he was arrested by police investigating an alleged offence. Police enquiries revealed that his nose had been broken two days before the arrest, whereupon he was charged with attempting to pervert the course of justice. The accused had in the meantime applied for legal aid to enable him to prosecute an assault action against the police. The prosecution sought production from the relevant area office of The Law Society of the accused's legal aid application form. Having held that the accused's communication to The Law Society for legal aid was *prima facie* privileged, the Court then considered whether the crime/fraud exception applied. As to this, Glidewell, LJ said:

---

25 See also Lord Parmoor in the same decision, at 622.
26 [1990] 1 WLR 1156.
27 [1995] 1 WLR 1238.
28 (1991) *The Times,* 22 April.
29 (1987) 137 NLJ 451.
30 [1988] QB 532.

"But if it is to be said that his application for legal aid was... a communication made for the purpose of being guided or helped in the commission of a crime, then it seems to me that practically every time somebody makes an untrue statement for the purpose of obtaining legal aid in order to make a civil claim, he is equally liable to have it held that the communication is made for that purpose. I cannot think that that is correct".[31]

As to the application of the crime/fraud exception, this will in practise be rare:

"... litigants in civil litigation may not be believed when their cases come to trial, but that is not to say that the statements they had made to their solicitors pending the trial, much less the applications which they made if they applied for legal aid, are not subject to legal privilege. The principle to be derived from *Reg. v Cox and Railton,* applies in my view to circumstances which do not cover the ordinary run of case such as this is".[31]

In *Francis & Francis,* Lord Goff was "inclined to agree" with Glidewell, LJ that the common law principle of legal professional privilege cannot be excluded by the crime/fraud exception "in cases where a communication is made by a client to his legal adviser regarding the conduct of his case in criminal or civil proceedings, merely because such communication is untrue and would, if acted upon, lead to the commission of the crime of perjury in such proceedings".[32]

Nor will the exception apply so as to enable an applicant to seek discovery from one who is an innocent assignee from a fraudster. In *Banque Keyser Ullman SA* v *Skandia (UK) Insurance Co Limited,*[33] substantial loans were made on terms that the borrowers would lodge certain securities with the lending banks and also take out insurance cover to guard against a failure to repay. Three of the policies so taken out were issued to the borrowers directly who assigned them to the lenders. When the borrowers defaulted, the banks claimed under the policies. The insurers denied liability on the grounds that the policies had been obtained by the fraud of the borrowers or their associates. When discovery took place in the action, the insurers challenged the bank's claims to legal professional privilege. Such challenge was directed to documents, communications and

---

31 *Ibid.,* at 53.

32 [1989] AC 346 at 397. (The decision in *Snaresbrook* was overruled in *Francis & Francis* as regards the proper interpretation of s. 10(2) Police and Criminal Evidence Act 1984.) Note that in *Barclays Bank plc v Eustice* [1995] 1 WLR 1238, discussed in Section 3 below, Schiemann, LJ thought – but without deciding the point – that a "court would be reluctant... to force a legal adviser to give evidence or produce documents as to what a client had said when seeking advice as to how to respond to a criminal charge which had been preferred against him" (at 1250).

33 [1986] 1 Lloyd's Rep 336.

notes passing between the lenders and their solicitors at the time when the loans were made and at the time when the defaults occurred, and before any proceedings were contemplated.

The basis of the challenge was that because of the borrowers' fraud, the lenders must lose their privilege even though they were the victims of the fraud and themselves wholly innocent. The insurers argued that had the borrowers been the parties in the case who were claiming privilege (whether in litigation or in answer to a subpoena duces tecum), they could not have maintained a claim to privilege in relation to such documents. It followed, they submitted, that an assignee of an insurance policy from an assignor who is party to a fraud cannot be in a better position than the assignor. These submissions were rejected because:

> "Where, as in the present case, it is sought to contend against a wholly innocent party that a privilege does not exist, whether as assignee of a fraudsman or not, it is not in accordance with the law as previously laid down ... to [so extend the law] would involve the consequence that once there was a fraud, the party who was complaining could obtain discovery of documents otherwise covered by professional privilege not only against the fraud himself, but against anybody else who might be in a position to give evidence ...".[34]

Although the Court of Appeal rejected these propositions as unsustainable in *Banque Keyser,* it nevertheless appears from the House of Lords' judgments in *Francis & Francis* that the extension contended for by the insurers in the former decision is likely to be accepted where the person from whom the evidence is sought is used by the fraudster as his innocent tool. In *Banque Keyser,* the banks as assignees were not being used to further or to cover up the borrowers' fraud.

3. THE CRIME/FRAUD EXCEPTION IN CIVIL CASES

It is evident from the discussion in Section 2 above that the crime/fraud exception is not a feature unique to criminal proceedings[35] and that it can be invoked in relation to claims to privilege made in civil cases. Indeed, although the court's judgment in *R v Cox and Railton* was delivered in the context of criminal proceedings, Stephen, J's judgment expressly approved earlier decisions where the crime/fraud exception had been applied in civil

---

34 Parker, LJ *ibid.,* at 338.
35 Where the exception has been codified in s. 10(2) Police and Criminal Evidence Act 1984.

cases.[36] However, in *Williams* v *Quebrada Railway, Land and Copper Co*[37] it was argued that the crime/fraud exception only applied in civil cases where there was more than a charge of fraud against the defendant, for example where the defendant's lawyer was also a party to the fraud. Kekewich, J rejected this and appeared to indicate that the scope of the exception as it applies in civil proceedings was potentially very wide. In his view:

> "... where there is anything of an underhand nature or approaching to fraud, especially in commercial matters, where there should be the veriest good faith, the whole transaction should be ripped up and disclosed in all its nakedness to the light of the Court".[38]

Quebrada concerned an action by debenture holders against a company which had defaulted on payments of interest. The plaintiffs alleged that the defendant company had entered into further charges (without revealing the pre-existing ones) with a company which was its sole agent at a time when the defendant company was insolvent and its stoppage imminent. It was alleged that these charges had been entered into solely to defeat or delay the debenture holders. When the defendant's affidavit of documents was served by its liquidators (the company having gone into voluntary winding-up in the meantime), this revealed the existence of legal advice obtained with reference to the subsequent charges. The plaintiffs applied for discovery of these materials which was granted after the judge had inspected the relevant documents. As to the nature of the case before him, Kekewich, J commented:

> "... it is said that is not a charge of fraud. It is difficult to say it is not commercial dishonesty. It is, in my opinion, commercial dishonesty of the very worst type; and that is fraud".[39]

Despite the width of some of the judge's remarks, this was clearly a case which justified the application of the exception.[40] Indeed, in all subsequent cases, the Courts have been astute to ensure that the exception remains confined in civil proceedings to cases involving some element of fraud. In *Crescent Farm Sports* v *Sterling Offices*,[41] an attempt was made to invoke

---

36 *Follett* v *Jefferyes,* 1 Sim NS 3 and *Russell* v *Jackson,* 9 Hare 387.
37 [1895] 2 Ch 751.
38 *Ibid.,* at 755.
39 *Ibid.,* at 755.
40 Both Goff, J in *Crescent Farm Sports* v *Sterling Offices* [1972] Ch 553 and Vinelott, J in *Derby & Co Ltd* v *Weldon (No 7)* [1990] 1 WLR 1156 thought that the decision was in fact concerned with conduct of a fraudulent character, *i.e.* in line with the principles enunciated in *Cox and Railton.*
41 [1972] 1 Ch 553.

the exception in an action brought for breach of contract, unlawful interference with contract and damages for conspiracy. The plaintiffs, in attempting to get access to the defendant's privileged documentation, argued that the exception was not limited to crime or fraud but extended to any act or scheme which is unlawful in the sense of giving rise to a civil claim. Alternatively, it contended that "fraud" should be liberally construed so as to cover the facts of this case.[42] Goff, J rejected these contentions:

> "Apart possibly from *Williams v Quebrada Railway, Land and Copper Co* ... the exception has always been stated as confined to cases of crime or fraud ... the wide submission of the plaintiffs would endanger the whole basis of legal professional privilege. It is clear that parties must be at liberty to take advice as to the ambit of their contractual obligations and liabilities in tort and what liability they will incur whether in contract or tort by a proposed course of action without thereby in every case losing professional privilege".[43]

As regards the types of civil action in which the exception will apply, Goff, J agreed that fraud for this purpose was not limited to the tort of deceit but included all forms of fraud and dishonesty such as fraudulent breach of trust, fraudulent conspiracy, treachery and "sham contrivances".[44] However, it did not extend in his view to the tort of inducing a breach of contract or the "narrow" form of conspiracy pleaded in the case before him.

The same judge revisited these issues in the unreported Court of Appeal decision in *Gamlen Chemical Co (UK) Ltd* v *Rochem Ltd*.[45] This concerned, *inter alia*, actions against individuals who were senior employees of the plaintiff who had used their employer's time and money to promote their own interests and to set up a computing business. It was accepted before the Court of Appeal that in the case of one transaction the plaintiffs had sufficiently established (by reference to their pleadings and their unanswered affidavit evidence) that the employees had been guilty of fraud. Applying the crime/fraud exception, Goff, LJ said:

> "Where you draw the line in the infinite gradation of good and evil between [the *Quebrada* case] and the *Crescent Farm* case... I do not attempt to say but I have no doubt the present case is on the same side as [the *Quebrada* case] and that discovery ought to be given".

---

42 These are described in Chap. 6, Section 4.
43 [1972] 1 Ch 553 at 564–565.
44 [1972] 1 Ch 553 at 565.
45 Extracts from the judgments were cited in both *Derby & Co Ltd* v *Weldon (No 7)* [1990] 1 WLR 1156 and *Barclays Bank plc* v *Eustice* [1995] 1 WLR 1238.

However, he went on to warn that in every case the court has to be satisfied that what is *prima facie* proved for the purpose of the rule "really is dishonest, and not merely disreputable or a failure to maintain good ethical standards". The decision in *Gamlen Chemical Co* was relied on by Vinelott, J in *Derby & Co Ltd v Weldon (No 7)*[46] where he reviewed the relevant authorities in detail. This decision arose out of complicated and protracted litigation involving claims for breach of contract, negligence, breach of fiduciary duty, deceit and conspiracy to defraud. In the event, the judge accepted that the plaintiffs had established a strong *prima facie* case of fraud in relation to certain aspects of the claim which justified the loss of the privilege. As to this, a submission was made that there was no foundation for a finding that the creation of certain trusts and the transfer of assets to them were steps taken in furtherance of an initial fraud. The judge rejected this:

> "These steps were taken in furtherance of the initial fraud in that they were taken to conceal and render irrecoverable profits to which the plaintiffs asserted a proprietary claim. Moreover, the steps, even if taken in isolation from the initial fraud were ... themselves so dishonest as to negate the claim for professional legal privilege. They involved, in the words of Goff J. in the *Crescent Farm* case ... 'trickery and sham contrivances'".[47]

In *Skuse v Granada Television Ltd*[48] Drake, J, relying on the *Derby v Weldon (No 7)* decision, appears to have been ready to apply the exception in relation to "a form of improper conduct" in the context of a taxation of costs. That improper conduct allegedly consisted of the plaintiff being secretly maintained and his solicitors improperly financing him by giving him credit on a speculative or contingency basis to enable him to prosecute an appeal. Whilst no doubt reprehensible conduct, it is, with respect, a little difficult to see that this falls on the *Quebrada* side of the "gradation of good and evil" (although, in the event there was insufficient evidence of the improper conduct to justify the application of the exception).

More recently, the Court of Appeal has held that the crime/fraud exception can be invoked in the context of proceedings under section 423, Insolvency Act 1986, the side note to which refers to "Transactions defrauding creditors". In *Barclays Bank plc v Eustice*,[49] the bank sought declarations under this section seeking to set aside certain transactions in respect of farmland which was already charged as security for loans it had

---

46 [1990] 1 WLR 1156.
47 *Ibid.*, at 1174.
48 [1994] 1 WLR 1156.
49 [1995] 1 WLR 1238.

made to the defendant. Those transactions were entered into on favourable terms which amounted to undervalues within the meaning of section 423; further, because those transactions occurred with family members at a time when action by the bank was clearly anticipated by the defendant debtor, with the result that what remained in the defendant's hand barely if at all covered his debt, the Court held there was a strong *prima facie* case that the purpose of the transaction was to prejudice the interests of the bank. Accordingly there existed a strong *prima facie* case that the preconditions for making an order under section 423 were fulfilled.[50] Did these findings entitle the bank, on an interlocutory application for discovery, to an order for disclosure of communications between the defendant and his legal advisers relating to such transactions?

For the defendant it was submitted that the cloak of privilege should not be lifted because neither he nor his solicitors were a party to a crime, nor were they seeking or giving advice for a criminal or fraudulent purpose. Rather, the defendant and his solicitors had jointly and openly engaged in a purpose which was both overt and lawful, namely seeking and giving advice as to how to remove the defendant's assets out of the temporary reach of the bank without rendering the transactions liable to be set aside under section 423.

The Court's response to this was to consider whether public policy required that the documents concerned be disclosed or not. The court accepted that the case was "essentially one about advice sought on how to structure a transaction", albeit in circumstances where it must have been obvious to the defendant that the bank would challenge it once it learnt of it.[51] Nonetheless, having regard to its earlier findings in relation to section 423, the Court held that the defendant's conduct was:

> "... sufficiently iniquitous for public policy to require that communications between him and his solicitor in relation to the setting up of these transactions be discoverable".[52]

Furthermore, it made no difference whether or not the client or solicitor shared that view, since public policy does not require the communications of those who misapprehend the law to be privileged in circumstances where no privilege attaches to those who correctly understand the situation. The Court did not think that the result of its decision would discourage "straightforward citizens" from consulting their lawyers:

---

50 Per Schiemann, LJ at 1248.
51 *Ibid.*, at 1250.
52 *Ibid.*, at 1252.

"Those lawyers should tell them that what is proposed is liable to be set aside and the straightforward citizen will then not do it and so the advice will never see the light of day. Insofar as those wishing to engage in sharp practice are concerned, the effect of the present decision may well be to discourage them from going to their lawyers. This has the arguable public disadvantage that the lawyers might have dissuaded them from the sharp practise. However, it has the undoubted public advantage that the absence of lawyers will make it more difficult for them to carry out their sharp practice".[53]

There can be no objection to this decision in so far as it applies the crime/fraud exception to claims involving fraudulent conduct under the insolvency legislation. Transgression of related provisions of the Insolvency Act 1986, such as the fraudulent trading provisions in section 213, could presumably also attract the application of the exception, though not the wrongful trading provisions in section 214. What is of some concern however is that the decision was reached in circumstances where, apparently, the client did not set out to commit a crime or engage in fraudulent conduct (in contrast to the position of, say, *Cox and Railton* 110 years earlier). Furthermore, unlike *Cox and Railton*, Mr Eustice appears, so far as one can tell from the report, to have acted in accordance with legal advice sought to enable him to stay within the boundaries of the law. Even though, in the event, the court concluded there was a strong *prima facie* case that Mr Eustice had contravened section 423, and that his purpose in seeking legal advice was "iniquitous", "sharp practice" perpetrated on the advice of legal advisers is pushing at the boundaries to which this exception should be taken. Perhaps the scope of this exception is subtly changing, for "sharp practice" is, arguably, different from "crime", "fraud", "trick" or "sham contrivance". Whatever, lawyers who are asked to advise their clients how they can stay within the boundaries of the law in cases such as these now need to warn of the potential consequences if the court takes a different view of steps taken in consequence of their advice.

4. INVOKING THE CRIME/FRAUD EXCEPTION

Important, but competing, public policy considerations underlie the rationale for the legal professional privilege generally and the basis of the crime/fraud exception. Nonetheless, the courts have consistently made it clear that negativing privilege by applying the exception will rarely occur.

53 *Ibid.,* at 1252.

As Stephen, J warned at the end of his judgment in *Cox and Railton:*

> "... the power in question ought to be used with the greatest care not to hamper prisoners in making their defence, and not to enable unscrupulous persons to acquire a knowledge to which they have no right, and every precaution should be taken against compelling unnecessary disclosures".[54]

Such warnings are periodically repeated.[55] In *R v Snaresbrook Crown Court, ex p. DPP.*[56] Glidewell, LJ thought that the crime/fraud exception only applies to circumstances which do not cover the ordinary run of case.

However, what precisely is required from an evidential viewpoint in order to persuade a court to do this? The problem, as Earl Halsbury, the Lord Chancellor, pointed out in *Bullivant v Attorney General for Victoria,*[57] is the tension between waiting until the defendant has been proved guilty of a crime, which would have the result that relevant documentation would never be produced at all until too late; as against a party demanding production on the basis that what he is endeavouring to enquire into is possibly illegal, with the result that the privilege may wrongly be displaced. In *Bullivant,* the Lord Chancellor said:

> "The line which the Courts have hitherto taken, and I hope will preserve, is this – that in order to displace the prima facie right of silence by a witness who has been put in the relation of professional confidence with his client, before that confidence can be broken you must have some definite charge either by way of allegation or affidavit or what not ... there must be some definite charge of something which displaces the privilege".[58]

In *Bullivant,* the House of Lords rejected the attempt to displace the privilege because of the lack of a definite charge – there was nothing there which the Court could regard as an allegation of fact sufficient to displace the privilege.

The House of Lords returned to this issue in *O'Rourke v Darbishire.*[59] This action was brought by representatives of the heiress at law of the late Sir Joseph Whitworth against the representatives of his executors. The plaintiffs' claims included ones to the effect that testamentary dispositions made in favour of the executors had been obtained by their fraud. In the

---

54 (1884) 14 QBD 153 at 176.
55 Donaldson, LJ commented in *Buttes Gas & Oil Co v Hammer (No 3)* [1981] QB 223 at p. 252 "something exceptional is called for" in order to displace the privilege; and in *Derby v Weldon (No 7)* [1990] 1 WLR 1156 Vinelott, J commented at 1173 that "... the court will be very slow to deprive a defendant of the important protection of legal professional privilege on an interlocutory application".
56 [1988] QB 532.
57 [1901] AC 196.
58 At 201.
59 [1920] AC 581.

light of these allegations, the defendants' claims to privilege in respect of certain trust documents were challenged. This claim was unanimously rejected by the House of Lords whose members all emphasised the insufficiency of merely alleging fraud in order to invoke the crime/fraud exception. According to Viscount Finlay:

> "... there must be, in order to get rid of privilege, not merely an allegation that they were made for the purpose of getting advice for the commission of a fraud, but there must be something to give colour to the charge. The statement must be made in clear and definite terms, and there must further be some prima facie evidence that it has some foundation in fact.... It is obvious that it would be absurd to say that the privilege could be got rid of merely by making a charge of fraud. The Court will exercise its discretion, not merely as to the terms in which the allegation is made, but also as to the surrounding circumstances, for the purpose of seeing whether the charge is made honestly and with sufficient probability of its truth to make it right to disallow the privilege of professional communications".[60]

Other speeches in this decision canvassed whether a sufficient charge of fraud might be comprised in allegations in a statement of claim, apart from any other source of information.[61] Lord Sumner indicated[62] that an unsuccessful motion to strike out a plaintiff's pleading which alleges fraud does not thereby lead to the result that the plaintiff has established a sufficient *prima facie* case for the purpose of the crime/fraud exception: all the materials must be weighed, such as they are.

Although some of the early decisions, particularly *Bullivant* and *O'Rourke,* declined to specify precisely what is required by way of substantiating the prima facie case of fraud so as to invoke the exception, those cases in which this has been done successfully provide some pointers. Obviously, the prosecution's success in *Cox and Railton* was in part due to the surrounding evidence adduced at the trial. This made it probable, according to Stephen, J, "that the visit to the solicitor really was intended for the purpose for which, after he had given his evidence, it turned out to have been intended".[63] In *Derby & Co v Weldon (No 7)*[64] Vinelott, J had substantial material before him (particularly in the form of affidavit evidence made as a consequence of a number of previous interlocutory applications arising out of, *inter alia*, the granting of Mareva injunctions

---

60   *Ibid.,* at 604. See also *Nationwide Building Society* v *Various Solicitors* (1998) *The Times,* 5 February.
61   See Lord Parmoor and Lord Wrenbury at 622 and 632. Lord Sumner, at 613, appeared to doubt this; see also Vinelott, J in *Derby v Weldon (No 7)* [1990] 1 WLR 1156 at 1173.
62   At 614.
63   (1884) 14 QBD 153 at 176.
64   [1990] 1 WLR 1156.

and related relief) which enabled him to find that the plaintiffs had established a strong *prima facie* case of fraud such that the privilege should be displaced. In *Gamlen Chemical Co*,[65] the court had the plaintiff's statement of claim and uncontradicted affidavit evidence;[66] similarly, in *Barclays Bank plc* v *Eustice*[67] the Court of Appeal evidently had considerable surrounding or background information available to it enable it to decide to displace the privilege.[68]

It is also worth noting a dictum of the Divisional Court in *R* v *Governor of Pentonville Prison, ex p. Osman*[69] which indicated the court's view that it could see no objection to a court looking, if necessary, at documents in order to determine whether they came into existence for a criminal or fraudulent purpose.[70] Even if this is right, it must be the case that a court would not inspect unless the applicant had already gone some way to discharging the burden on him, by way of giving "some colour" to the charge.

Finally, in order to invoke the exception, it is sufficient if the communication concerned relates merely to an issue in the action. The fraud relied on need not be the foundation of the claim: see *Dubai Bank* v *Galadari (No 6)*.[71]

5. POLICE POWERS OF SEARCH AND SEIZURE

Privilege issues, including the application of the statutory version of the crime/fraud exception contained in section 10(2) Police and Criminal Evidence Act 1984, occasionally arise in the context of police powers of search and seizure both under the 1984 Act and in relation to other statutes, such as the Forgery and Counterfeiting Act 1981 and the Drug Trafficking Offences Act 1986. It is not the intention of this work to

---

65 [1980] 1 WLR 614.
66 See p. 233 above.
67 [1995] 1 WLR 1238.
68 In contrast, in *Re Konigsberg (bankrupt), ex p. the Trustee* v *Konigsberg and Others* [1989] 3 All ER 289, an attempt to invoke the privilege on the basis of a single sentence in an affidavit failed. Peter Gibson, J commented that any allegations relied on as a ground for breaching privilege should be made "clearly and with sufficient supporting evidence to enable the Court to conclude that there is a prima facie case resting on solid grounds". See also *Skuse* v *Granada Television Ltd* [1994] 1 WLR 1156, where there was "no strong evidence" to support the allegations of improper conduct.
69 [1989] 3 All ER 701, at 716 per Lloyd, LJ
70 The court found some support for this view in *Cox and Railton, op. cit.,* at 175.
71 (1991) *The Times*, 22 April.

examine these issues in any great detail. Nonetheless, given that the law reports evidence the police's willingness on occasions to use these powers to search the offices of solicitors, as well as their clients, some reference should be made to these matters. This necessitates a brief description of the powers available to the police in the conduct of criminal investigations to obtain access to relevant[72] evidential material under the Police and Criminal Evidence Act 1984 ("the 1984 Act").[73]

Section 8 of the 1984 Act empowers the police to seek warrants to enter and search premises for materials upon application being made to a justice of the peace. If however the materials sought comprise "excluded materials"[74] or "special procedure material"[75] that application is made to a circuit judge pursuant to section 9. Except in exceptional circumstances (permitted by para. 14(d) of Schedule 1 to the 1984 Act), the application for an order under Section 9 is made on notice to the person against whom it is applied for. Further, Schedule 1 to the 1984 Act sets out a stringent set of "access conditions" (which thereby impose much greater safeguards than in the case of applications under section 8[76]) which must be satisfied before an order can be made under section 9.

The powers available under sections 8 and 9 are both subject to the restriction that items subject to legal privilege, as defined in section 10(1) of the 1984 Act, "are placed beyond the reach of any of the investigative powers conferred":[77] see, for example, section 8(1)(d). Further, section 9(2) provides that any Act (including a local Act) passed before the 1984 Act under which a search of premises for the purposes of a criminal investigation could be authorised by the issue of a warrant ceases to have

---

72 Which, in the context of the 1984 Act, means "admissible evidence": s. 8(4) of the 1984 Act.

73 As to which, see *e.g.* Lord Bridge in his dissenting speech in *Francis & Francis (a firm)* v *Central Criminal Court* [1989] AC 345 at 369–371 and Leggatt, LJ in *R* v *Leeds Magistrates' Court, ex p. Dumbleton* [1993] Crim LR 866. The procedures which the police must follow under other Acts, such as the Drug Trafficking Offences Act 1986, are not necessarily exactly the same as those outlined here under the 1984 Act.

74 Defined in s. 11 of the 1984 Act as including personal records (*e.g.* relating to the health of an individual) and journalistic material, all of which are held "in confidence".

75 Defined in s. 14 of the 1984 Act as material, other than excluded material and privileged material, which the person who possesses it has acquired or created in the course, *e.g.* of any trade, business or profession and which he holds, inter alia, subject to an express or implied undertaking to hold in confidence.

76 Per Parker, LJ in *R* v *Guildhall Magistrates' Court, ex p. Primlaks Holdings Co (Panama) Inc* [1990] 1 QB 261 at 268.

77 Lord Bridge in *Francis & Francis,* [1989] AC 345 at 369. He made the same comment in relation to the investigative powers available under the Drug Trafficking Offences Act 1986. Note however, that the Inland Revenue's powers of document seizure under *e.g.* s. 20C Taxes Management Act 1970 entitle it to seize privileged material from the client (but not his solicitor, barrister or advocate).

effect so far as it relates to the authorisation of searches for privileged material. Additionally, section 19(6) restricts the wide powers of seizure conferred by section 19(2) and (3) where a constable is lawfully on any premises, by providing that no power of seizure conferred under any enactment can be taken to authorise the seizure of an item which the police constable exercising that power has reasonable grounds for believing is subject to legal privilege.

Section 10 of the 1984 Act defines items subject to legal privilege in a manner which caused Lord Goff in *Francis & Francis*[78] to comment that "... the intention of the legislature was to encapsulate in Section 10 the common law principles relating to ...legal professional privilege".[79] As discussed in Section 2 above, the definition in section 10(1) is subject to the statutory crime/fraud exception contained in section 10(2) which similarly reflects the common law position.

As the House of Lords confirmed in *Francis & Francis,* while the privilege is that of the client and not his solicitor, it is nonetheless the duty of the solicitor to protect his client's privilege unless he waives it.[80] Where therefore the police obtain a search warrant under their investigative powers, the following issues may arise:

- First, the solicitor will need to be astute to ensure that the warrant does not seek privileged materials. This will be particularly so in the case of search warrants executed in respect of the solicitor's own premises. Similar issues may also arise in relation to privileged material maintained by the client himself, whether at his home or place of business.

---

78 *Ibid.,* at 395. The definition of legal privilege contained in s. 10(1) of the 1984 Act is also relevant when privilege issues arise in the context of applications made under the Criminal Justice (International Co-operation) Act 1990: see *Crown Prosecution Service on behalf of Director of Public Prosecutions for Australia* v *Holman Fenwick & Willan (a firm)* (unrep., 13 December 1993), noted in Chap. 2.

79 Specifically, s. 10(1) defines "items subject to legal privilege" as meaning "(a) communications between the professional legal adviser and his client or any person representing his client made in connection with the giving of legal advice to the client; (b) communications between the professional legal adviser and his client or any person representing his client or between such an adviser or his client or any such representative and any other person made in connection with or in contemplation of legal proceedings and for the purposes of such proceedings; and (c) items enclosed with or referred to in such communications and made – (i) in connection with the giving of legal advice; or (ii) in connection with or in contemplation of legal proceedings and for the purposes of such proceedings, when they are in the possession of a person who is entitled to possession of them".

80 See, *e.g.,* Lord Griffiths, *op. cit.,* at 383.

- Secondly, having regard to the provisions of the 1984 Act described above, it would also be open to the client (or the solicitor) to apply to quash the warrant if this was granted under an incorrect procedure.
- Thirdly, as Lord Bridge observed in *Francis & Francis*,[81] all documents and other records in the possession of a solicitor in relation to the affairs of his clients are special procedure material (unless they are subject to legal privilege). This means that any attempt by the police to obtain access to them can only be achieved by way of an application made under section 9 of the 1984 Act (and not s.8).[82]
- Fourthly, in *R v Guildhall Magistrates' Court ex p. Primlaks Holdings Co (Panama) Inc*[83] the Divisional Court held that even where the police seek materials in relation to which they assert privilege has been lost by virtue of section 10(2) of the 1984 Act, then the loss of the privilege does not automatically result in there being no express or implied undertaking to hold those materials in confidence. This has the consequence that the police must seek a warrant for such documents as being "special procedure" materials, under section 9 and not section 8.

As to this last point, the Divisional Court in *ex p. Primlaks* expressed the view that Parliament could not have intended that a justice of the peace on an *ex parte* application under section 8 should be able to authorise the search and seizure of documents *prima facie* privileged, when it had expressly created a procedure (under s.9) by which any question concerning the loss of that privilege ought to be determined by a circuit judge. Here, warrants issued under section 8 of the 1984 Act permitting the police to search solicitors' offices were quashed because the police could not have been satisfied that the material to be seized was not *prima facie* privileged. The application should therefore have been made under section 9.

In contrast, the challenge to the search warrant issued in *Dumbleton*[84] under the Forgery and Counterfeiting Act 1981 failed. Here, the applicant, a dishonest solicitor, contended that the application for warrant ought to have been made under section 9 of the 1984 Act (in view of the restriction contained in s.9(2)) because the warrant allegedly sought items subject to legal privilege within the meaning of section 10(1) of the 1984 Act. The

---

81 *Op. cit.*, at 370.
82 See also the *Dumbleton* case (n. 73 above), transcript at p. 11.
83 [1990] 1 QB 261 at 271, per Parker, LJ
84 See n. 73 above.

Divisional Court disagreed: they did not comprise communications in connection with legal proceedings, even though two of them were forged letters used in and by inference made for the purposes of deceiving a court in relation to certain prior civil proceedings. Nor was this material special procedure material because:

> "... from its nature it cannot have been acquired or created in the course of the profession of a solicitor. Parliament cannot have intended to protect forged documents on the ground that they were forged by a solicitor or supplied to him by a fraudulent client. In any event, a dishonest solicitor cannot be said to hold a forged document subject to an implied undertaking (or an express undertaking) to hold it in confidence".[85]

Finally, the Divisional Court's decision in *R v Southampton Crown Court, ex p. J and P*[86] should be noted. Here, solicitors who were being investigated by the police for suspected theft of client money successfully quashed warrants issued under section 9 of the 1984 Act for the search of their office premises. Their application succeeded because of the excessive width of the warrants and because the police were not justified, in the circumstances, in obtaining them on an *ex parte* application. A further ground on which the application succeeded was that the warrants wrongly included material subject to legal privilege, as certain of the materials sought included files involving transactions relating to named individuals and companies which were likely to include privileged material. The court held that there was a need to balance the competing interests of the investigation of crime against the confidentiality of communications between solicitor and client. Accordingly a judge had to be given information upon which he could reasonably infer that the material sought was not privileged. Here the judge should have considered this issue and whether or not privilege had been lost by the crime/fraud exception in section 10(2) of the 1984 Act. There was no evidence that he did. The court went on to observe that the police should draw a judge's attention to material arguably subject to legal privilege and provide him with sufficient information to reach a decision on it.[87]

---

85 Transcript.

86 [1993] Crim LR 962.

87 In the event, it was noted that notwithstanding the solicitors' successful application the police could have made a further application, *inter partes,* for any of the materials which would be properly within the scope of the warrant. See also *R v Inner London Crown Court, ex p. Baines & Baines (a firm)* [1988] QB 579.

Chapter 9

CLAIMING PRIVILEGE

1. INTRODUCTION

This Chapter looks briefly at some of the procedural aspects which arise when a claim to privilege is made or contested; at the circumstances in which the Court will exercise its right to inspect documents in respect of which the claim to privilege is made; and what happens when an order for production is made in respect of materials which are only privileged in part.

2. THE RULES OF COURT

Most privilege disputes arise at the discovery stage of litigation. A litigant must always give discovery of his privileged documents, in the sense that he must disclose them in his list of documents. However, he is not obliged to produce them to his opponent, in the sense of making them available for inspection (unless his claim to privilege is successfully challenged or is waived). In High Court civil litigation the relevant provisions are currently contained in RSC Order 24 rule 5(2) which provides that:

> "If it is desired to claim that any documents are privileged from production, the claim must be made in the list of documents with a sufficient statement of the grounds of the privilege".[1]

RSC Order 24 rule 5(1) requires that the list of documents be in Form No. 26 in Appendix A to the *Supreme Court Practice*. Form 26 requires the litigant to state in paragraph 1 of his list that he has documents in his possession, custody or power relating to matters in question in the action which he will describe in Schedule 1 to the list. The claim for privilege is usually made in paragraph 2 of the list. A typical claim will assert that:

> "The Plaintiff/Defendant objects to produce the documents enumerated in part 2 of schedule 1 on the grounds that..."

followed by a "sufficient statement" of the grounds of the privilege which he makes for the documents concerned. As is discussed at page 248 below,

---

1 The "privilege" will include those discussed in Chaps. 10 and 11, namely the without prejudice privilege and the privilege against self-incrimination. Note that the rules relating to discovery will change when the Woolf reform proposals are introduced.

the description of the privileged documents listed in part 2 need not be as detailed as for those listed in part 1.

By RSC Order 24 rules 2(7) and 3, a party serving the list can be required to verify his list on oath, in which case the prescribed form of affidavit (as per RSC O.24 r.5(3)) is in Form No. 27 in Appendix A to the Supreme Court Practice. Current practice necessitates a simple form affidavit (assuming the claim to privilege is adequately made in the list) and it will usually be sufficient to depose shortly to the effect that the statement of facts by which the claim to privilege is made in paragraph 2 of the list of documents is true.

It is a common feature of many of the nineteenth-century decisions considered in this book that they were concerned with disputes as to the adequacy of the claim to privilege, including where the claim was made on oath. However, following the Court of Appeal decisions in *Taylor* v *Batten*,[2] *Jones* v *Monte Video Gas Co*[3] and *Bewicke* v *Graham*,[4] such disputes become increasingly uncommon as, together, they established first the conclusiveness of an affidavit verifying the claim to privilege, so long as the claim was good on its face, and secondly they endorsed the practice of the party who objects to disclosure giving a non-informative description of the documents concerned. As a result challenges to claims for privilege became increasingly more difficult.

The consequence of these decisions is that if an affidavit sworn pursuant to RSC Order 24 claims or verifies a claim for privilege and observes the rules set out in *Jones* v *Monte Video Gas Co*,[5] it is effectively incapable of challenge.[6] So, unless it is apparent from the list or verifying affidavit, or the documents they refer to, or from an admission in the pleadings of the party from whom the discovery is sought, that the claim to privilege is insufficiently made, the court will normally accept it at face value: the opposing party is not permitted to persuade the court by means of a contentious affidavit that the verifying affidavit is inadequate or that the claim to privilege is not made out. These rules have been consistently

---

2 (1878) 4 QBD 85.

3 (1880) 5 QBD 556.

4 (1881) 7 QBD 400. As to this case, see the Law Reform Committee's Sixteenth Report Privilege in Civil Proceedings Cmnd. 3472 at para. 28.

5 See Brett, LJ (1880) 5 QBD 556 at 558 and Cotton, LJ in *Jones* v *Andrews* (1888) 58 LT 601 at 604. Thus, leading counsel for Mrs Waugh in *Waugh* v *British Railways Board* [1980] AC 521 at 539 (discussed in Chap. 3) accepted he could not challenge the assertion made on oath on behalf of the Board that litigation was anticipated when the report in issue in that case was prepared.

6 As to challenging privilege, see Section 4 below.

applied throughout the last century,[7] and were recently reaffirmed by the Court of Appeal in *Fayed* v *Lonhro plc*[8] where Stuart-Smith, LJ, after a review of the authorities, stated:

> "[These] lead me to the conclusion that on whatever ground the order for a further affidavit is made... the oath of the deponent in answer is conclusive; it cannot be contravened by a further contentious affidavit and cannot be the subject of cross-examination".[9]

Furthermore, he indicated that even if the power to order cross-examination on the verifying affidavit existed,

> "... the exercise of that power should... be reserved for those cases where the existence or non-existence of the document raises a discreet issue which does not impinge to any serious extent on the issues in the action".[10]

3 . CLAIMING PRIVILEGE

In the nineteenth century the Courts placed considerable emphasis on the precision with which the claim to privilege was made. While the practice is now much more relaxed,[11] nonetheless, there must still be a "sufficient statement" of the privilege and careless claims to privilege can still provoke challenges, particularly in hotly contested litigation.[12]

Accordingly, there are some basic rules. So, if the claim to privilege is being made under the advice head, it is essential to refer at least to the confidential character of the professional communications which have been

---

7   See, *e.g.*, *Lyell* v *Kennedy (No 3)* (1884) 27 Ch D 1, per Cotton, LJ at 19; *Wiedman* v *Walpole* (1890) 24 QBD 626 (CA); and *Birmingham & Midland Motor Omnibus Co Ltd* v *London & North West Railway* [1913] 2 KB 850, per Buckley, LJ at 855.

8   (1993) *The Times*, 24 June.

9   Transcript.

10 Transcript. See also *Berkeley Administration Inc* v *McClelland* [1990] FSR 381 and *R* v *The Secretary of State for Transport ex p. Factortame* (1997) *The Times*, 1 September, both of which deprecated applications to ensure discovery has been properly given. In *Berkeley Administration,* the Court of Appeal suggested that if a deponent is not believed, his opponent should call for him to be cross-examined on his oath.

11 The Law Reform Committee noted in its Report on privilege produced in 1967, "Privilege in Civil Proceedings", Cmnd 3472, at para. 28, there is room for: "... honest errors of judgment in claims where the documents come into existence for more than one purpose, and it is easy for a practice to grow up making a claim to privilege for all documents of a particular type without considering the contents of the individual documents and the circumstances in which it came into existence, so as to see whether it is really entitled to privilege."

12 Model objections can be found in *Atkins Court Forms*, Vol 15 pp.142–144. Here, a few examples only from the reports will be briefly considered.

made for the purposes of seeking or obtaining legal advice.[13] So far as concerns litigation privilege, the claim must make clear that the documents concerned came into existence with the dominant or primary purpose for use in, or as evidence for, or to enable legal advice to be obtained in connection with actual, pending or contemplated litigation.

If the litigant is relying on the "once privileged, always privileged" rule, then he will need to describe the previous litigation in connection with which the documents came into existence. Similarly, if the claimant is relying on the "successors in title" rule, or on common interest privilege, some explanation of the entitlement will be expected.

Otherwise, the party on whom the list is served is not necessarily entitled to a full description of each document for which privilege is claimed, to the same degree as is required when listing those documents which are not privileged and which are disclosed in Schedule 1 of Part I.[14] In *Gardner* v *Irvin* Cotton, LJ said:

> "I think that the Plaintiffs are not entitled to have the dates of the letters and such other particulars of the correspondence as may enable them to discover indirectly the contents of the letters, and thus to cause the Defendants to furnish evidence against themselves in this action."[15]

In *Derby* v *Weldon (No 7)*,[16] counsel for the plaintiffs, in challenging the adequacy of a claim to privilege, accepted that he was not entitled to any information which might lead by a process of inference to a conclusion as to the probable nature or content of the legal advice sought. But he did submit that he was entitled to know at least the identity of the persons or firms from whom advice was sought, the time when it was sought and, subject to his concession, the "category" of advice sought. This submission was rejected, Vinelott, J accepting that "in modern times" the claim for privilege is usually treated as sufficient. In reaching this decision he rejected a further submission that more care is required in dealing with the basis of the claim to privilege in cases of exceptional complexity, an aspect he considered to be irrelevant. He also rejected the further contention that the plaintiffs were entitled to satisfy themselves as

---

13   Thus in *Derby & Co Ltd* v *Weldon (No 7)* [1990] 1 WLR 1156, Vinelott, J upheld a claim to privilege which was in "usual form" and referred to "Confidential correspondence, both original and copies, memoranda of instructions, opinions and other documents and other notes of meetings, telephone conversations between the first and second Defendants, their solicitors and Counsel and other legal advisors, or any of them, and drafts of the same for the purpose of obtaining legal advice."

14   See Eveleigh, J in *Crompton (Alfred) Amusement Machines Ltd* v *Commissioners of Customs and Excise* [1971] 2 All ER 843.

15   (1878) 4 Ex D 49 at 53. See also *Taylor* v *Batten* (1878) 4 QBD 85.

16   [1990] 1 WLR 1156 at 1176.

to the sufficiency of the claim to privilege by means of a fuller description of the documents for which the privilege was claimed. This contention arose because the evidence showed apparently that lawyers (especially in foreign jurisdictions) had been employed by the defendants more as business intermediaries than legal advisors. As to this, Vinelott, J was content to accept the general claim to privilege set out in the list of documents, taken together with a written assurance in letter form from the Defendants' solicitors that they had been through the documents and were satisfied that in each case there was a valid claim to privilege.

4. CHALLENGING PRIVILEGE

So long as there is an adequate claim to privilege in the list, properly supported on affidavit (where appropriate), then challenging the privilege is a very difficult task.[17] Clearly, where points of principle arise as to the scope of privilege, the courts will examine the claim carefully. Otherwise, as discussed in Section 2, a challenge to the privilege will usually cut little ice unless the facts which support the claim or which are verified on oath render it unsound on its face. In *Gardner* v *Irvin*,[18] a challenge was permitted because an affidavit stated merely that certain documents "are privileged", a claim which was highly dubious having regard to the fact that the documents concerned were described merely as "correspondence between ourselves and our solicitors; correspondence between our solicitors and their agents; cash books, ledgers and accounts...". Cotton, LJ held:

> "How can it be said that this affidavit is sufficient; in the body of the affidavit the Defendants simply say "that the same are privileged", and in the schedule they set out the documents, some of which clearly are not privileged. They ought to say not only that the documents are privileged, which is a statement of law, but they ought to set out the facts from which we can see that the Defendants' view of the law is right. Cash-books and ledgers prima facie are not privileged".[19]

More recently, the Court of Appeal in *Standrin* v *Yenton Minster Homes*[20] refused to accept the conclusiveness of a deponent's assertion that certain documents were privileged from production on the grounds of the "without prejudice" privilege. However, this was not a case of the court

---

17 See n. 10 above.
18 (1878) 4 Ex D 49.
19 *Ibid.*, at 53.
20 (1991) *The Times,* 22 July.

ignoring the rules described in Section 2 above. Rather, it was one in which the claim to privilege was bad on its face since it was made in respect of documents which post-dated the successful conclusion of the without prejudice negotiations of which it was wrongly asserted they formed part.

On the other side of the coin, it has already been noted that in *Derby* v *Weldon (No 7)*,[21] Vinelott, J was prepared to accept assurances given by solicitors in correspondence as to the validity of the claim to privilege (despite challenges to the "pleonastic" formulae by which the claim to privilege was made).

And yet the court will, sometimes, "go behind" a claim to privilege made on oath and look at the underlying documents before the court which go to support it. This happened in *Neilson* v *Laugharne*[22] where the Court of Appeal refused to accept, having examined some of the background documentation, a deponent's assertion that the dominant purpose for which the police took statements for which a claim to privilege was erroneously made was in respect of threatened litigation.

A similar issue arose in *Re Highgrade Traders*[23] concerning the adequacy of the evidence which had been sworn in support of a claim to litigation privilege. For the appellant, it was argued that in the light of the uncontradicted affidavit evidence it was not open to the judge at first instance to conclude that the dominant purpose for which the reports which featured in that decision had been obtained was to use them to obtain advice in relation to litigation then reasonably in prospect. In response, it was argued that the court could "go behind" the affidavit evidence in the same way as the court had done in *Neilson* v *Laugharne*. Oliver, LJ's response to this issue demonstrates the importance of making a proper claim to privilege since he was not able:

> "to subscribe to the view that the court is necessarily bound to accept a bare assertion as to the dominant motive of a deponent, unaccompanied by some explanation of the circumstances, at any rate in a case where more than one motive is possible".[24]

Accordingly, he was in no doubt that if there was something in the circumstances of the case which showed that the affidavit evidence was

---

21 [1990] 1 WLR 1156.
22 [1981] 1 QB 736.
23 [1984] BCLC 151 discussed in detail in Chap. 3.
24 *Ibid.*, p. 166.

wrong, as in *Neilson,* then the court was entitled to go behind that evidence.[25]

5 . INSPECTION OF DOCUMENTS BY THE COURT

Just as disputes in the nineteenth century over the sufficiency of the claim to privilege were common, so the courts were more willing to inspect the underlying documents in order to reach the right result. As to this, Sir George Jessel, MR referred in 1876 in *Bustros* v *White*[26] to the prevailing chambers practice:

> "in cases where affidavits have been produced to the judge which appeared to be defective; and where at the desire of both parties, and with a view of avoiding ... delay and expense ... the judge has taken upon himself the trouble and responsibility of looking into the documents and deciding whether they ought to be produced".

The practice at this time was voluntary, since rules of court did not then provide the courts with the power to inspect. However, despite the introduction shortly afterwards of rules which did permit inspection, the courts began to avail themselves of this opportunity less frequently. Although one can point to occasional examples of inspection, such as in *Ainsworth* v *Wilding,*[27] in 1951 the Court of Appeal in *Westminster Airways* v *Kuwait Oil Co*[28] made it clear that where the claim to privilege is formally correct, then inspection was to be discouraged. However, over the last twenty years or so the courts, led by Lord Denning, MR, have shown a renewed willingness to inspect.[29]

The rules governing the production to the court of privileged documents in High Court proceedings are now set out in RSC Order 24, rule 13(2) which provides as follows:

---

25 In the event, in the *Highgrade* case, there was no need to do so because the challenge to the appellant's evidence came at a very late stage and in fact the Court of Appeal allowed further evidence to be introduced. Compare the Court of Appeal's approach in *Westminster Airways Ltd* v *Kuwait Oil Co Ltd* [1951] 1 KB 134, discussed in Section 5 below.

26 1 QBD 423 at 427.

27 [1900] 2 Ch 315.

28 [1951] 1 KB 134.

29 Readers of the current (1997) *Supreme Court Practice* would be forgiven for thinking that the views expressed in the *Westminster* case still hold sway, for the notes to RSC O.24 r. 13(2) make no mention of any of the subsequent decisions referred to below in which the Courts have inspected.

"Where on an application under this Order for production of any document for inspection or to the Court, or for the supply of a copy of any document, privilege from such production or supply is claimed or objection is made to such production or supply on any other ground, the court may inspect the document for the purpose of deciding whether the claim or objection is valid".[30]

The notes to this provision in the *Supreme Court Practice* (1997), at 24/13/2, indicate, on the authority of the Court of Appeal's decision in *Westminster Airways v Kuwait Oil Co*,[31] that the courts will now be very reluctant to inspect. Generally speaking, this is entirely understandable where the claim to privilege is sufficiently stated in either the list of documents or any supporting or verifying affidavit. As it was put by Jenkins, LJ in the *Westminster Airways* case:

"The question whether the court should inspect the documents is one which is a matter for the discretion of the court, and primarily for the judge of first instance. Each case must depend on its own circumstances; but if, looking at the affidavit [and now the list of documents verified by affidavit] the court finds that the claim to privilege is formally correct, and that the documents in respect of which it is made are sufficiently identified and are such that, prima facie, the claim to privilege would appear to be properly made in respect of them ... the court should, generally speaking, accept the affidavit as sufficiently justifying the claim without going further and inspecting the documents".[32]

In the *Westminster Airways* case the defendants, who were sued when their truck ran into and damaged an aeroplane owned by the plaintiffs, wrote to their insurers about the matter and claimed privilege for this correspondence. The court was clear that this was an obvious case in which a claim could be anticipated following the accident and that the privilege was properly claimed in respect of documents coming into existence at a date considerably after the date of the accident. As Jenkins, LJ noted, the appellants did not argue that the privilege was "wholly bad on the face of it" but rather there was "a dubious claim for privilege which might, or might not, be justified". However, he held that that alone, in the circumstances of the case, did not compel the Court to inspect and it refused to do so.

---

30 The forerunner to this rule, O.31, r. 19A(2), which features in a number of the decided cases, provided that "Where on an application for an Order for inspection privilege is claimed for any document, it shall be lawful for the Court or a Judge to inspect the document for the purpose of deciding as to the validity of the claim of privilege".

31 [1951] 1 KB 134.

32 *Ibid.*, at 146.

Despite the court's observations in *Westminster*, judges have subsequently shown some willingness to inspect documents in order to cut through disputes over privilege. This "trend" appears to have been revived by Lord Denning, MR in the *Alfred Crompton* litigation (discussed in Chap. 3) where, in view of the difference of opinion as to whether litigation had been anticipated, he thought this was "eminently a case where the court should inspect the documents itself".[33] Lord Denning, MR again inspected in the *Buttes Oil* v *Hammer (No 3)* litigation, where he commented that the courts often "nowadays" ask to inspect the disputed documents.[34] It is also apparent that the Court of Appeal inspected the disputed documents in *Balabel* v *Air India*.[35] Further, judges will tend to inspect documents where there are disputes as to whether the remainder of a partially disclosed document should also be made available to an opponent.[36] It is difficult to draw any general conclusion from the foregoing save perhaps to speculate that there is generally a greater willingness on the Court's part to exercise its right to inspect where to do so will facilitate resolution of the underlying dispute.[37]

6. PARTLY PRIVILEGED DOCUMENTS

The recent past has seen some judicial controversy regarding a litigant's disclosure and production obligations in relation to documents which contain sections or passages which are privileged, and others which are not.

---

33 *Alfred Crompton Amusement Machines Ltd* v *Customs & Excise Commissioners (No 2)* [1972] 2 QB at 130. Lord Denning was evidently encouraged by the Law Reform Committee's recommendation (in para. 55) that the courts should be more ready to inspect. The House of Lords did not inspect when the case went on further appeal: see [1974] AC 405
34 [1980] 3 WLR 668 at 681.
35 [1988] Ch 317 at 321. See also *Standrin* v *Yenton Minster Homes Ltd* (1991) *The Times*, 22 July; *R* v *Governor of Pentonville Prison, ex p. Osman* [1989] 3 All ER 701; *R* v *The Law Society, ex p. Rosen* (1990) *The Independent*, 12 February. *Kupe Group Ltd* v *Seamar Holdings Ltd* [1993] 3 NZLR 209 is an example of the New Zealand Courts' approach to the issue of inspection. The European Court of Justice will also inspect privileged documents: see *A M & S Europe Ltd* v *Commission of the European Communities* [1983] QB 878.
36 See *Great Atlantic Insurance Co* v *Home Insurance Co* [1981] 1 WLR 529, *Derby & Co Ltd* v *Weldon (No 10)* [1991] 1 WLR 660 and *Sills* v *Tilbury Cargo Handling Ltd (and others)* (unrep., 2 November 1994).
37 Even so, there are exceptions as in *Derby* v *Weldon (No 7)* [1991] 1 WLR 1156. Lord Denning thought it unnecessary to inspect in *Neilson* v *Laugharne* [1981] 1 QB 736. Another case in which the court declined to inspect was *Crescent Farm Sports* v *Sterling Offices Ltd* [1972] Ch 553. Note that in applications for discovery of confidential documents the Courts will increasingly exercise the right to inspect. See *Wallace Smith Trust Co Ltd (in liq)* v *Deloitte Haskins & Sells (a firm)* [1996] 4 All ER 403, CA.

Does the litigant have to show his opponent the entirety of the document; or can he "mask" or "redact" or "seal" the privileged parts? The Court of Appeal in *G.E. Capital Group Ltd* v *Bankers Trust Co*[38] has recently clarified that a litigant need only produce for inspection at the discovery stage the unprivileged parts; further, in doing so he does not run the risk of waiving privilege over the remainder unless and until the privileged sections are put in evidence.

That there has been this controversy is in some respects surprising. As Hoffmann, LJ pointed out in *G.E. Capital*,[39] *Bray's Digest of the Law of Discovery*[40] had noted in 1910 that "generally speaking, any part of a document may be sealed up or otherwise concealed under the same conditions as a whole document may be withheld from production".[41] Indeed, Chapter 2 discusses two older cases in which this practise was adopted.[42]

Despite these authorities, certain dicta in the Court of Appeal's decision in *Great Atlantic Insurance Co* v *Home Insurance*[43] were interpreted as introducing into these rules the additional element of the so-called "separate subject matter" text. This derived from Templeman, LJ's judgment when he said:

> "In my judgment the simplest, safest and most straightforward rule is that if a document is privileged then privilege must be asserted, if at all, to the whole document unless the document deals with separate subject matters so that the document can in effect be divided into two separate and distinct documents each of which is complete".[44]

As a result of these comments, the previous practice started to change, with the result that, at the discovery stage, parties began to make claims to privilege in respect of the whole document, for fear of waiving privilege over the unprivileged parts.[45]

---

38 [1995] 1 WLR 172.

39 *Ibid.*, at 174.

40 2nd Edn., pp. 55–56.

41 McPherson, J's judgment (described by Hoffmann, LJ in *G.E. Capital* as "masterly") in *Curlex Manufacturing Pty Ltd* v *Carlingford Australia General Insurance Ltd* [1987] 2 QR 335, contains a detailed account of the history of the practise in relation to redaction.

42 See *e.g. Nicholl* v *Jones*, 2 H&M 588 and *Ainsworth* v *Wilding* [1900] 2 Ch 315.

43 [1981] 1 WLR 529.

44 *Ibid.*, at 536.

45 This was in spite of the decision in *The "Good Luck"* [1992] 2 Lloyd's Rep 540, which Hoffmann, LJ approved in *G.E. Capital*. For an account of the confusion which reigned immediately prior to the decision in *G.E. Capital*, see "Party privileged documents", by Colin Passmore and Jonathan Goodliffe, at (1994) NLJ, 3 June, p. 761 and (1994) NLJ, 16 September, p. 1240.

In *G E Capital*,[46] the Court of Appeal pointed out that Templeman, LJ's comments in *Great Atlantic* were said in the context of a party putting in evidence at trial part of a privileged document.[47] As we have seen in Chapter 7, in that scenario a party must expect to be treated as having waived privilege over the whole document in the interests of fairness to his opponent. But at the discovery stage of litigation, these rules do not apply, as the *G E Capital* decision has now confirmed.

This decision was, strictly, concerned with the redaction of irrelevant parts of a document. Nonetheless, Hoffman, LJ's judgment made clear that the underlying principles apply equally to documents which contain both privileged and unprivileged sections.[48] In this respect his judgment was followed by Rix, J in *The "Sagheera"*[49] and by the Divisional Court in *Factortame*.[50] In *G E Capital*, when serving their list of documents, GE's solicitors drew attention in an accompanying letter to the fact that in some cases they had disclosed copy extracts of documents. In these edited versions they had blanked out passages which they considered were privileged or commercially sensitive and irrelevant to the issues in the action. Bankers Trust's solicitors pressed for greater particularity as to the individual reasons for each blanked out passage. By the time the matter reached the Court of Appeal, the only documents in issue were those which were blanked out solely on the grounds of irrelevance. Hoffman, LJ had no doubt that GE were entitled to edit out the irrelevant parts since this conformed with longstanding practice. The "separate subject matter" test described in *Great Atlantic* did not extend to the discovery of parts of a document.[51]

According to Hoffman, LJ:

> "... the test for whether or not on discovery part of a document can be withheld on grounds of irrelevance is simply whether that part is irrelevant. The test for whether part could be withheld on grounds of privilege is simply whether that part is privileged. There is no additional requirement that the part must deal with an entirely different subject matter from the rest".[52]

However, the *Great Atlantic* decision is still correct having regard to the context in which it was decided, namely the introduction of a partly

---

46 [1995] 1 WLR 172.
47 The context in which this occurred is discussed in Chap. 7.
48 *Ibid.*, at 175. In contrast, Leggett, LJ, at 176, noted that the court was not concerned with privilege, only relevance. The third judge, Dillon, LJ, made no reference to privilege.
49 [1997] 1 Lloyd's Rep 160.
50 (1997) *The Times,* 11 September.
51 *Op. cit.,* at 175.
52 *Op. cit.,* at 175.

privileged document in evidence at trial.[53] So, had the plaintiff in *G E Capital* sought to introduce into evidence (*e.g.* at trial), documents which had only been disclosed in part at the discovery stage, then the whole of the document would become discloseable at that stage.

How do the redaction principles actually work? Evidently, whole sections of a document which comprise privileged matters can be redacted. In *G E Capital,* Hoffmann, LJ contemplated[54] that even parts of a sentence could be redacted provided this did not destroy the sense of the rest of the sentence, or make it misleading. As to particular examples, Hoffmann, LJ noted:

> "A solicitor may have a composite attendance note on which he records conversations with his client which are privileged and conversations with third parties on the same subject matter which, in the absence of pending litigation, are not.[55] Or a client's internal document may record advice from his solicitor which is privileged and internal commercial discussions on the same subject matter which are not".[56]

From this, it would appear to follow that a Court can order that the unprivileged elements of a professional lawyer–client communication be unravelled from the privileged parts. In reality, this is likely to prove easier to achieve in relation to written material than verbal communication. A judge is therefore likely to be reluctant – as in *In re Sarah Getty*[57] – to require a solicitor to try to recount what he told his client about an unprivileged communication with a third party, since this is likely to be difficult to unravel from any privileged parts of the conversation. Similarly, difficulties may arise where a solicitor sends an account of a matter which is not privileged which is accompanied by privileged advice and comment, as in *Ainsworth* v *Wilding*:[58] again, unravelling the two may not always be easy.

---

53   It is implicit that Hoffmann, LJ in *G.E. Capital* thought that this was so (*ibid.,* at 175), and the point is spelt out in MacPherson, J's judgment in *Curlex* (1987) 2 QdR 335.

54   *Ibid.,* at 175.

55   See also Bingham, LJ's judgment in *Parry & Whelan* v *News Group Newspapers Ltd* [1990] 141 NLJ 1720 discussed in Chap. 2, Section 7.

56   *Ibid.,* at 176. In *The "Sagheera",* [1997] 1 Lloyd's Rep 160 at 172, Rix, J held that a separate section of an attendance note of a conversation with third parties was privileged, and so could be redacted. The earlier part of the note was not and so had to be disclosed.

57   [1985] QB 956.

58   [1900] 2 Ch 315.

Chapter 10

WITHOUT PREJUDICE COMMUNICATIONS

1. INTRODUCTION

This chapter examines the without prejudice privilege which is similar in its effect to legal professional privilege but differs from it in concept in a number of important respects. Most fundamentally, this privilege arises as a consequence of certain types of communication which are made *between* opposing parties for the purposes of genuinely trying to compromise or resolve the matters in dispute between them. In contrast, as we have seen,[1] legal professional privilege cannot arise in respect of communications between opponents to litigation.[2]

2. WITHOUT PREJUDICE: THE GENERAL RULE.

Communications made between the parties to a dispute[3] which are written or made for the purpose of settling that dispute, and which are expressed or otherwise proved to have been made on a "without prejudice" basis,[3a] cannot generally be admitted in evidence, whether in the proceedings (if any) to which the dispute gives rise, or any other litigation in which the contents of such communications are relevant.

It is fundamental to the operation of the without prejudice rule that such communications are made for these purposes, since the courts will not apply this privilege to communications which have a purpose other than settlement of the dispute.[4] The rationale behind the rule is to enable the parties to the dispute to communicate more frankly or openly than

---

1 See Chap. 2, Section 8.

2 But see the Court of Appeal's decision in *Feuerheerd* v *London General Omnibus Co* [1918] 2 KB 565.

3 And with a mediator who is enlisted to help parties in dispute reach a settlement: see the cases discussed in Chap. 1, Section 8; and also *R* v *Nottingham Justices, ex p. Bostock* [1970] 2 All ER 641.

3a As will be seen, a party who believes he is conducting such negotiations will normally mark his correspondence with a "without prejudice" stamp.

perhaps they would do in "open" correspondence which is potentially admissible in evidence against them. So, for example, the parties might well in without prejudice correspondence make concessions or admissions – which they would not ordinarily make in "open" correspondence – with a view to facilitating a settlement.

It can be seen from this that the rule is founded on the public policy of encouraging litigants to settle their differences rather than litigate them to a finish and on the implied agreement arising out of what is commonly understood to be the consequences of agreeing to negotiate without prejudice.[5] Accordingly, parties who are trying to settle their dispute:

> "... should not be discouraged by the knowledge that anything that is said in the course of such negotiations (and that includes ... as much the failure to reply to an offer as an actual reply) may be used to their prejudice in the course of the proceedings. They should ... be encouraged fully and frankly to put their cards on the table.... The public policy justification, in truth, essentially rests on the desirability of preventing statements or offers made in the course of negotiations for settlement being brought before the court of trial[6] as admissions on the question of liability".[7]

The principal effect of the without prejudice privilege is to make the communications concerned inadmissible in evidence. But are they discloseable? Dillon, LJ appeared to suggest that they are when he commented in *Parry and Whelan* v *News Group Newspapers Ltd:*

> "Documents which are merely without prejudice and not governed by legal professional privilege[8] are discloseable, although it may be that they cannot be put in evidence until certain other matters have happened[9] to remove the "without prejudice" bar".[10]

However, disclosure as between the parties can hardly be necessary as they are well aware of what has passed between them.[10a] Furthermore, *Rabin* v *Mendoza and Co*[11] is authority for the view that "even as between the parties to "mere" "without prejudice" correspondence they are not

---

4　*Re Daintrey* [1893] 2 QB 116 at 120, per Vaughan Williams, J

5　*Rush and Tompkins* v *GLC* [1989] AC 1280 (discussed below). The two aspects of the rule are also discussed by Hoffmann, LJ in *Muller* v *Linsley and Mortimer* (1994) *The Times,* 8 December, a decision considered in Sections 5 and 6 below.

6　As regards the position in interlocutory applications, see Section 4 below.

7　Per Oliver, LJ in *Cutts* v *Head* [1984] Ch 290 at 306, cited with approval by Lord Griffiths in *Rush and Tompkins* v *GLC* [1989] 1 AC 1280 at 1299.

8　See *Standrin* v *Yenton Minster Homes Ltd* (1991) *The Times,* 22 July, for an example of documents which are protected by both the without prejudice privilege and legal professional privilege.

9　As to which, see Section 6 below.

10　[1990] 141 NLJ 1720, transcript at p. 7. The decision is discussed in Chap. 2, Section 7.

10a　Per Lord Griffiths, in Rush and Tompkins, op. cit. at 1300.

11　[1954] 1 WLR 271.

entitled to discovery against one another".[12]

In contrast, the position is entirely free from doubt when it is a third party who seeks disclosure of the without prejudice materials, even though, normally, the right to discovery and production of documents does not depend upon their admissibility in evidence.[13] In *Rush and Tompkins* v *GLC*,[14] the House of Lords held that without prejudice communications should not be disclosed to third parties. Lord Griffiths said:

> "If the party who obtains discovery of the 'without prejudice' correspondence can make no use of it at trial it can be of only very limited value to him. It may give some insight into his opponent's general approach to the issues in the case but in most cases this is likely to be of marginal significance and will probably be revealed to him in direct negotiations in any event. ... [T]he general public policy that applies to protect genuine negotiations from being admissible in evidence should be extended to protect those negotiations from being discoverable to third parties".[15,16]

As with legal professional privilege, the without prejudice privilege survives beyond the litigation in respect of which it arose: in this respect, the "once privileged always privileged" maxim applies.[17] Nor does the privilege expire once a settlement is agreed between the parties. Such communications remain inadmissible in respect of all litigation on the same subject matter,[18] even between different parties, except to the extent that the without prejudice communications evidence the terms of any settlement[19] reached following without prejudice negotiations, and there is a dispute as to whether a settlement was in fact reached and/or, if so, on what terms.[20]

---

12 Per Lord Griffiths in Rush and Tompkins, *op. cit.* at 1304. In *Rabin v Mendoza and Co,* one party claimed the privilege for a report made following a without prejudice meeting with the other party. The Court of Appeal refused to order the report's production, it having come into being under an express or tacit agreement that it should not used to the prejudice of either party (per Denning, LJ [1954] 1 WLR 271 at 273–274).

13 See *O'Rourke v Darbishire* [1920] AC 581.

14 [1989] AC 1280.

15 *Ibid.,* at 1305.

16 Which means that relevant without prejudice correspondence between A and B should in litigation between A and C be disclosed in Sch 1 Pt 2 of A's list.

17 See Chap. 6, Section 5. This is the consequence of the decision in *Rush v Tomkins,* discussed below.

18 Strictly, the communications should be inadmissible in any litigation, irrespective of the subject matter. As explained in *The "Aegis Blaze"* [1986] 1 Lloyd's Rep 203, the communications are unlikely to be relevant in litigation involving another subject matter: see Chap. 6, Section 5.

19 *Rush and Tompkins v GLC* [1989] AC 1280; *Tomlin v Standard Telephones and Cables Ltd* [1969] 3 All ER 201.

20 See Section 4 below.

3 . WHEN ARE NEGOTIATIONS MADE "WITHOUT PREJUDICE"?

The leading authority is the House of Lords' decision in *Rush and Tompkins* v *GLC*.[21] Here, the plaintiffs had contracted to build a housing development for the GLC, the first defendant. The second defendants were the plaintiffs' sub-contractors. The project was subject to much disruption and delay. The sub-contractors put in claims for loss and expense to the plaintiffs who sought reimbursement from the GLC who would not agree them. To break the deadlock, the plaintiffs commenced proceedings against the GLC and the sub-contractors, claiming an inquiry into what the latter were owed; and a declaration as to the GLC's liability to reimburse them. Before trial, the plaintiffs settled with the GLC. The settlement, which required the plaintiffs to accept responsibility for the sub-contractors' claims, was disclosed to the sub-contractors.[21a] As it did not reveal the value placed on the sub-contractors' claim, the latter sought discovery of the negotiations leading up to the settlement in the hope that this would be revealed. The plaintiffs admitted such documents existed, but refused to give discovery of them. The House of Lords held that genuine negotiations with a view to settlement are protected from disclosure whether or not the "without prejudice" stamp has been expressly applied to the negotiations. Lord Griffiths said:

> "The ['without prejudice'] rule applies to exclude all negotiations genuinely aimed at settlement whether oral or in writing from being given in evidence. A competent solicitor will always head any negotiating correspondence 'without prejudice' to make clear beyond doubt that in the event of the negotiations being unsuccessful they are not to be referred to at the subsequent trial. However, the application of the rule is not dependent upon the use of the phrase 'without prejudice' and if it is clear from the surrounding circumstances that the parties were seeking to compromise the action, evidence of the content of those negotiations will, as a general rule, not be admissible at the trial and cannot be used to establish an admission or partial admission".[22]

The House of Lords expressly rejected a linguistic approach to the question of whether a communication is without prejudice. Accordingly, the question has to be looked at more broadly and "resolved by balancing

---

21 [1989] AC 1280.

21a In *Robert Hitchins Ltd* v *International Computers Ltd* (unrep.) 10 December 1996, the Court of Appeal held that a settlement agreement between a defendant and third party was not relevant to issues raised in the main action against the defendant since it would not advance the plaintiff's case "one iota".

22 [1989] AC 1299–1300.

two different public interests, namely the public interest in promoting settlements and the public interest in full discovery between parties to the litigation".[23]

Once settlement (or without prejudice) negotiations are commenced, the privilege will extend to all follow-up communications from either party which are part of the same chain of without prejudice correspondence, even if certain letters in the negotiations do not contain an offer of compromise.[24] Although the chain will be broken by "open" communications,[25] it is necessary for the party who is seeking to change the basis of the negotiations to spell out that change with clarity. However, even though the basis of the negotiation changes, it is not thereby permissible to refer to the content of without prejudice correspondence in later, open communications.

In *Cheddar Valley Engineering Ltd* v *Chaddlewood Homes Ltd*,[26] Mr Jules Sher QC, sitting as a deputy judge, considered the effect of the word "open" in a solicitor's attendance note of a telephone conversation with the opposing party. The litigation resulted from an agreement for the sale of certain property. A telephone conversation had taken place between the two parties' solicitors in which an offer had been made to purchase the land in question. The issue was whether the conversation was open or without prejudice. One party was clearly of the understanding that the offer was without prejudice. The other party said that he had used the word "open" and the follow-up letter was expressed to be "subject to contract" and was not marked "without prejudice". Although the court found that the word "open" was used it was not picked up by the other party. If the negotiations started off without prejudice and one side wished to make an open offer, then the change had to be bilateral. It had to be communicated to the other side and could not refer to earlier "without prejudice" discussions. It might not be enough just to say the word "open".

Conversely, an offer to settle can be made in open correspondence for which neither party can claim the privilege.[27] So, in *Dixons Stores Group Ltd* v *Thames Television plc*,[28-29] it was held that a party to an action could write a letter containing an offer to settle the action without *ipso facto*

---

23 Per Lord Griffiths at 1300.
24 See *South Shropshire DC* v *Amos* [1987] 1 All ER 340.
25 *India Rubber, Gutta Percha and Telegraph Works Co Ltd* v *Chapman* (1926) 20 BWCC 184.
26 [1992] 1 WLR 820.
27 Though it would be open to the receiving party to respond, and to make a counter offer, on a without prejudice basis.
28-29 [1993] 1 All ER 349.

attracting to that letter any privilege which could be claimed by the opposing party, provided the letter was not part of continuing negotiations. However, if the letter was a reply to a letter written without prejudice or was part of a continuing sequence of negotiations, whether by correspondence or orally, then it would be privileged and could not be admitted in evidence without the consent of *both* parties. Drake, J stated:

> "The mere fact of heading a letter 'without prejudice' is not in the least decisive as to whether or not the letter is in fact privileged. The privilege exists in order to encourage bona fide attempts to negotiate a settlement of an action and if the letter is not written to initiate or continue such a bona fide attempt to effect a settlement it will not be protected by privilege. But, conversely, if it is written in the course of such a bona fide attempt, it will be covered by privilege, and the absence of any heading or reference in the letter to show it is written without prejudice will not be fatal".[30]

It is not necessary in order to qualify for the without prejudice privilege that the negotiations should be concerned with the substantive issues in dispute. Negotiations aimed at resolving interlocutory disputes can also fall within the scope of this privilege. So, in *Forster* v *Friedland*,[31] Hoffmann, LJ in the Court of Appeal said that:

> "... there is no basis in authority or in principle for limiting the rule to negotiations aimed at resolving the legal issues between the parties. There must be many without prejudice negotiations which do not address the issues at all. They are attempts to find an agreed solution which will make it unnecessary for the issues to be debated either in negotiation or in court. All that is necessary, as Lord Griffiths said in *Rush and Tomkins Ltd* v *GLC,* is that the negotiations must be 'genuinely aimed at settlement', that is, the avoidance of litigation. Provided that this criterion is met, the nature of the proposals put forward or the character of the arguments used to support them, are irrelevant. One party may ask another for more time, or a reduction in what he has to pay. In support of such a proposal he may urge the weakness of the plaintiff's case or his own lack of money, or their friendly business relations in the past. The communication will be protected if there is an intention to speak without prejudice followed by a genuine proposal or genuine negotiations aimed at avoiding litigation."

However, the without prejudice privilege will not apply to communications which cannot properly be regarded as "negotiating documents". This can give rise to difficulties of application. In *Norwich Union Life Assurance Society* v *Tony Waller*,[32] Harman, J held that a landlord's "trigger notice" in a rent review could not successfully be headed "without prejudice". This was because the parties could not at that

---

30 *Ibid.*, at 351.
31 Unrep., 10 November 1992.
32 (1984) 270 EG 42.

stage be said to be in dispute because there had been no response from the opposing party. However, in *South Shropshire DC v Amos*,[33] the Court of Appeal expressly disapproved this reasoning, since otherwise no one could safely proceed directly to an offer to accept a sum in settlement of an as yet unquantified claim. In *South Shropshire*, the Court of Appeal held that, although documents marked "without prejudice" were only inadmissible in evidence if they came into being because there was an existing dispute which the parties were seeking to settle, thereafter documents so marked were privileged if they formed part of the negotiations, whether or not they were documents making an offer: furthermore they could include documents which initiated the negotiations.

In contrast, in *Buckinghamshire County Council v Moran*,[34] the Court of Appeal held in relation to a title dispute that a letter which was the opening shot in negotiations could not be protected by the without prejudice privilege because it did not put forward any offer or make any proposals of compromise. Slade, LJ said:

> "... as the letter itself indicated, the defendant was writing the letter in an attempt to persuade the council that his case was well founded. As I read the letter, it amounted not to an offer to negotiate, but to an assertion of the defendant's rights, coupled with an intimation that he contemplated taking his solicitor's advice unless the council replied in terms recognising his asserted rights".[35]

Lloyd, LJ summarised the principles to be derived from these decisions in *Standrin v Yenton Minster Homes Ltd*[36] where he said that:

> "... the opening shot in negotiations may well be subject to privilege where, for example, a person puts forward a claim and in the same breath offers to take something less in settlement, or... where a person offers to accept a sum in settlement of an as yet unquantified claim. But where the opening shot is an assertion of a person's claim and nothing more than that, then prima facie it is not protected."

Once the without prejudice negotiations have resulted in a binding settlement which resolves all issues in dispute, continuing communications between the parties to that dispute cannot be privileged under the without prejudice rule.[37]

On the other hand, the use of the expression "without prejudice" in the

---

33 [1986] 1 WLR 1271.
34 [1989] 2 All ER 225.
35 At 231.
36 (1991) *The Times*, 22 July, per Lloyd, LJ. This decision is an example of the situation in which communications can be protected both by without prejudice privilege and legal professional privilege.
37 See *Standrin v Yenton Minster Homes Ltd* (1991) *The Times*, 22 July.

body of a letter may not indicate an intention that the letter as a whole should be treated as without prejudice and so inadmissible. In *Peterborough City Council* v *Mancetter Developments Ltd*,[38] the defendants served a notice under section 146 Law of Property Act 1925 because the plaintiffs were making unauthorised use of the premises let. The plaintiffs applied to the court for relief against forfeiture. Subsequently, the plaintiffs wrote the defendants a letter seeking temporary consent for their use of the land "without prejudice" to their application. The Court of Appeal held that, in using that expression, the plaintiffs' intention had been to give notice that they intended to avail themselves of an alternative right and were doing so without prejudice to their application. They had not intended that the letter as a whole should be treated as without prejudice and so inadmissible in evidence.

4. EXCEPTIONS TO THE RULE

There are a number of exceptions to the rule that the court will not, at the trial of an action, take note of the content of without prejudice negotiations for the purposes of determining liability. In most cases, these exceptions are more apparent than real, since it is the fact of the negotiations, rather than their content, which is of interest to the court, especially where one party seeks to explain away his delay. In these situations – nearly all of which occur in an interlocutory context – the underlying policy of the rule is not infringed. However, on rare occasions, the content of the negotiations will be received in evidence.

Dispute as to settlement

The most important exception concerns disputes as to whether settlement negotiations resulted in a binding compromise. Given that the underlying purpose of the "without prejudice" rule is "to protect a litigant from being embarrassed by any admission made purely in an attempt to achieve settlement",[39] it follows that without prejudice material will be admissible in evidence if the only issue for which it is relied on is whether or not the negotiations resulted in an agreed settlement. This necessarily points to the fact that some care should be taken in drafting without prejudice communications. Accordingly, where a party does not, in any event, wish

---

38 [1996] EGCS 50.
39 Per Lord Griffiths, *Rush and Tomkins* [1989] AC 1280 at 1300.

to be bound by the terms of an offer made in a without prejudice letter, that letter should also be marked "subject to contract".[40]

In *Tomlin v Standard Telephones and Cables Ltd*,[41] the Court of Appeal considered the admissibility of "without prejudice" correspondence between the plaintiff's solicitors and his employers' insurers in which the plaintiff's solicitor had written that the plaintiff would agree to settle his case on a fifty–fifty basis, with the question of quantum being left for subsequent agreement. This was later referred to in correspondence by the insurers as an "agreement". The Court of Appeal held that the letters were admissible as it was not possible to determine without looking into the correspondence whether there was a binding agreement.[42-43]

The limits of this exception should be appreciated in that only those parts of the without prejudice correspondence which establish the existence of the agreement which is the result of the negotiations may be adduced in evidence. Any admissions made by either party for the purposes of pursing a compromise remain protected.

Rebuttal of a suggestion of delay or laches

It is well established that the fact of without prejudice negotiations having been conducted can be used to explain away procedural and other delays. In *Walker v Wilsher*, Lindley, LJ stated:

> "No doubt there are cases where a letter written without prejudice may be taken into consideration, as was done the other day in a case in which a question of laches was raised. The fact that such letters have been written and the dates at which they were written may be regarded, and in so doing the rule ... would not be infringed".[44]

A more recent case dealing with this point is *Redifusion Simulation Ltd v Link Miles Limited*.[45] This involved an attempt between the parties to resolve their differences on an issue of patent infringement by alternative dispute resolution ("ADR"). The attempt failed and one party issued proceedings. The plaintiff applied to amend its patent. In its particulars of objection the defendant relied upon the plaintiff's delay in making the

---

40 See also the comments on this issue in Style and Hollander, *Documentary Evidence,* 6th Edn., pp. 261–262.
41 [1969] 3 All ER 201.
42 Ormerod, J dissented because in his view the parties were negotiating towards a "packaged deal" and that only a settlement of both liability and quantum was intended to be binding.
44 (1889) 23 QBD 335 at 338.
45 [1992] FSR 195.

application and the plaintiff responded by filing an affidavit relying on the fact that it had mentioned in the course of the without prejudice meetings connected with the ADR that it intended to apply for leave to amend. The defendant conceded that the fact that without prejudice negotiations had taken place was admissible to explain delay but objected to the filing of any evidence of what had been said in such negotiations. Mummery, J stood over the defendant's motion to strike out the relevant passages from the plaintiff's affidavit. He considered that the plaintiff's case for including the passages was "arguable" and that the question of admissibility should be dealt with by the trial judge.

Finally, the fact of settlement negotiations having been conducted is sometimes before the court on an application to extent the validity of a writ.[46]

Strike-out application

On certain types of application, the court may hear evidence not only of the fact of negotiation, but also of its contents, even though no compromise has been reached. In *Family Housing Association (Manchester) Ltd* v *Michael Hyde and Partners*,[47] the Court of Appeal held that the substance – as opposed to the fact – of without prejudice correspondence could be admissible in applications to strike out for want of prosecution. The defendants in this case challenged the common practice whereby "without prejudice correspondence is regularly exhibited to affidavits without objection from the court or counsel on interlocutory applications, for example to strike out for want of prosecution, or for discovery".[48] Hirst, LJ stated:

> "The main considerations of public policy in favour of the general rule excluding the reference to without prejudice correspondence ... seem to me to have little or no application in the present context, seeing that I do not think the parties' willingness to talk frankly about the strengths and weaknesses of their case, and to make provisional offers or admissions for the purposes of negotiation only, will be to any significant extent inhibited by the knowledge that the negotiations may be referred to in this very narrow field, not for the purpose of showing that such provisional offers or admissions were made, but solely for the purpose of explaining delay and the conduct of the parties at any relevant period. On the other hand the content

---

46 Although the fact of such negotiations is not of itself a good reason for the Court extending the writ's validity: see *Easy* v *Universal Anchorage* [1974] 1 WLR 899, and *The "Mouna"* [1991] 2 Lloyd's Rep 221.
47 [1993] 1 WLR 354.
48 See *Phipson on Evidence*, 14th Edn. 1990 para. 20–65.

of the negotiations may well be of much more significance in this context than the mere fact that they have taken place ..."[49]

In the result, the Court of Appeal agreed that the plaintiff could file affidavit evidence which included details of without prejudice negotiations. Such evidence included references to suggested trial dates and might indicate which side was trying to delay the proceedings. In these situations, it appears all of the without prejudice correspondence will be admissible:

> "... in practice, it would often be difficult to obtain the flavour of the severed part without reference to its context in the letter as a whole, and severance would often lead to controversy as to where the line should be drawn".[50]

Security for costs

In other interlocutory arenas, a different approach has been taken. In *Simaan General Contracting Co v Pilkington Glass Co*[51] the privilege applied to exclude evidence at the hearing of an application for security for costs. The court held that although evidence of negotiations between parties to an action would assist it when considering a plaintiff's prospects of successfully prosecuting an action – and might also indicate whether a defendant was endeavouring to prevent a plaintiff maintaining the action – it was contrary to public policy that without prejudice correspondence should be admitted in evidence on a summons for security for costs. Judge Newey, QC said:

> "Defendants... would be deterred from exploring possibilities of settlement and making sensible offers for fear of prejudicing their prospects of being able to obtain security for costs. In particular a defendant who has obtained an order for a security intended to relate to preparations for trial only would be most unwilling to take any action which might prevent him from obtaining a second order for security in respect of trial costs... defendants who make payments into court... are making offers, which they intend should be mentioned in court in appropriate circumstances. They do so, instead of making fully 'without prejudice' offers, for tactical reasons and because of possible costs advantages. A defendant... should not be at a disadvantage in obtaining security, because he has, for whatever reason, made attempts to settle the case".[52]

However, in a decision on 21 May 1992,[53] His Honour Judge Marshall

---

49 *Op.cit.*, 363.
50 Per Hirst, LJ, *ibid.*, at 364.
51 [1987] 1 WLR 516.
52 *Ibid.*, at 520.
53 Unrep., referred to in Foskett *The Law and Practice of Compromise*, Supplement to the 3rd Edn., paras 9–27.

Evans QC, sitting as an Official Referee in Liverpool, refused to follow *Simaan*. He considered that a "serious substantial offer" made in the course of protracted "without prejudice" negotiations concerning the resolution of a building dispute should be a relevant factor on an application for security for costs.[54]

Limitation issues

In certain circumstances, a defendant might be estopped from raising a limitation defence if an agreement has been reached on the settlement of the dispute, or if the defendant has admitted liability.[55] In *Lubovsky v Snelling*[56] an agreement between plaintiff and defendant that liability in damages for the plaintiff's cause of action was "once and for all definitively accepted by the defendant and his insurers" was held to prevent either the defendant or the insurer from raising any defence which might contest that liability, so that an agreement not to plead the Limitation Act 1939 could be implied.[57] In *Wright v Bagnall and Sons Ltd*,[58] the plaintiff applied out of time for compensation under the Workmen's Compensation Act 1897 in respect of an accident suffered in the course of his employment. Before the expiry of the time limit the employer had started paying the plaintiff a weekly sum expressed to be on account of his compensation under the Act, and the parties negotiated on the payment of a lump sum to the plaintiff. The plaintiff's application, made after the negotiations were unsuccessful, was initially rejected as being time-barred. On his appeal, the Court of Appeal held that there was evidence of an agreement that compensation should be paid, leaving only the amount to be determined, so that the defendants

---

54 *Quaere* whether a "without prejudice" offer would be admissible on an application for an interim payment of damages. In *Fryer v London Transport Executive, The Times* (1982) 4 December, the Court of Appeal held that a payment into court was admissible in evidence on an application for an interim payment.

55 See *Lade v Trill* (1842) 11 LJ Ch 102; *Lubovsky v Snelling* [1944] KB 1944; *Wright v Bagnall and Sons Ltd* [1900] 2 QB 240.

56 [1944] KB 44.

57 Some doubt was cast on this principle in *The "Sauria" and the "Trent"* [1957] 1 Lloyd's Rep 396. Lord Evershed, MR noted that: "As a matter of principle, I confess that whatever may have been the facts in the *Lubovsky* case... I have the greatest difficulty in seeing how you can formulate an agreement which will have the effect... of binding the defendants contractually not to raise the plea of Section 8 of the [Maritime Conventions Act 1911] in any action the plaintiffs may choose to bring for finding that the damage suffered apparently was done by the barge Trent, however long after the cause of action they may elect to start those proceedings". See also *Asianic International Panama SA and Transocean Transport Corporation v Transocean* [1990] 1 Lloyd's Rep 150.

58 [1900] 2 QB 240.

were debarred from raising a limitation defence.[59] It was suggested that in that case the defendants were also debarred because they had allowed the six-month limitation period to expire while negotiations were still proceeding.

In cases where a limitation defence has been raised under the Marine Conventions Act 1911, the fact that the parties were still negotiating when time ran out has been held to give grounds for the court to exercise its discretion to extend the limitation period.[60] However, it must always be dangerous for a defendant who is negotiating to ignore limitation problems: the existence of ongoing negotiations will not prevent the defendant relying on a limitation defence where, as with cases where the 1980 Act is pleaded, the court does not have a general discretion to extend the limitation period.[61]

Where the "without prejudice" document would prejudice recipient

In *Re Daintrey, ex p. Holt*[62] it was held that a letter headed "without prejudice" which clearly contained an offer to settle pending litigation but which was also a clear act of bankruptcy, could be put in evidence on the hearing of a bankruptcy petition on the ground that it was "one which, from its character, might prejudicially affect the recipient whether or not he accepted the terms offered thereby".

Threats, abuse of rule and lack of good faith

Although improper threats cannot be protected by the "without prejudice" privilege, it is not improper for a party to restate his position that there was no legally binding agreement and that if his opponent resorted to law rather than reliance on his commercial honour he would deny that there

---

59 *Rendall v Hill's Dry Docks and Engineering Co* [1900] 2 QB 254, a case which also involved a claim for compensation under the Workmen's Compensation Act 1897 made out of time, though decided against the plaintiff on the facts, seems to have accepted that had the parties agreed that the employers were liable to pay compensation, the agreement would have had the effect of waiving their right to raise a limitation defence.

60 See *Asianic International Panama SA and Transocean Transport Corporation v Transocean Ro-Ro Corporation (the "Seaspeed America")* [1990] 1 Lloyd's Rep 150, and dicta in *The "Sauria" and the "Trent"* [1957] 1 Lloyd's Rep 396.

61 The Law Reform Committee noted in its Twenty-First Report (Final Report on Limitation of Actions) (1977) that the fact that negotiations were proceeding when the limitation period expired would not, without more, enable the plaintiff to defeat a limitation defence (see paras 2.55–2.61).

62 [1893] 2 QB 116.

had been any agreement. In *Forster v Friedland*,[63] Hoffmann, LJ said:

> "I accept that a party, whether plaintiff or defendant, cannot use the without
> prejudice rule as a cloak for blackmail. [Counsel] cited two cases[64] which
> illustrate this proposition. ... These are clear cases of improper threats, but
> the value of the without prejudice rule would be seriously impaired if its
> protection could be removed from anything less than unambiguous
> impropriety. The rule is designed to encourage parties to express themselves
> freely and without inhibition. I think it is quite wrong for the tape recorded
> words of a layman, who has used colourful or even exaggerated language, to
> be picked over in order to support an argument that he intends to raise
> defences which he does not really believe to be true."

In *Alizadeh v Nikbin*[65] the Court of Appeal followed *Forster v Friedland*
and held that a tape recording of unsuccessful settlement negotiations
should only be admitted in evidence if it contained an unambiguous
admission of impropriety.

Admission of "independent fact"

There is also authority – albeit sparse – for the proposition that the
admission of an "independent fact", in no way connected with the merits
of the case, is admissible even if made in the course of negotiations for a
settlement. In *Waldridge v Kennison*,[66] an admission that a document was
in the handwriting of one of the parties was received in evidence. This case
was described by Lord Griffiths in *Rush and Tompkins v GLC* as
"exceptional" and one which should not be allowed to "whittle" down the
extent of the protection.[67] More recently, the issue arose in *McDowell v
Hirschfield Lipson and Rumney*.[68] This was a solicitor's negligence action
concerned with the issue of whether there had been a severance of a joint
tenancy of property. His Honour Judge Eric Stockdale, sitting as a High
Court Judge, ruled as admissible certain "without prejudice"
correspondence between solicitors arguing that a severance had been
effected. This was considered an investigation of an "independent fact".

Leading text books do not think highly of this category of exception.
Phipson on Evidence (14th Edn) states as follows:

> "Although it is always said that what is collaterally admitted in without

---

63 Unrep., 10 November 1992.
64 *Greenwood v Fitts* [1961] 29 DLR (2d) 260 and *Hawick Jersey International Ltd v
  Caplan* (1988), *The Times*, 11 March.
65 (1993) *The Times*, 19 March. This decision was itself followed in *Michael Mallis SA
  Packing Systems v Harold Supplies plc*, Garland J (unrep., 23 March 1996).
66 (1794) 1 Esp 143, 170 ER 306.
67 *Op. cit.*, at 1300.
68 [1992] 2 FLR 126.

prejudice negotiations is not protected, there is little authority which supports this proposition, and we think that it ought to be treated with some circumspection. [After referring to *Waldridge* v *Kennison*[69]]... now that it is clear that the protection for without prejudice negotiations is a species of privilege, it is thought that the whole of the negotiations are protected".[70]

Correspondence relevant otherwise than by reference to any admissions

In *Muller* v *Linsley and Mortimer*,[71] the question arose whether when:

A sues B,

A has without prejudice negotiations with B,

A settles with B,

A then sues his solicitors, C, whom he had instructed at an earlier stage of the claim (but before the negotiations took place), and

A pleads in his statement of claim that the settlement with B was a reasonable attempt to mitigate his damages in connection with the claim against C,

should C be entitled to discovery of A's without prejudice correspondence with B?

The Court of Appeal held unanimously that he should. Hoffmann, LJ, with whom Leggatt and Swinton Thomas, LJJ concurred,[72] indicated that the public policy aspects of the without prejudice rule were not concerned with the admissibility of statements which are relevant otherwise than as admissions, that is independently of the truth of the facts alleged to have been admitted. Here, A's statement of claim put in issue the reasonableness of his conduct in settling the claim with B, and the without prejudice correspondence formed a part of that conduct. Its relevance lay, not in its admissibility to establish the truth of any express or implied admission it might contain, but in whether A acted reasonably in concluding his settlement with B. Hoffmann, LJ thought that interpreting the rule in this way would not infringe the policy of encouraging settlements. This view is not, with respect, easy to reconcile with *Rush and Tompkins* v *GLC*,[73] where, on not dissimilar facts, the House of Lords held that A's without prejudice negotiations with B were not discloseable in litigation with C concerning the same subject matter.[74] The result in *Muller* may be

69 (1794) 1 Esp 143, 170 ER 306.
70 At paras 20–64.
71 (1994) *The Times*, 8 December.
72 Leggatt and Swinton Thomas, LJJ gave other reasons for arriving at the same conclusion. See Section 6 below.
73 [1989] AC 1280.
74 See also *Hodgkinson and Corby* v *Wards Mobility Service* [1997] FSR 178 and the further discussion of this decision *Muller* in Section 6 below.

justifiable on the basis that A put in issue, by his plea that the settlement with B was reasonable, documents otherwise covered by the privilege: see further on this in Section 6 below.

5 . COSTS

In *Walker* v *Wilsher*[75] the Court of Appeal held that letters or conversations, declared to be "without prejudice", cannot be taken into consideration in determining whether a litigant can recover costs. However, in *Calderbank* v *Calderbank*[76] the principle was confirmed in a matrimonial case that reference could be made in an application for costs to a without prejudice offer to settle which had been made subject to a clearly expressed reservation of the right to refer to it on the costs issue. Thus has grown up the practice of marking certain correspondence "without prejudice save as to costs".

In *Cutts* v *Head*,[77] the Court of Appeal confirmed that this so-called "*Calderbank* principle" extends across all civil litigation.[78] Oliver, LJ said:

> "The protection from disclosure of without prejudice negotiations rest in part upon public policy and in part upon convention (i.e. an express or implied agreement that the negotiations shall be so protected). ... There is no public policy which precludes a conventional modification to the extent suggested in *Calderbank*.... As a practical matter, a consciousness of a risk as to costs if reasonable offers are refused can only encourage settlement ...".[79]

This rule has been codified in RSC Order 22, rule 14, which provides as follows:

> "(1) A party to proceedings may at any time make a written offer to any other party to those proceedings which is expressed to be 'without prejudice save as to costs' and which relates to any issue in the proceedings.
>
> (2) Where an offer is made under paragraph (1), the fact that such an offer has been made shall not be communicated to the Court until the question of costs falls to be decided".

---

75 (1889) 23 QBD 335.

76 [1976] Fam 93.

77 [1984] Ch 290.

78 In arbitration proceedings a "sealed offer", the existence of which is not revealed to the tribunal until it has made its award on the substance of the dispute, will be treated in the same way as a *Calderbank* letter. See *The "Toni"* [1974] 1 Lloyd's Rep 489, *Ahrenkel Liner Service* v *Wilhelm Sen Enterprises* (unrep., 26 September 1988) and *Re London Arbitration No 14/94* [1994] LMLN 386.

79 *Op. cit.* at 306.

However, a *Calderbank* offer should not be made, and will not be effective as to costs, "if at the time it is made, the party making it could have protected his position as to costs by means of a payment into court under Order 22".[80]

Where a bill of costs is lodged for taxation and an offer of payment by the unsuccessful party to litigation is rejected, that party may make a *Calderbank* offer "without prejudice save as to the costs of taxation" in respect of the costs within fourteen days of delivery of the bill. This offer may be taken into account by the taxing officer when dealing with the costs of the taxation.[81]

6. WAIVING WITHOUT PREJUDICE PRIVILEGE

Privilege can normally only be waived in respect of "without prejudice" communications with the consent of *both* parties to the correspondence.[82] In *Blow v Norfolk County Council*,[83] the Court of Appeal found that the Lands Tribunal had acted erroneously in failing to take into account the amount of a settlement offer in "without prejudice" correspondence after the parties had agreed the correspondence should become open.

In *Muller v Linsley and Mortimer*,[84] discussed in Section 4 above, Swinton Thomas and Leggatt, LJJ considered that there had been an implied waiver of privilege by A. Leggatt, LJ commented:

> "Discovery is sought not for the purpose of diminishing the protection afforded to the plaintiffs for any admissions that they may have made, but for the purpose of proving what they did. If they invoke the settlement for their own purposes, they must expect its worth to be evaluated by reference to the means by which it was achieved. There is no reason to suppose that the plaintiffs would have conducted themselves differently if they had appreciated that they might have to reveal what was written in the course of settling the... action".

Leggatt LJ added that he regarded this as an application of the principle established in *Lillicrap v Nalder and Sons*.[85] Whilst the analogy with that

---

80 RSC O.62 r. 9(1)(d). Lord Woolf's final "Access to Justice" Report (1996) has recommended that this rule be abolished.

81 RSC O.62 r. 27(3). See *Chrulew v Borm-Reid and Co* [1992] 1 WLR 176 and *Platt v GKN Kwikform Ltd* [1992] 1 WLR 465.

82 See, *e.g.*, *McTaggart v McTaggart* [1949] p 94 and *Dixons Stores Group v Thames Television plc* [1993] 1 All ER 349.

83 [1967] 1 WLR 1280.

84 (1994) *The Times*, 8 December.

85 [1993] 1 WLR 94. See the discussion of this decision in Chap. 7, Section 4.

decision is tempting, it ignores the fact it was the plaintiff's own privilege which was there waived; whereas here the privilege was enjoyed by B as well.[86] In this respect, then, the decision is difficult to reconcile with the well-established rule that without prejudice privilege can only be waived with the consent of both parties to the correspondence in question. Against that, one possible explanation is that the consent of A and B is required before without prejudice correspondence may be used in litigation between A and B, but not where A alone waives the benefit of without prejudice privilege in litigation with C. If so, then the effect of this decision would not be to prevent B from asserting the privilege in litigation in which he (but not A) is involved in which the without privilege materials are relevant.

7. STATUTORY OVERRIDES

We have seen in Chapter 1[87] that various statutes which empower certain types of bodies, such as the police, the revenue, etc., with the right to seize documentary materials in specific situations except from those powers the right to seize material which is properly subject to a claim for legal professional privilege. The question may therefore arise whether communications subject to the without prejudice privilege are within the scope of these exceptions. To answer this requires analysis of the phraseology used in the statute concerned. However, in most instances, the without prejudice privilege is likely to be outside the ambit of any exception, as for example with section 10 Police and Criminal Evidence Act 1984, where the definition of "items subject to legal privilege" was held by the House of Lords in *R v Central Criminal Court, ex parte Francis and Francis (a firm)*[88] to accord with the common law legal professional privilege.

---

86 The conflicting views to which this issue can give rise are also reflected in two decisions concerned with whether legal professional privilege is waived by a pleading which refers to a "reasonable" settlement. See the decision discussed in Chap. 7, Section 6. Note that in one of those decisions, *X Corporation Ltd v Y (a firm)* (unrep.) 16 May 1997, Moore-Bick, J noted that the Court in *Muller v Linsley and Mortimer* was concerned with inter partes correspondence and that it was understandable there that exchanges between the parties were relevant in deciding whether the plaintiffs acted reasonably in making the compromise. In *X Corporation,* Moore-Bick, J was concerned only with documents passing between the plaintiffs and their legal advisers which he held did not shed any light on the question whether the steps which the plaintiffs took were reasonable.

87 See Section 5.

88 [1989] AC 346, discussed in Chap. 8, Section 2.

Chapter 11

THE PRIVILEGE AGAINST SELF-INCRIMINATION

1. INTRODUCTION

This chapter considers a further privilege which entitles a party to civil proceedings to refuse to answer any question or produce any document or thing, if to do so would tend to expose that person to proceedings for a criminal offence or for the recovery of a penalty.[1] This "privilege against self-incrimination" was restated in section 14 Civil Evidence Act 1968 which provides as follows:

> "The right of a person in any legal proceedings other than criminal proceedings to refuse to answer any question or produce any document or thing if to do so would tend to expose that person to proceedings for an offence or for the recovery of a penalty–
>
> (a) shall apply only as regards criminal offences under the law of any part of the UK and penalties provided for by such law; and
>
> (b) shall include a like right to refuse to answer any question or produce any document or thing if to do so would tend to expose the husband or wife of that person to proceedings for any such criminal offence or for the recovery of any such penalty."

As the section makes clear, the privilege:

- also allows a person to refuse to provide evidence which tends to incriminate his or her spouse, but
- only applies to offences under the law of any part of the United Kingdom.[2]

---

1 *Blunt v Park Lane Hotel* [1942] 2 KB 253.

2 Which includes EC law: *Rio Tinto Zinc v Westinghouse Electric* [1978] AC 547. The possibility of self-incrimination under the law of a foreign state may be taken into account in the exercise of the court's discretion as to whether to order a document to be produced or a question answered: *Arab Monetary Fund v Hashim* [1989] 1 WLR 565.

The privilege is not, however, universally popular. In *AT&T Istel Ltd* v *Tully* Lord Templeman said:

> "I regard the privilege against self-incrimination exercisable in civil proceedings as an archaic and unjustifiable survival from the past. ... Events have ... shown that in this day and age the exercise of a right to silence affords protection for the guilty and is unnecessary to safeguard the innocent".[3]

This approach is shared by many English judges who have, over the last eight years or so, tended to construe the privilege narrowly. A large number of statutory provisions have in any event been construed as excluding the operation of the privilege in relation to particular types of proceedings. Moreover, Part III of the Criminal Justice and Public Order Act 1994 now allows adverse inferences to be drawn in criminal proceedings when the accused exercises his right to silence.

On the other hand a number of well-publicised recent cases, in which convictions based on false confessions have subsequently been quashed by the Court of Appeal, suggests that the privilege may sometimes serve a useful function. Moreover, Lord Templeman's views are not shared by other European judges. In *Funke* v *France*[4] the European Court of Human Rights held that a conviction under Article 65 of the French Customs Code, for refusing to supply documents in relation to suspected customs offences, amounted to a breach of the right to a fair trial under Article 6 of the European Convention on Human Rights. It was, the court indicated, implicit in the Article that the accused should not be required to provide evidence for the case against him.

2. THE CLAIM TO PRIVILEGE

The privilege against self-incrimination, like legal professional privilege, excuses a party from producing documents or answering questions, but does not excuse him from disclosure of the existence of the documents. So, for instance, in High Court civil proceedings an incriminating document would have to be disclosed by a defendant in Schedule 1, Part 2 of his list of documents, but he would not have to give inspection of it.

The privilege must be raised before the evidence is supplied. In *IBM United Kingdom Ltd* v *Prima Data International Ltd*,[5] *Mareva* and *Anton Piller* orders drew the attention of the defendant to his privilege and this

---

3 [1993] AC 45 at 53.
4 Case 82/1991/334/407, Series A, Vol 256-A.
5 [1994] 1 WLR 719.

was explained to him at the time of service. He did not, however, seek to raise the privilege until after the orders were executed. By that time it was too late as incriminating material had already been obtained by the plaintiffs. Now, however, where an *Anton Piller* provides for the production of documents, some of which it is apprehended may incriminate the defendant, the supervising solicitor may be requested to screen them to ensure that no incriminating documents are handed over to the plaintiff's solicitors. This precaution may prevent the effect of the order being frustrated by a subsequent invocation of the privilege.[6]

The privilege is only available in respect of the claimant's own documents and, probably, can only be claimed by natural persons. In *Garvin* v *Domus Publishing*[7] a defendant was ordered to produce a document belonging to his employer, a company. Walton, J held that he could only claim the privilege in relation to his own property. By contrast the decisions of the House of Lords in *Rio Tinto Zinc Corporation* v *Westinghouse Electric Corporation*[8] and the Court of Appeal in *Sonangol* v *Lundqvist*[9] have left open the question whether directors, servants or agents of a corporate body could claim the privilege on that body's behalf.[10]

The privilege against self-incrimination almost certainly extends beyond court proceedings to professional disciplinary proceedings. Sedley, J decided the privilege was available in relation to proceedings before the Disciplinary Committee of the Institute of Chartered Accountants in England and Wales in *R* v *Institute of Chartered Accountants of England and Wales, ex p. Nawaz*.[11] In the Court of Appeal,[12] Leggatt, LJ was "content to assume, without deciding, that the privilege from self-incrimination at least extends to investigations of a quasi-judicial character such as we are concerned with".[13] However, like Sedley, J, the Court of Appeal went on to hold that Mr Nawaz's acceptance, under the Institute's by-laws, "of a duty to provide information demanded of an accountant constitutes a waiver by the member concerned of any privilege from disclosure".[14]

---

6 See Hartle and Baring, "The Norwich Pharmacal Order", *Commercial Lawyer*, January 1996, p. 20.
7 [1989] Ch 335.
8 [1978] AC 547.
9 [1991] 2 QB 310.
10 As to the position under European law, see Section 9 below.
11 (1996) *The Times*, 7 November.
12 Unrep., 25 April 1997.
13 Transcript, p.9.
14 No reference was made in the court's judgment to the ruling of the European Court of Human Right's judgment in *Saunders* v *United Kingdom* (1997) 23 EHRR 313, considered in Section 8 below. Some authority exists for the view that some disciplinary proceedings are within the scope of the European Convention on Human Rights: *La Compte, Van Leuven and De Mayere* v *Belgium* (1982) 5 EHRR 183.

3 . THE RISK OF INCRIMINATION

A person who asserts the privilege must satisfy a court that disclosure gives rise to an actual risk of incrimination. Once he does so, then a defendant can claim the privilege even though he sets up an affirmative case which, if proved, would amount to a defence to an apprehended criminal charge.

In *R* v *Boyes* Cockburn, CJ said:

> "The danger to be apprehended must be real and appreciable with reference to the ordinary operation of law in the ordinary course of things - not a danger of an imaginary and unsubstantial character."[15]

More recently, Hoffmann, LJ held in *Tarasov* v *Nassif*[16] that the privilege could not be claimed on the basis of a mere possibility that the facts might disclose an offence with which the witness could be charged. To hold that this was sufficient to enable the privilege to be asserted would lead to a situation where any person asked to say what had happened to money which he held in trust could, without giving any further facts, refuse to answer on the ground that he might have given it to someone with whom he could be charged as a conspirator, yet without actually saying as much.

In *Renworth* v *Stephansen*,[17] it was common ground that there was a reasonable likelihood of charges being brought against the defendant under the Theft Act 1968 in connection with the subject matter of the plaintiff's claim against him. The privilege against self-incrimination has been excluded in relation to offences under that Act by section 31.[18] The defendant sought nevertheless to be excused from complying with an order requiring him to supply information on affidavit, on the grounds that he might also be prosecuted for conspiracy. This claim was rejected by the Court of Appeal: there was no likelihood of proceedings in conspiracy separate and distinct from proceedings under the 1968 Act.

Nor does the disclosure of assets, as such, amount to self-incrimination, as Leggatt, LJ pointed out in *Re Thomas (Disclosure Order)*.[19] A person does not, by making reparation, incur punishment. Where a defendant apprehends that he would be in personal danger (*e.g.* of violence) if he complied with an order requiring him to name those concerned with him in an infringement of intellectual property rights, that will generally not be

---

15 (1861) 1 B & S 311 at p. 330.
16 Unrep., CA, 11 February 1994.
17 [1996] 3 All ER 244.
18 See below.
19 [1992] 4 All ER 814.

grounds on which the court will withhold what would otherwise be the appropriate order.[20]

4. STATUTORY MODIFICATION OF THE PRIVILEGE

Section 31 of the Theft Act 1968 removes the privilege in relation to compliance with orders in civil proceedings[21] requiring information to be supplied or documents to be produced which might lead to charges for an offence under that Act. However the material thus provided is not then admissible in the subsequent, related criminal proceedings.

Similar provisions are contained in:

- section 9 of the Criminal Damage Act 1971 in relation to offences under that Act; and
- section 72 of the Supreme Court Act 1981[22] in relation to passing off or infringement of intellectual property rights.

In *Sociedade Nacional de Combustiveis v Lundqvist*,[23] however, the Court of Appeal held that a charge of conspiracy to commit an offence under the Theft Act 1968 is not an "offence under the Act" within the meaning of section 31.[25] Accordingly, when seeking to avoid complying with disclosure orders, defendants often rely on the risk of conspiracy charges, but in order to do so successfully they must show a likelihood that they will face proceedings for conspiracy separate and distinct from proceedings for offences under the 1968 Act.

A committee of judges appointed by the Judges' Council has recommended that section 72 Supreme Court Act 1981 should be extended to apply to the law of conspiracy to prevent *Anton Piller* applications from being frustrated by reliance on the privilege.[26]

Under section 2 Criminal Justice Act 1987 the Director of the Serious Fraud Office is entitled to require a person whom he believes has relevant

---

20 *Coca Cola Co v Gilbey* [1995] 4 All ER 711.
21 Civil proceedings do not include, for this purpose, bankruptcy proceedings: *R v Kansal* [1993] QB 244.
22 As amended by Trade Marks Act 1994, s. 106(1), Sched. 4, para. 1.
23 [1990] 3 All ER 283.
24 A similar issue arises under the Criminal Damages Act 1971 which is worded in a similar way to s. 31 Theft Act 1968, but not under s. 72 Supreme Court Act 1981, which is more widely drawn.
25 See *Renworth v Stephansen* [1996] 3 All ER 244, noted in Section 3 above.
26 "Anton Piller Orders, A Consultation Paper", Lord Chancellor's Department, November 1992.

information to attend to answer questions. Replies to such questions are generally inadmissible[27] in criminal proceedings but will often put the police on the right track which they might not otherwise have found.

5. STATUTORY ABROGATIONS OF THE PRIVILEGE

Modern statutes often contain provisions allowing regulatory authorities, liquidators, administrative receivers and inspectors of companies appointed under the Companies Act 1985 to require information and documents. Where those required to supply the material in question consider that to do so would tend to incriminate them, the question will arise whether the privilege has been abrogated by statute. Invariably the courts hold that it has. Thus the privilege has been held to be abrogated by implication in the following contexts:

- the right of the Bank of England to question under section 42 Banking Act 1987 where a breach of sections 3 or 35 is suspected;[28]
- application for disclosure of assets by affidavit pursuant to a restraint order under section 77 Criminal Justice Act 1988;[29]
- examination of an officer of an insolvent company under section 236 Insolvency Act 1986;[30]
- examination of witnesses under section 434 Companies Act 1985 by inspectors appointed under section 432;[31]
- public examination in bankruptcy under section 290 Insolvency Act 1986 and public examination in a company's liquidation under section 133.[32]
- application for affidavits of assets in support of a restraint order under section 8 Drug Trafficking Offences Act 1986;[33]
- requisition for information under section 71 Environmental Protection Act 1990.[34]

---

27 S. 2(8).
28 *Bank of England v Riley* [1992] Ch 475.
29 *In Re O and Another (Restraint Order: Disclosure of Assets)* [1991] 2 QB 520.
30 *In re Jeffrey S Levitt Ltd* [1992] Ch 457; *Bishopsgate Investment Management v Maxwell, Cooper v Maxwell* [1993] Ch 1.
31 *Re London United Investments plc* [1992] Ch 578.
32 *Bishopsgate Investment Management v Maxwell, Cooper v Maxwell* [1993] Ch 1.
33 *Re Thomas (Disclosure Order)* [1992] 4 All ER 814.
34 *R v Hertfordshire County Council, ex p. Green Environmental Industries* [1996] NPC 119.

6. RESTRAINING THE USE OF INCRIMINATING DOCUMENTS OR INFORMATION IN OTHER PROCEEDINGS

In *Re Arrows (No 4)*[35] the House of Lords held that it was a wrong exercise of the Companies Court's discretion, when granting an application by the director of the Serious Fraud Office for the production of transcripts of the examination of a witness under section 236 Insolvency Act 1986, to seek to prevent the director from using them in any subsequent criminal prosecution of the witness.[36] Note that, on the other hand, it was held in *Morris v Director of the Serious Fraud Office*[37] that the Serious Fraud Office is not at liberty voluntarily to disclose to liquidators documents which it had seized under its powers contained in section 2 Criminal Justice Act 1987. Those from whom such documents are obtained have to be afforded the opportunity to object to their further disclosure.

In *United Norwest Co-operatives v Johnstone*[38] the plaintiffs, in seeking an *Anton Piller* order against the defendants in relation to allegedly fraudulent activities, were willing to submit to an injunction restraining them from supplying the material thus disclosed to the prosecuting authorities. However, a majority of the Court of Appeal[39] held that this was not a sufficient reason for withholding the privilege against self-incrimination. Dillon, LJ pointed out that if the prosecuting authorities subsequently applied to the court, the court might well assist them in obtaining any information filed or disclosed in the proceedings, regardless of any order made against the plaintiffs.

Where, however, the prosecuting authorities have agreed not to make use of material disclosed in a civil action for the purpose of subsequent criminal proceedings, and the defendant can otherwise adequately be protected, it was held by the House of Lords in *AT&T Istel v Tully*[40] that the defendant would not be allowed to invoke the privilege. Undertakings by prosecuting authorities not to use such material have been given, inter

---

35 [1995] 2 AC 75.
36 However, the trial judge retains a discretion whether to admit them in evidence: s.78 Police and Criminal Evidence Act 1984. As to the position with documents obtained by the police and which are wanted in parallel civil proceedings, see *Marcel v Commissioner of Police of the Metropolis* [1992] Ch 225.
37 [1993] Ch 372.
38 (1994) *The Times*, 24 February.
39 Dillon, and Hobhouse, LJJ, Stuart-Smith, LJ dissenting.
40 [1993] AC 74.

alia, in proceedings pursuant to restraint orders under section 77 Criminal Justice Act 1988[41] and under section 8 Drug Trafficking Offences Act 1986.[42]

In *Re C*[43] an order for disclosure under the Drug Trafficking Offences Act 1986 had been made. The person against whom the order had been made sought an undertaking from the prosecution authorities not only that they should not use the information in any subsequent prosecution, but also that they should not use the evidence as an *investigative tool*. Ognall, J upheld this application. If the privilege against self-incrimination was to be overridden, it should be replaced by measures which give the person against whom an order was made equivalent protection.

The decisions considered in this section may now have to be reconsidered in the light of the European Court of Human Rights' decision in *R v Saunders etc.*,[44] discussed in Section 8 below.

7 . DISCRETION OF THE CRIMINAL COURT IN ALLOWING MATERIAL TO BE USED

Where the privilege has been abrogated by statute or cannot for other reasons be invoked, the judge in the criminal proceedings has a discretion to exclude any material the use of which might be unfair to the defence.[45] In *R v Saunders; R v Parnes; R v Ronson; R v Lyons*,[46] Henry, J allowed the prosecution in the "Guinness" trial to produce in evidence transcripts of the accused's interrogation by inspectors appointed by the Department of Trade and Industry under section 434(5) Companies Act 1985. The Court of Appeal dismissed the accused's appeal against conviction, holding that there had been nothing unfair in the use of the material, even though it contained self-incriminatory statements. As discussed in the next section, however, this decision is now suspect in the light of the European Court of Human Rights' subsequent ruling in this matter.

---

41 In *Re O and Another (Restraint Order: Disclosure of Assets)* [1991] 2 QB 520.
42 *Re Thomas (Disclosure Order)* [1992] 4 All ER 814.
43 Unrep., 17 February 1995.
44 (1997) 23 EHRR 313.
45 Ss. 76 and 78 Police and Criminal Evidence Act 1984. See *R v Seelig, R v Spens* [1992] 1 WLR 149; *Bank of England v Riley* [1992] Ch 475.
46 (1996) 1 Cr App R 463.

8. HUMAN RIGHTS

All of the decisions and legislation considered above are likely to require reconsideration in the light of rulings by the European Court of Human Rights and in the event that the government voted into office in May 1997 makes good its electoral promise to incorporate the European Convention on Human Rights[47] into domestic law. Generally speaking, the Convention is in any case already exerting some influence on English domestic proceedings;[48] and recent decisions of the European Court of Human Rights suggest that the Convention is already likely to impact on attempts to erode the privilege against self-incrimination before the domestic courts.[49] So in *Funke v France,*[50] the European Court of Human Rights held that an accused was entitled, under Article 6 of the Convention,[51] to remain silent and not to contribute to incriminate himself.[52]

In *Saunders v United Kingdom*[53] the European Court of Human Rights reviewed the decision of the Court of Appeal in *R v Saunders; R v Parnes; R v Ronson; R v Lyons.*[54] A majority of the court took the view that the use of the transcripts in evidence in that case was a breach of Article 6 of the European Convention on Human Rights. It distinguished between a requirement for a person to produce relevant evidence in support of the case against him (such as documents or a blood or urine sample), which was compatible with the Convention, and an infringement of the right to remain silent, which was incompatible with Article 6. Judge Walsh, in his concurring judgment, said:

---

47 European Convention for the Protection of Human Rights and Fundamental Freedoms (1953) (Cmnd 8969).

48 In his first speech in the House of Lords (Hansard, 3rd July 1996, Column 1465–1467) in his capacity as Lord Chief Justice, Lord Bingham identified six areas in which the Convention can presently impact on English law. These include cases involving the construction of a statute capable of two interpretations; where the courts have a discretion to exercise; and where courts must decide what public policy demands. It is beyond the scope of this book to consider these issues in any detail: see Murray Hunt, "Using Human Rights Law in English Courts", (1997).

49 As to the relevance of "human rights" law to legal professional privilege, see the brief discussion in Chapter 1, Section 10.

50 Case 82/1991/334/407, Series A, Vol 256-A.

51 Which, *inter alia,* guarantees everybody a fair and public hearing.

52 Article 14(3) of the International Covenant on Civil and Political Rights recognises more expressly a right not to give evidence against oneself, or to confess guilt. This, however, is narrower than the English privilege against self-incrimination, which focuses on the tendency of the information or documents sought to expose the person concerned to criminal proceedings.

53 (1997) 23 EHRR 313.

54 (1996) 1 Cr App R 463.

"In my opinion the privilege against self-incrimination extends further than answers which themselves will support a conviction. It is sufficient to sustain the privilege where it is evident from the implications of the questions and the setting in which they are asked that a responsive answer to the question or an explanation as to why it cannot be answered could also be dangerous because injurious disclosure could result."

The result obviously contrasts with the approach adopted in the domestic (English) court.

As noted, the European Convention on Human Rights, though not yet incorporated into English law, can nevertheless exercise an influence over the decision-making of the courts but the circumstances in which it presently does so are relatively limited (for example as where English law is unclear[55] or where the court is exercising a statutory discretion[56]). It did not assist in *R v Saunders; R v Parnes; R v Ronson; R v Lyons*,[57] discussed in Section 7 above, where the Court of Appeal held that there was no ambiguity in the relevant English law and therefore no room for the exercise of the court's discretion.

A similar conclusion was arrived at in *R v Morrissey; R v Staines*.[58] Section 177 of the Financial Services Act 1986 expressly authorises the use, in criminal proceedings, of statements made by a person to investigators appointed by the Secretary of State under that Act. Lord Bingham, C.J, giving the judgment of the court, regarded that as a statutory presumption that the use of such statements was fair, and therefore the Convention did not come into play.

Bank of England v Riley[59] is an earlier decision which might now require reconsideration if the Convention is incorporated into English law. Here it was held that the right of the Bank of England to question under section 42 of the Banking Act 1987 where a breach of section 3 or 35 was suspected impliedly abrogated the privilege against self-incrimination. There was nothing in the statute, however, expressly authorising the use of evidence thus obtained in criminal proceedings. The court indicated that the question of any possible unfair use of information and documents in a subsequent prosecution should be left to the court where such proceedings might be brought. Now the ruling of the European Court of Human Rights in *Saunders v United Kingdom*[60] might be relevant to the exercise of a

---

55   As with interpreting a statute: see *R v Secretary of State for the Home Department, ex p. Brind* [1991] 1 AC 696.
56   *Regina v Khan*, unrep., 2 July 1996, House of Lords.
57   (1996) 1 Cr App R 463.
58   (1997) *The Times*, 1 May.
59   [1992] Ch 475: see section 5 p. 180 above.
60   (1997) 23 EHRR 313.

criminal court's discretion to admit evidence obtained under the Banking Act 1987 and other statutes in similar terms.

9. EUROPEAN COMMUNITY LAW

The Court of Justice of the European Communities has also recognised the privilege in narrow terms. In *Orkem SA (CdF Chimie SA) v EC Commission*[61] the Court accepted that in general the laws of Member States grant an individual the right not to give evidence against himself in criminal proceedings.[62] However, as a general principle of European law this did not extend to "legal persons", that is companies, when faced with proceedings in relation to infringements in the economic sphere. Thus in *Orkem*, the Court held that the European Commission could compel an undertaking to provide all necessary information concerning such facts as may be known to it and to disclose to it relevant documents in its possession, even if these could be used to establish, against it or another undertaking, the existence of anti-competitive conduct. It could not, however, undermine the rights of defence of the undertaking concerned. The Commission could not compel an undertaking to provide it with the answers which might involve an admission on its part of the existence of an infringement which it is incumbent on the Commission to prove.

In the result, the Court accordingly upheld questions of a factual nature but annulled questions put by the Commission which in effect sought an admission of guilt.

---

61 [1991] CMLR 502.

62 This right may, perhaps, be extended by the CJEC in the future in the light of the judgment of the European Court of Human Rights in *Saunders v United Kingdom*, *supra*.

INDEX